MANAGING IN
CHANGING TIMES

MANAGING IN CHANGING TIMES

A Guide for the Perplexed Manager

Edited by

Sid Lowe

Response
Business books from SAGE
Los Angeles ▪ London ▪ New Delhi ▪ Singapore ▪ Washington DC
www.sagepublications.com

First published in 2010 by

Response Books
Business books from SAGE
B1/I-1 Mohan Cooperative Industrial Area
Mathura Road, New Delhi 110 044, India
www.sagepub.in

SAGE Publications Inc
2455 Teller Road
Thousand Oaks, California 91320, USA

SAGE Publications Ltd
1 Oliver's Yard, 55 City Road
London EC1Y 1SP, United Kingdom

SAGE Publications Asia-Pacific Pte Ltd
33 Pekin Street
#02-01 Far East Square
Singapore 048763

Published by Vivek Mehra for Response Books, typeset in 11/14pt Minion by Tantla Composition Services Pvt. Ltd., Chandigarh and printed at Chaman Enterprises, New Delhi.

Library of Congress Cataloging-in-Publication Data
Managing in changing times : a guide for the perplexed manager / edited by Sid Lowe.
    p. cm.
  Includes bibliographical references and index.
1. Management. I. Lowe, Sid.

HD38.15M365	658—dc22	2009	2009037163

ISBN: 978-81-321-0233-5 (PB)

The SAGE Team: Reema Singhal, Meena Chakravorty, Sanjeev Kumar Sharma and Trinankur Banerjee

Dedicated to

Kieran Allen Lowe

CONTENTS

PART ONE
Perplexity, Management and Organisation Theory

PART TWO
Perplexities in Selective International Contexts

PREFACE

At the time of writing, in the midst of a financial crisis and at the start of a recession in the West, there is perplexity everywhere. The centre of economic and political power appears to be beginning to shift towards Asia and globalisation is an issue that is talked about endlessly using a variety of meanings. The election of Barak Obama signals that the blind faith in 'free' markets as a panacea and neo-Con experiment in the USA appears to have failed. The War in Iraq appears to have been an unmitigated disaster. In the UK, huge investments in public services appear to have made them less effective and more 'bureaupathic'. America and Europe appear to be facing the revisitation of stagflation or debilitating deflation and all the threats to social cohesion that come with them. In the midst of all this, management and organisation theory appears to be fragmenting. The old hegemony of 'neo-classical' scientific management is being challenged by new ideas. The old ideas, however, continue to be taught in most business schools, particularly run by those trained in scientific management who have risen through the ranks of massive higher educational bureaucracies that are products of old thinking.

This of course cannot last. Scientific management, the 'paralysis of analysis', unrestrained casino financiers, the excesses of hyper-individualistic over consumption, irresponsible personal debt, the unquestioned preoccupation with economic self-interest, corrupt and greedy management such as that within Enron, widening income inequality and social malaise have brought the West to a time where re-examination of values is critical. In the East, there are also problems with corruption but there is an impetus to grow, which means that development potential is high. However, is it in the interest of the East to adopt Western scientific management? There are plenty of Western business schools in the East and other developing regions promoting simplistic and easily sold 'old' thinking that takes no account of local cultures, morals or socio-economic conditions.

In this book, various possibilities are explored for the future development of understanding managing and organising in the context of new conditions in both East and West (and for that matter North and South). In the first two chapters the potentials for the ideas of Schumacher and Capra are presented. These are not simplistic ideas that can be regarded as 'off-the-shelf' and 'quick-fix' solutions. They require a certain amount of concentration and reflection to be of benefit to the reader. The hope is that the reader will accept that nothing of lasting value comes very easily and this will encourage persistence in attempts to understand the complex arguments presented.

The complexity of the argument follows David Boje's (2008) challenge to move studies of Management and Organisation out of the outmoded 'systems theory' era. This had as an unquestioned agenda, a desire to comprehensively understand the World from a position of unitary coherence. In support of this desire, modernist 'centripetal' narratives dominate and control through the imposition of monological, coherent, rational logic. This book follows Boje's (2008) challenge to move beyond narratives of coherent order within 'dead-machine' theories and to cultivate 'centrifugal' stories that liberate change through 'dialogism' (Boje 2008: 21). There is a positive attempt, therefore, to promote different styles, discourses, temporalities and voices and a conscious agenda to avoid a 'final vocabulary' of immutable, unitary truth. This is not comfortable for most of us conditioned to seek such unitary knowledge but it is now essential to brave the insecurity of Wisdom. The approach followed, therefore, is 'plurivocal' and 'polytheistic'; there is no single reliable way to understand complexity and multiple viewpoints are crucial.

In the chapters that follow, the contributors use the first two chapters as a catalyst to explore further a post-scientific global management era. In Part One, Chapter 3, Kathryn Pavlovich and Robert Chia explore how processes-based practice using a 'rhizome' metaphor may be perplexity reducing. In Chapter 4, John Shotter is also concerned with the potentials for practical wisdom. For him, ascending Schumacher's hierarchy involves dedicated focus upon emergent phenomena and the descriptive concepts needed to illuminate their nature. In Chapter 5, Richard Ennals takes a human-centred approach to building technological systems to avoid the perplexity inducement of 'dead map' technology development. In Chapter 6, Ian Steers takes an embodied approach to human ethics, which emerges through bio-social processes of questing and narrating. Questing and narrating, self-enacting and self-disclosing managers are celebrated as complex and perplexed humans who organise part of their lives within organisations. In Chapter 7, Sławomir Jan Magala explores how relational identities involve weaving our 'red thread' of personal identity through the rich texture of social processes dwelling in cultural 'tempospaces'. In Chapter 8, Jonathan Gander promotes an 'enrolment advantage paradigm' using Actor–Network Theory as an antidote to the perplexity inducing dominance of prescriptive 'neo-classical' strategy models.

In Part Two, Chapter 9, Karl-Eric Sveiby rediscovers 'pure', traditional horizontal leadership styles within Australian Aboriginal traditional knowledge and contemporary African Bushmen bands. He proposes that a primordial horizontal leadership paradigm is one of the unique contributions that Indigenous Leadership can make to the mainstream leadership discourse. In Chapter 10, Balakrishnan Muniapan also focuses upon an ancient wisdom with relevance to perplexed modern leaders; namely the *Bhagavad-Gita*, which provides the spirit of Indian *Vedic* thought. In Chapter 11, Astrid Kainzbauer shows how a practical and sensitive approach to self-awareness can pay necessary dividends for expatriate managers. In the final chapter (12), Ronnie Lessem et al., provide a useful 'global compass' metaphor, termed *Oikomorphosis*, for navigating the kind of transformation required for coping with perplexity.

REFERENCE

Boje, D.M. 2008. *Storytelling Organizations.* London: Sage Publications.

NOTES ON THE EDITOR AND CONTRIBUTORS

Editor

Sid Lowe is Reader, Strategy, Marketing and Entrepreneurship at Kingston University, London, UK.

Contributors

Robert Chia is Professor, Management at University of Aberdeen, Scotland.

Richard Ennals is Professor of Corporate Responsibility and Working Life at Kingston University, London, UK.

Jonathan Gander is Senior Lecturer, Strategy, Marketing and Entrepreneurship at Kingston University, London, UK.

Astrid Kainzbauer is at Mahidol University, Bangkok, Thailand.

Ronnie Lessem is a Professor in Trans-cultural Management and Director of the Social and Economic Transformation programmes at the University of Buckingham, UK. He is also the co-founder of Trans4m, Geneva.

Sławomir Jan Magala is Professor of Cross-cultural Management at Rotterdam School of Management, Erasmus University, Rotterdam, The Netherlands.

Balakrishnan Muniapan is Senior Lecturer at School of Business & Enterprise, Swinburne University of Technology, Sarawak Campus, Malaysia.

Sudhanshu Palsule is Visiting Professor at Duke Business School, USA and at the Indian School of Business in Hyderabad.

Kathryn Pavlovich is Associate Professor, Strategy and Human Resource Management at University of Waikato, Management School, New Zealand.

Alexander Schieffer received his Ph.D. from St. Gallen University, Switzerland and he is presently founder and managing partner of Centre of Excellence for Leadership and Learning (CELL). He is also the co-founder of Trans4m, Geneva.

John Shotter is Emeritus Professor of Communication in the Department of Communication, University of New Hampshire.

Ian Steers is Lecturer at Thames Valley University, UK.

Karl-Erik Sveiby is Professor, Department of Management and Organisation, Hanken Business School, Helsinki, Finland.

PART ONE

PERPLEXITY, MANAGEMENT AND ORGANISATION THEORY

1

SCHUMACHER'S HIERARCHY

Sid Lowe

Schumacher's hierarchy arranges different ways of understanding realities in a succession of complexity. Lower forms of understanding are fixed and machine-like. They are 'one size fits all' dead-maps. Classical 'scientific' management occupies this level. Ascending this hierarchy requires new metaphors to explore more fluid, plural and contextual 'higher' understanding. Contemporary management theory appears to be moving up Schumacher's hierarchy and ready to begin trading in newer metaphors.

Scientific management had been a dominant perspective in business disciplines for most of the 20th century. The effectiveness of this approach in the contemporary uncertain global business environment is now in question. In this book, the source of the ideas surrounding scientific management is identified in Western culture and philosophy. Alternative ideas, from both East and West, are surveyed to suggest where contemporary, 21st century developments in management have and will continue to be taken increasingly from outside those framed by Western 'instructional' science.

Perplexed managers in the 21st century are pressed for time and are faced with an increasingly complex world. They do, of course, like to be introduced to fashionable panaceas that promise to solve their problems quickly, cheaply and effortlessly. Most have begun to realise that the 'how to control the universe', 'pop' management texts populating airport bookshops that come in and out of fashion do not really often provide sustained comfort. The reason seems obvious; there is no panacea. Dealing with a complex world is dangerous if you are relying on quick-fix, off-the-shelf solutions. The real solution is to be able to act-think through contemporary complexity and its consequences within local contexts. The objective of this book is to provide a means through which this kind of critical, practical, action-based thinking can be channelled.

In *A Guide for the Perplexed* (1977), Schumacher provides us with an approach to reality and our understanding of it. In this book, this view is enlisted to show how managers and researchers in the 21st century might best grasp and influence organisational realities and the ways of their understanding. Schumacher (1977) sees (multiple) reality and our understanding of it as a hierarchy. The hierarchy is one of a base reality of tangible substance that rises to a peak of the intangible and 'sublime' (see Figure 1.1). Schumacher challenges us to see that there are many different realities that require different types of knowledge to understand. Success, therefore, depends upon mental flexibility to be able to see in many different ways, using many different types of maps or 'lenses'.

Figure 1.1: Schumacher's Hierarchy

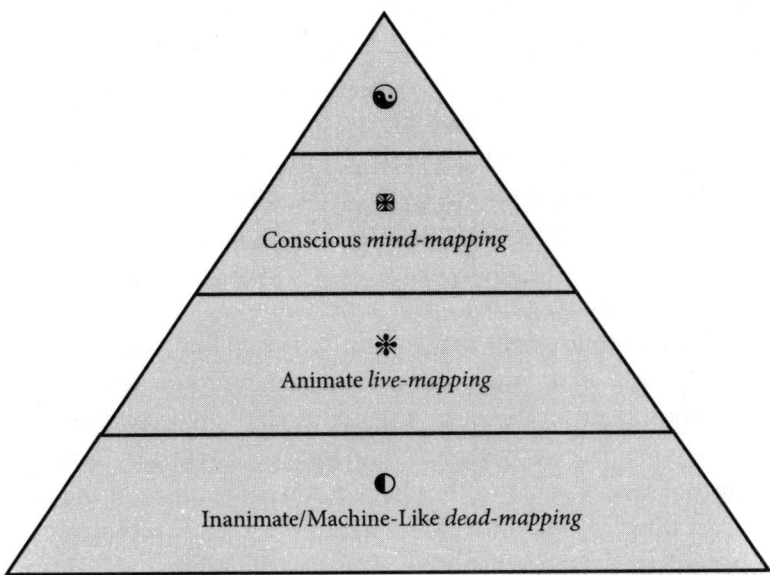

At the tangible base of Schumacher's hierarchy reality is non-living and machine-like. It is understood through scientific knowledge that leaves little room for uncertainty in determining Truth. At the top of the hierarchy, the 'sublime' is entirely intangible, uncertain, indeterminate and inexplicable. Art in its greatest form, attempts to express the inexpressible experience of the sublime by liberating aesthetic interpretations of paradox and wisdom. Schumacher (1977) implies that dominant modern 'scientific' thinking privileges the lower 'inanimate' or machine-like view of reality and creates a gravitational cultural force which cloaks higher levels of understanding and restricts access to them. Success, therefore, depends upon retaining scientific knowledge but not at the expense of exclusion of other (higher) kinds of knowing which are equally (if not more) relevant in a complex world.

Schumacher describes four Levels of 'Being'; namely inanimate (lifeless/machine-like), animate (life), conscious (thinking, feeling, talking) and, finally, sublime self-awareness. Movement up the 'ladder' of higher Being is only prevented through failures in being able to understand that level because of the lack of access to an appropriate map or 'paradigm'. Different kinds of mapping of reality (knowledge) need to be used to understand the territories of the different levels. The capability of the knower must be adequate to the thing to be known. In other words, the kind of mapping of knowledge required moves from 'dead' mapping through 'live' mapping, onto 'mind' mapping and, ideally, beyond. Schumacher proposes that moving up the hierarchical 'ladder' to the sublime level requires an increasing attention to 'inner' knowing and, in particular, to Socrates' requirement that you must, before knowing anything, 'know thyself' first. Success, therefore, would appear to require a revisitation of ancient wisdoms that our modern preoccupation with 'instructional' science has forced us to forget. This agenda, therefore, requires abandonment of the chauvinistic modernism of the 20th century when myopic 'modernists were more likely to accentuate the superior value of the farther view' (Hatch and Cunliffe 2006: 37) that scientific progress requires 'new ideas' and not ancient wisdoms.

Schumacher's hierarchy requires us to realise that there is more than one type of map or 'paradigm' of reality and more than one type of knowing. If reality and knowing are restricted to only one type, the implication is that such impoverishment will lead to ineffective and sterile decisions and actions. In increasingly turbulent environments the 'double-loop' learning organisation that can change its operating paradigms when required is essential for survival. Consequently, 'successful learning organizations need to be skilled in the art of representation. They need to be able to create appropriate maps of the reality with which they have to deal' (Morgan 1997: 91). Acquiring more than one way of mapping/ knowing reality, however, requires considerable effort, dedication and determination. The 'process has to be active rather than passive. It has to embrace views of potential futures as well as of the present and the past' (ibid.). The message from Schumacher, therefore, may be unwelcomed. There are no simple, 'quick-fix' and easy solutions to the problems of the contemporary perplexed manager. Success requires 'endeavour' and, above all, a mental dexterity that avoids one-dimensional, single-lens, scientific myopia. The problem has been that 'in understanding organization as a rational, technical process, mechanical imagery tends to underplay the human aspects of organization and to overlook the fact that the tasks facing organizations are often much more complex, uncertain, and difficult than those that can be performed by most machines' (Morgan 1997: 27). The perplexed manager has a decision to make. Does (s)he want to find a sustainable way out of perplexity or want to continue buying the kind of easy, 'sticking-plaster' solutions of procrastination that haven't worked in the past?

MAPPING STYLES

In the contemporary world, it is becoming clear that the maps or 'paradigms' that orient our identities, our relations with others and our constructions of the strategic questions 'where are we now?' and 'where do we want to get to?' are subject to Baudrillard's (1996) observation that 'Maps precede the territory' (a phrase/notion that can be originally attributed to Alford Korzybski). In other words, we do not see the territory facing us; we see through the map that represents the territory. We quite soon readily assume that the maps 'are' the territory because this invests confidence in the assumption that we know where we are and where we are going. If, however, we use maps that only see tangibles, then we are unable to navigate the all-important invisible territory. The mapper without wisdom 'entirely fixed in the philosophy of materialist scientism, denying the reality of the "invisibles" and confining his attention solely to what can be counted, measured and weighed, lives in a very poor world' (Schumacher 1977: 45).

The impoverished modernist mapper's omission of all but the explicit and measurable is a serious problem. That is to say, the Age of Discovery is all but over and The Age of Unreason is upon us when the time for 'thinking the unlikely and doing the unreasonable' (Handy 1989: 4) becomes the *sine qua non* for survival through inspirational change. Hatch, Kostera and Koźmiński (2005: 5) spell out the consequences in claiming 'art and ethics are the natural realms of creativity and inspiration' so that their 'describing how respected business leaders show the faces of the artist and the priest' will enable improvement of currently dominant institutionalised, scientific management which lacks adequate inspiration.

The 'discovery myth' that the world is simply real and 'out there' for us to objectively find, map and conquer is becoming absurd. Such Cartesian landmarks of certainties fail to show us more important, invisible places that are more alive, human-like, animate and extraordinarily wise. Inner mapping of invisibles requires individual 'inner' cartography that cannot be easily identified, taught or communicated directly. Only 'Ancient wisdom succeeds where corporate wisdom does not, by helping us see the unseen and hearing the unheard' (Siddiqui 2005: 30). Such higher 'invisible connectedness' cannot be understood except by the determined, self-motivated mapper, as this kind of 'seeing' is a personal and reflexive agenda. No objective, 'outside' influence is of much use and no simplistic, transferable 'source of material' is generally applicable to allow schools to run courses on how to see vital, invisible connections.

INANIMATE/MACHINE-LIKE 'DEAD-MAPPING'

What are Dead Maps?

Scientific 'dead mapping' of reality enables us to see only lower levels of Schumacher's hierarchy. It is an important and adequate contribution to knowledge but far from a sufficient condition for wisdom. Knowledge within dead-mapping is purely explicit, measurable and explicable. It involves a kind of 'epistemic cleansing' of all subjectivity and indeterminacy and the promotion of objective, detached certainty as 'epistemic purity'. The mission is to provide a 'final vocabulary' (Rorty 1999) which, once and for all, eliminates all pluralism, polysemy and imposes a unitary, legitimately rational understanding.

The predominant metaphor for reality of this intellectual disambiguation is the 'machine'. Anything not conforming to the perception of knowledge as mechanistically real is purged. The cognitive style of

NB; Epistemic Involving knowledge/ understanding

dead-mapping is a kind of monochrome 'photographic' one. The world is to be captured, with the assistance of a quantitative camera, in a fixed, black and white image and then presented as an unquestioned corresponding representation of reality. It is an assumption of the 'immaculate perception', which enables the objective rationalist to see reality 'perfectly logically' through perfectly articulated reason. That which is subjective, intangible, immeasurable, uncertain, moving and tacit does not count as knowledge until it is converted to explicit, objective and certain tangibility. This approach to understanding is not unimportant but on its own it is a dangerous and myopic form of cognitive constipation. The dead-mapping approach assumes that reality is fixed and tangible, that we can see it, and describe it without complication, using the correct form of quantifiable measurement. The assumption is that it is possible to produce a positivist, structural functionalist, alpha-numerical map that exactly represents the territory. The territory is, therefore, regarded as real and tangible and 'numbers maps' are considered the only credibly realistic representations corresponding to physical certainties. If the map or 'paradigm' fails to aid our orientation of the territory, it is assumed that the map requires further quantification of the inanimate, to produce in response a better 'model' or more precise camera, in order to be able to represent the territory even more objectively.

Scientific mapping involves identifying measurable certainties and then manipulating them through action executed not central to moral or any other 'higher' considerations. Such 'dead' mapping therefore portrays a universalistic, objective purpose of control through the illusion of a cartography of impartial certainty. Such machine-like 'maps of the dead' abandon traditional wisdom and leave out most of what is invisible, transitory, intangible, imaginary, indeterminate and indispensable for understanding the world. Dead maps perpetuate an absurd view 'that counts as "real" only inanimate matter and treats as "unreal", "subjective" and therefore scientifically non-existent the invisible dimensions of life, consciousness and self-awareness' (Schumacher 1977: 34). Their one-dimensional reductionism is 'fixed in the philosophy of materialistic scientism, denying the reality of the "invisibles"' (ibid.: 45). It reduces it to the representation of a 'dead map of the visible' so that we don't have to cultivate 'science for understanding' (ibid.: 65) or 'wisdom'. Social scientists and management theorists are able to file reports about the dead maps and do not have to get too directly involved with their actual use and abuse and do not have to engage with everything else that is important, invisible and inconclusive.

The dominant 'home' paradigm of Western functionalism is characterised by adherence to rationalism and scientism, and a unitary mode of representing a discovered absolute 'Truth'. As a result 'what passes as knowledge essentially reflects the views and visions of those who inquire' (Gergen 2003: 453) with limited vision of the visible. Dead-map modelling is a search for universal truth that sits comfortably within a dominant, intellectual sub-culture wedded to the presumption of discoverable Truth. The global colonialisation of objectivist, logico-scientific methods is the only assumed legitimate route to establishing such self-evident, universalistic and unquestioned reality constructed within 'self assertive' and 'dominant' (Capra 1996: 10) forms of knowledge.

Maps or 'paradigms' governed by scientism displaced pre-modern, subjective maps of experience that provided animation through beginning with our *capax universi* (Schumacher 1977: 45) or interior perspective as analogy for exterior orientation (Cummings and Wilson 2003: 4). Traditional knowledge involved a 'practical wisdom' requiring dedicated practice through apprenticeship involving 'dwelling' with the world pragmatically through the acquisition of skills necessary for 'being-in-the-world' (Heidegger 1962 [1927]). Mastering life involved practicing life skills honed through dedicated direct experience. In traditional, ancient wisdom, personal empathetic and involved understanding of the object by the 'helmsman' likened steering a skilfully polyvalent course between certainty and chaos (*metos*) to the 'wisdom of *oscillating* between different positions and perspectives toward a particular purpose' (Cummings and Wilson 2003: 4). The 'steersman' or 'kubernetes' (the Greek derivative of cybernetics) is a 'double-loop' skilled learner in that she is able to adjust to conditions and adjust her 'paradigm' or map of understanding when attempted adjustments to conditions are not working (Morgan 1997: 83). Dead maps of impoverished mechanistic, analytical reductionism fall short of the potentials of inspirational double-looping. Inspiration is possible through changing our maps, paradigms, minds, purposes and beliefs, enabling a change of perspective, which offer the promise for development of understanding higher hidden and important phenomena. Dead maps construct information that 'flushes out knowledge and knowledge flushes out wisdom-in-practice' (Chia 2003: 975). These 'maps produced by modern materialistic scientism leave all the questions that really matter unanswered' (Schumacher 1977: 14). Such illusory 'maps of *real* knowledge, designed for *real* life, [do] not show anything except things that allegedly could be *proved* to exist' (ibid.: 12).

Where did they come from?

Dead maps are a product of the dominant metaphysical assumptions of the West. These are towards an underlying fixity to reality; an 'essentialist' or 'foundationalist' assumption that underlying everything is a fixed and concrete existence. Dead mapping also emanates from a selective interpretation of Aristotle. Aristotelian metaphysics prescribes 'proper' knowledge as requiring accurate representation of phenomena as 'simple location' described through (alphabetic) language, classification of phenomena within a general or universal schema, and attribution of their identity and underlying causes. In other words, the world is founded by fixed realities and knowledge requires identifying them and their relations in a well-articulated theory prior to taking action.

Aristotle's legacy is to privilege that which facilitates articulate representation of a generalisable underlying causality. The lasting legacy of Aristotle has not been the wisdom of his organic holism, or his political and moral philosophy, but the residue of causality co-opted and embedded in modern Western languages. Aristotle's legacy is to privilege objectifying language that facilitates articulate representation of a generalisable underlying causal Truth. Truth is expressed here as a noun rather than as an adjective, reflecting the latent assumption in Western Enlightenment philosophy of its existential reality, as an unquestioned object with uncomplicated correspondence in empirical evidence. Truth, within this worldview, is 'found' rather than made (or socially constructed). It is found through factist rationalism and is universal and uniform rather than pluralist and multiform. Truth, in other words, is tangible, rather than spiritual for dead-mappers. Aristotle also permeates an imbalanced self-organisational sense making in that linear, 'narrative' (a centripetal centring force for control and order) becomes privileged over 'story' (a centrifugal non-linear counterbalance of disorder, de-centring and creativity) (Boje 2008).

Two broad Western theories of truth derive from mathematics and science. Mathematics is the vehicle through which logical truth is established through 'coherence' and science is the vehicle through which factual truth is established through 'correspondence' (Kosko 1994: 83). Logical truth is achieved within the tautological system of coherent rules of mathematics. Statements are logically true if they cohere within the bivalent symbolism of mathematics.

A logically true statement is true by the way the words it contains relate as internally consistent. Factual truth is achieved with reference to facts that correspond (or not) to statements. The latent assumption in Western Enlightenment philosophy is of Truth's existential reality, as an unquestioned object with uncomplicated correspondence in empirical evidence. This conception underlies assumptions in functionalism and scientism, which is that the world is a real, mechanistic, measurable, controllable and understandable by legitimate, objective, logical empirical scientific method only. Truth is assumed 'found' rather than made (through socially constructed imagination). It is presumed found through factist rationalism and is universalistic and uniform rather than pluralistic and multiform.

Both logical and factual Truths, however, trade accuracy for the simplicity of a black and white bivalent 'scorecard' (Kosko 1994: 80). They are culturally derived through the development of Western philosophical thought and particularly derive from the thinking of Aristotle and the Enlightenment philosophers. It is critical to identify that the Western lens thus produces results in vast gaps in 'understanding'. The bivalent filter of 'black and white' photographic logical and factual truth claims miss all 'shades of grey'; all aspects of contradiction, every sense of paradox and avoids understanding the synergies of the whole as a non-linear phenomena greater than the sum of its parts. As a result Truth, rationalism, science and logical positivism 'explains' phenomena on its own reductionist, bivalent, 'black and white' terms and 'understands' little of its inherent greyness. Consequently 'In an applied field such as management studies, therefore, the central task is to first make empirical observations of practice, theorise these practices in terms of established conceptual schemas and systems of explanations, verify these principles empirically, and then offer them as written recipes to an eager practitioner audience' (Chia 2003: 960).

This all may seem natural and reasonable but, in fact, it is a cultural consequence of dominant Western metaphysical assumptions. It privileges knowledge before action and, therefore, diminishes the inspirational potentials of knowing through direct experience or action-based learning that is characteristic of art, sports and Eastern cultures. Knowledge is not universally viewed as legitimate in the terms prescribed by Western alphabetic-literate rationalism, which somewhat restrict 'knowledge' to Schumacher's lowest level of Being; the inanimate level of dead-mapping. The Aristotelian way of knowing is consolidated by the mechanistic worldview of Descartes and Newton that has dominated Western society for centuries. The 'Cartesian' view 'persists, because it meets a profound need. We would all like to feel certain that there is an objective world "out there", different from the subjective world "in here"' (Magala 2005: 9). 'Keeping it simple', keeps you stupid and easily manipulated.

What do they lead to?

'Organizations that are designed and operated as if they were machines are now usually called bureaucracies' (Morgan 1997: 13). Bureaucracies are not malignant *per se* and are arguably the most appropriate vehicle for protecting civic rather than consumer demand (du Gay 1994). However, bureaucracies are a concomitant of scientism and cognitive determinism. They are the embodiment of rational choice and members must suffer 'hidden injuries' (Magala 2005: 39) as a result of adopting scientific dualisms and the marginalisation of human (relational and emotional) orientations. It is when bureaucracies exhibit 'bureaupathic' behaviour, a kind of hyper-rationalist hysteria, that they become dysfunctional. Bureaupathic behaviour is a consequent of an uninspired, dehumanised system that breeds apathy and alienation (Byrt 1973). Bureaucratic structures are appropriate in conditions of process technology use, large scale and relatively stable environments. Bureaucracy has grown under the influence of 'McDonaldisation' where Fordist/Taylorist principles (Fulop and Linstead 2004: 136) have sometimes been applied (for example in the UK) to public sector professional bureaucracies such as hospitals and universities. Building upon Byrt's critique, (Fulop and Linstead 2004: 135) propose that bureaupathic behaviour is really a product of applying the dead-mapping of excessively rigid instrumental rationalism that fails to take account of human considerations by assuming people can operate unquestionably as cogs in a mechanism. They argue that Weber's ideal type of bureaucracy, intended as a conceptual construct is too often adopted as a 'one best way' prescription ending in bureaupathic dystopia. Also Weber's characterisation of bureaucracy in terms of authority acceptance, centralised control and rule enforcement are rather differently perceived in the contemporary world than when Weber's theory was first published and found influence. Weber warned that formal, means-based rationality without the conscious consideration of 'purpose' provided by ends-based, substantive rationality would lead to an oppressive 'iron cage' machine-like prison (Hatch and Cunliffe 2006: 31) appears to have been ignored all too often.

Dead-mapping assumes that what is real is that which is identifiable with certainty. The scientific rationalist worldview explains the universe using a 'bivalent filter' (Kosko 1994: 13) of mathematical truth claims derived from Aristotelian binary logic. This bivalent ideology atomises the world by reducing it to bivalent facts about mechanistic elements that must be either true or false. The universe is explained by reduction to the 'substance' of its smallest parts or objects, which are explained through binary logic. These explanations of substance are then pooled as components to 'build' grander, nomothetic theories about the nature of the universe. The identity test of 'dualism' has to be passed for dead-mappers. To count as 'real', each element of reality is subject to the dualistic question: 'Is it or Isn't it?' Nothing that is indeterminate can get past the ultimate question of the reality of Being. 'To be or not to be, that is the question.' Phenomena that are processes (constantly changing in the rhizomic processes of 'becoming') do not count as real or worthy of the attention of knowledge activity within dead-mapping. To be valid, something has either to be or not to be. If it is both/and instead of either/or, it doesn't exist for dead-mappers. Organisational 'science' too frequently reduces realities to such bifurcated polarities and either/or antinomies (Lewis 2000). The relegation of 'both/and' processes to the unrealistic, fanciful and inauthentic is the main means of limiting reality to the lowest level of Schumacher's hierarchy. Life, mind and the sublime are only valid through the myopic prism of fixed, objectively identifiable, measurable and certain reality.

Derrida (1978) labelled this dead-mapping cognitive style 'logocentrism'. The 'logos' is the word that expresses the underlying concrete reality or the rational language that perfectly represents a certain reality. Reality is perfectly represented by rational discourse. Reality is fixed and certain and the quest is to find a perfectly certain language that represents it without doubt. Dead-mapping, therefore is a product of the quest of Reason to eliminate uncertainty. Its mission is to take the perfect 'photographic' black and white picture of 'substantial' underlying mechanical reality using the advanced 'camera' of rational and mathematical language. Because 'the camera never lies' a correspondence to the truth is assured. Knowledge therefore, is the most appropriate film for an aperture and shutter speed that captures the perfect, rational photograph that looks exactly like 'still' or 'steady-state', machine-like reality.

NB; Epistem-ological. Concerning knowing/ understanding

Within Western thought, 'knowledge' has become that which precedes action and expects the knowledgeable to be able to perfectly understand and articulate causal determinants that can be explained preferably through written communication (Chia 2003). Everything within this 'epistemological culture' (knowledge culture) is affected (or infected) by the pursuit of certainty and the frantic avoidance of indeterminacy. This rather unwise mindset, we might call a culture of 'epistemania'. Western languages become logocentric accomplishments of the 'metaphysics of presence' that promotes the delusion of certain and homogeneous meaning of words and numbers as true representations of reality. The only things worth knowing are those articulated and explained within theories, measurable using 'tried and tested' or 'rigorous' methodologies and suitably certain to warrant the ultimate legitimacy of results being 'significant' and universally 'generalisable'. God-like knowing from above (the outside) becomes the desired level of certainty and the mortal parochialism of the actor (on the inside) is too humanly subjective, local and insufficiently rationally intelligent to warrant credible explanation.

In Western metaphysics, logocentric thought relies upon a series of dichotomies of opposition. The photograph is black or white. This is the consequence of a 'metaphysics of substance' (Chia 1999) where phenomena are conveyed as existing 'as such', and being represented (without complications by managers and modelled by theorists). The 'dead' or 'machine-mapping' of the metaphysics of substance is 'trapped in a Parmenidian intellectual legacy which implicitly elevates permanence over change, discreteness over immanent interconnectedness, linear progress over heterogeneous becoming, and equilibrium over flux and transformation' (ibid.: 226). Binary opposites involve privileging one term over its opposite and as a result the creation of truth and meaning is an outcome of the illusion of the 'metaphysics of presence' (Derrida 1976). This is the dubious assumption that the meaning of a word is present in the speaker's mind and communicable to the listener without any slippage of meaning. The distinctions between metaphysics of presence and the metaphysics of substance are summarised in Table 1.1.

In other words, modern Western languages (particularly) force us to see phenomena as only superficially dynamic because of the subconsciously assumed imposition of an underlying, substantive and more significant world of fixed Platonic 'forms'. Reality, as derived through language, assumes there is a 'presence' or an underlying absolute that is either reality or is not reality involving

Table 1.1: Metaphysical Distinctions

	Metaphysics of substance/ presence	*Metaphysics of change/ process*
Metaphors	(Dead or Machine-mapping), networks, variance modelling Reality is something there to be 'still' photographed	(Mind-mapping), Rhizomes, Net-workings, Second-order thinking Reality is something 'we' are making through a 'movie'
Intellectual sources	Parmenides, Plato, Descartes, Newton	Heraclitus, Buddha, Lao Tsu, Whitehead, Heidegger, Bateson, Derrida, Serres, Deleuze
Ontology	Ontology of Being. Emphasis upon stability, permanence and order. Truth as fixed and underlying (foundational). An entitative conception of reality	Ontology of Becoming. Emphasis upon process existentialism—every 'thing' is a stability wave within a sea of indeterminate process. Things are not real, only processes are real
Epistemology	Substance/Representationalist Epistemology. A 'logocentric' correspondence theory of truth involving 'simple location' whereby 'essential or foundational' presence of matter and hence causal mechanisms are assumed locatable at specific co-ordinative points in space-time. Linguistic terms provide an 'immaculate conception' and are taken to accurately represent an external world of present, discrete and identifiable objects, forces and generative mechanisms	Process Epistemology The primacy of process and change requires realisation of the mutual implication of process and structure. Each structure is a stabilised moment in a process of continuous becoming. There is no inert or invariable object as a thing that changes, only changes that produce heterogeneous becomings of objects. Change, seen as a series of differences in objects over time through one stage of fixed stability to another, is reification

(Table 1.1 contd.)

(Table 1.1 contd.)

	Metaphysics of substance/ presence	Metaphysics of change/ process
Process viewpoint	Representationalism depicts change outcomes as transitory temporal phases necessary for bridging the various stages of the rest of evolution. Change is only an epiphenomenal and unreal stage between periods of 'real' fixity/stability. Change requires organisation and management	Process and change are the only reality. Fixity, stability, management and organisation are linguistic bewitchments that disguise the reality of flux, indeterminacy and *duree*. Organisational change is an oxymoron because change is process and organisation is substance/presence/ representation. The idea of net-workings (a verb) better encapsulates a Deleuzian conception than 'networks' (a noun). Change cannot be managed

Source: Chia (1999).

the dichotomous reductionism of différance (Derrida 1976). Différance implies the indeterminacy of meaning resulting from deferral of differentiated chains of suspended signifiers, which are unstable, shifting and arbitrarily related to a signified truth. This involves reducing phenomena to bivalent, black and white categories, one of which is privileged as 'subject' and the other is denigrated as 'object'. In other words, 'our Western world is framed by the black and white reductionism inherent in the structure of our modern languages'. Western language judges, reduces and simplifies the richness of narratives while at the same time politically loading the narrative to favour the rational, individualistic perspective, language, knowledge and communication (or discourses) require scrutiny for meanings and their political intentions if we want to ascend Schumacher's hierarchy.

A principal concomitant of the 'dead mapping' of the metaphysics of substance is that reality is depicted as essentially discrete, substantial and enduring resulting in a requirement for scientific obsessions with precision, accuracy and parsimony in representing 'rigorous' explanations of a concrete social reality. Western scientism breaks down in certain contexts, however. In art or Eastern culture where knowledge is something acquired principally through practice, it is incoherent (Chia 2003). In the study of culture, for example, the problem (within scientism) of needing to know how to explain and compare 'rationally' from the outside using 'etic' models frustrates a more vital 'emic' and local understanding from the inside. The unfortunate compulsion towards certainty, theorising and explaining causalities through logocentric language ends up with epistemological (involving assumptions about knowledge) productions or artefacts of scientism. The 'method' or map determines the reality, and understanding is confined to understanding entirely on the abstract terms of the 'understander' rather than from the viewpoint of those being understood.

Epistemania: A 'real' identity problem and lifeless knowing

The Western mind has inherited the structural representationalism of Aristotle and of Descartes' *Cogito*. Descartes sought an absolute, certain knowledge. Applying rigorous, sceptical, universal doubt through mathematical method he found that he could only be certain of knowing one thing; namely that he was exercising this doubt and, therefore, he could be certain of his existence. The certainty myth of the existence of the self is established through the use of Platonic Reason in processing external phenomena. The

NB; Ontological Concerning what is reality, truth, veritable, actual

problem we inherit from Descartes is Cartesian anxiety. It is an ontological (involving assumptions about reality) delusion. Thousands of years of Western philosophy leaves the Western mind in a state of anxious delusion in the search for certainty through acquisition of knowledge. The inherited problem of Cartesian anxiety for Zohar (1991) is the principle source of a contemporary Western, atomised, egocentric, alienated, 'I-centered culture'. Capra (1997: 287) sums up the consequent contemporary Western condition of atomised alienation of the isolated narcissist from each other and from the rest of the world. We are autonomous individuals, shaped by our own history and structural changes. We are self-aware, aware of our individual identity and yet, when we look for an independent self within our world of experience we cannot find any such entity. The origin of our dilemma lies in our tendency to create the abstraction of separate objects, including a separate self, and then to believe that they belong to an objective, independent existing reality.

Cave (1995) proposes that the internal 'I' and the external 'Me' are reciprocal and mutually constitutive but the latter is denigrated under the privilege offered, during an 'inward turn', to the former in modern identity narration. Modern, Western identity, therefore, is characteristically egocentric and internalised so that plots of identity are narrative attempts at the verisimilitude of the individual ego.

> NB;
> Verisimilitude
> Truth claims-
> contested
> plots of reality

Added to these are the problems we inherit from Newton. Newton's mechanistic model of the universe is a bleak and lifeless system that follows immutable rules. For Zohar (1991), Newton's mechanism is still a principal influence of everyday Western life and a principal influence on our relentless search for a deluded, fixity requirement of knowing the world. As a result 'Newton's vision tore us out from the fabric of the universe itself' (ibid.: 2). Newtonian fixity has inspired equally lifeless, deterministic social theorising from Marx, Darwin, Freud and others (ibid.). 'Knowing' over 'Being' in Western philosophy, from this viewpoint, has cultivated a culture of individualistic modernism that is lifeless, exploitative, inhuman and alienating.

The resulting problem in the West is not simply knowledge institutionalisation, commodification or marketisation

(Gabriel 2002; Hassard and Keleman 2002), but 'an unwise obsession with knowledge itself' (Chia 2003). This Western epistemania is characterised by a 'preoccupation with knowledge-creation and knowledge management' where knowledge is 'rigorously' restricted to 'that which has been produced through the process of observation, reflection and reasoning, and which has then been systematically articulated in a written form through the medium of language' (ibid.: 953). More knowledge within epistemania, it goes without saying, is better in the 'hyped' knowledge economy occupied by knowledge-intensive industry, knowledge-based firms and knowledge workers dedicated to 'lifelong learning', which is a form of epistemological (knowledge based) servitude. This obsession is predicated on the illusion that more knowledge, created through rationality in an explicit representational form, will produce improved performance once effectively applied (ibid.). As a result, we end up with totalitarian, wisdom-free social science rather than social inquiry as social philosophy concerned to identify what is important to happiness, how to resolve human problems and conflicts and how to establish moral cohesion in a world of plural moralities.

A Cartesian-Newtonian mechanistic worldview, Zohar (1991) argues, produces an inherited dualism pervading our everyday lives. She argues that this has created, in the West, an alienating fragmentation at different levels. She cites Lawrence Cahoones's 'three pernicious dichotomies' of 'mind–body', 'self–other' and 'nature–nurture' dualisms as sources of contemporary, multi-level alienation. She states, (ibid.: 216):

> The three 'pernicious dichotomies' left us wondering how we conscious human beings related to ourselves (our own bodies, our own past and future, our own sub-selves), to each other or to the world of nature and facts.

Restriction to the machine-maps or 'pointer readings' of Cartesian scientism leads to 'the abomination of desolation' of modern abstract, meaningless, inhospitable and inhuman existence that creates life within a socially bankrupt, amoral, narcissistic, voluptuous consumption machine. The machine-maps of scientism are maps of 'real' things that don't 'really' matter and offer representations of the living through a cartography of visible, dead and measurable things. Such maps or 'paradigms' lead to the dead-end of nowhere important because 'the quantitative factor is of preponderant weight only at the lowest level of Being' (Schumacher 1977: 64) cultivating a 'science for manipulation' whose misplaced purpose becomes power over nature and man.

Dead-maps denigrate the wisdom of 'pre-modernity's acceptance of subjectivity and different interpretations' (Cummings and Wilson 2003: 13) of the territory resulting in the centralisation of state-sponsored essentialist or foundational 'replication of arboreal-triangular form toward greater certainty and order of explanation' (ibid.) promoting a Cartesian 'fallacy of detachment' between thinking (mind) and doing (body). The metaphor of the thinking mind (*res cognitans*) using rational certainty to control the inert body (*res extensa*) where power is wasted and dangerous is foundational to neo-classical strategic theory where structure (body) follows strategy (mind). This Cartesian '"a withdrawal from wisdom" and the exclusive concentration on knowledge as firm and indubitable as mathematics and geometry' (Schumacher 1977: 14) promotes that dead, machine-like and lower external realities govern all sensory expectations.

The increasing tendency, therefore, is for values that are determined to optimise managerialist value at the expense of social, moral, spiritual and intellectual values are a consequence of the unwitting, impoverished incremental materialism of what J.K. Galbraith (2004) terms 'The Economics of Innocent Fraud'. Quantifiable knowledge, amoral action and inanimate Being of impoverished and illusory certainty ensure that the 'will to power' of planning and associated fallacies maintains the power in thinking and the thinking in the 'hands' of the powerful (Clegg et al. 2005: 22). The consequence is a domination of modern economic society by the corporation and the superintendent materialism of management who constitute the high priesthood of legitimised exploitation. That which detracts from the pecuniary interests of management and their sponsors is most severely scorned. It is in the nature of the institutionalisation of delusion of managerialism that its progenitors are more often without agency in justifying the legitimation of greed in that they, in the main, are unaware of its moral and spiritual deficit and are also victims of an 'innocent fraud' (Galbraith 2004: 2).

The outcome is that 'much of the apathy, carelessness and lack of pride so often encountered in the modern workplace is thus not coincidental: it is fostered by the mechanistic approach' (Morgan 1997: 30). The fraud is innocent because social identity becomes so overwhelmed by the cash nexus that everyday constructions of reality succumb to the inevitability and tacit acceptance of the 'TINA' principle that 'there is no alternative' to the delusion that material advancement can bring happiness and avarice has no relevant social, moral, ecological or spiritual costs. The implication of this is not that corporatist interests overtly purchase political, professional and civic society but that cash becomes the quasi-object that pervasively controls the consciousness of the politician, professional and civilian-consumer. In other words it becomes impossible to think outside the money box 'plot' when the lowest level of Schumacher's hierarchy is dominant. As a result 'in understanding organization as a rational, technical process, mechanical imagery tends to underplay the human aspects of organization and to overlook the fact that the task facing organizations are often much more complex, uncertain and difficult than those that can be performed by most machines' (ibid.: 27). Aldous Huxley suggested that 'A really efficient totalitarian state would be one in which the all-powerful executive of political bosses and their army of managers control a population of slaves who do not have to be coerced, because they love their servitude' (Huxley 1962: xii). Has the 'innocent fraud' not already produced Huxley's 'brave new world' dystopia, where freedom has been mortgaged to ubiquitous, amoral self-absorbed, rationalist materialism?

ANIMATE MAPS OF ORGANIC LIFE

Uncomfortable with the machine-maps of scientism, many management authors began to develop an alternative metaphor of 'organism' to describe a more life-like reality. Organic approaches developed in response to the obvious limitations of Taylorism and the machine-metaphor. Mary Parker Follett, Elton Mayo's Hawthorne Studies, Abraham Maslow, Chris Argyris, Frederich Hertzberg, Douglas McGregor, the Tavistock Institute of Human Relations and Peter Drucker all contributed to the humanisation of management theory and a realisation of the critical importance of the social domain in establishing work motivation (Morgan 1997).

This organicism constitutes another, less rigid, form of 'modernism', namely a post-classical modernism drawing upon von Bertalanffy's General Systems Theory. This approach, as for Schumacher (1977), identifies phenomena as formed within a hierarchy of complexity of systems. Boulding (1956), also identifies 'transcendental' systems (of 'inescapable unknowables') at the top of a hierarchy of systems. However, for systems theorists, these levels are all subject to generalisable laws that permit a theoretical and universal unity of understanding. Bertalanffy, according to Hatch and Cunliffe (2006: 37)

> ... did not expect the theory to do away with the varied branches of science, he predicted that the branches would continue to investigate the unique features of their phenomena of interest. Instead systems theorists would focus on the law-like regularities underlying and uniting all phenomena across the various branches of natural and social science.

In terms of Schumacher's hierarchy, therefore, General Systems Theory is a principal source of continued privileging of essentialism, universalism and foundationalism. It is theory that is generalisable and subject to universal law that is the priority. Differences within different levels are the 'colouring in' required to complete the universal picture. The assumption is that the same scientific laws

NB; *Essentialism* Reality is assumed as caused or based upon 'real', underlying factors

govern the inanimate, the animate, the cognitive and the sublime.

Organicism drew heavily upon the inherited assumptions of Darwinism and promoted the rise of Contingency Theory, Resource Dependency Theory, Population Ecology, Institutional Theory, and Complexity Theory (Hatch and Cunliffe 2006; Morgan 1997). It was also a principal metaphor underlying Mintzberg's 'more "organic" view of organisations' that mapped a more bottom up, emergent and processual view of organisations (Cummings and Wilson 2003: 18). These organic views are sensitive to patterns and 'survival' processes of organisational relationships 'in terms of organic functioning, relations with the environment, relations among species, and the wider ecology' (Morgan 1997: 66).

These new 'organic' modernist maps or 'paradigms', however, fail to escape adequately from the problems of classical modernism. Contingency Theory, for example, still adopts a causal deterministic approach 'that is, of seeing organizational structures as being determined or pushed by contingencies' (Fulop and Linstead 2004: 143). It 'takes an objectivist stance and is typically assessed on criteria of technical rationality and efficiency' (Hatch and Cunliffe 2006: 41). The agency of managers and their tendency to 'enact' their environments, which are invented more by their choices about what to notice and respond to, is overlooked. Contingency theory, therefore, as an organic, animate, 'live mapping' approach 'tends to reify organizations (and indeed environment)' (Fulop and Linstead 2004: 143) as kinds of 'immaculate perceptions' under the influence of lower dead-mapping. We are still, according to Morgan 'led to view organizations and their environments in a way that is far too concrete' and deny the capacity to permit organisations to be 'understood as socially constructed phenomena' (Morgan 1997: 66) that involve political struggles in language games that reflect interests in what is projected-invented as 'efficient', 'organisation', 'environment' and 'survival'. The problem with adopting Darwinism in the social sphere is its abuse, when 'In effect, natural law is invoked to legitimize the organization of society' (Morgan 1997: 71) and the prospect of change in terms of liberatory democratic, social and civic reform is diminished in the name of the imperative of 'survival of the fittest'.

Organismic metaphors replace linear causality with misplaced political, economic, social and technological 'multi-linear' causality that retains an epistemological (knowledge assumption) addiction to certainty. Complexity, for example, is often used as a 'smokescreen to justify the exploration of higher levels of Being with lower inanimate matter' (Schumacher 1977: 116). As with Darwinism, such organicism is 'descriptive science' that is more holistic and tolerant of uncertainty than the 'instructional' science of classical modernist mapping. However, like Darwinism, it fails to escape from science fiction or 'hoax' (ibid.: 129) of proof of causation that 'complexity' is an effect of accumulated tangible, simpler 'visible' causes, rather than the uncertain, indeterminate 'invisibilia' of Aristotle's higher 'final cause' or 'purpose'. Aristotle was the arch advocate of causation but in his schema he maintained that ultimate causation is a 'final cause' attributable 'teleologically' to sublime influences and required a poetic sensibility. For 'essentialists', this is anathema and so this aspect of Aristotle's philosophy is selectively ignored and only 'real' causation is regarded as legitimate.

At times, complexity theory spins out of credibility and into a kind of hippy-foundationalist fantasy. So, for example, Beck and Cowan (2006) piggybacking upon the neo-Darwinist Richard Dawkins and the American psychologist Clare Graves elicit the metaphor of 'spirals' to advocate a sort of essentialist mimetic cultural DNA to explain human behaviour. Some complexity theorists, therefore, appear hamstrung by their dead-mapping past. They bring with them all the baggage of assuming that natural sciences are a model for the development of social science. They are captivated by methodological individualism, by the ideas that there are causal cognitive determinants to complex cultural outcomes and by the mentalism of innate ideas (another Cartesian inheritance promulgated by Chomsky). What results is a reiteration of rational choice modelling in a more contemporary situation that explains complexity through essentialism and foundationalism. Another (better) way of viewing organisations as complex systems 'is to explore complex ways of thinking about organisations as complex systems' (Tsoukas and Hatch 2001: 980). Such a 'second order' examination of the meanings ascribed to 'complexity' needs to take account of what and why 'statements' about complexity come to be held to be true. It also needs reflection upon language itself, in that 'the history of language is a seamless story of gradually increasing complexity' (Rorty 1999: 74). Complexity, in other words is a projection/invention of complex language rather than a 'discovery' of complex systems.

Schumacher (1977) distinguishes two types of problems. The first type of problems are 'convergent' and are solved through the pursuit of greater analysis, greater certainty and more knowledge. These, of course are the principal concern of those in 'instructional science' who see the world through inanimate dead-maps. Divergent problems, by contrast, do not respond to greater analysis and more certainty. The more that dead-mapping is applied to such problems, the more paradoxical they appear. These are 'process' problems more familiar to those concerned with animate and cognitive mapping. The solution to these problems is not in the more applied dead-mapping but in the engagement of wisdom, which begins with synchronous application of knowledge from all successive levels in Schumacher's hierarchy.

According to David Boje (1999)

Since the 1960s much of the organization theory (OT) writing is a never-ending debate between the machine/organ analogies, and attempts to develop growth models of how simple mechanistic forms can grow into the more complex organic forms. Few have stopped to question the silliness of this theory of semantic illusions, or to look at the five-century debate in philosophy about the machine philosophies of Locke, Hume, Newton and the reemerging organic philosophy.

The consequent problem is due to a kind of 'Snakes and Ladders' dualistic reality-game with too many snakes and not enough ladders. The snakes are convergent problems that can be coped with through lower forms of knowledge using instructional certainties, quantification and other dead-mapping techniques. Here, differences can be resolved with choice between either/or options and yes/no dualisms using the 'correct formulae' (Schumacher 1977: 141) of lower, simplistic, economic utilitarian rationalism. The 'ladders', of course, access 'divergent problems' that are replete with dilemma, paradox, contradiction. These are insoluble at lower levels of Being and can only be transcended through ascendance 'up the ladder' of Schumacher's hierarchy to higher levels, where previous differences disappear when faced with higher virtues (ibid.). Because snakes outnumber ladders, the potential for climbing the order of Being and reaching a transcendent 'home' is thwarted by the gravitational pull of impoverished dead-mapping knowledge, lower Being and the politics of warfare between incommensurable, intransigent views transfixed by lower externalities. Schumacher's four levels of Being are ontologically 'different, incomparable, incommensurable and discontinuous' (ibid.: 33) but the dilemma is that a wise understanding requires somehow transcending these incommensurabilities.

In Strategy, for example, the 'descriptive' science of Mintzberg has been involved with the 'instructional science' of Ansoff and Porter in a protracted war of attrition between 'design' and 'emergence' paradigms for decades. In Schumachers terms, these paradigms occupy different onto-epistemological levels. Whittington's (1993) strategic paradigms or 'theories of action' are mapped in Schumacher's hierarchy in Figure 1.2.

Whittington is highly critical of the hegemony of the 'classical' school in strategy, characterised by an addiction to 'banalysis'. The implication is that strategists need to be aware of different lenses and be competent and pragmatic in their contextual use. Within strategic paradigm warfare, wisdom is marginalised. Wisdom is an

Figure 1.2: Whittington's Schools of Strategy within Schumacher's Hierarchy

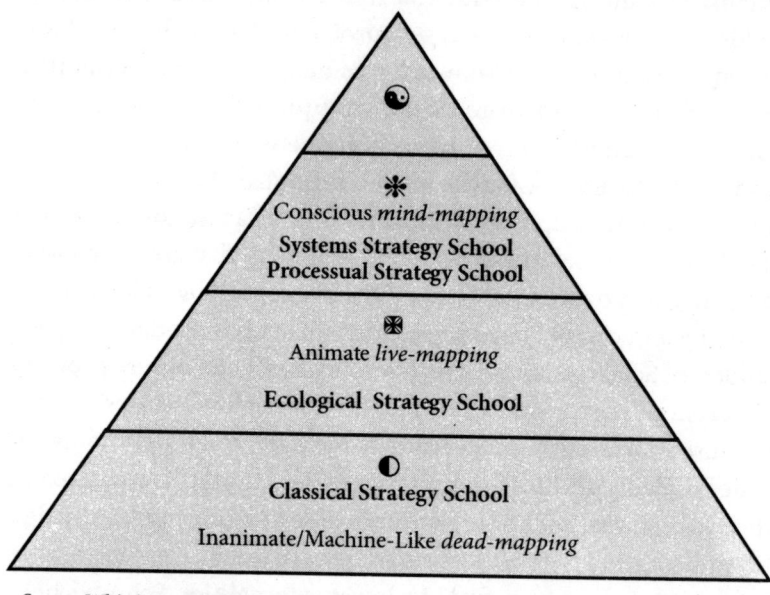

Conscious *mind-mapping*
Systems Strategy School
Processual Strategy School

Animate *live-mapping*

Ecological Strategy School

Classical Strategy School
Inanimate/Machine-Like *dead-mapping*

Source: Whittington (1993).

attitude that maintains a healthy balance between overconfident knowing and debilitating uncertainty (Weick 2001). It is paradoxically increasingly absent, yet needed more urgently in the midst of language and paradigm war-gaming among management theorists.

MIND MAPS

Mind mapping began after the 'crisis of representation' in art, anthropology and other areas of understanding. The crisis of representation realised the untenability of the modernists in their assumption of the 'immaculate perception'. This is the logocentric assumption that photographic 'logic' enables the rationalist to see reality 'perfectly logically' through perfectly articulated Reason.

In art, Magritte provided a representation that challenged such essentialist 'representationalism'. In the 'pipe' (Figure 1.3), he shows us a picture of a pipe.

Figure 1.3: Ceci n'est pas une pipe

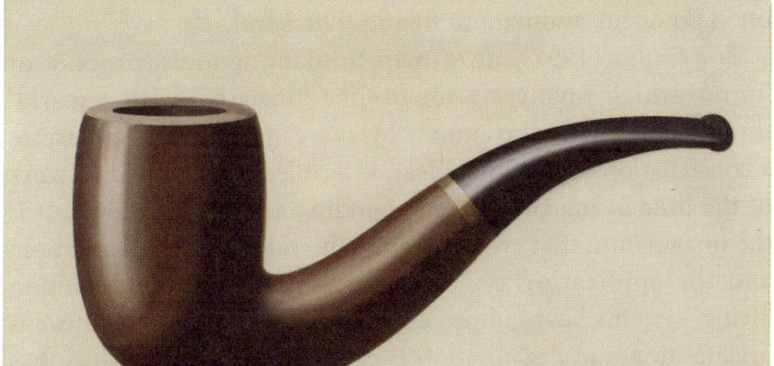

Source:	La Trahison des images (ceci n'est pasune pipe), 1929 by Rene Magritte
	Museum Number. 78.7; Medium : Oil on Canvas. Size Overall: 25 3/8 × 37 in. (64.45 × 93.98 cm). Unframed Canvas: 23 11/16 × 31 7/7 inches, 1 1/2 inches deep, 39 5/8 inches diagonal.
Credit:	Los Angeles County Museum of Art, Purchased with funds provided by Mr and Mrs William Preston Harrison Collection.
Copyright notice:	Photograph © 2009 Museum Associate/LACMA.

He at the same time provided text which says: 'This is not a pipe.' Magritte is asking us to realise that pictures (paradigms or maps) are not realities (or territories) and require us to reflect on our modernist propensity to reify representations and objectify reality. If the prevailing picture metaphor for dead-mapping is the photograph, then the equivalent for mind-mapping is cinema. Reality for mind-mapping is a more 'cinematographic' projection, from minds and language, of a moving reality. The 'movie', perceived as reality, as an image seen on the silver screen of meaning by the audience is a product of the enactment of scripts and organisation involving directors, screenplay writers, actors and technicians (and, of course, often powerful, anonymous financial backers).

For Capra (1997), dead-map thinking ignores 'process' or 'mind' which involves a movie-like 'bringing forth a world' through imaginative invention. Ideas are imagined and culture, as a constellation of dynamic ideas, is a collective dynamic network of the human imagination surrounding a group of people. It is the imagination that creates reality, the rules for such a creation, and the application or 'enactment' of those rules. Human 'living' systems have culture as an emergent property. Culture is organisation and organisation is cognition or 'mind', which has network characteristics. Mind enables change and transformation through learning processes that formulate and reformulate, (most actively during periods of instability) images of self, relationships and environment. As a result, networks are central to human life because they are cultural. Culture as 'mind' is central to life because it is organised through networks. Networks are cultural and culture is an ideational network, a phenomenon best suited to the metaphor of mind and imagination. Such cognitive or 'conscious' systems theories focus upon networks as the principal organisational metaphor.

Culture and society, from this viewpoint is conceivable as an organisation of a matrix of meanings, which emerge from the process of interaction of its members using information as a relation or carrier of meanings. This produces the notion of culture as consisting of 'intensional objects that comprise a society's information system' (Brownstein 1995: 329). 'Intensional objects' are non-physical entities or psychological manifestations organised into interacting structures such as religious beliefs or propositional attitudes constituting a societal information system. Brownstein explains culture by using a metaphor to reflect on the relationship between society and culture (Brownstein 1995: 330). Society as a system of apparent interactive relationships can be likened to the 'brain' whereas culture as a system, which organises society's information, is likened to the 'mind'. The brain and the mind are reflections of each other and co-determined, but the main differentiation is that the brain (society) is manifest, more explicit and empirically examinable, whereas the mind (culture) is less so.

Culture as 'mind' is, therefore, the distinctive, non-temporal and non-spatial aspect of 'self-organising' human systems (Capra 1982: 316). The human mind creates a subjective inner world (constituted by self-awareness, concepts, art, experience, values and expectations, purposes, symbols, perceptions) that mirrors an outer reality (ibid.: 320). The environment is, therefore, 'made' through these subjective perceptual filters. Response to the environment is governed by the interplay between the changing outer and inner world. The environment thus shapes and is shaped by the collective conscious 'mind' of human culture. Culture as mind 'is a multi-levelled and integrated pattern of processes that represent the dynamics of human self-organisation' (ibid.: 322) which enables social evolution in dynamic cycles of rhythmic fluctuation (ibid.: 326) between continuity and change. The mind of the system is what specifies which perturbations from the environment are significant and how a network system responds to a selected disturbance through changes in its patterns of connectivity. Mind, or cognition, is therefore synonymous with learning and development, which allows intelligent interaction with the environment. Human cognition (or 'culture'), which is highly sophisticated, allows such coupling with its environment and itself. As a result, human culture 'brings forth not only an external but also an internal world. In human beings, the bringing forth of such an inner world is intimately linked to language, thought, and consciousness' (Capra 1997: 263). In other words, humans invent both the 'outside' and their 'inside'.

Understanding the non-physical world of networks requires emphasis upon social construction. This involves understanding *verstehen* or meaning, interpretations of meanings and rules of interpretation. This represents a theory-of-knowledge or epistemic dimension of the concept of meaning wherein reality exists nominally only through meaning (Alasuutari 1995: 27). Ideas are imagined and culture, as a constellation of dynamic ideas, is a collective dynamic network of the human imagination surrounding a group of people. It is the interaction of imagination that creates reality, the rules for such a co-creation, and the application or 'enactment' of those rules.

Hatch and Cunliffe (2006: 43) term the focus on mind-mapping, the 'symbolic–interpretive' perspective. This involves the creation or invention of reality by communicative interaction within social groups through sense-making and exchange of meaning using language and symbols. It is, in terms of the 'picture' metaphor introduced above, it corresponds to a 'cinematographic' view of reality. Language within this metaphor is the celluloid film; it's the software of an invented moving picture. Hatch and Cunliffe identify four important influences on the development of this 'movie-like' perspective as; social construction theory, enactment theory, institutionalisation and reflexivity (ibid.).

Social constructionism emphasises how knowledge of reality is accessed through communal interchange using language. It also emphasises that knowledge, as a product of this inventive process, is ideologically saturated (Gergen and Gergen 2003). The communal reality-generating practices that configure rules for judging acceptable truths of everyday life are 'ethnomethods'. They 'go without saying' in that they come to be taken for granted 'accomplishments' as unquestionably correct and create frustration followed by anger if challenged. They help us frame and configure reality in context because 'our constructions of the situation influence what rules and codes of behaviour are to be summoned' (Morgan 1997: 140). Questioning the meaning of words can create havoc when words are seen as the vehicle of the 'immaculate conception' of their meaning within a correspondence theory of truth.

Karl Weick is the central figure in enactment theory and 'sensemaking'. Weick 'brought social construction into organization theory with his theory of sensemaking' (Hatch and Cunliffe 2006: 44). Organisations are consequences of cognitive maps of organisational members' sensemaking. Weick (1995) famously also used the map metaphor in the story of the Hungarian troop of soldiers lost in the Alps. In this story the soldiers save themselves using a map of a different territory mistaken for the one they are lost in. For many, the emphasis upon the mimetic animation or 'enactment' of the map, rather than the map itself was a welcome improvement. Such social constructions of reality result in maps that are projections of negotiated, often contested meaning of what is objectified as real territory. The symbolic–interpretive agenda finally liberated subjective and uncertain influences from their previous denigration by of dead map obsession with the notion of objective certainty.

Culture as 'mind' is, therefore, the distinctive, non-temporal and non-spatial aspect of 'self-organising' human systems (Capra 1982: 316). The environment is, therefore, 'made' through these subjective perceptual filters. Response to the environment is governed by the interplay between the changing outer and inner world images. The environment, thus, shapes and is shaped by the collective conscious 'mind' of human culture. Such self-organisation enables social evolution in dynamic cycles of rhythmic fluctuation (ibid.: 326) between continuity and change.

We move from life mapping to mind mapping conceptions of organisation and organising change. Morgan outlines a metaphorical shift from conceptions of organisations as 'brains' from informational processing, through cybernetic 'double-loop' learning to holographic, self-organising cognitive systems 'where qualities of the whole are enfolded in all the parts' (Morgan 1997: 100). Within Schumacher's hierarchy, this transition of metaphor is depicted in Figure 1.4.

Figure 1.4: Schumacher's Hierarchy and Morgan's (1997) 'Brain' Metaphors

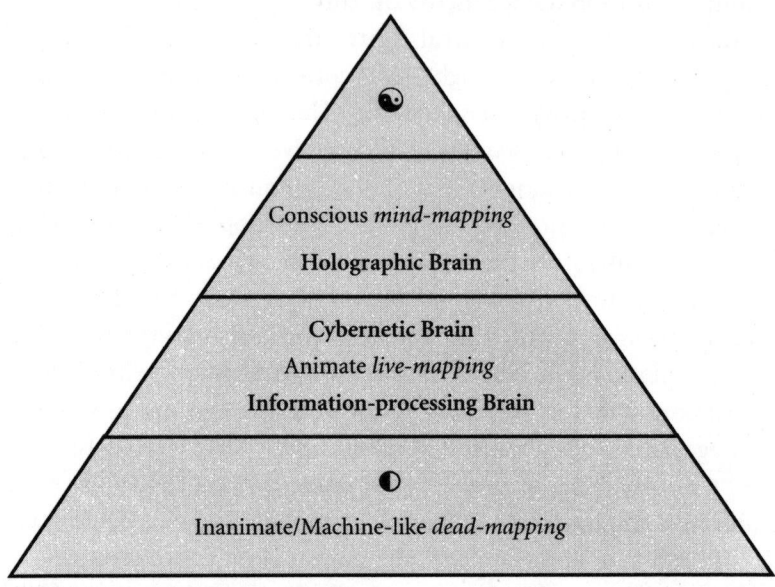

When the organisation metaphorically acquires a brain, it is capable of learning. In particular, it is capable of learning that it is using a map. It is also potentially capable of learning that changing the map will change the nature of embarkation, journey and destination; in other words it is capable of learning how to learn.

The emergence of the brain and mind metaphor in organisational analysis is largely due to Morgan's (1986, 1997) equating self-organisation and learning with images of the brain. Morgan (1997) surveys the 'maps' and 'paradigms' of organisation and management thought and demonstrates how each mapping style is characterised by a dominant metaphor. The mind metaphor as the consequence of the emergence of an 'evolutionary' paradigm which is in the process of displacing 'mechanistic' and 'organismic' paradigms, has been explored through the idea of the holographic brain (ibid.) and 'triune-brain' (Broekstra 1996). The suggestion is that the consciousness of complex, multi-levelled, living systems, means that the self-organising network is likely to become the normative organisational metaphor in the coming era. This conscious 'mind' metaphor shares considerable 'domain similarities' with the adaptive, relational networks of management in that it evokes a conception of a conscious, intelligent and learning system. It is also consistent with the postmodern view of culture as relationally based meaning production within a symbolic environment. This symbolic environment as a process is constantly changing and subsumed within the context of power.

Metaphors of Change

Morgan's (1986, 1997) metaphors of change assume that experience is a surface feature of a deeper dynamic logic or a basic 'implicate' transformation. In other words change at deeper structures of a 'flowing and unbroken whole' universe is manifested, realised and expressed in the 'explicate' world around us. Stability is therefore always a surface appearance underpinned by constant transformation. Science has focused upon the surface phenomena, assuming that change is a product of reality. The metaphors of implicate, changing reality require an assumption that surface, explicate reality is a production of immanent continuous change. This in turn requires an emphasis upon understanding the logic of the generative processes that link dynamic implicate change with explicate experience.

Culture in the context of these metaphors is a surface phenomenon generating patterns of meaning that produce how the explicate world is interpreted. Meanings regarding the environment, self-identity and relationships with others are principal cultural inventions. In other words, culture involves the means by which the world is made and enacted or socially constructed through imagination. Culture is differently learned and created in different discourses. These have equal validity but differentially frame human conceptualisation of surface 'reality' involving a symbolic environment, which are images and fictions with an existence of their own.

The worldview that this kind of thinking evokes is noticeably different from the rational worldview dominant in management theory generally. The alternative view presented by an index of possibilities serves as a promising lens to develop a more 'binocular' view of culture. The differences between the two lenses are comprehensive and substantial and a binocular view requires an ability to understand and command them both and to treat them as equally valid perspectives.

Metaphors of the unfolding logics of change essentially replace rationalist linearity with systems circularity which feature a recognition of holism and organic 'form' involving flux and transformation and pattern of relationships within an organised whole. They assume self-referential closure or enactment in relation to environments. In other words environments do not 'exist' as ontologically 'real' and separate variables, but as nominally created by humans. Environments then are seen as a created projection of self-image or identity. Another principal assumption is the fundamental interdependence of all phenomena, which are embedded in the cyclical processes of nature as integrated wholes or fields of relations so that all elements are engaged in maintenance of self and others.

Postmodernism

Postmodernism and poststructuralism is a sustained attack on dead-mapping. It focuses upon how meaning is established through language and communication. In doing so it exposes the instability and uncertainty of meaning and reveals how established meaning reflects the power interests of establishment elites. In terms of Schumacher's hierarchy it remains within the realm of 'mind-mapping' because its focus is upon meaning and knowledge and not (principally) wisdom, the central issue within the domain of the sublime.

Postmodernism may be said to involve a transition in styles of belief creating new schisms and non-ideological, issue-based 'culture wars'. A breakdown of the Enlightenment Project of scientism or universal rationalism as a single correct, objective mode of representing immanent or metaphysical 'truth'. This promotes an end of the dead-mapping ideology of 'progress' and associated beliefs of linear progress, absolute truths, and rational planning of ideal social orders. This, in turn, promotes an end of other modernist 'metanarratives' or grand unifying discourses along with a critique of legitimatisation of authority and power, and atomisation of the individual from the context of her relationships.

Postmodernism is consistent with an emergence of pluralism and acceptance of multiple 'truths' and relative rather than absolute objectivity, for example regarding identity and morality, which are socially constructed or 'made' rather than 'found'. Such relativism favours an acceptance that such truths are human creations produced through language and communication so that 'where there are no sentences there is no truth' (Truett 1996: 8). This lends itself to an identification of the construction of truth or meaning within science and management as a strategy of exercising power through knowledge and a focus upon the 'linguistic turn' which assumes that ideas cannot be understood outside the language system that produced them locally and specifically. Language is to humans like water is to fish; it configures everything about us without our realising it. Unwittingly immersed in a 'pool of nouns and verbs' (Gergen 1992: 207), we swim around socially unaware of the flowing textuality of our existence. In this respect, it is assumed that 'our languages of description and explanation do not so much map an independent reality as they create the very sense of its existence' (Gergen 2003: 453). Reality, from this viewpoint is talked into existence within cultural contexts. This approach is consistent with an acceptance of cultural or moral relativism, eclecticism, 'cultural bricolage' and multiple worldviews both within groups and for individuals. Postmodernism promotes the centrality of culture, as a kind of symbolic DNA, as differently learned and created discourses of equal validity which frame human conceptualisation of surface 'reality'. The focus is upon a symbolic environment involving images and fictions with an existence of their own that we are increasingly becoming conscious of, acting upon and trading with.

Significant differences between modernist and postmodern discourses are evident and contiguous to this are different conceptions of organisation and organising. Modernist discourse is characterised by transcendent yet anthropocentric criteria such as 'reason' and 'progress'. In modernist discourse, 'organisation' concerns enacting or legitimising rationality as a totalising ambition. Organisation is therefore promoted as a legitimate social tool for the totalisation of rationalism, reason and progress. It is an objective, administrative-economic function that enables planned activity. By contrast, postmodern discourse is characterised by a rejection of such modernist, structural certainties. Postmodern discourse involves the need to 'absorb ambiguity and uncertainty into our theorizing' (Hatch and Cunliffe 2006: 48) through engagement with paradox, contradiction and indeterminacy. Organisation is, in postmodern terms therefore, an anthropocentric defence against a chaotic, uncertain and uncontrollable and 'disorganised' universe. From this viewpoint organisation has an inherent 'automaticity'; a life of its own that is beyond human control (Cooper and Burrell 1988) or management.

Postmodernists often share many of the assumptions and foci of social constructionism. Knowledge is regarded as ideological and language is regarded as formative of reality, rather than as the modernists would have it; as a mirror of reality or a 'photographic' means of representing Truth. In its attack on dead-mapping assumptions that progress requires the universal spread of rationalism, postmodernists seek to privilege the local over the global. Postmodernism requires above all that local culture be taken seriously. Culture involves thinking, talking and acting locally according to a socially constructed world where meaning or 'reality' is produced through symbolic creations. Culture is therefore made locally through symbols and, particularly, through language. A universal culture is therefore an impossible agenda since all ideas will pass through local symbolic transformation. The postmodern mantra could be 'think local, act local'.

Put another way, postmodernism requires the realisation that people are cultural beings and this means that all of us (together) are 'making it up as we go along'. This equally applies to sober and rigorously scientific management professors as to local street vendors. The 'hawkers' worldview is 'different' but in no way inferior to the management professors' worldview. If the latter claims a privileged position, this is no more than a 'strategy of power' of modernist thinking which seeks to maintain scientific 'truth' and logical rationalism as the sole criteria for legitimising decisions in a 'modern' world. This modernist discourse claims, amongst other things, the validity of transcendent anthropocentric criteria of 'progress' and 'reason' and the human subject as the vehicle for control of uncertainty through management and organisation (Cooper and Burrell 1988).

WISDOM MAPS BEYOND MIND, TALK AND TIME

Wisdom maps cannot be spoken or written so the following section must be regarded as only a poor proxy for their understanding. Wisdom maps concern what might be termed spirit or spirituality. They have been somewhat 'crowded out' of Western discourse by the twin pillars of science and materialism. In this section, we focus upon Eastern philosophy and mostly use Buddhism to exemplify the benefits of re-seeking the sublime. Eastern 'philosophy' retains what the etymology of that word reveals; namely a 'love of wisdom'. Most Eastern philosophy does not, by contrast to Western scientism, differentiate between knowledge and belief. It is polytheistic in recognition that no single perspective is adequate in pursuit of the Sublime. The true self is not individual but integral to the cosmic whole. Suffering lies in grasping onto the ego and salvation lies in virtuous living for the other and meditation on the Sublime. Escape to salvation lies in future lives as a karmic accrual from practicing virtue in this life that achieves transcendence from a false, egoistic self.

Eastern philosophy is sympathetic to the cultivation of the wisdom-based attitude of the *karmyogis*, namely the subordination of ends to the karmic benefit of virtuous action (Siddiqui 2005: 13) and consequent prioritisation of ethically positive 'processes' (*kaizen* in Japanese) whose ends will take care of themselves. Such wisdom involves awakening to the invisible, paradoxical, indeterminate and inexplicable. 'By helping us see the unseen and hearing the unheard' (ibid.: 30), we sensitise ourselves to significant and uncontrollable intangibles of nature. To deal with these sublime influences, Chinese philosophy, for example, has always relied upon a balance of combined opposites. The interventionist, rationalistic and anthropomorphic virtue of Confucian *Li* (order) is combined in dialectic balance with the Taoist *habitus* of nature or *Wu Wei* that promotes action through intuitive or spiritual engagement with the paradoxical, natural, dynamic stability of 'manifestation' in the 'anchorless moment' (ibid.: 47) of living interconnectedness.

In Eastern culture knowing by doing is preferred over abstract theorising and mastery is sought through sustained and dedicated practice beginning with extensive apprenticeships of direct experience (Chia 2003). Motivation derives from a desire to achieve 'pure experience'; namely a reality of 'being' that is primary to constructions of identity of self and others. Chinese philosophy has always been inclined towards the primacy of change over fixity and permanence. Eastern art and philosophies, such as Buddhism and Taoism, have in common a dedication towards direct experience and dedicated, practical action (ibid.).

Within Eastern thought an ontological (reality assuming) restlessness in the pursuit of pure experience is a normative motivation. The ultimate experience is a pre-literate engagement with an undifferentiated sublime reality that transcends individual identity or self. Eastern cultures 'despite their apparent cultural diversities and ideological differences, the invisible, the tacit, the spoken and the implied are inevitably privileged over the visible, the explicit, the written and the articulate' (Chia 2003: 957). Buddhism in particular seeks enlightenment for all living beings. All objects and experiences are products of the mind and so are mentally made rather than discovered. Buddha is attributed as saying that 'with our thoughts we make the world'. For Buddhists reality and the self are made by the mind and Man has a spiritual agency in that his deeds will either improve or detract from his karma. Karma is not mysterious. It is a Sanskrit word which means intentional 'action' and it 'denotes an active force, the inference being that the outcome of future events can be influenced by our actions' (Tenzin Gyatso 1999: 141). Buddhist enlightenment can only be achieved through experiencing meditative practice and practicing virtuous action and so cannot be 'taught' in a conventional didactic manner. In Buddhist meditative practice, the objective is to cultivate a 'communion with the present' where reality is beyond words or belief and does not deal with the past or the future. The Buddha requires 'Don't just do something, stand there' (Siddiqui 2005: 59). Living the moment requires the giving up of self in favour of focus upon the happiness of others, and arriving at the juncture where mind (thought) and body (experience) are synonymous (Watts 1951).

Knowledge is problematic in the context of Eastern ontological (reality assuming) restlessness. Particular problems arise under conditions of bad karma resulting from distorted and negative perceptions, attitudes, values and beliefs. Academic disciplines 'have unknowingly developed under the influence of these' (Payutto 2001: 66) perceptions and attitudes. In particular, the social sciences have focussed upon the divisive 'interests' of mankind rather than upon a moral agenda that seeks to overcome divisiveness by focussing on the potential for transcending greed and hatred. An amoral agenda on the part of knowledge producers becomes immoral when used by powerful others as a strategy of power. Knowledge has become a vehicle for preventing human development under these circumstances. It in itself becomes a source of *macchariya*: greed, avarice or covetousness. Academics are locked into as an ego-epistemological (ego-based on knowledge accomplishment) hierarchy characterised by aggressive competition and the self-cherishing protection of personal interests. Academic competitive achievement and attainment is based upon winning arguments and therefore upon denigrating arguments of others to the inflated benefit of self. The promotion of self through knowledge is complete through its unconscious promotion of the ideas of the desirability of Man's separation from and control over nature and the illusion that happiness through material advancement is possible and desirable (Payutto 2001). The obsession with the self means that it has to be filled up with material things that affirm its over-inflated significance. As a consequence, 'Science, technology and the development of information and communications technology have been used to lull humanity into heedless consumption, dullness and intoxication, rather than for the development of the individual or quality of life' (ibid.: 65).

Buddhism is a nominalist philosophy because it encourages us to realise that the mind creates reality rather than interprets it. Speaking of the world is to create it and this is reflected in the organisation of Eastern languages. Chinese languages, for example, are ideographic, which serves to promote communication, information and knowledge (or 'discourse') that is contextual, nominalist and tacit. Mandarin has developed as 'non-alphabetic' through the use of ideogrammatic characters. As a consequence it tends to avoid the preoccupation with literal meaning characterised in 'alphabetic-literate' cultures (Chia 2003: 957). In reflection of this, Chinese language is not a receptacle of Truth but a nominalist vehicle for communicating social virtues and an inadequate vehicle for communicating or understanding spiritual virtues. Language for the Chinese is not the vehicle for communication of wisdoms, which cannot be spoken. Nothing sublimely worthy is ever worth saying as one can learn about eternal truth but such understanding cannot be expressed in language (Siddiqui 2005: 25) or grasped by a logical mind (ibid.: 29). Chinese is, therefore, a multi-valued language that appreciates 'fuzzy' 'intervening shades of grey between the extremes of black and white' (Emmet 1991: 45).

Similarly within Taoism, the ultimate can only be experienced not spoken of, explained or analysed. The Tao is eternal flux and transformation that cannot be represented by language except as metaphor in relational context (Chia 2003: 958). Within Taoism 'he who speaks does not know and he who knows does not speak'. The Tao is the spiritual, processual, dynamic, nominalist guiding 'discourse' (Hansen 1996: 177) of the 'way of Virtue'. This encompasses notions of the flowing course of nature and the universe's simultaneously ordered and chaotic patterns, which can only be experienced intimately through virtuous practice, the *Té* (or *Dé*), an inner spirit, a special character. *Dé* involves the 'everything' of complementary opposites within, and a uniqueness of the individual which derives from his/her paradoxical association with the unfolding pattern of the Universe. Engagement with change and transformation engenders a preference for correlative rather than linear causal thinking in Chinese culture (Chia 2003: 963). The cognitive imperative is 'emphatically dynamic, non-discrete and urges the "harmonizing of internal wills" through concrete existential engagement rather than external causal relations' (ibid.: 963).

The Eastern archetype can be described as favouring 'aesthetic' rather than scientific constructions (Lessem and Palsule 1997: 48) and does not seek an absolute Truth. An aesthetic construction is oriented towards 'virtue'. This means that action is not determined by the rationalist identification of what is 'true' and proven but by a nominalist consensus about what is acceptable and what 'we', together, can work with. The wisdom of virtuous leadership is in the humanistic capacity to harmonise the imagination of the family, group, clan or nation.

'Ancient wisdom is fathomable, yet beyond the grasp of a logical mind' (Siddiqui 2005: 29). So the need to address Schumachers highest level of Being cannot be accomplished whilst dead-mapping is dominant to excess. Siddiqui predicts the end of the dominance of scientific management as 'The emerging post-scientific/post-modern era of business management will be the era of ethics and spirituality where purpose, vision, values, virtue, wisdom will be the new gods of worship' (ibid.: 39).

Wisdom mapping requires climbing the ladder to a 'self-aware' level of Being where the consciousness of paradigm warfare and emphasis on the privilege of knowledge before wisdom is reversed. Wisdom mapping would seek to make management fields more conscious of the contemporary obsession with knowledge gained through representational language as a culture of epistemania. This is a culture locked in the cognitive realm, a sort of catholicon cognitive compulsion to comprehend, in which 'wisdom' has become cast as the denigrated opposite of knowledge. The solution, to epistemological (knowledge based) warfare is not, therefore, in more 'one track minded' epistemology (knowledge) but in cultivating more wisdom.

Schumacher's (1977) solution is worthy of reflection and (re)engagement by all academic 'thinking communities' and management 'practising communities'. The attrition warfare of paradigm commensurability is an ontological (reality assuming) problem that cannot be resolved by epistemological (knowledge based assumptions) skirmishing. Schumacher posits that it is Levels of Being that are ontologically 'different, incomparable, incommensurable and discontinuous' (ibid.: 33). He prescribes four Levels of Being: namely inanimate (lifeless/machine-like), animate (life), consciousness and self-awareness. Movement up the ontological ladder of higher Being is only prevented through failures in *adequatiorei et intellectus*; namely understanding of the knower must be adequate to the thing to be known. Moving 'up the ladder' requires an increasing attention to 'inner' epistemologies and, in particular, to Socrates's requirement that you (rather than the 'actor' or the 'interlocutor' outside of 'you') must 'know thyself' first. To know thyself, however, is an epistemology of wisdom above cognition. It is an inner 'knowledge without thinking' that many academics and intellectuals will find identity threatening, 'inconceivable' and 'mindless'. It requires critical reflection of 'the hierarchical arrangement by which the academic discipline is situated as the generative source of knowledge, and the practitioner as the potentially enlightened user' (Gergen 2003: 453). Episto-ontological (or knowledge/realism based assumptions) progression is a remedy for incommensurable warfare which takes place outside this field of wisdom. Paradigm warfare is a product of egocentric minds with undeveloped 'consciousness' pilots and incommensurable intolerance in turn is a product of mutual incompetence usually between the dead-mapper and the mind-mapper. The dead-mapper hasn't the *adequatio* to understand the episteme of consciousness and the mind-mapper hasn't the *adequatio* to rise above the conscious mind to the wisdom of peace settlements that emerge from self-awareness. Such warfare is 'wisdom incompetence' and a symptom of failures of *adequatio* because such egotistical epistemania is impossible once the ladder to wisdom has been climbed. The *adequatio* of wisdom provides higher competences and 'awakening' of virtues from crucial and necessary mindful 'mindlessness' that make paradigm warfare futile, silly, spiritless and cognitive life-imprisonment. In such a higher 'self-aware' level of Being, the supposition that 'politics is everything' that perpetuates 'epistemanic' warring factions to continue battling for fear of losing can be seen as a trap of the lower Level of Being of consciousness. That power problems are 'divergent' can be seen as capable of being transcended only above and outside the rhetoric of win/lose politics. War stops when thinking stops and the heart, virtue, morality, love and of course peace, finally, 'as they must', win out.

The implication of Schumacher's hierarchy (and as we shall see in Chapter 2, also of Capra's Kite) is that different levels of reality (or ontologies), require different approaches to knowing (or epistemologies). These levels of knowing and being are incommensurable. To overcome perplexity the manager has to simultaneously have knowledge at different levels that appear incompatible with each other. (S)he has to be able to think and act with 'multiple' minds and contextual action, and transcend the incommensurabilities of different realities and ways of knowing them. Successful organising requires seeing the potential of mixing organisational metaphors to match the situational context and changing metaphor mixes to accommodate requirements for appropriate change to match changing conditions. This ambitious cognitive and behavioural dexterity that requires considerable effort and adaptability in cultivating reflexive wisdom is far from an easy agenda.

There is of course no map or 'paradigm' available for the highest 'self-awareness' Level of Being because it is a non-place which has no space and no time. The accomplishment of getting to this important nowhere does not need to involve the map, paradigm or the journey metaphor, although the notion of the 'path' or the 'way' has assisted many. To provide specific directions is, however, equally inappropriate because the discourse involved is futile in the ultimate stages of finding the timeless eternal, still, empty non-location of the invisible wisdom of self-awareness. It requires abandonment of the subliminal Cartesian dictum of 'I think, therefore I am' for a silent, knowing wisdom of 'I am not separate' in order to move to an important nowhere from nowhere important.

Wisdom Mapping of the Sublime

The logic of both Schumacher and Capra's argument, is that theory as with all 'social facts', takes its specific form from the interpretative framework of the viewer. Greenfield (1993a: 94) argued that 'if our theories create the facts that are relevant to them, we can only explore truth within a framework that defines what it is'. A move away from theory and toward a discourse that overtly embraces philosophy might be in order, particularly in the direction suggested by T.B. Greenfield. Essentially, Greenfield's position was to advocate a philosophically oriented, normative and moral alternative. Greenfield came to the conclusion that theory was not simply an assemblage of 'facts', but was 'also a moral vision of the world' (1993b: 217). If it can be said that management and administration are fundamentally about the production of desirable outcomes, then the implication of Greenfield's vision is for us to initiate a discourse related to values, for values are viewed as the very 'stuff' of management. The Greenfield vision has yet to make a conspicuous presence in discourses related to management and organisation.

Unfortunately the wisdom of self-awareness is albeit erased from Western thought under the gravitational cultural force of scientism that regards only rational thought as worthy of the label 'knowledge'. The greatest delusion of certainty in Western individualistic cultures is the compulsive certainty of knowing the 'realist' self. This requires the reification of the self as an independent entity. In the modern Western era under the corrupting realist interpretation of Plato, 'know yourself' has obscured pre-Socratic emphasis upon 'take care of yourself' (Foucault 1988). This is also reflected in the central question for Sankara (of the Advaita-Vedanta School in India during the 8th century AD) being 'what is our true self?' when only the Brahman (the Sublime) is real.

Within Eastern thought an ontological restlessness in the pursuit of pure experience is a normative motivation. The ultimate experience is a pre-literate engagement with an undifferentiated sublime reality that transcends individual identity or self. Eastern cultures 'despite their apparent cultural diversities and ideological differences, the invisible, the tacit, the spoken and the implied are inevitably privileged over the visible, the explicit, the written and the articulate' (Chia 2003: 957). Buddhism in particular seeks enlightenment for all living beings. Enlightenment can only be achieved through experiencing meditative practice and cannot be 'taught' directly.

As scholars begin to deconstruct 'self', some likely consequences are uncertainties resulting from reducing reliance upon knowledge. This journey is a personal one and will likely involve different individuals travelling different routes. The postmodern death of the self is consonant with the Buddhist conception of self which, along with other realities, is a conception of mind that does not exist on its own side (Zwei, 1996). Self can be realised as a form of belief created in various guises through speech. Contemporary Western culture stimulates us to avoid submission to change and insecurity by the promotion of the illusion of 'self'. For the 'knowledge elite', knowledge is the cement that constitutes the foundations of the self. Letting go of the idea of a true self is necessary in Buddhism to the realisation of emptiness and in the postmodern world this letting go is a strategy of irony essential for contemporary survival (O'Hara and Anderson 1996).

In particular for Buddhists, 'self-cherishing' is the most harmful of afflictive emotions. It involves the distorted view of a 'what about me' preoccupation that puts the happiness of the constructed self above the happiness of others. This self-preoccupation is destructive of wellness because of the stress and unhappiness caused by the impossibility of self-satisfaction. Buddhism is a philosophy of mind and Buddhist meditation requires suspension of the stream of consciousness by single-pointed focus on an object of virtue, such as love or compassion. In this way wisdom is achievable in that the root delusions of hatred, greed, jealousy, attachment and ignorance can be eliminated along with the unhappiness they cultivate. The object is to cultivate a 'communion with the present' where reality is beyond 'mind', words or belief and living the moment requires 'faith' rather than belief and the giving up of self in favour of focus upon the happiness of others, where mind (thought) and body (experience) are synonymous (Watts 1951). For any academic 'thinking community', a crumbling foundation of self as a result of the disintegration of the foundational cement of knowledge may provide an opportunity. The opportunity is to escape the illusion of self that is built upon the delusion of superior knowledge.

Because knowledge can never provide wise understanding, wisdom and other virtues need to be cultivated to facilitate greater balance and a dialectic source of the development of greater understanding and a better future. Cultivating the virtues of wisdom, morality, spirit and soul will be very difficult because it requires a substantive cultural change and identity shift for 'thinking communities'. One source of inspiration might be Buddhist philosophy.

Schumacher's Four Fields of Knowledge

The consequence of *adequatio* is that to comprehend higher levels of Being requires cultivation of appropriate organs or instruments or lenses. Schumacher implies that scientific lenses are restrictive and captive of lower, machine-like 'inanimate' onto-epistemologies. To create a fuller picture, Schumacher (1977) proposes a classification that distinguishes the I (between 'inner' invisible and 'outer' visible that correspond to what we are calling the 'I' and 'Me') and between inner and outer aspects of 'the world' (you/other). The implication of this schema is that *adequatio* requires simultaneous attention to all four fields of knowledge which provide emergent and synergistic understandings. From the viewpoint of the study of identity, Schumacher (1977) requires us to add two types of 'you/other' to the two types of self (I and Me) for a more comprehensive understanding. First, there is the more visible outside of the other, what might be called the 'persona' and second, there is the more invisible inside of the other, which we might call 'the spirit'. From this viewpoint, identity is both a consequence of interaction between the 'I', the 'Me' and 'the variously constructed aspects of the You'.

The I and the Me are, from this perspective, also a product of what 'you' feel like and look like. My impressions and projections of the identity of the other are critical influences of my constructions of what I imagine you think of me and how I react to that perception. So for example, if I like and admire you I am likely to construct a different I and Me than if I detest or am afraid of you.

The potential human identity described by Schumacher (1977) is one of self-awareness which has enacted a 'pilot of consciousness'. This potential identity has transcended ego and has reached the highest level of being (the level of becoming). Such an identity is self-aware and self-directed. It is not slavishly governed by reactions to the mirror of 'Me' or by the ego-narcissism of 'I'. These are prerequisites to 'know thyself'. In organisational terms, it is neither dysfunctionally 'narcissistic' nor 'hyper-adaptive' (Hatch and Schultz 2002) but has, through contemplative empathy and compassion directed to the 'other', accomplished the potentials beyond identity. An organisation needs, from this perspective, to follow an ambition to 'know thyself'. The implication for studies of identity is to introduce the necessity of moral and spiritual avoidance of the identity's obsession with the mirror and to appreciate the relatively greater importance of alterity.

In studies of strategic decision-making, it should not be forgotten that constructing difference and otherness is an inseparable aspect of organising, a critical part of this labour of division (Hetherington and Munro 1997). Otherness is not an end result; it is part of a constant process, where similarities and difference are articulated and visions of the world are contested. The move within, for example, marketing thought towards relational aspects is an implicit acknowledgement of differentiation and identity within the supply chain and the broader market. This process is, however, rarely identified within the marketing literature (Smith and Higgins 2000). Schumacher's (1977) ideas offer a great deal to the study of organisational identity. By introducing the prioritisation of the 'other', identity in its present mirror-obsessed form can be seen as profane, corrupt and a disastrous route to dysfunctionalism as evidenced in the cases of Enron, WorldCom and Parmalat.

The inner experience of the other is, therefore, the most pertinent contribution to understanding identity emanating from Schumacher (1977). The implication is, that identity without attempted insight into the invisibilia of the other is vacuous because such curious concern is essential for mutual understanding, good relationships and healthy identities. Schumacher posits that 'knowing thyself' is a precondition to knowing the other in such depth because the depth of inside knowledge of the self provides the *adequatio* for the competence to know deep inside of the other. Without the *adequatio* provided from knowing thyself 'We tend to see ourselves primarily in the light of our intentions, which are invisible to others, while we see others mainly in the light of their actions, which are visible to us, we have a situation in which misunderstanding and injustices are the order of the day' (ibid.: 96).

In organisational terms, this offers us an appreciation of why no organisation is an island (Håkansson and Snehota 1990). As such deep and empathetically wise understanding of You, I and Me are critical to successful business relationships just as egocentric, superficial and sentimental orientations are recipes for relationship disasters. A dedication to understanding the interiority of self and others is concomitant with a quality of communication that encompasses bodily emotion rather than simply through the rational mind. Schumacher asserts that without an empathetic 'feeling' for the self and other, with emotional and intuitive *adequatio*, it is impossible to get into a deeper understanding of identity deriving from the accomplishment of 'knowing thyself'.

The 'Me' therefore is complementary to the 'I' and the 'You'. For Schumacher (1977) a healthy 'Me' is able to see through blinkered narcissism and vanity and see the paradox of views from the other, which are both/and favourable/critical. A balanced view, therefore, ponders the fallibility of the self without judgement. The object is seeing the fallibility of the self by 'putting the self in the shoes of others'. To accomplish this 'uncritical self-observation' (Schumacher 1977: 112), however, requires a prior achievement in the ambition to 'know thyself' and enable the pilot of consciousness to accomplish self-awareness.

The fourth field of knowledge for Schumacher (ibid.) is that of behavioural observation accessed through scientific, empirical observation. The scientific field has a not unimportant (but only) contributory role when it comes to identity, which is an issue that belongs at onto-epistemological levels above the level of inanimate 'dead mapping' of science. Confinement to the empiricist 'field of appearances' on its own is inadequate for understanding identity, which is an issue located in animate and consciousness mapping of life and mind. In the context of identity, confined scientific hegemony is a form of dangerous myopia, where all that can be seen is that which is visible, measurable and relatively unimportant. The machine maps of scientism are maps or 'paradigms' of 'real' things that don't 'really' matter and offer representations of the living through a cartography of visible, dead and measurable things. Such maps lead to nowhere important because 'the quantitative factor is of preponderant weight only at the lowest level of Being' (ibid.: 64) cultivating a 'science for manipulation' whose purpose becomes power over nature and Man.

The proposition is that identity is a 'divergent problem'. Divergent problems do not respond to greater analysis and more certainty as with 'convergent problems'. The more that fourth field logic, which is suitable for convergent problems, is applied to such problems, the more paradoxical they appear. The solution to identity problems is not therefore in more applied 'fourth field' knowledge but in the engagement of wisdom, which requires synchronous application of all four fields of knowledge.

As a result process based study that also accommodates other fields of knowledge is preferable to sole use of simple causal logic. Identity is perceived as a process of 'becoming' that never ends. Process and becoming is an ontology accessible through intuition (and not rational analysis) of the flow of duration that makes change the only certainty and rejects the entitative fixity or eternity of 'things'. Process based approaches to meaning construction are a common aspect of post-structuralism. The 'becoming' self is a meaning that is continuously constructed, maintained and communicated but not rationally controlled or 'manageable'. It can be regarded as a text (a collection of signs whose meaning is iteratively constructed and interpreted) within a genre (cultural conventions or codes providing repertoires about what a 'self' constitutes) and using media of communication (verbal and non-verbal). The convincing self is, therefore, not a fixed achievement of signification but a protean process and an in-between accomplishment between certainty and uncertainty.

Identity as a 'between' process is a non-entitative and ongoing accomplishment of bricolage, involving a creative dialogue among ready to hand resources (such as language), adaptive action (such as speech) and purposes. This diachronic and protean, in-between process is, consequently, indeterminate and subject to the 'failings' of an identity crisis. This occurs when the verisimilitude (truth claims) of the self ceases to convince the audience or the actor of a tolerable certainty. In Freudian psychoanalytic tradition, identity is conceived as somewhat in a state of flux, emerging from a playing out of the dynamic between 'self' and 'other'. Following Freud, other psychodynamic theorists were to argue that it was this dynamic that was crucial to our sense of coherence, an 'ontological security'.

Perhaps the best example of processual analysis of organisational identity is that provided by Hatch and Schultz (2002). Their model combines the processes of establishing the organisational 'Me' and 'I', which means that identity is a process that develops through the interpenetration of organisational culture and external images. Hatch and Schultz (ibid.) aim to show that a balanced and healthy identity is one which avoids over-emphasis upon internal culture (narcissism) or upon sycophantic response to external images (hyper-adaptation).

What Schumacher (1977) brings with his processual approach is a realisation that the quality of the 'I' and the 'Me' is intimately bound up with a commitment to alterity; the addition of the wisdom of privileging the other or the 'You'. Without an exploration that includes the other, identity involves the ontic superficiality of inauthentic Being. Such being-with-others, through unquestioned care about what matters to 'them' (Heidegger 1962 [1927]) is a temporal inauthentic trap. For Schumacher (1977) the trap is a result of a moral neglect for an inside view of the other and an amoral sycophancy towards reflected images in a Hall of Mirrors. Because identity is a divergent problem and the 'I' and 'Me' are products of knowledge, solutions do not lie in further knowledge or analysis, in obsession with identity but in wisdom. It is the wisdom of self-transcendence that accrues from privilege of the other that provides the possible solution to the 'identity problem'. Solutions therefore lie in morality rather than mathematics, and in traditional wisdom rather than logocentrism. From this viewpoint, the identity balance that avoids narcissism and hyper-adaptation that Hatch and Schultz (2002) advocate, can only be achieved through effort to create a moral economy and not self-absorbed manipulation of organisational culture or external image.

Schumacher and Lévinas; It's the Morality, Stupid!

The dangers of a modern preoccupation with identity that ignores or marginalises alterity is that the existential outcome is a hall of mirrors that distorts any ambitions for a virtuous 'examined life'. Schumacher (1977) sensitises us to the need to include a morally oriented view of the inside of the other. Lévinas (1996 [1968]) also challenges the 'inward turn' of modern identity and, in developing the notion of 'substitution', he critically re-examines modern essentialist identity as egoistic self-possession, as the deluded ontological realism of the 'I' and as an illusion of separateness.

The modern self is a constantly recuperating reflexive encrustation which answers its own identity question 'who am I' with the deceit of the use of the signifier 'I' in the question. In promoting 'one-for-the-other', Lévinas appears to be presaging Schumacher's (1977) concern for understanding other-centred interiority as a prerequisite to a healthier, holistic identity. Schumacher's 'self-awareness' that comes at the top of his hierarchy (above conscious mind-mapping) is consonant with Lévinas's call for dedication of substitution in the prioritisation of assignation responsibility for the other.

A hall of mirrors, therefore, is the source of narcissism that prevents a moral self from emergence. Images are delusions whose egocentric glare and attention-getting consequences negate the sentience required for the assignation of responsibility towards the other. Lévinas's target is the self-awareness that Schumacher places at the top of his hierarchy. Self-transcendence, self-awareness, and 'knowing thyself' are all the objects of ancient wisdom and prerequisites of acquisition of all four fields of knowledge and reaching the *adequatio* of the highest level of knowing/being; namely sublime wisdom above cognition. In this supra-ontological realm, the gateway to understanding is a communion with the other, rather than a reflection on the self. A communion with the other involves recognition of the irreducibility to comprehension of her identity to the rhetorical assimilation of the same. The other puts the 'I' of 'my' identity into question. An ethical relation with the other is a responsibility not dependent or conditional upon the illusion of the self. By implication, therefore, identity requires a rediscovery of such ancient wisdom; namely that identity is ultimately unidentifiable. This involves a 'rhizomic' axiom of the logic of otherness, which requires a realisation of 'identity' as a process in the context of creation and interaction of self and other. As a result 'meaning is never fully and immediately present in a term, rather each term contains the traces of its "other" which as the other serves to supplement and complement it' (Chia 1999: 220).

Such morality for Bauman (1989) is not a societal construct, or a means of ensuring civilisation. Morality exists prior to language, and it arises through the notion of being with others. Morality cannot be apportioned or calculated in order to supplement a relationship 'with' the other for which benefit is reciprocally intended. Drawing upon Lévinas (1989), morality is defined as the encounter with the 'other'; as 'face'. Morality is personal and felt. Real responsibility for the 'other' must include the responsibility for determining what is required to exercise that responsibility. Legislating for ethics is thus presented as a barrier to morality. Whilst arguably the foundations of Bauman's moral impulse is to be found in metaphysics, issues of morality become a process of negotiation, a dialogue among parties. One approach to understanding this process (and by implication moral intent) requires research that begins to examine the construction of realities through language. Indeed, for Lévinas, language is the basis of the ethical since it enables links to be made among people.

The 'problem of identity' of the academic 'thinking community' and the manager's 'practicing community' appears to have been almost totally wrapped up in being more knowledgeable of dead, machine-like things of scientism. This is a condition where 'information flushes out knowledge and knowledge flushes out wisdom-in-practice' (Chia 2003: 975). 'In our books and journals we speak increasingly to each other, employing descriptive and analytic argots that are increasingly removed from the domain of organizational life' (Gergen, 2003: 453). 'We', therefore as the thinking community need to do less 'thinking' and more wise 'community' practice. 'We', as researchers and managers, need to begin a journey by 'getting out more' and participating in the construction of a moral economy in a suitably reflexive manner. As a result, a new, rebalancing and participative pursuit of wisdom and other virtues is perhaps the greatest potential offered to 'thinking communities' by daring to become 'thinking communities of practice' by developing pragmatic wisdom or a 'science for understanding' (Schumacher 1977: 64). For Aldous Huxley (1962) cultivating such 'sanity', as an alternative to the contemporary dystopia, would require an improved situation where 'Science and technology would be used as though, like the Sabbath, they had been made for man, not (as at present and even more so in the Brave New World) as though man were to be adapted and enslaved to them' (ibid.: viii).

Organising in pursuit of a moral economy and after the 'linguistic turn' no longer involves discoveries of a territory scrupulously mapped and supposedly perfect representation of reality. The linguistic turn requires sensitisation to the reification role of language in concocting reality. The 'maps' made by language 'precede the territory' (Baudrillard 1996) and are 'inventive' of the territory, which is then orientated with reference to the created fictional map. Maps, therefore, are 'paradigms' or sense-making devices. However, mapping is a 'process' because

> ... we do not simply make sense of the world by honing our linguistic and analytical skills, and by discovering once and forever 'the world out there'. We continue deciphering and constructing (or reconstructing, deconstructing or destroying), meanings in our communications and continually redraw 'maps' of reality. (Magala 2005: 99)

It is also clear that these maps are not of our individual making because 'In an increasingly complex and "mediated" social reality, in which our "maps" of social relations are formed with the aid of multimedia, we become crucially dependent upon them' (ibid.). Some maps, of course, have durable hegemonic influence. In particular science and managerialism are the Royal ordinance paradigms of most management theory. They invent 'weapons of mass deduction' and then go to epistemological war in the deluded search of defensible Truth and accompanying tolerances of absolute certainty. They insist upon imposing 'despotic signifiers' and 'final vocabularies' (Rorty 1999) to solidify, unify and fix an unchallenged rational unity. They conflate organisation with 'order' and 'control' and forget that effective organising requires navigation between order and chaos (Clegg et al. 2005). Without counterbalancing maps to provide alternative directions, totalising 'one size fits all' scientific maps are in danger of leading us to certain disaster.

CONCLUSIONS

When we follow the lead of Schumacher and set our sights on cultivating ways of knowing above scientism all kinds of benefits open up. It has to be said that all kinds of difficulties in acquiring the requisite *adequatio* also present themselves. Objects such as 'organisations', for example, no longer unquestionably 'exist'. They are now to be seen as 'texts'; a non-entitative process of a dynamic 'shifting network of signifiers' (Westwood and Linstead 2001: 4). They are a product of a kind of 'smoke and mirrors' magical performance that fixes their identity on a politically contested stage.

The dominance of reason in Western philosophy and theories of management has brought benefits to the West. However, increasing problems of imbalance and excess have resulted in a 'turning point' (Capra 1997) requiring ascendance of Schumacher's hierarchy through a striving for wisdom. The obsession with knowledge must come to an end and be compensated by wiser, reflective practice. This sentiment is expressed eloquently by Eckhart Tolle (2003: 9) who asks:

> Do you need more knowledge? Is more information going to save the world, or faster computers, more scientific or intellectual analysis? Is it not wisdom that humanity needs most at this time?

REFERENCES

Alasuutari, P. 1995. *Researching Culture Qualitative Method and Cultural Studies* (2nd edn). London: Sage Publications.
Baudrillard, J. 1996. 'The Map Precedes The Territory' in W.T. Anderson (ed.), *The Fontana Postmodernism Reader*. London: Fontana Press.

Bauman, Z. 1989. *Modernity and the Holocaust.* Cambridge: Polity Press.

Beck, D. and Cowan. 2006. *Spiral Dynamics.* Oxford: Blackwell.

Boje, D.M. 2008. *Storytelling Organizations.* London: Sage Publications.

Boulding, K. 1956. 'General Systems Theory: The Skeleton of Science', *Management Science*, 2197–208.

Boje, D. 1999. 'Five Centuries of Mechanistic-Organic Debate', Available online at http://business.nmsu.edn/~dboje/between.html.

Broekstra, G. 1996. 'The Tribune-Brain Metaphor: The Evolution of the Living Organism', in D. Grant and C. Oswick (eds), *Metaphor and Organisations.* London: Sage Publications.

Brownstein, L. 1995. 'A Reappraisal of the Concept of Culture', *Social Epistemology*, 94: 311–51.

Byrt, W. 1973. *Theories of Organisation.* Sydney: McGraw-Hill.

Capra, F. 1982. *The Turning Point.* London: Wildwood House.

———. 1996. *The Web of Life.* London: Flamingo.

Cave, T. 1995. 'Fictional Identities', in H. Harris (ed.), *Identity*, pp. 99–127. Oxford University Press.

Chia, R. 1999. 'A Rhizomic Model of Organizational Change and Transformation: Perspectives from a metaphysics of Change', *British Journal of Management*, 10 209–27.

———. 2003. 'From Knowledge-Creation to the Perfecting of Action: Tao, Basho and Pure Experience as the Ultimate Ground of Knowing', *Human Relations*, 56(8): 953–81.

Clegg, R., M. Kornberger and C. Rhodes. 2005. 'Learning/Becoming/Organizing', *Organization*, 12(2): 147–67.

Cooper, R. and G. Burrell. 1988. 'Modernism, Postmodernism and Organizational Analysis', *Organization Studies*, 9(1): 91–112.

Cummings, S. and D. Wilson. 2003. 'Images of Strategy', in S. Cummings and D. Wilson (eds), *Images of Strategy*, pp. 1–40. Oxford: Blackwell.

Derrida, J. 1976. *Of Grammatology.* Baltimore. The Johns Hopkins.

———. 1978. *Writing and Difference.* London: Routledge and Kegan Paul.

du Gay, P. 1994. 'Colossal Immodesties and Hopeful Monsters', *Organization*, 1(1): 125–48.

Emmet, E. 1991. *Learning to Philosophise.* Harmondsworth: Penguin.

Foucault, M. 1988. 'Technologies of the Self', in R. Martin, H. Gutman and P. Hutton (eds), *Technologies of the Self*, pp. 16–49. London: Tavistock.

Fulop, L. and S. Linstead. 2004. 'A Critical Approach to Management and Organization', in S. Linstead, L. Fulop and S. Lilley (eds), *Management and Organization: A Critical Text*, pp. 1–14. London: Palgrove.

Gabriel, Y. 2002. 'On Paragrammatic Uses of Organization Theory: A Provocation', *Organization Studies*, 23(1): 133–51.

Galbraith, J.K. 2004. *The Economics of Innocent Fraud.* London: Penguin.

Gergen, K. 1992. 'Organization Theory in the Postmodern Era', in M. Reed and M. Hughes (eds), *Rethinking Organization: New Directions in Organization Theory and Analysis*, pp. 207–26. London: Sage Publications.

———. 2003. 'Beyond Knowledge in Organizational Inquiry', *Organization*, 10(3): 453–55.

Gergen, M. and K. Gergen (eds). 2003. *Social Construction: A Reader*. London: Sage Publications.

Greenfield, T.B. 1993a. 'The Man Who Comes Back Through the Door in the Wall: Discovering Truth, Discovering Self, Discovering Organizations', in T. Greenfield and P. Ribbins (eds), *Greenfield on Educational Administration*, pp. 92–121. London: Routledge.

———. 1993b. 'Re-forming and Re-valuing Educational Administration: Whence and When Cometh the Phoenix?' In T. Greenfield and P. Ribbins (eds), *Greenfield on Educational Administration*. pp. 169–98. London: Routledge.

Håkansson, H. and L. Snehota. 1990. 'No Business is an Island: The Network Concept of Business Strategy', *Scandinavian Journal of Management*, 4(3). Reprinted in D. Ford (ed.), *Understanding Business Markets: Interaction, Relationships and Networks*, pp. 526–40. London: Academic Press.

Handy, C. 1989. *The Age of Unreason*. London: Business Books.

Hansen, C. 1996. 'Duty and Virtue,' in P.J. Ivanhoe (ed.) *Thought and Culture: Nivision and his Critics*, Chapter 8. Chicago and La Salle, III: Open Court.

Hassard, J. and M. Keleman. 2002. 'Discourses of Production and Consumption in Organizational Knowledge: The Case of the "Paradigms Debate"', *Organization*, 9(2): 331–56.

Hatch, M-J and A. Cunliffe. 2006. *Organization Theory*. Oxford: Oxford University Press.

Hatch, M-J, M. Kostera and A. Ko mi ski. 2005. *The Three Faces of Leadership: Manager, Artist, Priest*. Malden, MA: Blackwell.

Hatch, M-J and M. Schultz. 2002. 'The Dynamics of Organizational Identity', *Human Relations*, 55(8): 989–1018.

Heidegger, M. 1962 [1927]. *Being and Time*. Oxford: Blackwell.

Hetherington, K. and R. Munro. 1997. *Ideas of Difference: Social Ordering and the Labour of Division*. Oxford: Blackwell.

Huxley, A. 1962. *Brave New World*. New York: Bantam Classic Edition.

Kosko, B. 1994. *Fuzzy Thinking*. London: Famingo.

Lessem, R. and S. Palsule. 1997. *Managing in Four Worlds: From Competition to Co-Creation*. Oxford: Blackwell.

Lévinas, E. 1989. *The Levinas Reader*. Oxford: Blackwell.

———. 1996 [1968]. 'Substitution', Chapter 5, in A.T. Peperzak, S. Critchley and R. Bernasconi (eds), *Emanuel Lévinas; Basic Philosophical Writings*, pp. 79–96. Bloomington, IN: Indiana University Press.

Lewis, M. 2000. 'Exploring Paradox: Toward a More Comprehensive Guide', *Academy of Management Review*, 25(4): 760–76.

Magala, S. 2005. *Cross-Cultural Competence*. London and New York: Routledge.

Morgan, G. 1986. *Images of Organization*. Beverly Hills, CA: Sage Publications.

———. 1997. *Images of Organization* (2nd edition). Beverly Hills, CA: Sage Publications.

O'Hara, M. and W. Truett Anderson. 1996. 'Psychotherapy's Own Identity Crisis', in W. Truett Anderson (ed.), *The Fontana Postmodernism Reader*, pp. 166–77. London: Fontana Press.

Payutto, P. 2001. *Buddhist Solutions for the Twenty-First Century*. Translated by B. Evans. Bangkok, Thailand: The World Buddhist University.

Rorty, R. 1999. *Philosophy and Social Hope*. London: Penguin.

Schumacher, E.F. 1977. *A Guide for the Perplexed*. London: Jonathan Cape.

Siddiqui, M. 2005. *Corporate Soul: The Monk Within the Manager*. London: Sage Publications.

Smith, W. and M. Higgins. 2000. 'Reconsidering the Relationship Analogy', *Journal of Marketing Management*, 16(1): 81–94.

Tenzin Gyatso (His Holiness the Dalai Lama). 1999. *Ancient Wisdom, Modern World: Ethics for the New Millennium*. London: Abacus.

Tolle, E. 2003. *Stillness Speaks*. London: Hodder Stoughton.

Truett Anderson, W. 1996. '"What's Going on Here?", Introduction' in W. Truett Anderson (ed.), *The Fontana Postmodernism Reader*, pp. 1–11. London: Fontana Press.

Tsoukas, H. and M-J Hatch. 2001. 'Complex Thinking, Complex Practice: The Case for a Narrative Approach to Organizational Complexity', *Human Relations*, 54(8): 979–1013.

Watts, A. 1951. *The Wisdom of Insecurity*. New York: Vintage Books.

Weick, K. 1995. *Sensemaking in Organizations*. London: Sage Publications.

———. 2001. *Making Sense of the Organization*. Oxford: Blackwell.

Westwood, R. and S. Linstead. 2001. 'Introduction', Chapter 1, in R. Westwood and S. Linstead (eds), *The Language of Organization*, pp. 1–19. London: Sage Publications.

Whittington, R. 1993. *What is Strategy and Does it Matter?* London: Routledge.

Zohar, D. 1991. *The Quantum Self*. London: Flamingo.

Zweig, C. 1996. 'The Death of the Self in the Postmodern World', in W. Truett Anderson (ed.), *The Fontana Postmodernism Reader*, pp. 141–47. London: Fontana.

2

CAPRA'S KITE

Sid Lowe

Capra's Kite is a vehicle that helps us to ascend Schumacher's Hierarchy. It enables the integration of various ways of understanding without destroying their differences. Such 'polyvalent' integration is tolerant of multiple perspectives and enables us to overcome the problem of incommensurability using multiple focus on mental process, relational pattern, communicative adaptability and structural dexterity. This promotes a practical dialogue between different ways of understanding.

Capra's 'kite' (as shown in Figure 2.1 and framed by an outline of Schumacher's Hierarchy) suggests that to comprehend complex, living systems requires simultaneous focus upon four interdependent and inseparable criteria.

Figure 2.1: Capra's Kite

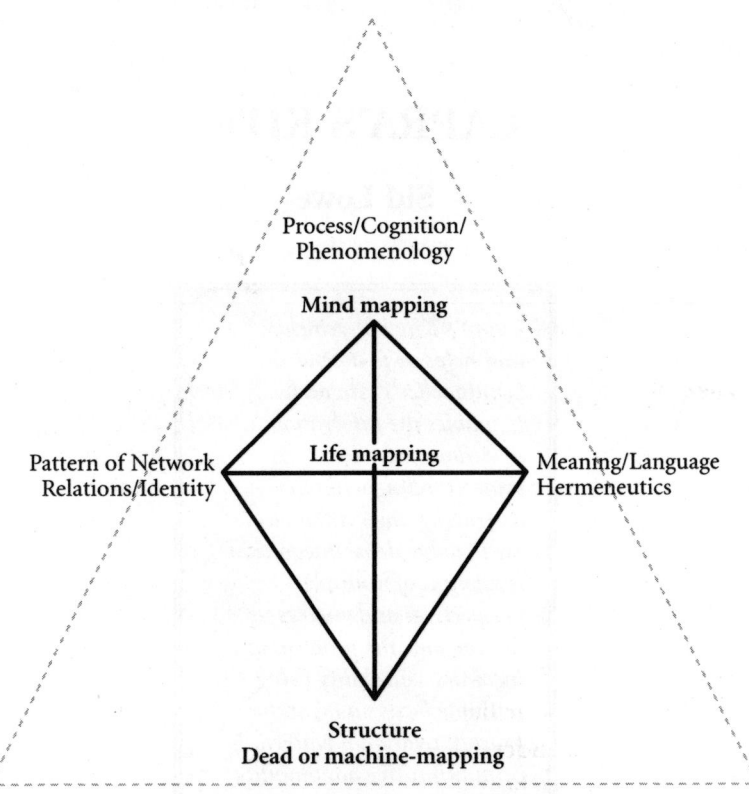

This approach constitutes a non-mechanistic, post-Cartesian and 'cultural' conception of social and other living systems that are characterised by an 'autopoietic' (self-making) network pattern of organisation. There is no longer any credibility in the 'realist', Cartesian split between 'mind' and 'body'; the biological machine is no longer occupied by the ghostly software of the mind as a simple dualism. Now we see minds and bodies and communication and identities as co-created and co-evolving in a networked, dynamic and fluid process or a 'multidimensional stream of events twisting space and time' (Magala 2005: 8). Dualistic attributions of simple, linear determinism are now inept, conveniently misleading and potentially dangerous.

Inside Capra's kite is a 'rhizomic' space; a 'non-linear milieu', a 'labyrinth interconnected with multiple, non-hierarchical entry and exit points'. The apparently static, flat, two-dimensional, hierarchical logic implied by the picture of a kite is actually illusory; an equivalent to Magritte's pipe. Appearances are deceptive; there is no kite, only a picture of a kite we might try to fly together.

Living 'autopoietic' systems, consist of internal non-linear communicative feedback enabling self-regulation, self-organisation and, therefore, adaptive development through learning. Network patterns enable 'self making' involving components of the system producing and transforming each other whilst maintaining the circular integrity of the system. The four inseparable criteria for understanding such complex, living systems are 'pattern', 'process', 'meaning' and 'structure'. Cartesian science emphasises structure and has largely ignored pattern, process and meaning. For Capra (1997, 2002) the agenda of escaping Cartesian-Newtonian fixity starts with the liberation of process. The main problem is that Enlightenment thinking ignores 'Process' which involves the 'bringing forth a world' through imaginative invention. Capra (1997: 287) maintains that the consequent Western condition is one of atomised alienation from each other and the world.

Capra (1997, 2002) proposes that four criteria are mutually implicated, co-evolving or 'panrelational' in that each one can only be defined in the context of the other three. As a consequence, any assumed incommensurability among different paradigms avoids the need to understand the simultaneous influence of these criteria by tending to justify a parochial privileging of one or two criteria at the expense of denigrating another. Schumacher's four levels of Being are ontologically 'different, incomparable, incommensurable and discontinuous' (Schumacher 1977: 33) and Capra's four criteria for understanding provide the same dilemma; a wise understanding requires somehow transcending these incommensurabilities. As a result, Capra's kite, is a call to transcend incommensurability assumptions (but not an agenda to create a unitary paradigm) through pluralistic, holistic mapping of living systems. The call is in keeping with a polytheistic approach adopted by various traditional wisdoms. The idea then is to promote multiple-mapping and a dialogue among map-makers in order to find particular, local, workable solutions to particular contexts; to find which maps (or combination of maps) appear to provide the most suitable route out for any particular group of lost travellers. 'There isn't any one true map of the earth, of human existence, of the universe, or of "ultimate reality", a map supposedly embedded inside these things; there are only maps we construct to make sense of the welter of our experience, and only us to judge whether these maps are worthwhile for us or not' (Fay, quoted in Weick 2001: 9). Such mapping requires cultivation of 'epistemic consciousness' (Capra 1997) in realising all knowledge as approximate and cultural. In other words, this means understanding that when we know, we know through a map of epistemology (knowledge assumptions). It is necessary to be aware what our knowledge map is letting us understand and to appreciate what it is putting in the background. Polytheistic mapping lets us see more by switching maps to optimal effect.

An adoption of all four criteria, as equally important, results in a conception of structure that reveals the mechanistic, foundational certainties of Cartesian science as deluded and their analytical methods as contrived. Structure, in Capra's (1997, 2002) view, is merely a manifestation of the 'process' of embodiment of the 'pattern' of organisation of a system enacted through meaning created by language and communication. As a result, 'structure' is not ontologically 'real' as such, because it is always a 'reification' of language, process and pattern. Living structures, which are self-organising are 'dissipative' and are structurally open to flows of energy and matter but organisationally closed. They are self-organising in that order and behaviours are established internally and not imposed by the environment. Such living structures are paradoxically, therefore, characterised by the coexistence of structural change and organisational stability. Contrary to mechanistic, Newtonian perception of time as linear, determinate and reversible, they are subject to the 'arrow of time' and are indeterminate and irreversible. Living systems are characterised by non-equilibrium and non-linearity. As they fluctuate further away from equilibrium, they reach a 'bifurcation point' of instability, where feedback communication produces newly emerging forms of order, evolution and development (Capra 1997: 167).

A living system is an integrated and interdependent whole of interconnected parts. Networks are the basic metaphor used to describe complex, living systems. Such systems are hierarchical in that they are networks within networks of higher complexity. They have emergent properties in that they are more than the sum of their parts. Emergent properties are a consequence of complexity in that any network system is a product of the relationship among its parts (which are themselves networks of lower complexity). Understanding of these systems requires an emphasis upon mapping their pattern (or form) of organisation, which involves the qualitative configuration of relationships. Pattern is the configuration of relationships that gives a system its essential characteristics (Capra 1997: 167) or identity.

Living systems are commonly characterised by an autopoietic or 'self-making' network pattern of organisation. Relational patterns in living systems are dynamic non-material and non-physical processes rather than a static, mechanistic set of relations among components. They, therefore, are not conducive to structural, deductive and reductionist analysis because they are only understandable through holistic mapping. Living systems process, as the embodiment of pattern in structure, is one of cognition or knowing. This mental process means that all living systems have or even are 'mind' in that they can think, perceive, feel and do. A human system has a mind that we recognise as 'culture'. Culture, therefore, is a process of the social mind of a human group. It is the mental process that enables the embodiment of social pattern in social structure. Because of the complexity of human systems, there is an 'inner world' of concepts, ideas and symbols arising from human thought, consciousness and language. The human mind creates this subjective inner world (constituted by self-awareness, concepts, art, experience, values and expectations, purposes, symbols, perceptions) that mirrors an outer reality, which means 'human social systems exist not only in the physical domain but also in a symbolic social domain' (Capra 1997: 206). In this social symbolic domain the social rules generated by the system, unlike rules in physical systems, can be broken and are subject to interpretation and development through language and communication. Indeed, language and communication are so important to Capra, that in his latest book, language and hermeneutics serve as critical fourth criteria for holistic understanding (Capra 2002).

Human cognition is characterised by self-awareness as well as an awareness of the environment. Human consciousness involves the bringing forth of an inner world in a process intimately linked to language. In the Santiago theory, communication is regarded as involving a coordination of behaviour, which enables 'structural coupling', rather than a simple transmission of information. Linguistic communication involves learned communicative behaviour and language is linguistic communication involving 'communication about communication' (Capra 1997: 280). Human language provides words as tokens for linguistic coordination and enable, through further 'distinctions of distinctions' the creation of the notion of objects. Objects are the basis upon which abstraction is possible. Self-awareness arises when we employ the notion of an object and associated abstractions to describe ourselves. The implication is that, because identity is an abstraction that we 'bring forth into the world', we must realise that in examining a living system we cannot differentiate ourselves from it and view it objectively. We are always bringing forth images of systems through the epistemologies we use. There is no objectivity because the Cartesian duality that constructs it has been discredited. The objective 'body' as opposed to the subjective 'mind' is now seen as a fallacy because 'minds evolve with their bodies, and viewing them separately and independently from their environments, both natural and social, distorts our understanding of both of them' (Magala 2005: 9).

This allows us to put a frame around how pictures or images of truth have been constructed within any 'discipline'.

Figure 2.2: Existing Position of Management Research within Capra's Kite

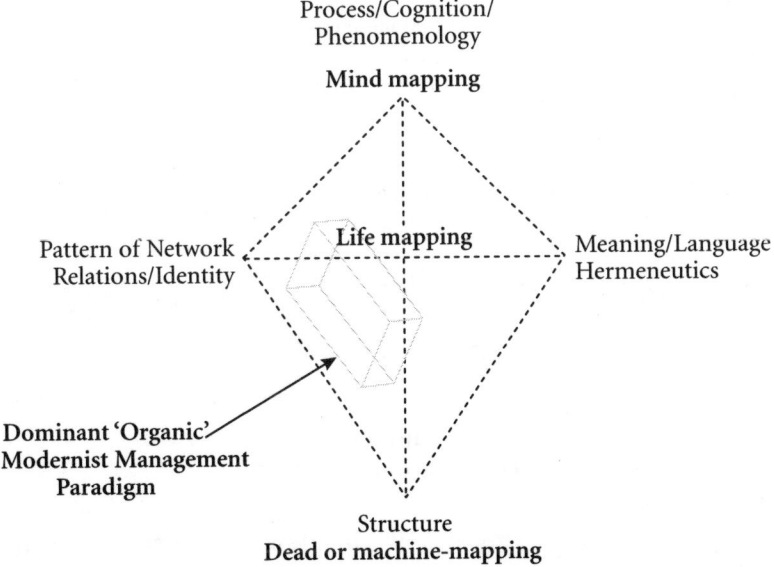

In Figure 2.2, the dominant paradigm within management is the organicist metaphor, largely derived from Darwin's theory. It is depicted as occupying a restrictively narrow frame within Capra's kite. It pictures the dominant paradigm as a restricted and somewhat myopic concentration on substance with tolerance of 'pattern' and marginalisation of focus upon 'process' and 'language' or 'meaning'.

THE ORGANIC METAPHOR FOR ORGANISATION

Take, for example, Contingency Theory, Resource Dependency Theory and Population Ecology.

Figure 2.3: Existing Position of Four Modernist Management Theories Within Capra's Kite

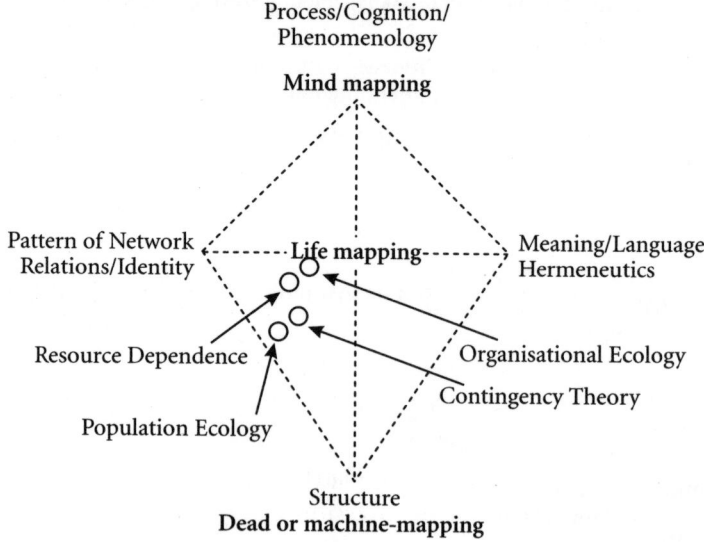

These 'modernist' theories are located in Figure 2.3 within Capra's kite.

Population Ecology, for example, places emphasis upon environmental resource dependency but the focus is upon patterns of interdependence within resource pools at the ecological 'niche' level. The focus in comparison with Resource Dependency Theory (discussed below) is more emphatically at the 'ecological' level involving 'populations' of patterns of network relations/identity (in Capra's terms). Population Ecology, as its name suggests, most emphatically 'brings Darwin's theory of evolution right into the centre of organizational analysis' (Morgan 1997: 61) clearly reflects 'natural selection' orientation by emphasising a viewpoint more critical of organisations ability to adapt to environments. It applies a theory from the natural sciences and applies it to the human condition. It adheres to an environmental determinism which affords little agency for 'imagining' environments and, in Capra's terms, is furthest away from orientation towards 'mind' and 'meaning' than Contingency Theory or Resource Dependency Theory. Where such imagination is recognised it is constructed as cognitive inertia of unimaginative organisational 'mid-sets' (ibid.: 62) which promote subjective (and therefore inferior) inability to adapt to objectively real environments.

The Darwinism that underpins population ecology privileges a 'survival of the fittest' notion of ecological pessimism that masks the potential for realising, through a greater focus upon 'mind' and 'meaning' of an approach heading toward understanding the significance of 'survival of the fitting' (Boulding 1981). Population ecology 'applies most readily to populations that are highly competitive. Not all populations fit this description' (Hatch and Cunliffe 2006: 85). In many institutional and cultural conditions, the theory looks out of place. For example, in more traditional, paternal cooperative (such as Neo-Confucian) cultures providing situations where competition is not an obsession, an atmosphere of collective and cooperative goodwill and cohesion in holistic organising cultivates a narrative or context-based knowledge. Such a cultural environment provides for processes of elastic, creative adaptability and innovation within chaotic environments. Long-term failure is avoided and survival is enhanced by the transformational and self-transformational capacities of the holistic 'non-entity' or virtual form of network organising (Lessem and Palsule 1997: 55) whose constituents are 'irrepressibly participative and creative' (ibid.: 56). Population ecology, therefore, in its 'emphasis on resource scarcity and competition, which lie at the basis of selection, underplays the fact that resources can be abundant and self-renewing and that organisms can collaborate as well as compete' (Morgan 1997: 62).

The premise of Contingency Theory is that environmental conditions should determine organisational structure. The contingency approach identifies technology, organisational size and environmental conditions as the principal situational factors to be considered in organisational design. The prevalent assumption is that 'organic' structures are preferable to 'mechanistic' structures under environmental conditions (Hatch and Cunliffe 2006) 'perceived' as more complex and dynamic. Because of this recognition of the view of the environment as 'perceived', Contingency Theory within Capra's kite in Figure 2.3 is positioned to reflect a greater but implicit tolerance towards 'process' and 'meaning' (than the more purely scientific management approach of population ecology) without tacitly taking these influences as centrally important. Contingency theorists still 'tend to reify organizations (and indeed environments), that is, give them a "life" or existence which is independent of organizational participants and organizing processes' (Fulop 2004: 143).

Resource Dependence Theory regards the identity of the organisation in terms of power/dependence relations and their consequences for access to resources and consequent environmental vulnerability. Successful management, therefore, is assumed to involve identifying critical resources in the context of network relations and reducing dependence upon them. This calls for 'imagination with respect to balancing the power of others by developing countervailing power within your own organization' (Hatch and Cunliffe 2006: 83). Resource Dependence Theory in this call for 'imagination' is implicit in its recognition of the significance of 'process' and 'meaning'. However, the limitation appears to be to a restricted mind and discourse relating to meaning as it effects one thing; resource dependency within the pattern of network relations. In order to survive, the organisation must trace sources of resource dependencies and vulnerabilities within the inter-organisational network with regard to resource criticality and scarcity. The strategic focus of the organisation must then 'seek ways to avoid dependency or make other environmental actors dependent upon your organization' (Hatch and Cunliffe 2006: 83). The positioning of Resource Dependence Theory within Capra's kite in Figure 2.3 recognises, therefore, that its preoccupation is mainly with the tangibilities of structure and the power implications of inter-organisational 'patterns' of identities.

Organisational Ecology or Socio-Technical Systems Theory is depicted within Capra's kite (in Figure 2.3) as positioned as the approach within the organic metaphor most attuned to issues of 'mind' and 'meaning'. It is the organic approach most centrally located in Schumacher's 'life mapping' and the least, of all organic' approaches influenced by the cultural gravity of 'dead-mapping' scientism. Organisational Ecology owes its intellectual inheritance to Boulding, Trist and Bamforth (and others such as Fred Emery, A.K. Rice and E.J. Miller also of the Tavistock Institute) and was concerned to explore the 'humanistic dimension' (ibid.: 40) in determining the best fit 'joint optimisation' between social and technical systems and the value of autonomous teams in its achievement. In emphasising the importance of more visible social psychological influences of technological and environmental change and the communicative advantage of autonomous work groups, Organisational Ecology moves further away from the gravitational influence of 'structure' and 'pattern' and further towards catering for influences of 'mind' and 'meaning'.

In summary, the organic metaphor in organisational theory in the main moves us away from the addiction to solely structural, mechanistic approaches of pure scientific management and particularly toward an appreciation of the influence of 'patterns' of relation within environments and the implications for 'survival'. These metaphorically 'organic' approaches are more relativistic than pure mechanistic scientific management perspectives. They are, to varying degrees, still rooted to concerns with 'structure' and to varying degrees accommodate the issues surrounding relational 'pattern' of organisation within environments they inhabit. They abandon the purely technical focus of Taylorism and pure scientific management and seek to accommodate concerns with social as well as technical needs and the human element in organisations. They all owe an intellectual inheritance to Bertalanffy's General Systems Theory and the notion of organisations as 'open' systems which takes 'the living organism as a model for understanding' (Morgan 1997: 39).

Process is mostly regarded as an epiphenomenon and an emergent interest with both open systems and survival implicitly regarded as processual. However 'process' as a notion within organicism is somewhat impoverished by its restriction to physical and real processes. Process as understood by the 'deep ecology' approach of Capra (1997, 2002) 'also' involves, when it comes to human systems, more invisible ideational, cultural and communicative processes that create meaning. These 'invisibilia' are, of course, the subject of a higher level of knowing/being in Schumacher's (1977) hierarchy and are therefore mostly marginalised or ignored by the 'organic' approach because of the problems of *adequatio*. The organic metaphor simply does not have the requisite appropriate instruments or lenses to be able to recognise the comprehensive invisible influence of ideas, culture, meaning and language. Confidence in its effectiveness as the dominant metaphor is, consequently, misplaced and its predominance within organisation theory needs to be urgently replaced with approaches more inclusive of Capra's (1997, 2002) four essential criteria and Schumacher's (1977) successive levels of knowing/being.

SYMBOLIC INTERPRETIVE
METAPHORS FOR ORGANISING

Symbolic-Interpretive approaches seek to move further away from the gravitational pull of 'dead-mapping' scientism and classical management theory. The emphasis is upon processes of mind and meaning construction. The intellectual inheritance for the 'interpretivist' paradigm goes back a long way but, most often, attributions to its beginning refer to Immanuel Kant's philosophy (Burrell and Morgan 1979: 227). Kant's awakening from his rationalist 'dogmatic slumbers' was a result of David Hume's recognition of simple 'impressions' as forceful, unrepresentable perceptions that are prior to ideas. For Hume, therefore 'being' is prior to 'knowing'. Hume's 'impressions' are simple because they admit no distinctions or separation; they are pure ontological (unmediated reality) experiences. Ideas are, as they become more complex, epistemological phenomena that can tend to cover pure experience in a blanket of explicit, representational, causal knowledge. For Hume causality was pure belief. Kant's underlying noumenal world is prior to the phenomenological world of causation that appears to us. The mind is a constitutive contributor to the knowledge of reality and not a simple photographic camera of a separate reality. For Kant this underlying noumenal world is only accessible through escaping the phenomenological world of causation by adopting the essential morality exercised by free will and overcoming our desires (Allen 1962). Kant preserved ideas as foundational by his insistence upon *a priori* knowledge that precedes experience. For Kant, therefore prior knowledge constitutes mental apparatus or 'mental programming' upon which subsequent experience builds a cognitive understanding of the world.

The contemporary influence upon symbolic interpretivism is inspired less by Kant's *a priori* knowledge than by the 'crisis of representation' in art (as famously depicted by Magritte's pipe in his picture; 'The Treachery of Images', as shown in

Chapter 1), the humanities, anthropology and other areas of knowledge. The modernist notion of objective reality accessible by a separate observer was challenged by this crisis. Reality becomes the product of 'make believe' and objective knowledge is revealed as an outcome of objectified belief; a reification of images. The consequences of Kant's idea of 'mind' as a constitutive contributor to the knowledge of reality (and not a simple 'photographic' camera) is pursued further by symbolic–interpretivists. 'The logic of symbolic–interpretivism is based on the belief that organizational realities are socially produced as members interact, negotiate and make sense of their experience' (Hatch and Cunliffe 2006: 42). Minds 'make' and 'project' moving pictures of reality, and don't simply 'take' still pictures of reality.

The interpretive paradigm derives influence from the intellectual source of German idealism. The German idealists shared the neo-Platonic sense that the 'spirit' and 'idea' was the antecedent of sensuous empirical reality. It provides an alternative to positivist orthodoxy in sociology and an abandonment of many of its assumptions, such as the acceptance of the methods of 'natural science' in the study of human culture and society (Swingewood 1991: 128).

Within the sociology of regulation and the subjective–objective debate and 'in the wake of Berger and Luckmann's treatise on the sociology of knowledge (1966), Garfinkel's work on ethnomethodology (1967) and a general resurgence of interest in phenomenology, the questionable status of the ontological and epistemological assumptions of the functionalist paradigm have become increasingly exposed (Burrell and Morgan 1979: 21).

Berger and Luckmann (1966) were an early and important influence on the symbolic–interpretivists (Hatch and Cunliffe 2006: 43). Reality is a cultural creation of intersubjectively understood meaning facilitated by shared history and experience and created by language and communication. Reality and our descriptions of it are 'spun' networks of relationships that enable the 'brought forth' construction of 'webs of significance'

(Geertz 1973: 5). Within these meaning webs, the 'spiders and the flies' of interaction, compete, cooperate and strive for survival. Objective understanding is, therefore, a fallacy because we cannot abstractly separate from this 'brought forth' reality and our description of it because we are a part of it and it is a part of us. The 'interpretivists', therefore, argue that human systems are phenomenologically different from natural phenomena. Humans are regarded as a species that subjectively constructs, interprets and creates the environment that they inhabit. This subjective interpretivism is 'cultural' and, as such, culture distinguishes analysis of human experience from other phenomena.

Burrell and Morgan identify theorists within the interpretivist paradigm within sociological thought as characteristically and implicitly subscribing to the 'sociology of regulation'. There is an emphasis upon understanding the nature of the social world within the realm of the subjective interpretations of the participant actor and that reality lies in the 'spirit' or 'idea'. As it is based upon the Kantian ontological assumption of *a priori* knowledge, as a product of the 'mind', structurally underpinning all sense data of empirical experience (Burrell and Morgan 1979: 227), the approach is therefore more nominalist, anti-positivist, voluntarist and ideographic and rejects the validity of methods and assumptions employed in the natural sciences for the human subject in contrast to functionalism. The consequence of this subjectivism, non-rationalism and emphasis upon 'mind' and intuition are the constituent schools within sociology of hermeneutics and phenomenology; and within organisational analysis the schools of ethnomethodology and phenomenological symbolic interactionism.

This movement in sociology and social studies came to be known as 'the linguistic turn'. The linguistic turn highlights the significance of processes of 'mind' and the constitutive role of language in establishing perceptions and enactments of reality (Alvesson and Karreman 2000; Callas and Smircich 1999). In this worldview, reality is assumed to be processual and not 'thing-like'. It is not directly accessible through language because language is a structuring agent that parcels, substantiates, reifies, slows down and stabilises process by converting it to a thing (Chia and King 2001). Language, from this understanding, translates intangible and indeterminate processual reality into a falsely tangible reality. Central to the linguistic turn is the notion of meaning as contested. This is based upon poststructuralist and social constructionist perspectives of reality, knowledge and language. These perspectives challenge conventional organisation theory which tends to take an essentialist view of social reality (Alvesson and Willmott 2002), and instead refuse to take meanings for granted (Musson et al. 2007). Orientations derived from the linguistic turn consider constructs laterally, thus acknowledging what it means to use language and communication resourcefully as part of a reflexively thinking and practicing community.

In the context of Schumacher's (1977) hierarchy of onto-epistemological levels of Being/Becoming, the linguistic turn is mapping in Figure 2.4 in juxtaposition to the dominant paradigm of modernism. To help us make sense of the linguistic turn approaches, we have positioned them in Schumacher's hierarchy as encompassing both 'life' and 'mind' mapping. Part of the reasoning behind this positioning is the dilemma highlighted by Koivunen (2007) of how to reconcile the notion of process as change with the way that some social phenomena (for example, 'the market') appear to retain a powerful sense of permanence. The position also reflects the fact that most linguistic turners attempt to come to terms with meaning and consciousness using the *adequatio* of a process cosmology. This is what Chia (1999) has called a 'metaphysics of change' and Capra (2002) calls 'hidden connections'. This involves the development of approaches to show the social construction of meaning at the higher levels in Schumacher's hierarchy. Developing meaning involves the dynamic process of both the shared and the disputed, between 'heteroglotic' dynamism (Bakhtin 1986) and competing discourses; in other words, allowing multiple discourses to be

Figure 2.4: Schumacher's Hierarchy: Positioning Modernist Theory and The Linguistic Turn

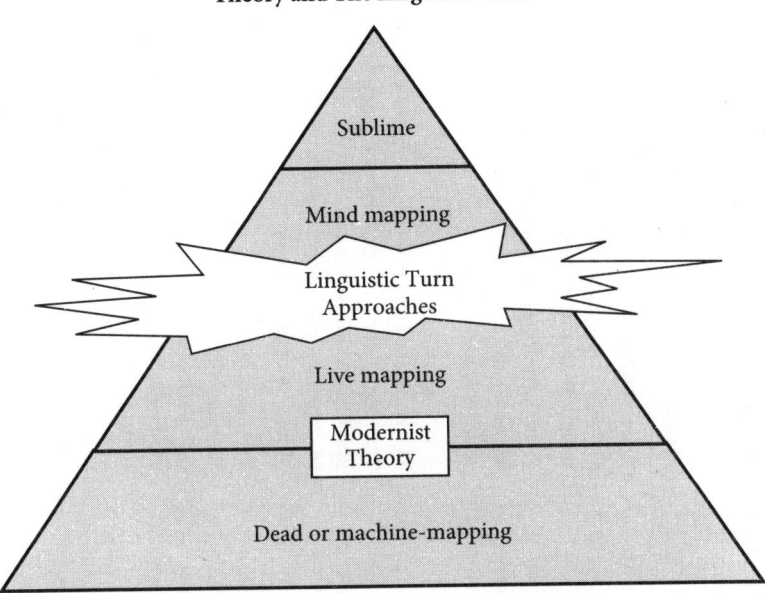

developed rather than concentrating on, say, the vocabulary of a particular model as the only language articulated.

Some influences of the linguistic turn thinking and their implications for organisation theory are shown in Table 2.1.

These contributions are not, of course, homogeneous. Most of the contributors mentioned would eschew being labelled as a 'movement' such as 'postmodern'. What they do offer us is a view of our own (Western) minds; the inheritance towards essentialism or foundationalism and the consequent Platonic cave of dualistic thought and talk. When we get to look at this 'mind', we find that purposes and beliefs dictate and perpetuate world views. To change our purposes and beliefs becomes increasingly difficult as they take hold and stifle inspiration (or change) beyond current purpose and belief. So we are stifled by the academic rhetoric of 'making a contribution'. What this particular cave does is to perpetuate the delusion that there is some grand aim that we haven't found yet but

Table 2.1: Post-Linguistic Turn Thinking: Implications for Organisation and Management

Author	Constructs	Implications for Organisational and Management Research
Frege (1848–1925)	Language is not logical. It has the dual creative function of symbolic sense or meaning and of reference to truth or falsehood.	The researched and the researchers create interactively, through language, the meaning and identity of organisation and management.
C.S. Pierce (1839–1914)	No ultimate truths about reality only ideas tested through pragmatic usefulness. Words are constructs of invented symbols that don't refer to the presence of their referent.	Organisation and Management concepts are symbols that are only valid as long as they have equitable pragmatic or actionable usefulness.
Nietzsche (1844–1900)	Modernist obsession with a will-to-truth hides that truths are illusions which we have forgotten to be illusions. Truth is contextual and situational. We are what we do in a process of 'becoming'.	The researched and researchers are unaware that they are 'making up' the truth and imposing their foundational illusions on themselves and each other. Organisation and Management concepts are 'processes of becoming' not 'things' of objective being.
Sigmund Freud (1856–1939)	Rational consciousness expends energy to bar desire within the non-rational unconscious from itself. Psychoanalysis allows access from analysing language emanating from the conscious mind to the naturalistic 'energetics' of the unconscious.	Psychoanalysis of managers and researchers will enable, through language, an understanding of their non-rational unconscious motives with relation to identity as actors, libidinally motivated activities and desire for resource control.
H. Bergson (1859–1941)	Process and change is the stuff of life. Concepts and language impose a fixity converting the real dynamic into unreal stasis.	Organisation and Management concepts are linguistic inventions of fixity; of things that exist, which cloaks their really processual character inexpressible by words but accessible through intuition and experience.

Alfred North Whitehead (1861–1947)	Process philosophy is a focus on time as duration, which is not discrete or measurable but is experienced as event.	Organisations must be experienced as creative 'events' coming into being through creative patterns. A changing poetic rather than a fixed categorising language is needed.
Deleuze (1925–1995)	Concepts are not solutions to problems, but constructions that define (limit) a range of thinking. Instead of asking, 'is it true?' or 'what is it?', better questions would be 'what does it do?' or 'how does it work?' For Deleuze the instrument of contemporary social control is marketing. Marketing facilitates the commodification of life and establishes business, commerce, entrepreneurship and shareholder value as hegemonic values turning human life 'machine-like'. The alternative construction is a *rhizomic* network.	Actionable effectiveness not nomothetic models are the legitimate pursuits of the observed manager and the observing researcher. Organisational theory is ideological. Turning the ideology towards the encouragement of human identity against repressed 'desiring machine' prevents emancipation from social control. Deleuze and Gauttari (1980) favour *rhizomes* to hierarchical arborial or 'tree like' networks as having more democratic potential. Rhizomes have no fixed, central authoritative order, they are fractal networks of unfolding labyrinths of discursive creativity that are non-linear, indeterminant and defiantly unmanageable.
Husserl (1859–1951)	Consciousness only explorable through *epoche* that suspends preconceptions about truth.	Organisational modelling is a preconception that needs 'bracketing' in the field. Focus should move to consciousness of actors.
Dewey (1859–1952)	Exaggerated dualisms do not clarify experience and lead to categorisation that can prevent pragmatic action.	Experience and action are the only valid learning vehicles for actors and researchers.

(Table 2.1 contd.)

(*Table 2.1 contd.*)

Author	Constructs	Implications for Organisational and Management Research
Elias	Networks are 'figurations' or on-going processes in the context of their historical creation through the 'gaming' of actors.	To understand such games requires focus upon the linguistic and communicative rules and practices of actors within the context of issues of power, culture, knowledge and identity.
Heidegger (1889–1976)	'Being' is even more fundamental than consciousness. It is realised by both acts of free choice and by being 'thrown' into inauthentic roles.	Actors are acting and being acted upon. Activities are freely chosen/authentic as well as imposed by expectations placed upon roles. The language and the created 'reality' of being a manager are inseparable.
Schütz	Schütz starts from everyday experiences in the *lebenswelt* which is constructed intersubjectively among actors. Actors in this intersubjective construction of the 'reality' of the world employ 'common sense' typifications to configure 'common sense' meaning and understanding so that the individual structures the life-world through consciousness: the stock of knowledge, typifications and relevance.	Commonsensical typifications of actors, their activities and the resources they use are ongoing everyday accomplishments of organising.
Wittgenstein	Meaning is in use and is inseparable from language. It is not 'essential' but a production of language games that use conventions of 'forms of life'.	Organisational theories tending towards 'meta-language' attempting to explain universal truth about managing and organising are an illusion, a language game in itself.
Saussure	Meaning derives from the relationship among signs and not from correspondence with referent objects outside the sign.	Language of actors and research observers has an arbitrary relation to the world. The language of management and organisation is about the language, a system of self-referential signs and signifiers, not any independent 'reality' of organisation and management 'as such'.

	Signification is the learned association of signs and signifiers. Language is a system of codes functioning through binary opposition that produces imaginative symbolic combinations that create meaningful fictions.	
Weick	Humans socially construct maps of reality and then orient themselves to enact a reality that 'makes sense'. The map, not an objective reality, provides reasoning for behaviour.	Organisations are images and appearances in the mind enacted and reified so that experiences of the social world make sense. Organisations are convenient fictional 'maps', talked into existence.
Goffman	Performances of actors in playing scripts equate claims of what's going on (meaning) with explanations with what is true about it (verisimilitude) in everyday presentations of self-legitimation.	Managers are miming, activities are scripted and ad-libbed. Resources are props. Organisation is drama.
Barthes (1915–1980)	Words are 'polysemic': their meaning is fragmented and contextual according to the situation and who is saying them to whom. Marketing and advertising are popular cultural 'mythologies' framing meaningful grammars of activity.	Organisation and Management concepts mean different things in different contexts, times and places. The meaning is not determined by the authors of these terms but by their ephemeral use in local context. The mythology managerialist materialism disguises itself as natural, innocent and impartial but is a grammar that legitimises meaning, action, activity and resource use.
Foucault (1926–1984)	Power is knowledge.	Organisation and management concepts and models are discourses that can be used to control the less powerful by the more powerful.
Berger & Luckman	Language is the site where the social world is constructed as objectified based upon interpretations found in intersubjectivity framed by shared experience and history.	Organisations and managers are intersubjectively produced through the linguistically fuelled processes of externalisation, objectification and internalisation.

(Table 2.1 contd.)

(Table 2.1 contd.)

Author	Constructs	Implications for Organisational and Management Research
Geertz	Man is an animal suspended in webs of significance he has spun.	Organisations and networks are webs made significant through symbols, requiring 'thick description' of how significant meaning is attributed to organisational and management concepts.
Derrida	*Différance* means that any word always depends for its meaning, not in a bond with the 'real', but on associations with other words in a network of significations with which it differs—language then is indeterminate as these associations change. There is nothing outside the text—meaning is imposed by the current dominant 'modernist' ideology of logocentrism.	Organisation and management concepts have no stable determinate meaning. A nomothetic model disguises the nominal fluidity of these constructs. 'Resources', for example, can change from meaning something to be exploited in one set of circumstances to something to be preserved and saved in another. Such indeterminacies do not need to be resolved, fixed or assimilated. Logocentrism and managerialist ideology impose fixed meanings of their own.
Lyotard	When different and incommensurable languages are used between parties, this causes a dispute of *differend*, normally resolved with recourse to power.	Organisation and management concepts create discourses that must find accommodation with incommensurable discourses, rather than trying to impose meaning uncritically.
Rorty	There is nothing to be known about an object except what sentences are held true about it.	Organisations and networks are 'panrelational', self-referential and 'relative' nominalist phenomena. Organisation and management concepts are formed in sentences held true of organisation and management concepts.

Bakhtin	To be means to communicate dialogically. Dialogues are heteroglotic (multiple/varied and simultaneously differential)—subject to counterveiling Centripetal (established ideology/official unifying language/monoglossia) or Centrifugal (behavioural/ unofficial and everyday practical language).	Modernist organisation and management concepts model are 'centripetal' and seek a nomothetic understanding, that is they seek to be a monoglossia (the only coherent language).
Bourdieu	The cultural *habitus* tacitly determines the field or the feel for the 'game', which is in turn determined by the relative field capital of actors.	*Habitus* configures positionality of the agent and their access to activities, rules of engagement and resources in structuration processes. Organisation and management concepts are culturally negotiated as a process that is power-laden.
MacIntyre	Tropes (figures of speech) are important because they allow us to see how social and moral life is an enacted narrative.	Organisations and networks can be socially and morally beneficial only as pro-social and pro-moral narratives. As one-dimensional, market materialistic tropes, social and moral progress is unlikely.
Baudrillard	Existence is 'hyperreal' where we are immersed in a 'simulacrum' where reality is a fantasy of images.	Actors, their activities and their images of resources are fantasies and created simulations that govern identity. Organisations and networks are a little like Disneyland or reality TV; fantastic illusions governed by the images of managerialist scripts.

Source: Hatch and Cunliffe (2006); Sim (1998); Solomon and Higgins (1996).

will do if we stay persistent in what we have been doing until now. It perpetuates a belief that we will not get anywhere inspirationally. Inspiration means changing your mind/beliefs/ways of seeing—all too often the academic rhetoric of making a 'contribution' means the perpetuation of a received 'wisdom' of foundationalism by moving us towards a putative 'essence' of truth—a 'contribution' of more of the same that fails, in the end, to improve anything.

The linguistic turn, then, offers the potential for inspiration. The 'turn' helps our realising that language configures our purposes and beliefs which iteratively configures what we think and say. Inspiration begins with the realisation that changing language changes the phenomena's appearance, and so its perceived reality. Interconnected talk and related action configures our relational schemas which reinforce our interconnected talk and action. Language is a vehicle of situated usage; of practice and action. In Wittgenstein's terms it is a game that is part of a 'form of life' and meanings are generated in situated use as paradigms or 'maps' of reality acted upon and persevered with as long as they provide satisfactory orientation in the navigation of action. The 'form of life' is of course, a dominant 'discourse' or 'world map' that has evolved to reflect particular purposes and beliefs. By determined reflection, we can free 'inspiration' that is trapped by engrained purposes and beliefs. In this strange world, many of us who have achieved (or have ambitions of) purposes of fame and recognition through isomorphic foundationalism may feel threatened. However, the potential for theorists is to realise that everything, including the self, is a nominalist (non-foundational or panrelational) network of 'labyrinthine inferential relations' (Rorty 1999: 134) which can be changed for the better through the inspirational reward of release from purposes and beliefs that have become cognitive prisons. With this 'poetic' ambition, the 'linguistic turn' only really tolerates one heuristic distinction 'between knowing what you want to get out of a person or thing or text in advance and hoping that the person or thing or text will help you want something different—that he or she or it will help you change your purposes' (Rorty 1999: 143).

Nevertheless, as the positioning of the linguistic turn in Figure 2.4 suggests, if we are to provide helpful advice to the community of managers and organisational scholars, some sort of decision needs to be made over a discursive way forward. One step in making sense of this is to emphasise a metaphysics of change rather then a metaphysics of substance/presence (Chia 1999). These positions equate with what we have been calling 'mind mapping' and 'dead mapping'. After Deleuze and Gautari (1988), Chia proposes 'a rhizomic model of the change process in which the precarious, tentative and heterogeneous network-strengthening features of actor–alliances are accentuated' (1999: 211). For example interaction processes can be described as communication exchanges where processes of identity clarification and repositioning occur, ultimately changing actors' images of themselves relative to all others. Communication exchanges may better be described, not in the amount of information exchanged, but rather in processes undertaken in relation to power games and developing self images.

The axiom of conceiving organising as a 'heterogeneous becoming of change' (Chia 1999: 218) within a Deleuzian conception of rhizomes is a useful one. Rhizomes are healthily disorganised fractal networks in that links are acentred, non-linear, indeterminate and asymmetrical. Such a view comes with two other complementary axioms. First, it involves the logic of otherness, which requires a realisation of 'identity' as process in the context of creation and interaction with others. As a result 'meaning is never fully and immediately present in a term, rather each term contains the traces of its "other" which as other serves to supplement and complement it' (ibid.: 220). That other is 'organisation' which is not a "thing" or "entity" with established patterns, but the repetitive activity of ordering and patterning itself' (ibid.). Change in such contexts cannot be rationally or objectively analysed, managed and organised. Organisation is a 'space' in between order and chaos.

Organising and learning are 'mutually constitutive and unstable, yet pragmatic, constructs that might enable a dynamic appreciation of organizational life' (Clegg et al. 2005: 147).

Second, the axiom of rhizomic understanding involves viewing the processual nature of time through the principal of immanence. Time is not a self-evident linear progression represented by the clock. Time as process means that the present absorbs and incorporates the past but is a novel and emergent outcome rather than a linear succession of it. Halinen (1997: 7) has a similar understanding where she posits an evolutionary model of time that is expressly not like 'predictive process models ...[which] try to capture the content of the relationship in dynamic concepts that are themselves defined in relation to temporal modes: to the past, present and future. This releases the models from the absolute time dimension'.

MAPPING SYMBOLIC–INTERPRETIVE APPROACHES IN CAPRA'S KITE

Approaches within 'interpretivism' are not as clearly delineated as compared to those within 'organic' modernism. However, for purposes of consistency, an artistic license is taken advantage of in locating them in a similar fashion in Figure 2.3.

Focusing upon language, communication and process requires substantial epistemological and ontological innovation. The linguistic turn requires researchers to cultivate a competence as 'bricoleurs of method', escaping from traditional limitations of logico-scientific, structural-functionalist and positivist methodologies. Organisational phenomena are regarded as non-physical, linguistic, nominal and web-like, and therefore not suited to such methodologies. Under the influence of the linguistic turn, language and communication processes are beginning to emerge as the principal legitimate topic of enquiry and a central focus in organisational research (see Grant et al. 1998; Weick et al. 2005).

**Figure 2.5: Positioning of Selective Interpretivist-sensitive
Organisational Theories within Capra's Kite**

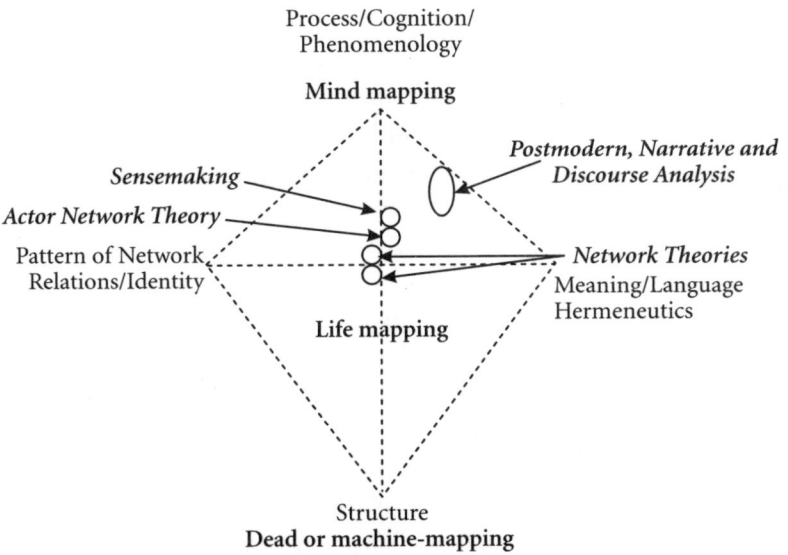

Network analysis has its antecedence firmly in modernism. More
recent developments, however, appear more obviously to be
locatable in symbolic-interpretivism. Within Capra's kite, in Figure
2.5, therefore, network theories are located as boundary spanning
both modern and symbolic domains. This may be a consequence
of the observation that 'very few theorists study networking from
a single perspective and multiperspective approaches dominate the
field' (Fulop 2004: 550).

Historically, network analysis, with few exceptions, adopted
a modernist discourse emphasising the potential for human
advancement through the adoption of rational thought, reason
and progress. The basic focus has been upon the structure of
'interests' within networks. This has often been accompanied by an
inevitable structural functionalist bias with its attendant adherence
to ontological realism, nomothetic modelling and positivist

epistemology. For example, social network theory, the privileged source of network analysis, has its antecedence firmly in 'objectivist' social anthropology, which has an underlying predisposition to structural–functional, structuralist and foundationalist principles (Araujo and Easton 1996: 64). It rejects explanations of behaviour from cultural and processual perspectives (ibid.: 72). Where culture is accommodated in network studies, the tendency is to co-opt it into an objectivist worldview. Culture is regarded regulatory and as something a human group 'has' rather than something that it 'is'. The regulatory approach, favoured by most economists, treats economic behaviour and culture as analytically distinct and stresses how culture constrains and configures the individual's economic efforts (DiMaggio 1992: 28). In this view, the assumption appears to be that the relationship between culture and economy is not mutually generative but exists as a dependent and independent variable.

Network thinking is felt to have 10 schools of thought or epistemological approaches (Araujo and Easton 1996) or, alternatively, 17 approaches (Oliver and Ebers 1998) that can be distilled into four configurations. The 10 schools of network theory identified by Araujo and Easton all have their antecedence in social anthropology (1996: 64). Social anthropology has an underlying predisposition to structural–functional, structuralist and foundationalist principles through the influence of its principal proponents from Edward Tylor, through Bronislaw Malinowsky and A.R. Radcliffe-Brown, to Franz Boas, Margaret Mead and Claude Levi-Strauss. Despite the disparity in their foci, these principal social anthropologists shared a predilection for structural explanations of social phenomena. Within network theory this is translated into a schema where social network theory is privileged. Social network theory is the most highly cross-referenced field within Industrial Network studies and the majority of other forms of network analysis (ibid.: 68). Social network theory rejects explanations of behaviour from cultural and processual perspectives (ibid.: 72). Thus social network theory, the privileged source of network analysis, is also the field which is most highly oriented to analysis of structure and is the most dedicated adherent of the positivist epistemology of sociometric and 'block modelling' techniques along with other objectivist assumptions.

The four dominant perspectives identified by Oliver and Ebers (1998) are social network, power and control, institutionalism and transaction costs. The power and control approach whose principal author is Robert Howard, appears to coalesce with many of the presuppositions and preoccupations of Resource Dependency theory. The transaction cost approach, led by Oliver Williamson, sees networks as a 'hybrid' form of (modernist) organisation which ignores the importance of irrational, social and cultural factors as irrelevant to outcomes in comparison to the critical influence of rational decisions of asset specificity, governance and efficiency (Fulop 2004: 550).

In the main 'process' has been largely overlooked in such 'photographic' network analysis, which has been dominated by a snapshot mentality and a 'substantive' metaphysics. Process, as a reminder, is cognition or 'mind' in living systems which enables the 'bringing forth' of reality and an identifiable self through inventive imagination (Capra 1997, 2000). It has recently been argued that, within the different schools of network theory, this neglect varies from apparent purposeful avoidance of cognitive process to a more reluctant avoidance with recognition of its potential secondary importance (Ellis et al. 2006).

The main problem with overtly rationalist forms of network analysis has been is the employment of Western, rationalist repertoires to 'analyse' through the logocentric assumption of objectivity. The outcome is consequently culturally embedded in its own Western, rationalist cognitive style and its methodological, epistemological and ontological assumptions. Network analysis has tended to focus upon economic 'interests' and not cultural 'ideas' in the analysis of the human condition, using quantitative, logically empirical analysis to determine the structure of relationships. The domain of 'ideas', particularly morality, and analysis sensitive to the subjective interpretations of cultural actors and the hermeneutics of their ideas, is largely absent from such network theory.

Social network and institutionalist approaches, however, do take social and cultural influences more seriously than Araujo and Easton (1996) give credit. Hatch and Cunliffe (2006) characterise 'New Institutionalism' as a symbolic–interpretivist project. New Institutionalists in the U.S., such as W. Richard Scott, Walter Powell and Paul DiMaggio developed Organisational Sociology, sometimes referred to as Economic Sociology. In Europe, Selznick's (1948, 1949) institutional theory was also the basis for the development of the organisational symbolism movement. The associated Standing Conference on Organisational Symbolism (SCOS) 'was instrumental in legitimating the symbolic–interpretive perspective in organisation theory and helped establish culture as a mainstream concept' (Hatch and Cunliffe 2006: 46). Walter Powell, Paul DiMaggio and Mark Granovetter all seek to take network theory in the direction of a processual approach by emphasising the important processes of relationality. These authors focus upon trust, relationships and power as processes that differentiate inter-organisational networks from market or bureaucratic structures. Granovettor (1985) focuses on the embeddedness of economic activity in social and cultural contexts so that the 'relational dimension of networking is important in explaining how risks are managed in networking by the development of social capital and particularly trust' (Fulop 2004: 558).

There may be some problems in the reification of fixing the 'social' process with the structural rhetoric of 'capital' but such conflations are recognised by Paul DiMaggio (1992) as the principal paradox in understanding networks. Capra's (1996) thesis requires us to revisit the lamentations of DiMaggio (1992), Emirbayer and Goodwin (1994) and Gómez and Acebrón (2001) as to the limitations of network analysis. Culture as systems of meaning and ideas has been ignored generally in network analysis, which has adopted an emphasis upon objective measures of relational structures (DiMaggio 1992). Emirbayer and Goodwin maintain that network analysis 'either neglects or inadequately recognizes the crucial dimension of subjective meaning and motivation' (1994: 1413) and propose 'an adequate approach to historical explanation must encompass both social structural and cultural perspectives on social action' (ibid.). They conclude that

> ...network analysis as it has been developed to date has inadequately theorized the causal role of ideals, beliefs and values, and of the actors that strive to realize them; as a result, it has neglected the cultural and symbolic moment in the very determination of social action. Network analysis gains its purchase upon social structures only at the considerable cost of losing its conceptual grasp upon culture, agency, and process (ibid.: 1446).

The consequence is a general failure of network analysis to adequately grasp dynamic processes that transform networks and shape social reality over time.

The preoccupation with pattern/structure within most network analysis means that any understanding of the role of perceptions and attitudes in networks is as a 'consequence' of the structure of relations amongst actors and their individual positional location within the network structure. There is no equality of focus between structural pattern and ideational process here. Process is assumed to be determined by pattern and there is no sense in which the mutuality of pattern, process and structure, as required by Capra's (1997) hypothesis, is accommodated. Network analysis generally is recognised by such 'pattern determinism' and is generally devoid of an understanding of pattern as incoherent except in the context of cognitive process and dissipative structure.

When considering the relevance of cultural process (or 'mind' and 'meaning' in Capra's terms), there is a tendency within network analysis to unconsciously denigrate it. For example, in their stalwart attempt to incorporate culture into the AAR model of the IMP Group, Welch and Wilkinson (2002) reduce culture to a real, substantive, concrete, structured, measurable variable capable of being recognised within this nomothetic model. This cultural conflation unconsciously conspires to 'simply adding another "variable" to our complex explanatory equation, as if culture were itself nothing more than a residual category to be brought in after the fact' (Emirbayer and Goodwin 1994: 1440).

The result is a dominant, simplistic and predominantly 'regulatory' (norms, values, routines) view that regards values as 'essential', 'foundational' or 'core'. So for example, for Hofstede (1980), culture is metaphorically an 'onion' with foundational values at its centre. This reflects a dominant 'cross-cultural' or 'comparative management' theme, involving the intersection of functionalist anthropology and neo-classical management theory (Smircich 1983). This approach adheres to assumptions dedicated towards concern for the problem of social order and to objectivism. It invariably results in treating culture as an independent variable imported into organisations and revealed through the patterns of actions and attitudes of organisational members (ibid.: 343). It adheres to organismic metaphors in organised behaviour. It seeks to identify general and contingent causality in the relationship between the cultural variable and organisational variables. Identifying the deterministic causality of culture is, therefore, seen as critical in the search for predictable, modernist means of organisational management and control (ibid.: 347). An alternative, 'constitutive' approach, is favoured by most anthropologists. Culture from a 'constitutive' viewpoint is seen as providing systems of meaning, which frame actors' 'interests', so enabling economic action, which in turn generates categories and understanding in an iterative, rather than deterministic, process. Such an anti-foundational view is also an 'important postmodern conclusion' (Firat and Venkatesh 1995: 249), which derives from understanding socially constructed reality as a synthetic process of economic and symbolic structuration.

ACTOR NETWORK THEORY

Actor network theory (ANT) is more sensitive to social constructionist and symbolic interpretivist approaches compared with the network theories outlined above. It advocates a network epistemology by arguing that knowledge is relative to network position (Hatch and Cunliffe 2006: 333) and identity. Within Capra's kite, in Figure 2.5, therefore, as with network theories it is located as boundary spanning both modern and symbolic domains but is closer to the position of 'sensemaking' (discussed below) because it is comparatively more focused upon 'identity', 'process' and 'meaning' than other network theories.

In conducting an ethnography of a scientific community, Latour and Woolgar (1979) showed scientific knowledge to be the socially constructed product of network identity and power. ANT, consequently sees 'society organizations and identity as effects created in networks of heterogeneous materials' (Hatch and Cunliffe 2006: 334). In this technocultural view, material artefacts and symbols, therefore relationally interact and contribute to the social construction of reality and the configuration of legitimate knowledge. Some resemblance with socio-technical systems approach or organisational ecology is apparent. The difference is that the more relational and interactive view of human and non-human systems makes the distinction between them less obvious and capable of separate analysis.

SENSEMAKING

Karl Weick (1995) provides a focus upon the 'sensemaking' aspect of organising which focuses upon the inventiveness of organisational realities. Sensemaking is less about discovery than it is about invention, social construction and 'framing' (ibid.) of plausible reality and truth through selective perception and the linguistic production of reality. The reflexive practitioner is constantly evaluating the ability of the map or 'paradigm' to identify an appropriate route and destination. Essential '"double-loop" learning depends upon what is sometimes described as the art of framing and reframing' (Morgan 1997: 92). In making retrospective sense of reality humans bring connected sets of beliefs, values, cultural and social expectations to bear on what becomes regarded as acceptably comprehensible. Making sense involves an interactive, fragmented and multi-layered 'flowing soup' (Weick 1995: 4) of plural plausibility 'frames' of ideas, narratives and communications. Sensemaking, therefore involves the subjective, collective communicative 'making it up as we go along' processes of inventing social reality. The antecedent notion for sensemaking is 'cognitive dissonance'; a psychological notion that understanding and acceptance cannot take place outside a set of established cultural values, beliefs, meanings and expectations of what is understandable and acceptable. Sensemaking uses a 'constitutive' view of culture, which regards it as a network of ideas that is a constantly changing system of imaginative social invention of reality made and continuously remade by its members through cues, categories, typifications and scripts. From this viewpoint culture is an emergent property of living human systems. It is a process of meaning-giving and that permits the making of sense (Weick 1995, 2001) through enactment (the generation and implanting of interpreted reality).

Sensemaking is a part of the 'cultural' metaphor in understanding organisation and 'stresses the proactive role that we unconsciously play in creating our world' (Morgan 1997: 141). Culture has a holographic quality and the culture metaphor has many domain similarities with Morgan's 'holographic brain'. In Schumacher's (1977) terms, it is clearly locatable as 'mind mapping'. In Capra's kite, it is located in Figure 2.5 as a focus on accounting for both 'process' and 'meaning' as constitutive of reality. Weick, for example, prefers the use of 'process' verbs (such as 'managing' and 'organising') over 'structural' nouns (such as organisation and management). Sensemaking still maintains selective attention to issues of 'pattern' and systems viewpoints. Weick (1995) talks of 'sensemaking systems' and emphasises the significance of the grounded nature of sensemaking activity in identity construction processes. Sensemaking is more 'holographic' (Morgan 1986: 139) than structural or mechanistic. Weick is comfortable with the view that 'the map is the territory'. As mentioned in Chapter 1, Weick (1995) famously used the map metaphor in the story of the Hungarian troop of soldiers lost in the Alps who saved themselves through abductive use of a map that ended up being a map of a different territory. For many, the emphasis upon the mimetic animation or 'enactment' of the map, rather than the map itself was a welcome improvement. Such social constructions of reality result in maps that are realised as projections of negotiated, often contested or mistaken meaning of what is the selective perception of what is taken as the plausible 'real' territory. The symbolic–interpretive agenda finally begins to liberate subjective and uncertain influences from their previous denigration by 'dead mappers' of objective certainty.

POSTMODERN, NARRATIVE AND DISCOURSE ANALYSIS

Postmodern approaches are diverse but share a dedication to challenge the assumptions of modernism and the agenda of the Enlightenment project with regard to objectivist/realist 'notions of reality, knowledge and identity' (Hatch and Cunliffe 2006: 47). In Capra's kite, it is firmly located in Figure 2.5 as accounting for both 'process' and 'meaning' as constitutive of reality. Postmodernism, in Morgan's (1997) terms, adopts the culture metaphor alongside the 'psychic prison', 'flux and transformation, 'political systems' and, particularly, the political 'domination' metaphors of organisation. In this sense, therefore, the approach is experimental and flexibly 'polytropic', involving the 'play of tropes' concerns the dynamics of the 'transformative interaction of the various subtropes' (Fernandez 1991: 6) and avoids the single-metaphor myopia of modernist perspectives. This approach is consonant with the view that metaphors and other tropes operate within a 'cognitive comfort zone' (Oswick et al. 2000: 1) and suggest that this is culturally derived. They propose that the 'lesser' tropes of anomaly, paradox and irony, operating in a 'cognitive discomfort zone' (ibid.) are the principal source of new understandings that can result from a release from culture-bound discourse. Postmodernism may be said to involve a transition in styles of belief creating new schisms and non-ideological, issue-based 'culture wars'. This seeks a breakdown of the Enlightenment project of scientism or universal rationalism as a single correct, objective mode of representing immanent or metaphysical 'truth'. Associated with this, postmodernism promotes an end of the Western myth of 'progress' and associated beliefs of linear progress, absolute truths, and rational planning of ideal social orders above all other values. This, in turn, promotes an end of other modernist 'metanarratives' or grand unifying discourses along with a critique of legitimation of authority and power, and atomisation of the individual from the context of her relationships.

Postmodernism, in its challenge to the modernist preference for universal knowledge, stimulates an emergence of pluralism and acceptance of multiple 'truths' and relative rather than absolute objectivity. For example, identity and morality are regarded as socially constructed or 'made' rather than 'found'. Such relativism favours an acceptance that such truths are human creations produced through language and communication so that 'where there are no sentences there is no truth' (Truett Anderson 1996: 8). Language and communication no longer can be regarded 'as a mirror that accurately reflects reality' (Hatch and Cunliffe 2006: 48). This lends itself to an identification of the construction of truth or meaning within science and management as a strategy of exercising power through knowledge and a focus upon the 'linguistic turn' which assumes that ideas cannot be understood outside the language system that produced them locally and specifically. It also is consistent with an acceptance of cultural or moral relativism, eclecticism, cultural 'bricolage' and multiple worldviews both within groups and for individuals. Postmodernism promotes the centrality of culture, as a kind of symbolic DNA, as differently learned and created discourses of equal validity which frame human conceptualisation of surface 'reality'. The focus is upon a symbolic environment involving images and fictions with an existence of their own that we are increasingly becoming conscious of, acting upon and trading with.

Discourse analysis (DA), for example, is a particularly suited complementary, interpretivist methodology in juxtaposition to network modelling. Discourse is constituted by information, knowledge and communication (Cooper and Burrell 1988: 91). Significant differences between modernist and postmodern discourses are evident and contiguous to this are different conceptions of organisation and organising. Modernist discourse is characterised by transcendent yet anthropocentric criteria such as 'reason' and 'progress'. In modernist discourse, 'organisation' concerns enacting or legitimising rationality as a totalising ambition. Organisation is therefore promoted as a legitimate social tool for the totalisation of rationalism, reason and progress. It is an objective, administrative–economic function that enables planned activity. By contrast, postmodern discourse is characterised by a rejection of such modernist, structural certainties. Postmodern discourse involves paradox, contradiction and indeterminacy. Organisation is, in postmodern terms therefore, an anthropocentric defence against a chaotic, uncertain and uncontrollable universe. From this viewpoint organisation has an inherent 'automaticity'; a life of its own that is beyond human control (Cooper and Burrell 1988) or management.

DA asserts an identification of the construction of truth or meaning within science and management as a strategy of exercising power through knowledge. In other words, discourse analysis recognises that all human knowledge is subjective and a product of human imagination. All knowledge is communicated in the context of power. All discourse involves the contest of establishing which truth, from the many truths available, is established as most legitimate, valid and credible. Discourse analysis, therefore, focuses on how ideas or truths are socially constructed or 'made' rather than 'found' by human beings. In particular, this involves within 'critical' discourse analysis, a 'genealogical' emphasis upon 'how inequalities in power determine the ability to control the production, distribution and consumption of particular texts' (Oswick et al. 2000: 1116). This critical approach, therefore, is an agenda to expose the political motives constitutive of 'dominant' modernist discourse. In other words modernist discourse is exposed to reconnaissance for its role in establishing and maintaining power inequalities in modern societies. Within the 'hermeneutical tradition' (Gómez and Acebrón 2001: 15) of discourse analysis, the 'archaeology of knowledge' emphasises liberating local truths, meanings and voices denigrated by dominant, universal, globalising, modernist 'metanarratives'.

Language, within discourse analysis, is generally accepted to be the principal medium through which human subjective understanding of the world is mediated. Phillips and Hardy (1997) delineate three interrelated and 'mutually implicated' (Oswick et al. 2000: 1118) discursive entities that facilitate this mediation. The three discursive entities are discursive concepts, discursive objects and discursive subjects. Concepts are theories, ideologies and notions created through language that frame our understanding of identity and relationships. Concepts occupy the realm of ideas and closely resemble the notion of schemas. A 'network', for example, is itself a discursive concept in that it is an alternative organisational notion to the concepts of 'market' or 'hierarchy'. Objects occupy the practical realm and exist in the material world as well as the ideational domain. Within networks are 'actors' who are tangible beings who are discursive objects also carrying images of identity. Finally, discursive subjects are practices, structures, social responses and policies generated through discourse. Within networks, 'trust' would be an example of a discursive subject, and 'strategy' would be another.

So what can DA bring to management research? If we accept that discourse 'acts as a powerful ordering force in organizations' (Alvesson and Karreman 2000: 1127), then DA has much to offer. Managerial discourse may not necessarily contain a realist report of inter-organisational actions, but it does construct the reality (or world) into which the speaker acts. Indeed, for Phillips et al. (2004: 640), 'the discursive realm acts as the background against which current actions occur—enabling some actions and constraining others'. A further question then arises: how should we explore this important discursive realm?

As indicated positioning of the linguistic turn in Figure 2.4, DA embraces a multitude of approaches. For a useful overview of organisational DA, see Iedema (2003: 28–56) who notes that it 'relies on and grounds its arguments in empirically derived data to make its claims'. Taking this empirical perspective, the version of DA that we advocate is based upon a number of trends in the linguistic turn, including discursive social psychology, critical discourse analysis, social linguistics and elements of conversation analysis. Management scholars take on board the most pragmatically useful elements of these versions of DA, enabling 'a simultaneous focus on the function of talk and the devices of construction' (Coupland 2001: 1107). In this way, as Koivunen (2007: 288) puts it, discourses can be treated as 'context-dependent processes'.

In the context of management studies it is increasingly accepted that such a discursive approach can facilitate greater understanding. In particular, topics investigated in recent research on strategy have significance for industrial networks. For instance: Hardy et al. (2000) examine discourse as a resource that can affect whether or not a certain strategic statement 'takes'. Eriksson and Lehtimäki (2001) show how the strategy discourse can reproduce problematic assumptions concerning the role of specific actors. Similarly Varaa et al. (2004) have studied the discursive practices via which concepts like 'alliances' are legitimised.

Viewing organisational phenomena as complex constructions may involve the acceptance of multiple narratives and appreciation that discourses change depending on network position. Kornberger et al. (2006: 20) highlight that such polyphonic discourse 'constitutes organizational reality' and that all narratives expose contextualities even though this will create multiple different perspectives and applications of how to interpret plots. Such tension or *différend* brings out the conflicts or paradoxes that emerge through multiple narratives. Embracing the linguistic turn means not discussing optimal or 'conclusive' solutions but including all narratives as possible equal realities without automatically rejecting any perspectives. In other words, this requires not simply ignoring narratives that do not conform to the researcher's unswerving view of reality. Despite the resonance of these suggestions, they appear to have had surprisingly little impact management research practices. For instance, organisational researchers examining narrative or discursive data often betray a belief in the possibility of an 'immaculate conception' or direct access to reality. As Czarniawska notes, however, 'Braved by a constructivist reflection, I know that no such thing is possible and it does not worry me too much' (1998: 30).

CONCLUSIONS

The discontinuities between Schumacher's ontological levels do not lead automatically to incommensurability intolerances (cf. Burrell and Morgan 1979) among paradigms. Research needs to remain at least partly embedded in the material/machine-like level of understanding but both Schumacher (1997) and Capra (2002) require us to employ multiple epistemologies to access different ontologies.

Figure 2.6 depicts the potential for an expanded, integrated frame for management and organisational theory into a broader picture that would encompass all of Capra's four essential criteria. No point within the rhizomic, integrated space can be privileged

**Figure 2.6: Potential for Expansion of Organisational
Research within Capra's Kite**

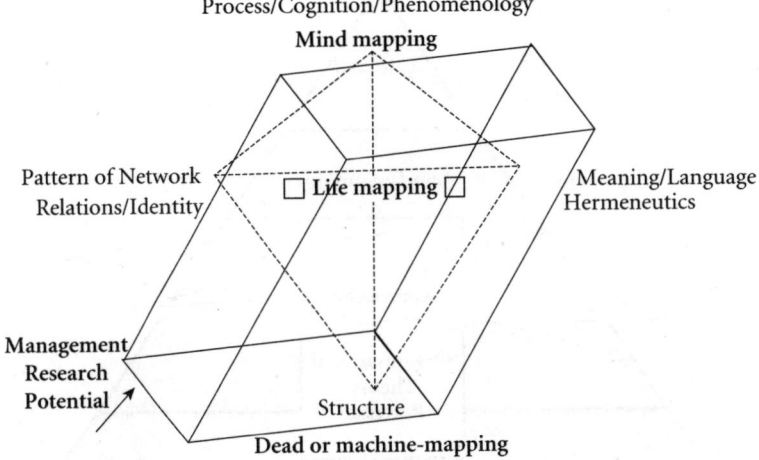

as no point actually exists except as panrelationally to all other points. Management must adopt a somewhat more practical and polyvalent, dialogical, polytheistic, holographic approach to accommodate this integrated frame.

Figure 2.7 depicts management scholarship moving up within Schumacher's hierarchy, towards mind-mapping and away from dead mapping. Achieving this requires organisational scholars to avoid using objectifying language during their own linguistic turn. Moving up the hierarchy involves positioning language as a discursive tool (or resource) used to define appropriate activity patterns, thus forming the basis of action (Palmer and Dunford 1996). Network researchers must therefore be prepared to study words as well as practices; and indeed, to study words 'as' practice. Reflecting Austin's (1962) maxim that 'words do things', it seems appropriate to consider issues of practice and discourse simultaneously (Oswick et al. 2007). The linguistic turn realises that practice and meaning are mutually constructive so that it is necessary to reflect upon the meaning of 'practice' as much as to

**Figure 2.7: Potential for Expansion of Organisational
Research within Schumacher's Hierarchy**

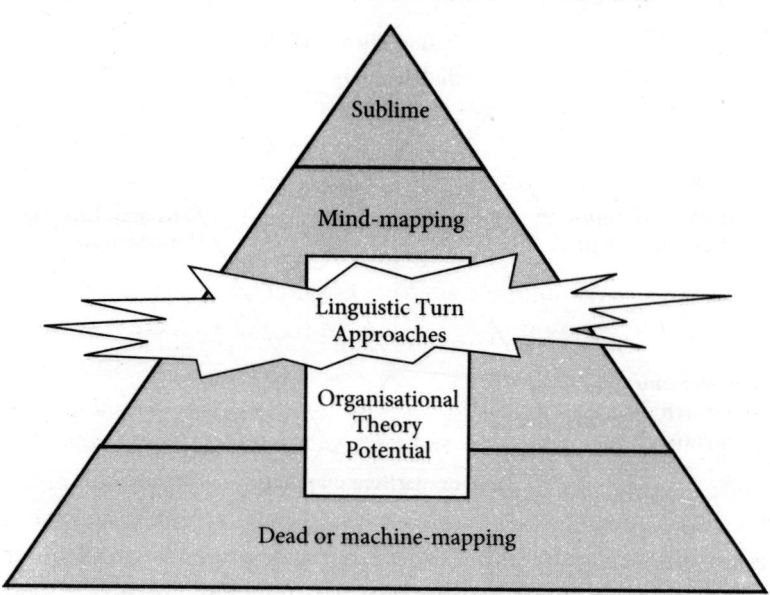

engage with the practice of meaning. Practicing managers may also benefit from extending their realm of sensemaking beyond the confines of individual rationalist cognition and including collective, social, communicative and emotional mind mapping (Magala 2005). This requires giving up some of our dead mapping certainties and acting in accordance with the tolerances of meaningful practice. Actors need to become aware of what improvised plots, scripts, words, gestures and intonations will be understood and held to be legitimate and meaningfully practical by other actors.

This integrative agenda requires the transcendence of incommensurabilities among paradigms regardless of the political and other barriers to such wisdom-based, integrative pluralism. This is a matter of appropriate intellectual competence: what is required is that the understanding of the knower must be adequate to the thing to be known. All 'knowledge is obtained *per modum cognescentis*—in accordance with the cognitive powers of the knower' (Schumacher 1977: 123).

For the practicing manager, the linguistic turn invites an acceptance of uncertainty, thereby encouraging the wisdom of 'appropriate certainty'. From this viewpoint, and building on an extended metaphor of Schumacher's, we suggest actors may find that while they are able to get a rock to respond to managerial action, and they may be able to exercise control over a dog, they will find it difficult to control a child, impossible to do so for a spouse, folly for an organisation and ludicrous for a network (cf. Schumacher 1977). Moreover, it is desirable to go beyond this and suggest that the practitioner can be seen as an author or writer of scenes or stories. This means going further than some commentators who highlight that a good manager has a certain scientific realism; that is, s/he is able to read situations in order to discover the images which are hidden in them somewhere (see Morgan 1986). In contrast Shotter proposes that a good manager is

> ...not *as if* involved 'in doing science', but as *actually* involved 'in the practical making of history'—thus besides being a 'reader', or a 'repairer', a good manager should also be something of an 'author' too. (1993: 157, emphasis original)

As a result, knowledge can, ironically, never provide wise understanding. Paradigms, their proliferation and incommensurability are inevitable within wisdom-free epistemania. Debates about them are facile, particularly if they assign intentions to change them or include an assumption of epistemological choice. In other words paradigms are a consequence of the nature of knowledge, which is to identify what it is in terms of what it isn't. Knowledge defies wisdom and in the end the 'thinking community' cannot help but set up epistemological silos that inoculate themselves from practical use.

Knowledge becomes a means masquerading as an end. It is the view here that an assumption of knowledge as an end in itself independent of purpose requires problematising. Gergen now encourages us to replace 'the search for Knowledge with the development of broadly actionable discourses' (Gergen 2003: 455) to avoid the 'discursive edifice' (ibid.) created by an obsession with esoteric knowledge. Similarly, Nicolas Maxwell, in *From Knowledge to Wisdom* (1984), argues that the modernist 'blunder' is not in the scientific revolution, but in a defective Enlightenment movement that seeks to apply un-adapted scientific methods to achievement of social progress. A problem arises from the quest for unified theories that represent a nomothetic comprehensibility of all phenomena. The outcome is a turn taking of scientific paradigms (Kuhn 1962). Maxwell accuses Enlightenment 'philosophers' of failing to identify and apply generalised progress-achieving methods adapted to the social domain. What results is totalitarian, wisdom-free social science instead of social inquiry as social philosophy concerned to identify what is important to happiness, how to resolve human problems and conflicts, and how to establish moral cohesion in a world of plural moralities.

Epistemania is compounded by 'epistemonopolies'. Paradigm wars within academia create cabals of communities of mutual referencing practice. Such communities are isolated and characterised by Balkanisation, paradigmatic warfare, persistent incommensurability frictions and epistemic apartheid. This sustains a culture of intolerance that results from over-reliance and unbalanced acquisition of knowledge to the detriment of wisdom. Combined with epistemania the outcome is a condition where 'information flushes out knowledge and knowledge flushes out wisdom-in-practice' (Chia 2003: 975). Knowledge within epistemania becomes an instrument of institutionalisation, commodification or marketisation (Gabriel 2002) in the language gaming of intellectual empire building through intertextual referencing. This is further compounded by uncontrollable 'bewitchment' (Wittgenstein 1953) or the unwitting incorporation into our knowledge of assumptions and modes of thinking that are embedded in the language used. As knowledge becomes increasingly marketable, its pursuit becomes obsessive and, paradoxically, knowledge also becomes effectively worthless as an emancipatory resource. Various limits to knowledge have long been identified. Knowledge is limited in terms of scope (there are many things of which we have little or limited knowledge); in terms of its utility (knowledge is used, sometimes hijacked, by individuals and groups for a variety of reasons); and in terms of restrictive paradigms which inform its development. Even if in investigating the social stratification of knowledge, the investigator's representation more often depends for its legitimacy on the very same social stratification (Winter 1991: 469). As a vehicle for exploitation, Foucault's (1980) characterisation of 'power as knowledge' sensitises us to the realisation that knowledge can construct repressive realities through being hijacked by the powerful. Knowledge lends itself to 'policing' and 'governmentality'. In other words, knowledge cannot be regarded as amoral or apolitical. It is the site of power struggles and the principal vehicle of oppression, surveillance and control.

This enslavement is facilitated by the underlying assumption that knowledge is good and more knowledge is better. Knowledge, constructed as an unquestioned 'good', is then often viewed unproblematically as the vital resource map and key 'driver' for success. However, 'If our guide, our annotated Map of life, cannot show us where The Good is situated and how it can be reached, it is worthless' (Schumacher 1977: 146). Knowledge has severe limitations and its over-emphasis actually denigrates other virtues, such as wisdom, morality, spirit and soul. Plato maintained that knowledge was an element of the soul, which requires moderation by wisdom. Plato's moderation of wisdom is absent in the obsessive and unbalanced knowledge-based societies. The obsessive Anglo-American knowledge-based society appears particularly imbalanced. We (that is, perplexed social scientists and managers) need to avoid the trap of limited solutions (of promised manageability) afforded within epistemania if balance is to be redressed and perplexity is to be left behind.

REFERENCES

Allen, E. 1962. *From Plato to Nietzsche.* New York: Fawcett Premier.

Alvesson, M. and D. Karreman. 2000. 'Taking the Linguistic Turn in Organizational Research: Challenges, Responses, Consequences', *Journal of Applied Behavioural Sciences*, 36(2): 136–58.

Alvesson, M. and H. Willmott. 2002. 'Identity Regulation as Organizational Control: Producing the Appropriate Individual', *Journal of Management Studies*, 39(5): 619–44.

Araujo, L. and G. Easton. 1996. 'Networks in Socioeconomic Systems: A Critical Review', in D. Iacobucci (ed.), *Networks in Marketing*, pp. 63–107. Thousand Oaks, CA: Sage Publications.

Austin, J. 1962. *How to Do Things With Words.* Oxford: Oxford University Press.

Bakhtin, M.M. 1986. *Speech Genres and Other Late Essays.* Translated by V.W. McGee. Austin, Tx: University of Taxas Press.

Berger, P. and T. Luckmann. 1966. *The Social Construction of Reality.* New York: Doubleday.

Boulding, K. 1981. *Evolutionary Economics.* Beverly Hills, CA: Sage Publications.

Burrell, G. and G. Morgan. 1979. *Sociological Paradigms and Organisational Analysis.* Oxford: Heinemann.

Callas, M. and L. Smircich. 1999. 'Past Postmodernism? Reflections and Tentative Directions', *Academy of Management Review*, 24(4): 649–72.

Capra, F. 1996. *The Web of Life.* London: Flamingo.

———. 1997. *The Web of Life.* London: Flamingo.

———. 2002. *The Hidden Connections.* London: Flamingo.

Chia, R. 1999. 'A "Rhizomic" Model of Organizational Change and Transformation: Perspectives From a Metaphysics of Change', *British Journal of Management*, 10(3): 209–27.

———. 2003. 'From Knowledge-Creation to the Perfecting of Action: Tao, Basho and Pure Experience as the Ultimate Ground of Knowing', *Human Relations*, 56(8): 953–81.

Chia, R. and L. King. 2001. 'The Language of Organization Theory', in R. Westwood and S. Linstead (eds), *The Language of Organization*, pp. 310–28. London: Sage Publications.

Clegg, R., M. Kornberger and C. Rhodes. 2005. 'Learning/Becoming/Organizing', *Organization*, 12(2): 147–67.

Cooper, R. and G. Burrell. 1988. 'Modernism, Postmodernism and Organizational Analysis', *Organization Studies*, 9(1): 91–112.

Coupland, C. 2001. 'Accounting for Change: A Discourse Analysis of Graduate Trainees' Talk of Adjustment', *Journal of Management Studies*, 38(8): 1103–19.

Czarniawska, B. 1998. *A Narrative Approach to Organization Studies.* London: Sage Publications.

Deleuze, G. and Gautari, F. 1988. *A Thousand Plateaus.* London: Athlone Press.

DiMaggio, P. 1992. 'Nadel's Paradox Revisited: Relational and Cultural Aspects of Organizational Structure', in N. Nohria and R. Eccles (eds), *Networks and*

Organizations: Structure, Form, and Action, pp. 118–42. Cambridge. MA: Harvard Business School Press.

Ellis, N., S. Lowe and S. Purchase. 2006. 'Towards a Re-Interpretation of Industrial Networks: A Discursive View of Culture', *The IMP Journal*, 1(2): 29–59.

Eriksson, P. and H. Lehtimäki. 2001. 'Strategic Rhetoric in City Management: How the Central Presumptions of Strategic Management Live On', *Scandinavian Journal of Management*, 17(2): 201–23.

Emirbayer, M. and J. Goodwin. 1994. 'Network Analysis, Culture, and the Problem of Agency', *American Journal of Sociology*, 99(6): 1411–54.

Fernandez, J. 1991. 'Introduction: Confluents of Enquiry', in *Beyond Metaphor: The Theory of Tropes in Anthropology*, pp. 1–13. Stanford, CA: Stanford University Press.

Firat, A. and A. Venkatesh. 1995. 'Liberatory Postmodernism and the Reenchantment of Consumption', *Journal of Consumer Research*, 22(3): 239–67.

Foucault, M. 1980. *Power/Knowledge: Selected Interviews & Other Writings, 1972–1977* (edited by C. Gordon). New York: Pantheon Books.

Fulop L. 2004. 'Interorganizational Networking', in S. Linstead, L. Fulop and S. Lilley (eds), *Management and Organization: A Critical Text*, pp. 539–88. London: Palgrove.

Fulop, L., H. Hayward and S. Lilley. 2004. 'Managing Structure', in S. Linstead, L. Fulop and S. Lilley (eds), *Management and Organization: A Critical Text*, pp. 123–54. London: Palgrove.

Gabriel, Y. 2002. 'On Paragrammatic Uses of Organization Theory: A Provocation', *Organization Studies* 23(1): 133–51.

Garfinkel, H. 1967. *Studies in Ethnomethodology*. Englewood Cliffs, NJ: Prentice Hall.

Geertz, C. 1973. *The Interpretation of Cultures*. New York: Basic Books.

Gergen, K. 2003. 'Beyond Knowledge in Organizational Inquiry', *Organization*, 10(3): 453–55.

Gómez Arias, J. and L. Acebrón. 2001. 'Postmodern Approaches in Business-to-Business Marketing and Marketing Research', *Journal of Business and Industrial Marketing*, 16(1): 7–20.

Granovettor, M. 1985. 'Economic Action and Social Structure: The Problem of Embeddedness', *American Journal of Sociology*, 91(3): 481–510.

Grant, D., T. Keenoy and C. Oswick. 1998. 'Introduction: Organizational Discourse: Of Diversity, Dichotomy and Multidisciplinarity', in D. Grant, T. Keenoy and C. Oswick (eds), *Discourse and Organization*, pp. 1–13. London: Sage Publications.

Halinen, A. 1997. *Relationship Marketing in Professional Services*. London: Routledge.

Hardy, C., I. Palmer and N. Phillips. 2000. 'Discourse as a Strategic Resource', *Human Relations*, 53(9): 1227–48.

Hatch, M-J and A. Cunliffe. 2006. *Organization Theory*. Oxford: Oxford University Press.

Hofstede, G. 1980. *Culture's Consequences*. London: Sage Publications.

Iedema, R. 2003. *Discourses of Post-Bureaucratic Organization*. Amsterdam: John Benjamins.

Koivunen, N. 2007. 'The Processual Nature of Leadership Discourses', *Scandinavian Journal of Management*, 23(3): 285–305.

Kornberger, M., S. Clegg and C. Carter. 2006. 'Rethinking the Polyphonic Organization: Managing as Discursive Practice', *Scandinavian Journal of Management*, 22(1): 3–30.

Kuhn, T. 1962. *The Structure of Scientific Revolutions*. Chicago: University of Chicago Press.

Latour, B. and S. Woolgar. 1979. *Laboratory Life: The Social Construction of Scientific Facts*. Beverly Hills, CA: Sage Publications.

Lessem, R. and S. Palsule. 1997. *Managing in Four Worlds: From Competition to Co-Creation*. Oxford: Blackwell Publishers.

Magala, S. 2005. *Cross-Cultural Competence*. London and New York: Routledge.

Maxwell, N. 1984. *From Knowledge to Wisdom*. Oxford: Blackwell.

Morgan, G. 1986. *Images of Organization*. Beverly Hills, CA: Sage Publications.

———. 1997. *Images of Organization* (2nd edition). Beverly Hills, CA: Sage Publications.

Musson, G., L. Cohen and S. Tietze. 2007. 'Pedagogy and the "Linguistic Turn": Developing Understanding Through Semiotics', *Management Learning*, 38(1): 45–60.

Oliver, A. and M. Ebers. 1998. 'Networking Network Studies: An Analysis of Conceptualization Configurations in the Study of Inter-Organizational Networks', *Organization Studies*, 19(4): 549–83.

Oswick, C., T. Keenoy, A. Beverungen, N. Ellis, I. Sabelis and S. Ybema. 2007. 'Discourse, Practice, Policy and Organizing: Some Opening Comments', *International Journal of Sociology & Social Policy*, 27(11/12): 429–32.

Oswick, C., T. Keenoy and D. Grant. 2000. 'Discourse, Organisations and Organising: Concepts, Objects and Subjects', *Human Relations*, 53(9): 1115–23.

Palmer, I. and R. Dunford. 1996. 'Conflicting Uses of Metaphors: Reconceptualizing Their Use in the Field of Organizational Change', *Academy of Management Review*, 21(3): 691–717.

Phillips, N. and C. Hardy. 1997. 'Managing Multiple Identities: Discourse, Legitimacy and Resources in the UK Refugee System, *Organization*, 4(2): 159–85.

Phillips, N., T. Lawrence and C. Hardy. 2004. 'Discourse and Institutions', *Academy of Management Review*, 29(4): 635–52.

Rorty, R. 1999. *Philosophy and Social Hope*. London: Penguin.

Selznick, P. 1948. 'Foundations of the Theory of Organizations', *American Sociological Review*, 13: 25–35.

———. 1949. *TVA and the Grass Roots*. Berkeley, CA: University of California Press.

Shotter, J. 1993. *Conversational Realities: Constructing Life Through Language*. London: Sage Publications.

Schumacher, E.F. 1977. *A Guide for the Perplexed*. London: Jonathan Cape.

Sim, S. (ed.). 1998. *The Icon Critical Dictionary of Postmodern Thought*. Cambridge. Icon Books.

Smircich, L. 1983. 'Concepts of Culture and Organizational Analysis', *Administrative Science Quarterly*, 28(3): 339–58.

Solomon, R.C. and K.M. Higgins. 1996. *A Short History of Philosophy*. New York: Oxford University Press.

Swingewood, A. 1991. *A Short History of Sociological Thought* (2nd edition). London: MacMillan.

Truett Anderson, W. 1996. 'What's Going on Here?' 'Introduction' in W. Truett Anderson (ed.), *The Fontana Postmodernism Reader*, pp. 1–11. London: Fontana Press.

Varaa, E., B. Kleymann and H. Seristö. 2004. 'Strategies as Discursive Constructions: The Case of Airline Alliances', *Journal of Management Studies*, 41: 1–35.

Wallemacq, A. and D. Sims. 1998. 'The Struggle With Sense', in D. Grant, T. Keenoy and C. Oswick (eds), *Discourse & Organization*, pp. 119–33. London: Sage Publications.

Weick, K. 1995. *Sensemaking in Organizations*. London: Sage Publications.

———. 2001. *Making Sense of the Organization*. Oxford: Blackwell.

Weick K., K. Sutcliffe and D. Obstfeld. 2005. 'Organizing and the Process of Sensemaking', *Organization Science*, 16(4): 409–21.

Welch, C. and I. Wilkinson. 2002. 'Idea Logics and Network Theory in Business Marketing', *Journal of Business-to-Business Marketing*, 8(3): 27–48.

Winter, R. 1991. 'Post-Modern Sociology as a Democratic Educational Practice? Some Suggestions', *British Journal of Sociology of Education*, 12(4): 467–81.

Wittgenstein, L. 1953. *Philosophical Investigations* (translated by G.E.M. Anscombe). Oxford: Blackwell.

3

PERPLEXITY, PROCESS AND PRACTICE

Kathryn Pavlovich and Robert Chia

The overwhelming presence of flux, fluidity and change in organisational activities requires the application of a 'rhizome' metaphor. The rhizome is an inter-connected processual network without structured organization. It is a panrelational network of mindful, reciprocal awareness and interactions among actors such that organisational continuity and change, identity and evolution are co-creative of each other. Practice-based process is about a ceaseless and interminable doing; a becoming of relationships that is always in the process of making and remaking. In such honing of organisational practices, an attitude of striving for perfection and silent self-awareness are vital.

Being aware takes attention away from thinking and
creates space... Through awakening, you find deep
purpose, a conscious connection with the universe.
(Tolle 2005: 244, 259)

INTRODUCTION

This chapter critiques the dominant world-view of organisations as 'objects' of investigation and argues that organising is a lot more tortuous and perplexing in practice than is generally acknowledged. We maintain that our accounts of organisation ought to acknowledge and incorporate the overwhelming presence of flux, fluidity and change in organisational activities rather than static representations of stable structures, bounded configurations and clear end-states. In this chapter we explore this notion of fluidity by proposing that organisation ought to be understood as rhizomically-linked networks of relations constantly in a state of tension and flux, and dependent on heedful processes among interconnected members that occur through mindful relationships. Indeed, the chapter proposes to offer the reader a radically alternative view of the nature of organisational reality by suggesting that all organising processes are realised through reciprocal awareness and interactions among actors such that organisational continuity and change, identity and evolution are co-creative of each other.

Thus, the practice of organising places process at its core. Practice is about a ceaseless and interminable doing; a becoming of relationships that is always in the process of making and remaking. In such honing of organisational practices, there is never a reachable end point but this does not deter the avid practitioner from pursuing ultimate stability, orderliness and predictability. Indeed, it is the interminable quest for certainty which provides the impulse for order and organisation. Like the song, 'The Impossible Dream', the strivings of practice towards perfection never ends: it is an impossible dream that we nevertheless dare to dream. This is the underlying message behind a recent Honda advertisement which drew its inspiration from this song in its unending search for the perfect automotive technology. Such an ontological attitude towards practice treats flux, continuous change and transformation at the centre of its epistemological priorities. Process metaphysicians and theoretical physicists such as Bergson (1911), Bohm, (1980), Capra (1996), Chia (1999), Prigogine (1996), Schumacher (1977) and Whitehead (1929) privilege becoming over being, activity over agency and process over substance. The 'building blocks' of reality are not discrete 'things' but events or 'actual occasions'; living units of elemental experience. Process philosophy rejects what Rescher (1996) calls the 'Process Reducibility Thesis'—that all processes necessarily reduce to the action of things and individuals. Thus, each of these process thinkers posit that process precedes structure and hence that the manner in which things are done is more fundamental than the outcome of the doing. As Whitehead (1929: 31, emphasis original) writes: '*how* an actual entity *becomes* constitutes *what* that actual entity *is*... Its "being" is constituted by its "becoming". This is the principle of process.' Consequently, the ontological priority accorded to process over outcome implies that attending to the micro-activities and actions carried out, 'tells us...more about the *coming-to-presence* of forms rather than the production of ready-made presences' (Cooper 2007: 1569). In other words, it reorients our attention, away from the overt manifestations and familiar forms displayed towards the hidden and less noticed emergence and becoming of things 'behind the scenes' or at the periphery of our conscious awareness. An acute 'subsidiary awareness' (Polanyi 1969: 55) of the mundane everyday practical coping activities becomes a crucial feature of a processual world-view, and we argue here that there is a need to include this more 'silent' and less 'spectacular' but deeper form of 'knowing' and instinctive 'doing' into our comprehension of the world of affairs, especially including the world of organisation. This is the intellectual reorientation and *modus operandi* that we advocate here in addressing the perplexity and complexity of the incessantly changing character of the modern world.

The current interconnected global environment is characterised by much uncertainty, volatility and rapidity in the pace of change with often dramatic consequences. The increasingly alarming fall-out and rapid spread of the domestic US sub-prime mortgage problem and its threatening escalation into a world-wide financial crisis of unprecedented proportions is one good example of how local occurrences can spread rhizomically like a subterranean stem or viral infection sprouting out and unsuspectingly 'infecting' other areas that are 'remote' from the scene of initiation. This illustration makes us aware of the non-linear character of the modern world where futures are uncertain and where low probability 'black swans' (Taleb 2007) can have catastrophic consequences. The need for instant clarification and readiness of access to support systems so as to assuage these innate anxieties therefore requires a shift in our attention to the underlying 'how' rather than on the manifest 'what' we are engaged in doing. As products, services and expertise are becoming increasingly commodified and virtualised in a contracting McDonaldised world, the future may well be determined by *how* such practices and dispositions are shaped and delivered rather than *what* is being delivered. Hence in both scenarios, a process orientation may help facilitate this redirection of attention towards the 'how' of things that prioritises relationships and their wider ramifications. This has implications for the management discipline, as in the world of homogeneity, the point of difference is likely to be on relational quality; on who you want to connect with in the future world of business rather than primarily on the strategic significance of the product or service itself. Product quality therefore is likely to depend on long term relationships between customers and suppliers (Powell 1990), leading to the priority given to habituated practices (*habitus*) or dispositions (Bourdieu 1990) over formal structures and outcomes. This relational quality, then, is set to prioritise emotional connectivity (who you know, like and trust) and suggest that business relationships in the future will be based on the ability of partners to work well together; that is, on how well they are familiar with each other's practices.

The practice of business therefore involves an intimate interactional process which reflects how relationships are forged, established and sustained in order to bring a degree of regularity and predictability in an inherently volatile and uncertain world. Durable interactions require an ability to connect and empathise, to feel compassion with partners in that their pain and suffering is not only noticed, but also felt (Lilius et al. 2008), and that there is a willingness to serve the interests of the partnership and the community, and not only one's personal interests. Thus, practice involves an inner development regarding *how* to engage appropriately with others to serve the interests of the planet, the community, the relationship and the partners' own interests. This confirms the move from an outward focus on tasks and measurable objectives to a more meaningful engagement on the people involved and how they interact. Indeed, in a discussion of entrepreneurial ventures, Schuyler argues that we need to better understand entrepreneurs as 'enlightened' individuals and not just as 'business entrepreneurs'. Schumacher's (1977) 'creative destruction', then, is a challenge for us to move from the material scientism of the modern world to a higher level of awareness that suggests a shift from a focus on the realities of the external world to the inner world of perceptions and mindsets. Pushing the ontological boundaries that define 'who are we' and 'why are we here' places self at the core of attention and draws our attention to fundamental questions that relate to the conscious mind mapping tasks at the peak of Schumacher's hierarchy.

In this chapter, then, the process of practice is explored in relation to conscious self-awareness. We begin by contending that process is a constant movement of 'becoming'; that change and becoming are at the core of our being, constituting and reconstituting our shifting identity rather than something external to us that we may merely apprehend. This recognition entails a radical shift in our intellectual mind-set and the conceptual categories needed to go along with it. Yet as Tsoukas and Chia (2002: 569) state, 'we lack the vocabulary to meaningfully talk about change as if change mattered—that is, to treat change not as an epiphenomenon, as a mere curiosity or exception, but to acknowledge its centrality in the constitution of socio-economic life.' There is, therefore, a need to re-examine ontological lenses commonly employed and to go beyond the 'outcome' oriented end-state mentality managers are so familiar with as to make it virtually unquestionable. Our chapter, then, examines conscious mind mapping though Capra's (2002) kite framework of *structure, process, relationships* and *meaning.* Thus, there are two parts to our inquiry. The first is a metaphysical consideration of movement and flow as quintessential as we question the 'nature of reality and what is real'. We begin by examining the rhizomic and anti-hierarchical reality of everyday life to explain how movement and change can be construed as central to organisational functioning with our reality becoming a continual ebb and flow of network connection. Based upon *structural* nodes and connections, we argue that while it is the connections that form change among nodes, it is the spaces in between which hold the possibilities of all creation. Connections, through *relationships*, are central to *process* and are based upon 'positive acts' at a micro-level that keep change and flow moving. Through the process of connecting, we actualise what is possible through heedful practice, highlighting the subsidiary awareness of a hidden reality based upon flow and indeterminism. The second focus explores conscious mind mapping and its relationship to the above consideration. We argue that it is the *meaning* of deep knowing that supports movement through self awareness and inner knowledge as we are 'other'. Thus, this second consideration concerns *our own nature.*Experience does not stand outside of us; we co-create through being in relationship with our inner knowing. Through a quantum lens, in changing ourselves, we change the whole world as we are connected through a unifying field of energy (Chu 2007) that is only created through conscious intention. Thus, we posit that self-awareness ought to be a central process for any perplexed manager who seeks to create positive change in the organisational context. The following section expands these two concepts as they relate to organisational practice.

There is no truth except
the truth that exists in you.
Everything else is what
someone else is telling you.
(The Buddha)

PROCESS

Being and Becoming

Process metaphysicists suggest that when challenging the modernist primacy of stability and certainty, it is uncertainty, fluidity and change that are central to what needs to be uncovered when addressing the nature of organisation (Durand and Calori 2006). As Tsoukas and Chia (2002: 567) suggest,

> Organization is an attempt to order the intrinsic flux of human action, to channel it towards certain ends, to give it a particular shape, through generalising and institutionalising particular meanings and rules... [thus] change is not a property of organization. Rather organization must be understood as an emergent property of change.

This reinforces that organisation is the outcome of process, a consequence of things changing and things moving. Bergson (1968: 222, emphasis original) too notes, 'There do not exist *things* made, but only things in the making, not *states* that remain fixed, but only states in the process of change.'

Yet our modernist world focuses on knowledge as a tangible asset, as an object to be manipulated for desired outcomes. Chia (2003: 959) claims that

> ...to know is to be able to define and say precisely 'what' a thing is, hence giving it an identity, and then to locate it in a system of causal relations. Naming, locating and the attribution of causal relations constitute the key steps in the knowledge-creation process.

Thus, conventional management is preoccupied with the lower order attention that Schumacher (1977) defines as inanimate mapping whereby the objects are fixed, controllable and mostly have a physical presence. The epistemological world of measurement and objects thus becomes questioned as things 'being' (fixed and immutable) rather than things 'becoming'. Yet there is a growing literature challenging these static and end-states approaches in organisational theory that favour change over persistence, activity over substance, and process over product (Rescher 1996). Indeed, Cooper (2007: 1569, emphasis original) contends that we need to think in terms of 'action as simple *doing* instead of *knowing, becoming* instead of *completing, starting* instead of finishing'. This places the uncertainty, the *not knowing* of this quest for understanding the nature of reality at the core of conscious mapping. Our challenge, thus, is to find the form of awareness that may hold these at the heart of our organising and practice endeavours.

Structure: Process and Anti-Hierarchy

'Becoming', then, implies movement and flow. One of Capra's (2002) central dimensions in understanding this ontological puzzle is that of structure. While structure is the embodiment of process and as such is not 'real', it does provide patterns and visual representations from which we can 'map' the organisation of a system—not to reify it, but to more deeply be aware of the flows of energy and matter. Understanding the structure of process, we claim, allows managers of organisations to appreciate why the anti-hierarchical structural form (visible through interdependent networks) denotes becoming as a practice of uncertainty, and thus such managers are more equipped to engage in practice that includes complexity, unknowing and indeterminable flux. Deleuze and Guattari (1987) insightfully provide a botanical metaphor for understanding this ontological premise. They claim that the more conventional hierarchical organising models follow a linear path somewhat like a root-tree, with central operating principles spreading predictably outwards through a fixed order. In contrast, they describe the network as more akin to a rhizome, with its underground tuber-like system that ramifies, divides and produces new buds. They call this 'anti-hierarchy', in that, 'It forms like a bulb. It evolves by subterranean stems and flows, along river or train tracks; it spreads like patches of oil' (Deleuze and Guattari 1987: 31).

Thus, the central feature of the rhizome is its undetermined nature of movement. The very essence of organisation within this ontological premise is its shifting nature of 'becoming' something else. The rhizome, (ibid.: 21) claim 'is composed not of units but of dimensions, or rather directions in motion. It has neither a beginning nor an end, but always a middle (milieu) from which it grows and overspills'. This perspective offers insights into movement as non-linear in that movement can emerge from anywhere in the system—without planning, without pre-determinism and without order. Rather, it is a fluidity of motion that moves according to its inner principles of generation as directions in motion. The measured results indicate the more transformative reality of the micro-practices supporting these outcomes.

An illustration of the anti-hierarchical form of 'becoming' is evident in the development of the PC computer. In the early 1980s, the future of computing appeared to rest in multi-user systems, with terminals connected to central systems. By the end of the decade however, distributed data processing had taken hold, with terminals replaced by PCs and users having the ability to directly access and control information. This change, from hierarchy to an anti-hierarchical network, has had profound consequences both socially and economically. Instead of information residing in the central terminals as in a hierarchy, the PC has enabled information to flow through every point within the system resulting in a greater equality of information transfer, primarily based on connectivity to the network. This rhizomic example illustrates how information travels through non-linear network links in an anti-hierarchical

(contd.)

(*contd.*)

form with change emerging at any bifurcation point in unpredictable ways. The 'emergence of things' through the non-linear spread of data allows for continual participation of all nodes within the system, with the flow of energy and matter always 'in-between'. This example illustrates the structural implications of a non-linear system that has movement and flow as its central organising mechanism.

The rhizomic form, therefore, highlights movement and flow among relationships, evident through its nodes and connections as structure. Yet the nodes are 'objects'—static, fixed and observable, while the connections indicate the strength of relationships—weak, strong, local and global. Cooper (2005: 1691) expands this by noting that such 'objects become more like markers around which dense networks of relationships are acted out instead of fixed objects which predetermine our mental and physical movement'. Process then, assists in the formation and maintenance of these connections, determining what outcomes may be.

Relationships as Structural Coupling

Thus, we need to shift our attention from the structural objects to relationships because it is from relationships that we manifest matter, the second aspect of Capra's (2002) kite. Relationships among people involve the flow of energy and information; thus relationships shape energy and information flow. Hierarchical structures have the ability to stymie the movement of energy as at some point energy may be halted as there may be no place for energy to move. Rhizomes however, allow an unbroken flow from node to node, in unpredictable directions and patterns. The constant coming together of structural coupling, the breaking off into new forms, and the re-territorialisation means energy continues: it moves from space to space, sometimes collecting more vitality, other times shrugging off what no longer works. Thus, it enfolds and unfolds into itself, representing what Bohm (1980) calls the 'implicate order' of constant movement. The way in which we relate constitutes the transforming process of connectivity. Practice therefore, is a way of transforming our relationships—not to fix things but to adjust one's perspective (Schuyler 2007). The 'objects' so commonly studied, then, are merely markers around which we mutually co-construct. It is therefore relationship—the structural coupling between nodes through connections—that shapes form. The rhizomic form is characterised by uncertainty and the not knowing, with only flow as its central movement. Thus, all is possible; limitation exists only through our focus on inanimate machine-like mapping.

In a study on Evidence Based Health Care (EBHC) Wood and Ferlie (2003) acknowledge that the organisation of health care knowledge follows a rhizomic path and cannot follow the principle of one single root because of the complexity of research processes involved through different patterns of relationality. This interdisciplinary research includes four sectors from health and social care, primary research care, cardiovascular research and health informatics, meaning that there are micro-politics of engagement that involve researchers, policy makers and practitioners, each with separate and sometimes conflicting goals. Thus, Wood and Ferlie identify that these different patterns of relationships involve 'connections, combinations, mergers, incorporations and associations across different interest groups and professional fields (ibid.: 62)' demonstrating a non-linear rhizomic flow of information, with a complex structural coupling of different nodal connection points 'becoming' something else. The essence of this form of organisation is the ability of managers to exist in the unknowing, to focus on the evolving process of practice rather than solely on administrative outcomes.

(*contd.*)

(contd.)

> Similarly, in a study on the transformation of a tourism destination, Pavlovich (2003) found that the most critical feature of this network evolution was the emergence of flexible structural coupling. The destination had historically been a single attraction, with limited resources flowing to the peripheral organisations (hierarchical). However, the emergence of a more comprehensive network system enabled plural pathways (rhizomic) where the sharing of information resulted in the development of specialised knowledge bases forming strategic capabilities in the destination. These structural couplings were based upon non-linear collaborative processes with complex and fluid reciprocal exchanges. This again highlights how it was the hidden practices that were quintessential for transformation, not the focus on outcomes.

Relationships as Actualisation

If objects are nodes and connections are relationships, what are the spaces in between? As Cooper (2007: 1559) states, 'process seems to emerge from a placeless place, an origin that refuses to be identified in space and time, where both before and after are impenetrably intertwined.' Merleau-Ponty (1962, cited in Cooper 2005: 1694) too agrees that 'instead of imagining [space] as a sort of ether in which all things float ... we must think of it as the universal power enabling them to be connected'. That which is unmanifested, the eternal, could be considered as of another dimension, and yet it is not separate from our dimensional form (Tolle 2005). Thus, form and formlessness are movement. The unmanifested flows into this dimension as awareness, inner space, presence.... It becomes form. This has a direct impact on perplexed managers as this understanding can assist in developing new products in new space. Thus, if all is possible, how can it be actualised into physical form?

An interesting paradox regarding the actualisation of space is the development of wireless technologies. We cannot see them, but they exist as transmitters of energy and flow. Indeed in decades past, such technologies did not exist in our consciousness, somewhat like the 'black swans' that Taleb (2007) identified. The wireless paradigm has been actualised from nothingness, from the virtual, and its physicality remains an act of faith; yet the process of its practice has and will continue to revolutionise the way business is enacted, freeing us from a 'being' state of constraint in location and mobility to 'becoming' location-free and mobile. This driving force of convergent technologies demonstrates how the emergence of things is non-linear and unpredictable and remains hidden until it becomes an experience of existence through a process of connection.

While some process metaphysicists comment on the neutrality of this latent space (see Cooper 2007), we also note the importance of creative endeavour through an enfolding and unfolding with the universe. We agree that the latent space is neutral, but we also posit that a central aspect of our humanness is to learn to create flourishing, vital and mutually inspired traditions, and we need to adopt 'positive acts' for such sustainable futures (Bergson 1911). To suggest the opposite would be to, 'Imagine that the world has no intrinsic character and that we could construct and differentiate the world according to our own interests.... . [This] essence is what allows for invention, creation or time in its pure sense' (Colebrook 2006: 14–15).

The Green Collar project in the USA was developed by Van Jones in an effort to build a green economy strong enough to lift millions of people from poverty. Jones and

(contd.)

(*contd.*)

Wyskida (2007) argue that the two important issues facing humanity at the moment are an ecological crisis and poverty (economic and spiritual), with a single solution: 'jobs for low income people to retrofit their communities'. Through the development of millions of wind, solar and wave farms, Jones and Wyskida contend that we have the power to create renewable sources of energy without destroying the planet (addressing the ecological crisis), providing jobs for low income people (addressing the economic crisis) and giving such people purpose and meaning in their lives (addressing the spiritual crisis). Such an example illustrates how positive action—through the inclusion of multi-dimensional relationships—has the ability to transform possibility into the actual. Again, the process of practice is based upon collaborative and positive relationships that Bergson (1911) and Deleuze (1991) argue for.

Thus, quintessential to metaphysicists is that only the collective is argued for. For to focus solely on the individual is what Deleuze and Guattari (1983) would suggest is a self-absorbed nomadic freedom, a form of schizophrenia based on lack, negation and desire. In considering the reality of practice and process, the relational quality comes to the fore, as positive acts and collaborative relationships require durability: that is, practice as an ever ceaseless striving towards perfection as the responsibility of all partners in the relationship. There is no 'other', as the outcome is co-created by the process of mutual connection.

Our focus, then, is on interdependent relations whereby we seek to manifest in the physical from the virtual possibilities. 'For, in order to be actualised, the virtual cannot proceed by elimination or limitation, but must create its own lines of actualisation in positive acts' (Deleuze 1991: 97). Through reciprocity, our positive acts and our engagement with others become central. Yet in noting the quality of 'otherness', there is no 'other', with creation and evolution a consequence of our interdependent engagements. Whitehead (1929: 24, emphasis original) too accords, 'That every condition to which the process of becoming conforms to a particular instance has its reason *either* in the character of some actual entity in the actual world of that concrescence, *or* in the character of the subject which is in process of concrescence.'

Space, the virtual (in a Bergsonian sense), therefore contains all that is possible; it is infinite and creation is only limited by the absence of relationship. That is, movement requires reciprocal connection through partnerships in order that connection be made to actualise the space. 'The work of process is the ceaseless alternation... between the mappable and the unmappable' (Cooper 2007: 1559). Thus, learning is created through partnerships. Specialisation and knowledge creation emerge from a synergistic movement of people, resources and information among the interconnected community as a consequence of the diversity and intensity of relational connectivity. Capra (1996) reinforces that this form of structural coupling is developmental rather than cyclical, again illustrating the coming to presence of a reality rather than the production of the ready-made. We can see that this structural coupling allows unpredictable and non-linear movement of Schumacher's (1977) second level of animate hierarchy, based upon partnerships and mutual reciprocity. While not intending to suggest taxonomy, this would imply that the third level map of consciousness requires personal intention and attention which may or may not be present within the actualisation process. This moves our focus from the nature of reality to our own nature.

> *Life is a series of nature and spontaneous changes.*
> *Don't resist them—that only creates sorrow.*
> *Let reality be reality.*
> *Let things flow naturally forward in whatever*
> *ways they like.*
> (Lao-Tse)

MEANING: MINDFULNESS
AS CONSCIOUS MAPPING

The 'space' referred to above has become the domain of quantum physicists, and this new science contends that what we have previously referred to as 'empty space' actually contains the secret of consciousness. They describe this space as inherently charged with an immense background of multi-dimensional energy. For instance, Bohm (1980) posits

> ... that what we perceive through the senses as empty space is actually the plenum, which is the ground for the existence of everything, including ourselves.... This plenum is, however, no longer to be conceived through the idea of a simple material medium, such as an ether, which would be regarded as existing and moving only in a three-dimensional space. Rather, one is to begin with a holomovement, in which there is the immense 'sea' of energy understood in terms of a multi-dimensional implicate order. (ibid.: 243)

The quantum perspective gives evidence to support the claim that the objects of our experience are enacted in a ground of consciousness. It is this consciousness, or field, that is the whole world in which objects appear (McTaggart 2001). We are able to feel this field through intimate experience, which hence illustrates why the power of connection is so much more important than the objects of our attention.

Thus, imagine a world where we privilege the virtual; the invisible; that which is latent; the spaces into which physical matter (the objects) reside. This supports the possibility of a something in the nothingness which contains the possibility of being actualised. Cooper (2007: 1569) reminds us that the work of process then, is 'pure action and ongoingness in which the significance of specific objects and specific tasks takes second place to their generation and movement in a field of generic relationship and transivity'. This sustains Bohm's (1980) call that the space, the hiddenness around us should be our primary place of focus, manifested through relationship.

Mindfulness

The perplexed manager will be asking that if all possibilities reside in this space, how can it best be co-created with for physical manifestation? Thus, the process of 'how' comes to the fore, and shifts this inquiry to our own inner awareness. Weick and Putnam (2006) offer insights in their noting of 'mindful-relating', whereby we need to 'pay attention to the internal processes of the mind [rather] than to content' (p. 276). The concentration and discipline demanded of mindfulness 'keeps the mind steady as a stone instead of letting it bob around like a pumpkin in water' (Bodhi 2000, cited in ibid.: 276). This allows more enhanced stability and clarity of attention whereby our connecting points are focused on an introspective and sensitive awareness of actions rather than the externalising of events, situations and consequences. In connecting with others through a mindful relationship, we reframe our relationship with each other through examining the impact of our actions, and thus we co-constructively relate more consciously. This very process allows more attention on the positive outcomes of a reciprocal learning activity and supports the notions of otherness and relationality. In this way, movement occurs through the quality of relationship that connects.

Mindfulness therefore is a slowing down to create stillness. In this stillness, we 'become' one with space within the infinite possibilities. Mindfulness allows us to let go of the objects and connect at a deep level of awareness through being present with the surroundings at each moment. This places the inner experience at the core of process. Chia (2003: 969–70) insightfully describes the conditions for experience and suggests three aspects that emerge in relation to 'becoming' part of the virtual:

> For, if experience is more fundamental than the individual and if such experience is one of flux and transformation, then it follows that the identity of the individual is the effect of the arresting and abstracting of experience. The individual self is only a by-product of perpetually shifting

constellations of relations, never a fundamental stable unity in its own right. First, pure experience is realised prior to self-awareness and the subject/ object distinctions. Second, pure experience is active and constructive, not passive, discrete and static as is generally understood in ordinary empiricism. Such experience grasped from within is systematically self-developing and self-unfolding—the self in ceaseless construction and reconstruction. Third, in pure experience, knowledge, feeling and volition remain undifferentiated. Ultimate reality is not merely registered cognitively but also felt emotionally and volitionally.

Our habitual routines and patterns of our object-focused behaviour then, are coping mechanisms that allow us to deal with uncertainty arising from our rhizomic experience. Perrow (1999: 214) explains that 'we construct an expected world because we can't handle the complexity of the present one, and then process the information that fits the expected world, and find reasons to exclude the information that might contradict it'. Yet it is this noise of our everyday routines that interrupt our coherent communication. We simply don't have the internal silence to listen carefully for the 'invisible' to become coherent. As Chia (2003) notes above, it is through our objective experience that we veil the possibilities available to us. Practice, then, ought to ally with the feeling of experience and being more comfortable with the uncertainty that flows from this. The ensuing self-awareness allows us to appreciate our 'becomingness' and widens our acceptance of the virtual space that we reside within. For in this place, 'There is no place for the flow to be known as flow, nor the individual the individual' (Carter 1990, in ibid.: 960). Everything is.

Conscious mind mapping as espoused by Schumacher then requires a 'letting go' of the objects with which we conventionally construct our experience. In 'letting go' we connect more fully with the 'other', and we appreciate the other as a manifestation of ourselves. The objective world of management needs to be guided by the inner awareness, the silence of connection. In that silence we are all knowing. As Chia (2003: 978) states that, 'To know is not so much to be able to explain the cause of things but to be able to effect a flawless and effortless performance'. Thus, through having an empty mind we develop clarity of thought. This accords with the concept of 'mindfulness' in that one focuses peacefully on the task as a moment of experience.

Process, then, is an outcome of intention. From the relational interaction with the 'other', movement is created. The moment of connection necessitates a harmonious becoming for the virtual to be actualised. Colebrook (2006: 53, emphasis original) explains, 'There are not things that perceive each other and *then* move, but a universal variation of imaging from which one movement reacts *in a certain way* to other movements.' Actualisation is seen as performance in that it exists in a world of reflective consciousness, in the unknown that becomes form. The individual 'becomes' secondary to the virtual. The virtual is overflowing with energy, with the spirit of life, filled with possibilities. Creation is the observable manifestation through reciprocal form. Positive acts allow the rhizomic world to expand, flow and move *into* through inner awareness of soul purpose and meaning. Capra (2002: 64) defines this 'meaning as a short hand notation of the inner world of reflective consciousness', transcending the objective world through virtuous endeavour. Thus, meaning embraces such expression as compassion, humility and gratitude. We suggest then, that 'I am the other'. Through an inner silence, we become still in order to be present to take in the life force that surrounds us. There is no separation from us and the 'other'—we are one and the same. Our choice, through will and intention, is to co-create with those possibilities. Buber (1970: 56, emphasis original) reminds us that, 'Those who experience do not participate *in* the world. For experience is "in them".... The world as experience belongs to the basic I-It world. The basic I-You world establishes the world of relations.'

Managers, we suggest, need to reframe their consciousness to see practice not so much as an objective task of control and implementation of resources, but as a shift to the inner awareness of the eternal flow of life. Reiterating Cooper (2007: 1569, emphasis original), we ought to think of 'action as simple *doing* instead of knowing, *becoming* instead of completing, *starting* instead of finishing'. Assisting in harmonic relationship with the 'other' through virtuous ways heightens creative expression when one is unattached to outcomes. Thus, it is who I am, not what I am, experienced through the inner guidance of self. Indeed, thinking very little, but thinking in the right way. Schumacher's (1977) conscious mind mapping then returns us to the technologies of self, yet realised through relationship in indeterminable, multi-dimensional and unpredictable rhizomic ways. The practice of process is a constant flow of becoming something else.

> *Ideas by themselves*
> *Cannot produce change of being*
> *Your effort must go in the right direction*
> *And one must correspond to the other*
> (P. D. Ouspensky)

CONCLUSION

Our advice to managers, then, is to spend more time reflecting in silence; to adhere to the principles of the inner tuition. We have argued that process is an outcome of doing with awareness, and from this we actualise in a manner that enhances sustenance with the earth. Rather than the world of objects and substance, we suggest it is that which is the invisible that needs attention. In a rhizomic world, we can practice actualisation through the inner processes of the mind; through reflective stances and inner meanings. Thus Capra's kite of structure (rhizomic), relationships (connections), process (doing) is governed by action from seeking deeper meanings into how and why we do things. 'Things' have no capacity to exist independently as we are inter-connected in a quantum of multi-dimensional energy. Economic generation (the pre-occupation of managers), therefore, are outcomes governed by the processes of positive action.

Hence the processual paradox of practice: becoming means to be in stillness.

REFERENCES

Bergson, H. 1911. *Creative Evolution* (translated by A. Mitchell). London: Macmillan.

———. 1968. *The Creative Mind*. [c. 1946]. New York: Greenwood Press.

Bourdieu, P. 1990. *The Logic of Practice*. Cambridge: Polity Press.

Bohm, D. 1980. *Wholeness and the Implicate Order*. Boston: Routledge and Kegan Paul.

Buber, M. 1970. *I and Thou* (translated by W. Kauffman). New York: Touchstone.

Capra, F. 1996. *The Web of Life*. London: Flamingo Press.

———. 2002. *The Hidden Connections: A Science for Sustainable Living*. London: HarperCollins.

Chia, R. 1999. 'A "Rhizomic" Model of Organizational Change and Transformation: Perspective from a Metaphysics of Change', *British Journal of Management*, 10: 209–27.

———. 2003. 'From Knowledge Creation to the Perfecting of Action: Tao, Basho and Pure Experience as the Ultimate Ground of Knowing', *Human Relations*, 56(8): 953–81.

Chu, E. 2007. 'Spiritual Capitalism: The Achievement of Flow in Entrepreneurial Enterprises', *Journal of Human Values*, 13(1): 61–77.

Colebrook, C. 2006. *Deleuze: A Guide for the Perplexed*. London: Continuum.

Cooper, R. 2005. 'Relationality', *Organization Studies*, 26(11): 1689–710.

———. 2007. 'Organs of Process—Rethinking Human Organization', *Organization Studies*, 28(10): 1547–73.

Deleuze, G. 1991. *Bergsonism* (translated by H. Tomlinson and B. Habberjam). New York: Zone Books.

Deleuze, G. and F. Guattari. 1983. *Anti-Oedipus: Capitalism and Schizophrenia*. Minneapolis: University of Minnesota Press.

———. 1987. *A Thousand Plateaus: Capitalism and Schizophrenia*. London: Althone Press.

Durand, R. and R. Calori. 2006. 'Sameness, Otherness? Enriching Organizational Change Theories with Philosophical Consideration on the Same and the Other', *Academy of Management Review*, 31(1): 93–114.

Jones, V. and B. Wyskida. 2007. 'Green-Collar Jobs for Urban America', Available online at http://www.yesmagazine.org/article.asp?ID=1551 (downloaded on 6 July 2008).

Lilius, J., M. Worline, S. Maitlis, J. Kanov, J. Dutton and P. Frost. 2008. 'The Contours and Consequences of Compassion at Work', *Journal of Organizational Behavior*, 29(2): 193–218.

McTaggart, L. 2001. *The Field*. London: HarperCollins.

Ouspensky, P.D. 1957. *The Fourth Way*. New York: Random House.

Pavlovich, K. 2003. 'All That Jazz: An Analysis of Dynamic Structures and Learning Networks', *Long Range Planning*, 36(5): 441–58.

Perrow, C. 1999. *Human Accidents*. New York: Basic Books.

Polanyi, M. 1969. *Knowing and Being*. Chicago: University of Chicago Press.

Powell, W. 1990. 'Neither Market Nor Hierarchy: Network Forms of Organization', *Research in Organizational Behavior*, 12: 295–336.

Prigogine, I. 1996. *The End of Certainty*. New York: The Free Press.

Rescher, N. 1996. *Process Metaphysics: An Introduction to Process Philosophy*. New York: State University of New York Press.

Schumacher, E.F. 1977. *A Guide for the Perplexed*. London: Jonathan Cape.

Schuyler, K. 2007. 'Being a *Bodhisattva* at Work: Perspectives on the Influence of Buddhist Practices in Entrepreneurial Organizations', *Journal of Human Values*, 13(1): 43–60.

Taleb, N.N. 2007. *The Black Swan: The Impact of the Highly Improbable*. London: Allen Lane.

Tolle, E. 2005. *The New Earth*. London: Penguin Books.

Tsoukas, H. and R. Chia. 2002. 'On Organizational Becoming: Rethinking Organizational Change', *Organization Science*, 13(5): 567–82.

Weick, K. and T. Putnam. 2006. 'Organizing For Mindfulness: Eastern Wisdom and Western Knowledge', *Journal of Management Inquiry*, 15(3): 1–13.

Whitehead, A. 1929. *Process and Reality: An Essay in Cosmology*. New York: The Free Press.

Wood, M. and E. Ferlie. 2003. 'Journeying from Hippocrates with Bergson and Deleuze', *Organization Studies*, 24(1): 47–68.

4

PERPLEXITY: PREPARING FOR THE HAPPENINGS OF CHANGE

John Shotter

Ascending Schumacher's hierarchy involves dedicated focus upon emergent phenomena and the descriptive concepts needed to illuminate their present nature.

A practical cultivation of 'habitus' involves a third realm of human activity: embodied spontaneously expressed expectations.

The pursuit of a descriptive science for understanding requires an apprenticeship of practical wisdom.

This involves practical comprehension of the present moment; quite a different kind from that we exert in our more intellectual accounts of the situations we face.

*The present—the concreteness of the present—as a phenomenon
to consider, as a structure, is for us an unknown planet: so we can
neither hold on to it in our memory nor reconstruct it through
imagination. We die without knowing what we have lived.*
(Kundera 1993: 129, emphasis original)

*If the social is always past, in the sense that it is always formed,
we have indeed to find new terms for the undeniable experience
of the present: not only the temporal present, the realization of
this and this instant, but the specificity of the present being,
the inalienably physical, within which we may discern and
acknowledge institutions, formations, positions, but not
always as fixed products, defining products.*
(Williams 1977: 128)

*If it be now, it is not to come; if it be not to come, it will
be now; if it be not now, yet it will come: the readiness is all.*
(*Hamlet*. Act V, Scene 2)

We cannot, I think, *plan* genuine innovative change, but we can *prepare* ourselves for it. Indeed, we can go further, we can *occasion* it, in the sense of 'setting the scene' for the *happening* of change. We can prepare ourselves by gaining some detailed, first hand experience of the actual situation in which the change is required. We can prepare ourselves also by learning what might be relevant 'descriptive concepts', that is, concepts which can be used to 'remind' (Wittgenstein 1953: §127) us of specific events and features in that situation that might be of importance, that might otherwise pass us by unnoticed. Supplying some of the descriptive concepts relevant to the actual workings of our everyday communicative activities is one of my overall themes in this chapter. The other is that there are two very different kinds of difficulties that we can face in life. Some are intellectual difficulties that we can formulate as problems and can solve by the application of clever and methodical thought. Others, as I see it, are difficulties of orientation or of relationship, to do with the kind of *expectations* with which we approach and relate ourselves to a particular situation, expectations that work selectively to influence what we *notice* and what we are *prepared* to respond to. Hence, overall, my concern is twofold: To try to describe the kind of activities that might prepare us, that is, 'get us ready' to act from within the midst of complexity, according to whatever opportunities to act in ways relevant to our aims that happen to present themselves to us in the situation we currently inhabit; but also, to try to describe the characteristics of these activities in ways that will make them memorable, and able to arouse in us again and again the original 'movement' that 'moved' us to a new way of acting, thus to make it unforgettable. As Merleau-Ponty (1964: 122) describes it: 'Our task is to broaden our reasoning to make it capable of grasping what, in our selves and others, precedes and exceeds reason.'

PREPARATIONS

Perception: 'Seeing Connections' Rather Than Having to 'Work Them Out'

> *... still the man hears what he wants to hear*
> *And disregards the rest, hmmmm.*

(*The Boxer*, Paul Simon 1968)

On the day I began to write this article, Wednesday 29 October 2008, the following few opening sentences appeared in an article on the Op-Ed page of the *New York Times*:

Roughly speaking, there are four steps to every decision. First, you perceive a situation. Then you think of possible courses of action. Then you *calculate* which course is in your best interest. Then you take the action. Over the past few centuries, public policy analysts have assumed that step three is the most important. Economic models and entire social science disciplines are premised on the assumption that people are mostly engaged in rationally calculating and maximizing their self-interest. But during this financial crisis, that way of thinking has failed spectacularly. As Alan Greenspan noted in his Congressional testimony last week, he was 'shocked' that markets did not work as anticipated.... So perhaps this will be the moment when we alter our view of decision-making. Perhaps this will be the moment when we shift our focus from step three, rational calculation, to step one, perception. Perceiving a situation seems, at first glimpse, like a remarkably simple operation. You just look and see what's around. But the operation that seems most simple is actually the most complex, it's just that most of the action takes place below the level of awareness. Looking at and perceiving the world is an active process of meaning-making that shapes and biases the rest of the decision-making chain.... (Brooks 2008, emphasis added)

And in the rest of his article, David Brooks wondered if the current financial meltdown was, perhaps, the harbinger of a cultural change: The turning of our attention away from the idea of calculating, that is, trying to 'figure out' what to do for the best in a situation, and more toward to how we *perceive the meaning* of events occurring around us, what some might call 'the *root* of the problem', and, let me add, a turn toward how we might better prepare ourselves to see their meaning more clearly and precisely. For, as we shall see, although we cannot predict in detail the nature of future events, we can anticipate their *style*, come to a grasp of their *logical grammar* as Wittgenstein (1953) calls it, a sense of the *way*[1] in which things and events are connected with each other.

Thus in what follows below, I want not only to build on these remarks of Brooks, but in doing so, to go more deeply into the distinction E.F. Schumacher (1977) made—in his book, *A Guide for the Perplexed*—between what he called the 'instructional' and the 'descriptive sciences'. Indeed, I want to go even further. I want to explore how the descriptive sciences (from now on, I will call them the descriptive disciplines[2]) can help us to *prepare* ourselves better for living out our lives, moment by moment, from within the midst of complexity in a way in which the *plans* we arrive at for our future—using the theories provided to us by the instructional sciences—do not and can not. Thus my aims in this chapter are, I hope, very practical ones. For I am not at all concerned to advance the kind of social science *theories* that Schumacher would see as falling into the domain of the instructional sciences. Instead, influenced especially by Wittgenstein (1953),[3] my aim is to *describe* certain of our social activities in some detail and to show how such conceptual descriptions can be of preparatory help to us—a switch away from dealing with numbers to working with words in giving shape to our actions.

Usually, we think it important to influence people by our arguments, we think it important to persuade them to think differently, to give them good reasons. Sometimes, we think we can change them by exhorting them to change, by preaching sermons that confront them with their guilty ways in the hope that they will cease their wrong doing. But the trouble with all such efforts is that at the time of their expression, no genuinely new ways forward seem to be apparent. Indeed, it is more often than not the case that seemingly 'new' proposals often turn out to have many of the same old assumptions hidden in them.

Instead of arguments, then, instead of the supposed 'content' of our utterances, I want to focus attention on our actual voicing of our utterances. I want to describe in some detail ways of speaking in which we make use of poetic metaphors, images, direct quotations of another's talk, special modes of intonation, use of pauses and many other vocal devices for influencing the way in which a listener is influenced, not in their *thinking*, but in how they *pay attention* to events in their surroundings. Remember that as children our parents influenced our actions by saying (along with the appropriate facial expressions, gestures and vocal emphasis): 'Stop!' 'Look at that!' 'Listen to this!'

Thus in what follows, I will be interested less in *what* is being said (the supposed *content* of an utterance), than in *how* it is being said, that is, in how the *saying* of it (its *form*) can exert its effects on us. But I want to go even further. I want also to emphasise the importance of using a form of talk (what I will call 'withness'—talk as distinct from our more usual forms of 'aboutness'—talk) in which people don't speak of their thoughts or opinions, of their professional knowledge, technical facts, or the such-like, but speak only guided by their own, lived, personal experience in voicing their utterances. This is a form of talk that we often call, 'speaking from the heart', and as we shall see, when used *at an opportune moment*, it can play a powerful part in the occasioning of change.

Thus, what I want to suggest here is that, only if we are prepared to live 'on the edge', that is, in the present moment, in the midst of complexity, can we find the new openings, the new possibilities we need to truly bring about innovative change. Not only shall I make this claim in this chapter, but I shall also try to describe what is actually entailed in doing so. We will find it difficult, however, to understand how this might be possible. For, as Kundera (1993: 129, emphasis original) notes, currently, given our present modes of factual and rational expression, 'the concreteness of the present—as a phenomenon to consider, as *a structure,* is for us a unknown planet: so we can neither hold on to it in our memory nor reconstruct it through imagination'. This is so because it is still *emerging*—that is what makes it so difficult for us to speak of its nature.

Category Mistakes and Temptations of the Intellect

One of the great temptations of the modern intellect is to concern itself only with facts. David Hume's stricture of 1748 is well known:

> If we take into our hand any volume; of divinity or school metaphysics, for instance; let us ask, Does it contain any abstract reasoning concerning quantity or number? No. Does it contain any experimental reasoning concerning matter of fact and existence? No. Consign it then to the flames: For it can contain nothing but sophistry and illusion. (1910: section XII)

However, if we are to concern ourselves with describing emergent phenomena, not as observers of them from the outside, but from within them while participating in their emergence, then we must concern ourselves with '... meanings and values as they are actively lived and felt....' (Williams 1977). We must concern ourselves with things that cannot be counted, that cannot be represented in the discrete symbols of a logical theory that cannot be manipulated experimentally. We must capture in some way the character of social experiences still in process,[4] experiences that are, says Williams

> ... often indeed not yet recognized as social but taken to be private, idiosyncratic, and even isolating, but which in analysis (though rarely otherwise) has its emergent, connecting, and dominant characteristics.... For structures of feeling can be defined as social experiences *in solution,* as distinct from other social semantic formations which have been *precipitated* and are more evidently and more immediately available. (ibid.: 134, emphasis original)

Yet we fail to do this. As Williams notes:

> In most description and analysis, culture and society are expressed in an habitual past tense. The strongest barrier to the recognition of human cultural activity is this immediate and regular conversion of experience into finished products, ... relationships, institutions and formations in which we are still actively involved are converted, by this procedural mode, into formed wholes rather than forming and formative processes. (ibid.: 128)

This is 'to lose the phenomena' (Garfinkel 2002: 264–67). It is to treat, say, the struggles of judgement involved in a speaker trying to sense what is 'called for' at a particular moment in an unfolding dialogue, the judgements involved in word choice, in emphasis, intonation, and so on, as something that can be represented retrospectively as being achieved by simply following a set of rules or social conventions. It is the *way*[5] in which persons must compose or arrange themselves to anticipate playing *their* part in such an activity—be it as a speaker or as a listener—that is lost, that is not represented in any factual record of the dialogue.

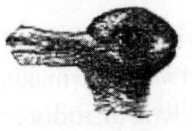 Our experiences with visually ambiguous figures can, perhaps, be informative here. For instance, with the well known faces/vase or duck/ rabbit figures, if we first look with the overall schema of a face to guide us in our expectations, we first could look *from* what might possibly be a forehead *to* an expected eye region, and then *to* an expected nose region, and so on, looking eventually *from* all these details (if each of these expectations is to

an extent fulfilled) *to* the overall perception of a face—in short, a face-way-of-looking can thus be satisfied by the figure. Similarly, with a vase-way-of-looking, we can look *from* a bowl region *to* a stem region *to* a base region, and find that *that* can be satisfied by the figure too. If we were just to say that first we see faces and then we see a vase, that is, describe our experience of the ambiguous figure in terms only of our achievements, we would lose the fact that in so doing, we switched from first *trying* to see faces, and what that trying consisted in.

Indeed, crucially in what is lost is the fact that intrinsic to all living activities, is their spontaneous responsiveness to events occurring in their surroundings. There are many implications of this fact, but here, with respect to our speech, I want to mention just one. As the Russian language and literary theorist Bakhtin (1986: 69, emphasis added) pointed out:

> All real and integral understanding is actively responsive.... And the speaker himself is oriented precisely toward such an actively responsive understanding. He does not *expect* passive understanding that, so to speak, only duplicates his or her own idea in someone else's mind.... Rather, the speaker talks *with an expectation* of a response, agreement, sympathy, objection, execution, and so forth....

It is the way in which speakers' utterances can, in the course of their utterance, arouse anticipations and expectations in their listeners as to their 'point' that is lost in a purely factual account of what they *said*. For a listener's actively responsive understanding is occurring in the speaker's *saying* of his or her utterance, with different words arousing different anticipations.

To think that we can get back to what occurs during the *saying* of an utterance from an examination of what was in fact *said*, is to make, as Gilbert Ryle (1949) terms it, a 'category mistake'. Ryle introduces the idea of a category mistake by imagining a foreigner asking to be shown 'the University of Oxford'. He is shown the various colleges, libraries, scientific departments, and so on, until there is no more to show. The foreigner then says: 'Thank you very much for showing me all these things, but can you now show me the university?' In other words, the foreigner has failed to recognise that notion of a university—as an *organised* collection of observable but disparate entities—is of a different logical type or category from the separate entities in which it consists. The most notable sphere is which we continually make such mistakes is in our attempts to *describe* human activities. For we continually use, Ryle points out, 'achievement-verbs' when we should have provided an 'orchestrated' sequence of 'task-verbs', along with their criteria of satisfaction—we talk of 'getting it' when we really should speak only of 'tryings'.

For instance, as I indicated above, it is the *way* which persons look or listen that in large part determines what they will hear or see. Hearing something, or seeing something, is an outcome, an achievement, of how they approach the tasks of listening or looking, what anticipations they have brought, as a result of their preparations, to the situation in which what they can hear or see is important. The anticipations and expectations a golf or a tennis coach might bring to a player they assess will be quite similar to those a choreographer would bring to a ballet dancer upon which they must pass judgement. *Achievement*-verbs, 'verbs like "spell", "catch", "solve", "find", "win", "cure", "score", "deceive", "persuade", "arrive", and countless others, signify not merely that some performance has been gone through, but also that something has been brought off by the agent going through it. They are verbs of success' (Ryle 1949: 125). People have performed something successfully, efficiently or correctly. But, Ryle asks: Is this enough? No, it is not. The people achieving these performances must also be *responsible* for these performances.

> A person's performance is described as careful or skilful, if in his operations he is ready to detect and correct lapses, to repeat and improve upon successes, to profit from the examples of others and so forth. He applies criteria in performing critically, that is, in trying to get things right. (ibid.: 29)

Description only in terms of *achievements* precludes the possibility for error and the need for *judgement* in the execution of our tasks.

In summary, category mistakes or mistakes in logical type occur when, in the service of *achieving general explanations*, we try to describe people's activities in terms of their general outcomes rather than in terms of their unfolding, particular, sequential details in a particular circumstance. As a consequence, instead of attending to something out in the world that can be *seen*, that can be *pointed out*, we talk of mysterious and imaginary entities, located somewhere in a Platonic world of ideas, whose only function is to play a part in our abstract theorising—we must return to talking always *from within* a context or situation. If we can, then say, as Wittgenstein (1953: §435) puts it, 'nothing is hidden'. Everything that we need to witness, if we are to understand the working of our communicative activities 'lies open to view' (ibid.).[6] In other words, as Schumacher (1977) notes, while the instructional sciences are concerned with how certain things can be manipulated to produce certain kinds of result, that is, they are based on evidence produced in experimental conditions, the descriptive disciplines primarily concerned with what can in fact be seen or otherwise experienced in everyday life settings.

The Role of 'Descriptive Concepts' in the Descriptive Disciplines: Their Non-Representational Nature

As we have seen, time and again, however, we find words, that is, concepts, of the wrong logical type being used to describe a human activity. Concepts designating what a collection of observable fragments of activity *would* amount to, *if* they were appropriately organised, are used in an *attempt* (a trying) to tell people of a new activity they *should* perform. In other words, the use of concepts, of words, of the wrong logical type, *mis*leads us into approaching a circumstance with the wrong *action guiding anticipations* at the ready (Shotter 2005), that is, ready to seek a mysterious essence, rather than to pay attention to the details observable in a person's voicing of his or her utterances. This is especially the case, as we saw above, when what are in fact tasks are described as achievements.

We can find mistakes of this kind arising continually in organisations, and in everyday life. For instance, the new 'leadership model' of a large, global company includes as a characteristic of *good leaders*, 'energising people'. But what does *energising people* look like in concrete detail in its execution? It may, for instance, mean *listening* to first line workers who have never before been listened to, it may mean giving and receiving honest feedback in ways never done before, and so on. Aware of this, a good section leader might suggest: 'The most powerful thing we can do is to share the model with our teams, talk through what it means, piece by piece, and then simply start to try to do it. Our teams will be the first to tell us when we're *not* doing it.' As this section leader realises, just to issue the exhortation—Energise People!—is not to issue an account of what *tasks* might make up the relevant *achievement*. Those on the receiving end of such an exhortation would remain mystified as to what they must actually *do* to achieve its aim.

Similarly, in everyday life, to understand what is involved in *insulting* someone, or in *respecting* them, we must describe the detailed dynamics of the unfolding inter-activities which constitute an insult or respect as their outcome or achievement. For example, a therapist *insults* a client by saying—after a client has spent time telling of an incident that mattered to them 'That's interesting', and then passing on to another topic without further reference to it. But a doctor *respects* a patient who says: 'The pain I feel is worst, strangely, when I'm trying to put my socks on', by responding: 'Oh, that's interesting. How are you sitting when you put your socks on, on the side of the bed, or on a chair? Show me what you do', but *insults* the patient by completely ignoring the comment and just passing on to the next question in her diagnostic check-list.

A common orientation toward concepts is to think of them as general representations of some kind. We think of good leaders as having good ideas, as having charisma, as inspiring those whom they must lead, and so on. We think of respecting someone, essentially, as something to do with holding them in high regard. We all, each of us, too easily think in terms of a 'picture', only to find that others have a somewhat different picture, and we then begin to argue as to whose picture is the 'right picture'. Thinking in terms of pictures, of representations—it can be argued—is connected with the idea that thinking is best thought of, that is, conceptualised, as a matter of calculation, as information processing, as the manipulation of symbols.

Although some of our thinking clearly does take the form of calculation, I want to suggest that much of it does not. It has much more the form of an inner dialogue or conversation unfolding among a number of different voices, influenced at each point as it unfolds by the anticipations as to a next step aroused by the words voiced by each participant. And we can thus imagine, instead of arguing as whose 'picture' is the best, a group of different people exploring in dialogue amongst themselves, their experiences of good leaders. As the dialogue develops and each participant adds yet another characterisation from their experience, they gradually arrive at a point when no one can think of any further relevant features to add. At that moment, if they can all remember each other's contributions, we can imagine each member leaving the group feeling that they have arrived at, that is, come to embody, a good grasp among them as to what constitutes a good leader. In other words, they have brought off a certain achievement.

Someone now says: 'Yes, but what's the *essence* of a good leader? Surely, we can express it in something like a dictionary definition. If we cannot, can we really claim to know what a good leader *is*?' The trouble is, as we have already seen, such a holistic sense cannot be captured in a single, simple definition. If we try, we are back into arguing as to who has the correct picture.

Why is this? Because like all living, dynamic, phenomena, such achievements have an *emergent* nature that cannot be captured in a single static representation; they simply cannot be pictured.

This, however, does not prevent us from applying such concepts to our experiences. We have already done this with the concept of emergence. What we seem to do in thinking conceptually in relation to such still incomplete phenomena, is not to compare the configuration of a state of affairs in reality with the configuration of a supposed mental representation, but something else much more complicated. We seem able to assemble and to organise in a socially intelligible way, that is, a way which makes sense to the others around us, bits and pieces of information dispersed in space and time in accordance with 'directions' provided by the words that they (and others) have used (or could use) in constituting the 'concept' in the first place. Many concepts, in fact, have this incomplete, still open character to them. Language, communication, organisation, political freedom, beauty, education, philosophy, mental illness, and time, to mention just a few, have this kind of *prospective* aspect to them, in that we feel we know exactly what they each designate, but we cannot exactly say it out loud. As St Augustine famously said about time: '*What, then, is time? If no one asks of me, I know; if I wish to explain to him who asks, I know not.*' Yet, with all these, and many other such concepts, we each have come to embody a conceptual schema which, in practical terms, seems to provide us with 'grammar' (or sense of sequencing) and a set of criteria for ordering events, against which the ordering of a set of events in an account of a circumstance—be it a claim of good leadership, political freedom, or whatever may be matched and tested.

I have called these incomplete or prospective concepts designating emergent phenomena 'descriptive concepts', as I want to draw attention frankly to their descriptive nature—they cannot be 'summed up' as having an essence, they need to be picked out from an otherwise amorphous background in terms of a whole set of distinguishing features.

As Wittgenstein (1953) remarks:

When philosophers use a word—'knowledge', 'being', 'object', 'I', 'proposition', 'name'—and try to grasp the essence of the thing, one must always ask oneself: is the word ever actually used in this way in the language-game which is its original home?—What we do is to bring words back from their metaphysical to their everyday use', to their countless different everyday uses in the countless different situations of their use ... it's the details that matter, give me the details.... (§ 116)

WHERE THE ACTION IS

Difficulties with 'Emergent' Phenomena

Central to our living out our lives from within the midst of complexity, is the task of acting for the best in *this* or *that* unique, concrete situation. While the instructional sciences deal with situations in general, and seek theories representative of the 'logic' of the repetitive patterns that can be perceived as occurring within them, the fact is, as Harold Garfinkel (1967: 9) so nicely termed it, in our everyday lives, everything always happens 'for "another first time"'. Indeed, as we begin below to bring into focus the nature of living activity, as distinct from the repetitive, mechanical activities of non-living, dead things, we will come to focus more and more on what is novel, on what is unique, on what some scientists call *singularities*. So, whilst it is true that a repetitive aspect can more often than not be recognised in our living expressions—for after all, the words on this page are, I hope, all words with common currency in the English language—the fact is, I hope, that they have—never appeared on any page before in quite this order, informed by quite the same intentions, that is, with quite the same retentions from the past and protentions toward the future, that are informing my use of them now.

In other words, as Bakhtin (1986) points out, as soon as we utter something in a responsive relation to the others and othernesses (things) around us, that 'utterance is never just a reflection or an expression of something already existing and outside it.... It always creates something that never existed before, something absolutely new and unrepeatable.... What is given is completely transformed in what is created' (ibid.: 119–20). Thus, as soon as someone replies to your claim—that the situation you are both in has *this* rather than *that* character to it—by saying: 'Well yes, but if you look at it *my* way, then...,' then the situation that you experience yourself as being 'in' can suddenly change! Sometimes, you can see it *their* way!

The occurrence of such a unique event as this—an event which is in fact quite a common *kind* of event in our daily affairs—brings us up against the need to understand what might actually be going on inside such actual moments as these, inside these unique 'first-time' events, events that Bakhtin (1993: 2) calls 'once-occurrent events of being'. Thus what we must deal with here, to put it somewhat paradoxically, is that in our everyday dealings with each other, only once occurring, first time events are the rule rather than the exception.[7] Or, to put it in the terms already introduced above, we must deal with *emergent* phenomena.

The notion of emergent phenomena was first outlined by G.H. Lewes (1875), in his *Problems of Life and Mind*. He distinguished among *resultants* (that we get, say, in a parallelogram of forces), and *emergents*:

> Although each effect is the resultant of its components, the products of its factors, we cannot always trace the steps of the process, so as to see in the product the mode of operation of each factor. In the latter case, I propose to call the effect an emergent. It arises out of the combined agencies, but in a form which does not display the agents in action. (ibid.: 412)

In other words, emergent phenomena are produced in interactions between two or more agencies in such a way that we cannot discover, from an examination of their outcomes, the part or parts played by each separate agency in their production.

Emergent phenomena can always occur, as we shall see, whenever two of more dynamic activities 'rub together', so to speak, to create a third. Holland (1998), for instance, details many different kinds of emergent phenomena occurring even in inorganic processes—in phase changes in ice crystal formation, for instance, and in solid state physics, and particularly in computer models—never mind in more organic processes. Prigogine (1996) has studied the emergence of order out of chaos (formlessness) in physical processes in far from equilibrium conditions, and has emphasised especially the importance of the irreversible flow of time in the continuous creation of novelty. This work is, I think, quite brilliant, and has changed our whole attitude to determinism even in the physical world. But as I see it, these achievements are still aimed at satisfying the goals implicit in the instructional sciences: Holland and Prigogine, it seems to me, still want to see their theories of complex systems as *representing*, that is, 'picturing', objective realities as something 'over there', as something that can be used to predict and plan the future. They talk 'about' complexity 'from the outside'.

My concerns here are of a very different kind: I want to talk in relation to complexity 'from the inside'. Thus I will not at all be concerned with explanations (especially ones of a generalised kind). I want to work 'from within the midst' of an already existing circumstance, towards 'evolving', 'unfolding' or 'articulating' the particular *potentialities for development* implicit in that circumstance in relation to the 'ends in view' of all those involved in it. My concerns will thus be of a quite local and particular kind. As I indicated above, for us to do this, to gain a 'feel for' what is involved in 'seeing' what to do from within the midst of complexity, we must be especially attentive to the practicalities involved in the forms of talk we use. For what seems to be crucial, is that use forms of talk that work to *orient* all concerned in our meetings, both to notice, and to be ready to respond to, certain kinds of subtle events that usually pass us by unnoticed, events that are (possibly) conducive to the development of new ways in which people might *relate* or *orient* themselves both to each other and to other features in their surroundings. But to do this, we must somehow gain a *sense* of a 'something' that, at the moment of acting, is still *invisible* to us, still in an *unrealised* state. Our task is thus to approach each new circumstance with an appropriate *readiness*, an appropriate *openness*, ready to allow that 'something' to 'call out' from us appropriate *embodied anticipations* as to how we next might act in relation to 'it'. Thus central to our functioning in this sphere of activity is our ability to *sense*, so to speak, the 'shape' of a circumstance, in everyday parlance to 'intuit' its character—what is involved in our doing this, to feel our way forward, will occupy much of our attention below.

As a first step in preparing ourselves for this shift of orientation, it might be useful to note that all the marvellous theoretical work done in chaos and complexity theory, is work done by human beings in the course of meetings between them and the others (and othernesses) in their surroundings. For even when working all alone, we must continually test out our theoretical formulations as to their public intelligibility (they must make sense to others). If we are to be truly reflexively self-aware of the parts we ourselves can and do play in our own cultural developments, then we must take account of this fact. The natural sciences are culturally and historically conditioned, and like the rest of us, natural scientists also must determine what constitutes the relevant facts, methods and theories in relation to what counts for them as 'nature'. These determinations are made on the basis of tacit practical skills and conventions acquired during training in the actual performance of scientific activities. Thus, instead of simply taking the theoretical *systems* such groups offer us—the achievements or outcomes they arrive at as a result of *their* meetings—if we are really to understand the nature of the 'first-time' events that can occur in the course of such meetings as they unfold, then, we must look into the work of such scientists in the same *descriptive* way that we need to examine the emergence of innovative changes in the rest of our daily affairs (Shotter 2007). Indeed, *their* theories might not be as essential to us as we have thought in the past.

Our descriptive investigations into people's uses of language, then, must work as Wittgenstein (1953) suggests, to give '... prominence to distinctions which our ordinary forms of language easily make us overlook' (ibid.: § 132)—where we must understand the word 'distinctions' here in a very practical sense, in terms of focussing on the particular difference made by the particular use of a particular word in a particular situation. This focus on detailed particularities, instead of generalities, is crucial. It is only too easy to think that when we use such words as 'leadership', 'organisation', 'strategy', 'planning', 'expertise', 'synergy', 'communication', 'story', 'knowledge', 'learning', and so on, that we all know what such words mean and that there is thus no need, when such words are used, to explore the *way* which they are being used any further. It is precisely the task of a descriptive discipline to bring out into the light of day these ways of using words, and what such ways of use can achieve.

To this end, although I will not be making any use of *explanatory theories*, I will be making use of what I will call 'descriptive concepts'—my use of the notion of emergence is already a case in point. Theories are of use in representing or picturing states of affairs, and we, as individuals, use them to *explain* events *after* they have happened, to determine their antecedent causes and to make predictions (on the assumption that the future will be like the past). Our use of descriptive concepts is quite different. Their use is pre-theoretical. If we wanted to be really technical about it, we could say that their use is ontological rather then epistemological, that it is to do with recognising that, currently, we are being confronted by a special kind of entity, an entity with a different way or mode of *being* in the world from any of the other previously known to us. Hence we must, perhaps, approach it in a way different from our usual ways, with different expectations. I have already used the concept of emergence to draw our attention to important differences in the phenomena around us—thus to orient us differently towards those phenomena that cannot be traced back to the contributions of the individual agents responsible for them, compared with those that can. What I want to do now, is to try to prepare us to 'see', that is, to pay special attention to, a certain special sphere of emergent phenomena, those that occur when two or more of us meet together and begin to participate in what we call a dialogue.

The Emergent and Creative Nature of Joint or Dialogically-structured Activity

As we have already noted above, Bakhtin (1986) has drawn our attention to the fact that our utterances, if they are uttered in a truly dialogically-structured situation, 'always create[s] something that

never existed before, something absolutely new and unrepeatable'
(Bakhtin 1986: 119–20). In fact, it is intrinsic to the very nature of
our living, bodily responsiveness to our surroundings, that something
genuinely new, *related to the context of interaction*, is always created
within our living, inter-activities. First-time events are the rule, not
the exception. But to understand how this is so, and what the nature
of the novelty that is created *is*, what it 'feels like' and 'looks like', let
me approach this issue in a slow, step-by-step manner.

First, let me note that traditional Western thought has it that
there are only two major spheres of activity: mechanical activity
that can be explained in terms of cause-and-effect theories and the
actions of individual agents acting in terms of reasons arising out of
their best rational judgements, or out of their rational 'calculations'.
In both these spheres of activity, we seem able to focus our thought
on clearly describable, that is, 'picturable' phenomena.

However, the nature of our living, spontaneously responsive
relations to each other, and the othernesses in our surroundings,
gives us the possibility of a third sphere of *emergent* activities—
elsewhere, I have introduced the descriptive concepts of 'joint
action' or 'dialogically-structured behaviour' (Shotter 1993a, 1993b)
to draw attention to the unique nature of activities in this third
sphere. Their emergent nature, as we have seen, means that they
have their being more in time than in space. Thus, in our imagining
of them, and how they might exert their influence in our behaviours,
we must think more in terms of 'shapes' unfolding in time, as a
speech or a musical 'shape' unfolds, and of their 'movements' as
mingling in with the 'movements' already under way within us as
they enter also to 'touch' or to 'move' us.

As I see it, activity in this special sphere, has three major features:
(1) As people coordinate their activity in with the activities of others,
and 'respond' to them in what they do, what they as individuals
desire and what actually results in their exchanges, are often two
very different things. In short, such joint action produces *unintended*
and unpredictable outcomes. They do, however, create a 'situation',
an 'organised practical–moral setting', which all the participants

experience themselves as 'being in'. But because its organisation cannot be traced back to the intentions of any particular individuals, it is *as if* it has a 'given', a 'natural', or an 'externally caused' nature; although to those within it, it is 'their/our' situation. (2) Although such a setting is unintended by any of the individuals within it, it nonetheless has an *intentional* quality to it: that is, it seems both to have a 'content', as well as to 'indicate' or to be 'related to something other than or beyond itself,'[8] that is, in finding themselves immersed 'in' an already *given* situation, participants find that it has a *horizon* to it, a horizon which provides them all with 'an end in view', and which makes it 'open' to their actions in relation to that end. Indeed, its 'organisation' is such that the practical–moral constraints (and enablements) it provides, 'invite' and 'motivate' their next possible actions. Indeed, (3) the very nature of all living activities is such, as we have seen, that we can come to *anticipate* how the others around us next might act. We thus experience their expressions as 'having a point'. However, while what people actually say may be recordable, their 'point' is, so to speak, invisible; it can only be grasped by those involved in the exchange. For example:

> CEO: We need to remember that next time we must talk to all concerned if we are to avoid getting ourselves into this mess again.
>
> Project Manager: Yes, but we also need to remind ourselves of the time pressures we have to work under.

Yet, once the exchange is over, the CEO can 'carry away' the Project Manager's point, and the Project Manager can 'carry away' the CEO's point. Clearly, then, joint action gives rise to *emergent* outcomes, due both to how what we are tempted to call 'past' and 'future' influences can intermingle, that is, can become 'entangled'[9] within each other.

The Need for Spontaneously Responsive Talk

Bush and his cohorts have been masterful splitters, employing a language that gives no room for exchange and necessarily distorts reality, which, unfortunately, is usually murky. This kind of speech does not recognise an interlocutor, a real human other. It is speech without empathy, and it is startlingly similar to the rhetoric of the Muslim radicals who spew venom on the West and 'the enemies of Islam'. (Hustvedt 2008)

With a monologic approach (in its extreme pure form) *another person* remains wholly and merely an *object* of consciousness, and not another consciousness. No response is expected from it that could change anything in the world of my consciousness. Monologue is finalized and deaf to the other's response, does not expect it and does not acknowledge in it any *decisive* force. (Bakhtin 1984: 292–93)

In such a spontaneously responsive sphere of living activity as this, then, instead of one person first acting individually and independently of another, and then the second replying by also acting individually and independently of the first, we always to an extent, act jointly, as a *collective–we*. And we do this bodily, in a 'living' way, spontaneously, without our having first 'to work out' how to respond to each other. For while listeners are responsively *feeling* the reactions aroused in them by a speaker's words, speakers also are spontaneously responsive to the facial expressions, to the nods and murmurs of agreement and the grimaces and frowns of disagreement, expressive of their listener's feelings as they speak. In a genuine dialogue—in which all involved hold themselves open to the utterance of those around them, and are *not* intent to speak only their own, pre-planned words—everyone's expressions are, to an extent, entangled or intertwined with each other. This, however, means that when someone acts, their activity cannot be accounted for as wholly their own activity—for one person's actions are partly 'shaped' by the actions of the others around him or her. So, although we tend to think that we are all, individually, the sole authors of our actions, this is not the case. For, even before I begin to choose my first words, I have a sense of the situation I must speak (or write) into, that I must respond to, and as I begin to utter (or write) my first words, I also begin to sense in anticipation how my listeners (or readers) will respond to them.

Consequently, my living speech—if it is not merely the routine mouthing of a set of pre-prepared words, but is voiced in a way that is spontaneously responsive to its surroundings—will in some sense be 'coloured' by features of the surroundings (immediate, historical and cultural) within which my words occur. So, although I can be (almost) wholly responsible for mechanically mouthing a speech or a PowerPoint presentation, say, written the night before in a way unresponsive to the context into within it is now being spoken, I cannot be wholly responsible for my spontaneously responsive speech in the same way. To the extent that I must always *try* to act in a way intended by me to be intelligible to you, the events that occur between us are always truly and uniquely 'ours'. For both your actual, and my expected, responsiveness to my speech will influence the 'shape' of my utterances as I express them.

In other words, human activity that matters to us is always emergent, it consists in 'passing', ephemeral, unrepeatable, dynamical events, events that occur only within our transitory meetings with the others and othernesses around us. It is this that makes it, at least in its everyday environment outside the controls exerted upon in experimental laboratories so intrinsically difficult to grasp.

But what else makes it difficult for us to attend to the character of these emergent events is, as I have already mentioned above, that they only occur *in our meetings* with the others and othernesses around us. While they have a very real existence, they exist only as passing or transitory events within the unfold dynamics of our interactions. Once our interactions cease, they disappear.

To return to the two spheres of activity mentioned above, they occur in a thick but fuzzy zone or region between *actions* (what I as an individual 'do'), and *events* (what merely 'happens' to, in or around me, outside of my agency as an individual to control). As such, they are multi-dimensional. We can characterise aspects of them in terms of our intentions, our deliberations, thoughts, ideas, plans, and so on; we can also talk of them in cultural and historical terms; we can describe them as well in biological, physiological, and genetic terms; or even physical and mechanical terms. We can see them as both to an extent orderly but also as disorderly, as to an extent objective as well as subjective, as having their existence within people as well as among them, as retaining features from the past, and so on. Although they have the character of a living whole, like all other living wholes (while still alive), they must remain for ever *unfinalised*, that is, incomplete, [10] and thus able always to arouse in others expectations of a next action. Indeed, to the extent that we can find in them *all* the dimensions of analysis that we have at one time or another applied to human phenomena in our attempts to explain them, they do not, as such, seem amenable to any clear characterisation at all.

This, however, is not entirely the case: It is their very lack of specificity, their lack of any pre-determined order, and thus their openness to being specified or determined by those involved in them, that is their central defining feature. [11] Indeed, it is not going too far to call this zone of joint or dialogically-structured activity, the *primal scene*[12] (with apologies to Freud) of human being.

The Happening of Change:
The Importance of 'Striking Events'

The 'otherness' which enters into us makes us other.
(Steiner 1989: 188)

Genuine innovative changes in institutions and organisations are 'deep' changes, in the sense that they are changes in our 'ways' of thinking, 'ways' of seeing, of hearing, 'ways' of 'making connections' among events, 'ways' of talking, and so on—in short, they are changes in our 'ways' of being someone, changes in the kinds of persons we are, changes in our *identity*, ontological changes, not epistemological ones. They are changes in what 'we think with', changes in how we relate to, or orient ourselves toward the situation we find ourselves to be 'in'.

Hence, these kind of changes cannot be produced by following intellectually devised plans, procedures or protocols; they cannot be done intentionally by people taking deliberate actions—this is because the coordinated execution of planned actions depends upon all concerned *already sharing* the set of existing *concepts* relevant to the formulation of the plan, thus all new plans depend on old concepts—the process results in the 'continuous rediscovery of sameness'. Nor can these kind of changes be produced by exhortation, by being *persuaded* to change—the simple fact is: people do not know how to 'guide' themselves toward the desired end; they have not yet embodied the norm against which they can 'measure' their own achievements 'so far' (are they 'on the way' towards success or not?). Yet change can, under certain conditions, happen.

It can happen, because crucial to all our routine, taken-for-granted, skilful actions, lookings, listenings, and so on, is an usually unnoticed *anticipation* of what should occur next. Such anticipations are the 'glue' holding all our 'habitual' actions together. Crucial to 'deep' change happening, that is, changes in how our more basic skills are 'glued' together in constituting more complex skills, is the occurrence of events that 'touch', 'move', or 'strike' us in such a way that we respond, spontaneously, in a bodily manner, in a new way. Suddenly, something unexpected, unanticipated, 'shows us' a new, previously unnoticed possibility. Such events give us a new feeling, a feeling that has a 'shaped' temporal contour to it, it arouses a 'something' that, at first, is unnameable, a bewildering sense of something happening that matters, even if at first 'we know not what' that something *is*. Crucial historical events have this character.

Consider the following vignette: A Safety Officer in a hospital does her duties diligently. She sends out reams of documents, memos, notice board pinups, and so on; she runs classes where she makes many PowerPoint presentations; she visits all the departments of the hospital and reports on her observations. She tells people continually what they must do for the safe running of the hospital. Yet, there are many lapses, infections that should not have occurred, injuries, and great deal of staff dissatisfaction with her expressed in mumblings behind her back. A TV journalist mounts an investigation into the hospital. She agrees to be interviewed. The journalist confronts her:

Journalist: 'You seem unaware of the failings at your hospital, what are you going to do about them? Do you care?'

Safety Officer (with tears in her eyes): 'Of course I care. I love those I work with. They are such good people. They care for the patients so well. I do everything I can think of to keep them and their patients safe. Of course I care.'

Staff member watching the TV programme (moved by the Safety Officer's expression of emotion): 'Why couldn't she tell *us* that!'

The staff member approaches her the next day: 'I saw you on TV last night. I was touched by how much you care about us here. Can we talk?' The Safety Officer starts the first of a series of more personal conversations with staff members (while still continuing her more 'official' communications). The safety record of the hospital slowly begins to improve. What is communicated in the Safety Officer's more personal communications that cannot be communicated in her more official documents?

At each unfolding step of our everyday, routine, taken-for-granted actions, our lookings and listenings, and so on, it is our *anticipation* of what might occur next, and where as a result we might go next, that is crucial. This is what makes our actions routinely skilful. As we 'gaze' at a 'something' in Foucault's (1973) sense of the term, we look from one expected feature of it to another, to see if 'it' conforms to what we *want* to see (for example, the doctor wants to see 'a disease' in the sequences of features 'surveyed'). Accidents can occur when we think we already know, that is, can anticipate, *everything* of relevance in the situations in which we work. The Safety Officer's communications are aimed at staff members' ideas, thoughts, their knowledge, and so on, not at their *way of being* in the hospital. As such, staff members can easily say to themselves: 'That's just her opinion. I know better.' They are unchanged in their perceptions. However, in her more personal encounters with staff members, the Safety Officer can—if she talks in an appropriate manner, through the use of vignettes, images, metaphors, tone of voice and emphasis, and so on,—'move' staff members in their very being. Striking, touching, moving, arresting events can *compel* our attention, can *direct* our attention towards aspects of our surroundings that we have not before noticed. In other words, in her more responsive, face-to-face talk, she can affect staff members, not in their thinking, but in their perceiving, how they 'look at' things and events in their surroundings.

If we are to understand, then, the happening of change, striking events, singular events, only once occurrent events of being are therefore crucial to us. An otherness that *can* enter us and make us other than we already are, is needed if we are to undergo any 'deep' changes within ourselves. I will call such striking events, events that *matter* to us, to distinguish them from events that we observe, but which leave us quite unchanged in our ways of being in the world. Wittgenstein (1980a: 31) describes their importance thus: 'The origin and primitive form of the language game is a reaction; only from this can more complicated forms develop. Language—I want to say—is a refinement, "in the beginning was the deed" [Goethe]'. And he adds elsewhere: 'But what is the word "primitive" meant to say here? Presumably that this sort of behavior is *pre-linguistic*: that a language-game is based *on it*, that it is the prototype of a way of thinking and not the result of thought' (Wittgenstein 1981: § 541).

Indeed, for a group of people, such mattering events can function as 'moments of common reference,' even if the people comprising the group are not all in face-to-face contact with each other, or experience the 'touching' events at different times. (As children, we were 'touched' in this way by our parents, in the games they played with us, in the stories they told us.) They can function as *exemplars* for new *ways* of acting—the beginnings of a new way of looking, thinking, acting, and so on. But, as a beginning, they are only a beginning: they still need further collaborative development. Those in the group must, among them all, develop such beginnings into new *ways* of acting, looking, listening, talking, evaluating, and so on, that *all* can come to embody. All this, of course, takes time and energy.

But how can we *prepare* ourselves to be open to such mattering events, and *keep* ourselves open? For such events *can be* the beginning of a whole new way of our relating ourselves to our surroundings, but they need not be. They certainly will not be if we are concerned only to see already well-known things repeated in them, if we give in to our temptation the try to codify them. Only if we can keep ourselves prepared 'to see what we have never seen before' (or better: to *feel* what we have never before *felt* within it) in the present moment of our lives, can we sustain the kind of 'living on the edge' required to occasion the continual happening of change. How can we do that?

A Third Realm of Human Activity: Embodied Spontaneously Expressed Expectations

What I have been trying to draw attention to above, then—with talk of emergent phenomena and the descriptive concepts needed to illuminate their nature—is the need to characterise the influences at work in a third realm of human activity, distinct on the one hand from the more objective and mechanical accounts of the external *causes* supposedly shaping our activities in the world, and the more subjective, cognitive accounts of people's *reasons* for their actions. Clearly, we possess a spontaneously operative, embodied, perceptual mode of understanding, an understanding of the specific field of possibilities in which we are, in each changing moment, embedded. For without it, we would lack all orientation. In other words, it is a kind of understanding to do, not with facts or information, but with our grasp of *what kind of context* we are in, with what our surroundings *require* of us, with the 'calls' they exert upon us to respond within them in *appropriate* ways—a kind of knowing[13] that shows up in our *readiness to respond* in a particular way, spontaneously, to a unique and particular circumstance. It is a readiness that shows up in how we *next act* in a situation 'to put an end to the ambiguity of its merely anticipated, suspected, character' (Todes 2001: 64).[14]

Prominent at the moment in explicitly noting the role of our *embodied* anticipations in shaping our spontaneously expressed actions in our social lives, is Pierre Bourdieu (2000), with his concept of *habitus*. He defines our 'practical comprehension' of our world as distinct from our 'intellectual comprehension' of it, by noting that:

> 'I' as an intellectual 'subject' concerned to execute a rational intention, concerned to take action on the basis of calculated profits and losses, can never be completely the subject of my own practices. As a social agent, I am endowed with *habitus*, it is inscribed in my body as a result of regularities encountered in my past experiences. Having acquired from this exposure a system of dispositions attuned to these regularities, it [my body] is inclined and able to anticipate them practically in behaviours which engage a *corporeal knowledge* that provides a practical comprehension of the world quite different from the intentional act of conscious decoding that is normally designated by the idea of comprehension. (ibid.: 135)

In other words, in the terms I have been using above, not only is this practical comprehension of quite a different kind from that we exert in our more intellectual accounts of the situations we face, the influence it exerts in orienting us towards the features we pick out to describe in those accounts, goes completely unnoticed.

DIFFICULTIES OF THE WILL AND DIFFICULTIES OF THE INTELLECT: OUR ORIENTATIONAL AND RELATIONAL NEEDS

Sensitive especially to issues of this kind, Wittgenstein (1980a: 17) notes that there are *two* very different kinds of difficulties we can face in our lives: difficulties of the *intellect*, and difficulties of the *will*. We can formulate difficulties of the intellect as *problems* which, with the aid of clever theories, we can solve by the use of reasoning. Difficulties of the will, however, are of a quite different kind. For they are to do with how we *orient* ourselves bodily towards events occurring around us, how we *relate* ourselves to them, the *ways* in which we see them, hear them, experience them, value them—for these are the *ways* that determine, that 'give shape to', the lines of action we further *resolve* on carrying out. But we must do all this while we are already in action, in motion, in spontaneous responsive contact with our surroundings. As soon as we stop moving in relation to one or another practical purpose in our surroundings, our relations to our surroundings cease to be structured by the aims and goals implicit in our movements, and become structured by a way of thinking—thus to substitute a very different system of organisational valences.

Wittgenstein (1980a) introduced these two kinds of difficulty thus:

> What makes a subject hard to understand ... is not that before you can understand it you need to be trained in abstruse matters, but the contrast between understanding the subject and what most people *want* to see.... What has to be overcome is a difficulty having to do with the will, rather than with the intellect. (ibid.: 17)

This distinction is not easy to grasp, for differences between difficulties of orientation and difficulties of the intellect cannot be captured formally, they can only be captured in practice with respect to practical criteria. Schumacher (1977), of course, also argued in a very similar manner, for a distinction between two types of problems[15] in the world: convergent and divergent problems. Convergent problems are those that arise in relation to non-living phenomena, and which can eventually give rise to a single, best answer or solution. Whilst divergent problems are concerned with the realm of the living, and do not converge on a single solution. The only solution for divergent problems, argues Schumacher, is to transcend them—but at this point, Schumacher turns to theological and mystical approaches to the 'purpose' of human life, and thus fails to give us the practical guidance we need to overcome our perplexity.

Nonetheless, recognising which type of problem one faces is, for Schumacher, one of the arts of living. Wittgenstein (1980a: 16) states the aim of work in (his kind of practical) philosophy similarly: Our aim in undertaking it, is not to provide ourselves with any new information, but to change ourselves, to change oneself in oneself, to change 'one's way of seeing things. (And what one expects of them)'. But how can we effect such changes in ourselves?

A NEW REALM OF INQUIRY: 'UNDERSTANDING FROM WITHIN' OUR OWN HUMAN EXPRESSIVE-RESPONSIVE ACTIVITIES

Traditional social science research—conducted on the model of the 'instructional sciences'—is oriented toward social worlds as already made and as already reflected upon worlds. It does not and cannot capture the aspects of actors' surroundings that they must attend to if they are to create these worlds in the first place. As Williams (1977) describes it:

> The mistake, as so often, is in taking *terms of analysis* as *terms of substance*. Thus we speak of a world-view or of a prevailing ideology or of a class-outlook, often with adequate evidence, but in this regular slide towards a past tense and fixed form we suppose, or even do not know that we have to suppose, that these exist and are lived specifically and definitively in singular and developing forms. (ibid.: 129, emphasis added)

In other words, conventional research insists on portraying actors as choosing and reflecting on already existing *achievements* (see section on 'Category Mistakes...' above), rather than as struggling to organise and sequence the *tasks* involved in the very making/ doing of an activity, successfully, for 'another first time' (Garfinkel 1967: 9).

Garfinkel's (1967) work demonstrates the importance of this distinction. As he sees it, rather than making our social worlds in our actions according to already existing rules or conventions, we try to cope with the uniqueness of the situation we face, by acting in ways that others *will* (we hope) recognise:

The anticipation that people *will* understand, the occasionality of expressions, the specific vagueness of references, the retrospective-prospective sense of a present occurrence, waiting for something later in order to see what was meant before, are sanctioned properties of common discourse. They furnish a background of seen but unnoticed features of common discourse whereby actual utterances are recognized as events of common, reasonable, understandable, plain talk. (Garfinkel 1967: 41)

But to do this, to act in this way, we must be attentive to a whole panoply of relevant events and features, including the responsive relations of our actions to events and features in the surroundings we share to the others around us, as well as their unfolding responsiveness to our responsive expressions. That attentiveness is so demanding that in most cases practitioners cannot reflect on what they are doing while they are doing it and act successfully in a seamless fashion.

What traditional research misses, and must always miss, in taking the events depicted in its objective transcripts or records as representative of already completed activities, are not only the invisible *action guiding anticipations* (Shotter 2005) felt by each of the participants, moment by moment, as they judge how best to take the next step in developing or progressing an activity towards its desired end, but also all the other 'background' features of our embodied perceptions of our current circumstances. Thus the way in which our judgements are tailored to the momentary local circumstances in which they are made—taking all those background features into account—is rendered invisible. We 'lose the phenomena', to repeat Garfinkel's (2002) phrase mentioned above.

BRINGING IT ALL TOGETHER: THE POWER OF 'REMINDERS'... IN PRACTICE: PUTTING 'STRIKING MOMENTS' ON 'FREEZE FRAME'

These are the days of miracle and wonder.
(Paul Simon, *The Boy in the Bubble,* 1986)

Above, I raised two questions: How can we effect the relevant 'deep' changes within ourselves to do with the embodied, spontaneous expectations with which we approach each new complex situation in which we must act, thus to change our ways of 'seeing' and 'hearing', that is, what we notice as significant in our surroundings? And how can we keep ourselves continually open to 'updating' ourselves in this respect? Or, to put it in other words, how can we *prepare* ourselves afresh to approach yet another uniquely new, complex situation, for yet another first time?

The answer to these questions lies, I think, in our use of certain kinds of 'reminders'. Like many other aspects of the *descriptive* approach that I have adopted in this chapter, I have taken this term from Wittgenstein (1953).[16] As he puts it, our task here, is not 'to hunt out new facts; it is, rather, of the essence of our investigation that we ... want to understand something that is already in plain view. For this is what we seem in some senses not to understand' (ibid.: § 89). Thus, to keep what we want to understand in plain view, 'the work of the philosopher consists in,' as we shall see, 'assembling reminders for a particular purpose' (ibid.: § 127).

But how can we keep what 'all goes by so quick ... as it were laid open to view' (ibid.: § 435)? How can we get inside, so to speak, such fleeting, only-once occurrent events of being sufficiently to be able to grasp their structure? To keep what we want to understand in plain view, we too must do that by assembling for ourselves here the appropriate reminders. For our task in conducting our investigations in a descriptive discipline is not that of bringing to our attention aspects of our own inter-activities that usually pass us by unnoticed, but also to portray these aspects to ourselves in such a way as to make them distinct and unforgettable. So let me proceed further in this final section, by trying to draw together what I have overall been trying to do in what I have written above.

First, let us remind ourselves that although our task, overall, has been one of a descriptive kind, it has not been an easy one, for we have faced the task of trying to describe (or to characterise) emergent phenomena, dynamic phenomena that cannot be pictured in any static representations. Further, our aim has been to arrive at a grasp *from within* of dynamically unfolding phenomena that we can sense as occurring *only* in the course of our meetings with the others and othernesses around us. These phenomena have no existence outside their fleeting existence within the unfolding of our living relations to our surroundings. Their only once-occurrent nature thus requires us to orient ourselves toward noticing, not what is simply a repetition of something previously experienced, but what is unique and distinctive for us in the unique situation we currently face. This is what makes our occasioning of change so difficult: we must focus on certain special but rare, transitory experiences that can provide us with 'openings' in which new steps can be taken, the 'striking' moments when an otherness that matters to us can enter us and make us other than we 'are' already—only if we can be sensitive to the new opportunities offered us in these rare moments, can we avoid simply relating ourselves yet again to our surroundings in our old ways 'dressed up' in new forms.

Central to the overall account I have tried to fashion above, then (among a number of other such innovations), are two focal concepts: the concept of 'striking moments' and the concept of 'descriptive concepts'—the notion of striking moment being itself, of course, just such a descriptive concept (others include, 'descriptive disciplines', 'emergent phenomena', 'preparing activities', 'the present moment', 'happening events', '*ways* of looking, listening, and so on,' 'embodied expectations', 'tasks', 'achievements', 'spontaneous, bodily responsiveness', 'expressions', 'withness versus aboutness talk', 'difficulties of orientation', 'difficulties of the intellect', to name some of them). Their task is, of course, to try to describe what important aspects of such passing events might look like, *if* they could be laid open to view, *if* we could re-experience them whenever required.

My point in emphasising the importance of striking moments, is that they can provide us with definable moments of a special kind, moments that can be noticed and remembered, and which can function as the basis for the description of a certain kind of happening: moments when the otherness of an other can enter us and make us other. Owen Barfield (1999: 79) talks of such moments as occasioning a 'felt change of consciousness,' a moment when there is 'the passage from one plane of consciousness to another'. He then goes on to add, most importantly: 'It lives during that moment of transition and then dies, and if it is to be repeated, some means must be found of renewing the transition itself' (ibid.)—a point I will expand on in a moment when I turn to the task of describing a kind of writing that can achieve the renewal, when required, of such felt transitions, for a *poetic* use of words would seem to be crucial to this task.

Such ephemeral transitions are important for they can often designate moments of 'getting it' (Shotter, in press), moments when we (imaginatively) see a connection among features of a situation we have not seen before. The most pure example of such an experience is, of course, in mathematics, in geometry—the moment when one writes QED (quod erat demonstrandum) at the moment of, say, proving Pythagoras's theorem. No wonder that we feel that unless we can prove things in numbers, our knowledge is still of an uncertain kind. Barfield (1999), however, is not talking above of our experience in mathematics, but of our appreciation of poetry: 'It is not simply that the poet enables me to see with his [or her] eyes, and so to apprehend a larger and fuller world,' the 'moment of appreciation depends upon something rarer and more transitory. It depends on the change itself' (ibid.: 78). For it is in that moment of appreciation that we can acquire a whole new *way* of orienting ourselves both to the world at large, *and* to ourselves—both we and our world become more full, not only of actualities, but of possibilities. What seems to happen in a moment of being struck is that a collection of unrelated facts or fragments of activity, which up till that moment have made no sense, suddenly do make sense. Our bodies find for us a *way* of interlinking all the fragments into an integrated whole, a whole in which the role of each part in constituting the whole can become clear.

It is as if, at that moment, events unfolding sequentially in time all become present at once, the temporal becomes spatial, a crucial and particular present moment has, so to speak, been put on *freeze frame* in such a way that one can now survey[1] it —'see it as it were laid open to view' (Wittgenstein, 1953: § 435)—to see first *this* detail and then *that*, and then, perhaps, to move closer in or further out, to see other kinds of relations among other kinds of detail.

But in all of this, it is the one with the experience, the one who has been 'struck', who must express in an articulated form the 'seeing' of these relations, who must talk *with* the guidance of the experience to give shape to their utterances. In other words, as we saw with the *ways* of looking people found occurring within them, spontaneously, in relation to the faces/vase ambiguous figure, so we can also find here, that once we have been struck by an event, we can 'go into' our body's experience of it, to find ways of articulating its meaning to those around us arising within us, spontaneously—in other words, we can put the event of being struck to *our* use, and not have its use determined *for us* by someone else's use of it.

THE IMPORTANCE OF SCENIC MOMENT AND DESCRIPTIVE CONCEPTS

Because of this, I am not interested (unlike many others at the moment) in 'narrative approaches' to organisational studies (see Boje 2008; Czarniawska 1998). For, a narrative is an achievement, as such it comes after, and is generated by, the practice of narrating. It succeeds (if it is successful, that is) in retrospectively *organising our understanding* of a past event (presumably, with a particular end in mind). Further, a narrative works in terms of an author controlling moment by moment, in its writing, in its expression, our expectations at any moment as to what will come next, against an overall background of what we have been led to think will happen next. The drama of a narrative belongs, in other words, to the author. Whereas, being struck just happens to us, spontaneously, irrespective of what our expectations were. Thus being struck is an event that belongs to the one who is struck, and as such, is open to whatever uses *they* might find for it.

Instead of narratives, then, our interest in the descriptive disciplines is in capturing a certain present moment in all its fullness. We are thus interested in *scenes* or *scenic moments*, moments which generate in those who experience in them a sense of 'something has happened', not in full-blown narratives. Kundera (1993), in his discussion of recent developments in the art of the novel, states our concerns well: 'The novelists who came after Boccaccio were fine storytellers,' he says,

> but capturing the concreteness of the present moment was neither their issue nor their goal. They were telling a story, without necessarily imagining it in concrete scenes. The scene becomes the *basic* element of the novels' composition (the locus of the novelists virtuosity) at the beginning of the nineteenth century. The novels of Scott, of Balzac, of Dostoevsky ... are composed as a series of minutely described scenes with their setting, their dialogue, their action: anything not connected with this series of scenes, anything that is not scene, is considered and felt to be secondary, even superfluous. The novel is like a very rich film script. (ibid.: 129)

The task is to capture the concreteness of the present moment.

Thus as Kundera (1993: 131) describes it, crucial to new developments in the art of the novel is 'a *discovery* that might be termed *ontological*: the discovery of the structure of present moment', the fact that 'in a single second, between two lines of dialogue, endless number of things occur ... a single second of the present becomes a little infinity'. As I suggested above, then, our task in capturing the concreteness of the present moment, is *not* to create a pattern, not to create a *chronology*, a temporal order or sequence, but moments of *kairos*, of times in relation to circumstances, as a series of *juxtaposed 'presents'*, of fragmentary events that in their occurrence motivate a sequence of tensions that those who experience them must *resolve* into meaningful wholes.

Elsewhere, Arlene Katz and I (Katz and Shotter 1996, 2004; Shotter and Katz 1998) have discussed the use of a 'social poetics' in our forms of talk and writing in the social and behavioural sciences, with respect to the task of putting our social realities on '*freeze frame*', so to speak, in ways that allow us to search over that *freeze frame* for ways in which to relate ourselves responsively to aspects of them that we might not otherwise have noticed. The kind of writing in which we can achieve this, is writing about concrete details, quoting actual voiced utterances, using metaphors, making comparisons, in short, writing in such a way that, in juxtaposing one's words in unconventional ways, writers create occasions in which readers must creatively complete—dialogically (not logically or cognitively), as in between two lines of dialogue—the process of understanding. As we see it, such a social poetics works noncognitively or nonrationally. For, as long as the gaps we create in juxtaposing our words in unusual ways are not too great, our bodies (our's and our listener's) will responsively create {Greek: *poiesis* = creation, making} ways of bridging them.

Indeed, we can now begin to see, perhaps, how each word in a text, just as each point we look at in a visual scene, can send us on to the next with a certain task already in hand. In this sense, the words in a text are hardly different from a set of 'signposts' staking out a 'journey' over a shared geographical landscape. But in working in this way, our words are doing something very much more than merely 'picturing' or representing such a landscape. Like signposts, they are pointing to a publicly shared reality beyond themselves. Indeed, along the same lines as his remarks above about the 'life of signs', Wittgenstein (1981) remarks about attempts to explain the process of intention in terms of 'pictures' as follows: 'When one has the picture in view by itself it is suddenly dead, and it is as if something has been taken away from it, which had given it life before ... it does not point outside itself to a reality beyond' (ibid.: § 236)—and our words in their speaking, in their embodied voicing, gesture to or call on the others around us in the same way.

But each striking moment is quite unique, a singularity, a first-time event. We need a way of characterising the *kind* of influences they exert on us both in shaping our actions at the moment of their occurrence, and in providing memorable resources that we can draw on in different ways at a later date. This is the function of the descriptive concepts I have outlined. Their task is to illuminate the *general* features of such unique events.

Our task in our writing, then, and our task in the descriptive disciplines in general, is to turn passing events, unique events which exist only in the moment of their own occurrence, into poetic accounts of events, into *scenes*, scenic events which can exist in their inscriptions, and which, on being read, or experienced in some other manner, can 'move' readers in a way similar to how people were moved by the original events. Further, by viewing such unique events in the light of descriptive concepts we have fashioned to capture certain of the general features of our ways of actively relating ourselves to our surroundings, my hope is that we can illuminate the unfolding, step-by-step details of how some of the best outcomes of our activities together are in fact achieved.

FINAL REMARKS

I began this chapter with an extract from the *New York Times*, in which the writer questioned our reliance in modern times on rational methods of problem solving: Our tendency to formulate theoretical schematisms and use such schematisms both to *explain* events *after* they have happened, and by the use of *rational calculations* to make *predictions* as to what will happen next (on the assumption that the future will be like the past). Instead, the writer switched attention to the first step in the problem solving process: our *perception* of the problem situation, our *readiness* to see this, that, or a number of other *possibilities* for what might occur next within it.

This has been central to my whole approach above. Instead of being concerned with explanatory and predictive schemes, especially ones of a generalised kind, my concerns have been quite different. In line with the idea of a descriptive discipline, I have been concerned to describe in some detail, what might be involved in working out (in practice, not in theory) how to act 'from within the midst' of an actual, already existing circumstance, to 'develop', 'refine', 'evolve', or 'unfold' further 'its' particular *potentialities for development* in relation to what our 'end in view' might be in that particular circumstance. But to do this, as we have seen, we must somehow gain a *sense* of a 'something' that, at the moment of acting, is still *invisible* to us, that is, available to us only as a *feeling*, a possibility, a felt tendency in a still *unrealised* state.

Our task is thus to prepare ourselves to approach each new circumstance with an appropriate *readiness*, an appropriate *openness*, ready to allow that 'something' to 'call out' from us appropriate *embodied anticipations* as to how next to act in relation to 'it'. My concern, then, in all the remarks making up the different sections in this chapter, is thus to do with *ways* of disciplining or of composing ourselves to act in this spontaneous fashion, and to do with appropriate *preparing activities* conducive to our coming to embody relevant *readinesses*. They are not at all concerned with *making plans*. They are also concerned with *ways of talking* (which also, of course, are *ways* of acting) that can exert a *formative* or an *organisational* influence within our practical collaborative activities as they unfold or emerge in this, that, or another particular surrounding.

NOTES

1. By the word 'way' here, I mean the way we organize a sequence of *task* activities in bringing off an *achievement* — see section on 'Category Mistakes...' below.
2. I do this to avoid the strictures of purists who may object that in lacking a clear methodology (but not *methods*, as we shall see) such *disciplines* lack the true stamp of science.

3. Wittgenstein (1953) describes his own mode of *practical* philosophical investigation thus: 'We may not advance any kind of theory. There must not be anything hypothetical in our considerations. We must do away with all explanation, and description alone must take its place ... problems are solved, not by giving new information, but by arranging what we have always known' (ibid.: § 109).

4. This, suggests Wittgenstein (1980b), is why it is so difficult to '... renouncing all theory: One has to regard what appears so obviously incomplete, as something complete' (ibid.: § 723).

5. By the word 'way' here, I mean the way we organise a sequence of *task* activities in bringing off an *achievement*—see section on 'Category Mistakes...' below.

6. But to this claim, that everything of importance lies open to view, Wittgenstein (1953) remarks, 'one would like to retort "Yes, but it all goes by so quick, and I should like to see it *as it were* laid open to view"' (ibid.: § 435, emphasis added). It is the task of 'descriptive concepts', as described in the next section, to achieve this aim, to describe what such passing events would *look like*, and *feel like*, if they could be, as it were, *laid open to view*.

7. But, as we shall see below, the 'specific variability' (Voloshinov 1986: 69), or the 'specific vagueness' (Garfinkel 1967: 40), in terms of which such uniqueness is expressed, depends upon the possibility of variations in the highly organised, orderly forms of interaction already existing among us.

8. 'Ahead of what I can see and perceive, there is, it is true, nothing more actually visible, but my world is carried forward by lines of intentionality which trace out in advance at least the style of what is to come....' (Merleau-Ponty 1962: 416).

9. Definition of *entanglement*: 'When two systems, of which we know the states by their respective representation, enter into a temporary physical interaction due to known forces between them and when after a time of mutual influence the systems separate again, then they can no longer be described as before, viz., by endowing each of them with a representative of its own. I would not call that *one* but rather *the* characteristic trait of quantum mechanics'.

10. Wittgenstein (1980b) describes the situation we face as follows: 'It is as if one saw a screen with scattered coloured–patches, and said: the way they are here, they are unintelligible; they only make sense when one completes them into a shape.—Whereas I want to say: Here *is* the whole. (If you complete it, you falsify it)' (ibid.: § 257).

11. Wittgenstein (1953: 227) formulated the difficulty in relation to such situations, in which we judge, for instance, that one person's judgement is better than another's, as follows: 'What is most difficult here is to put this indefiniteness, correctly and unfalsified, into words' (ibid.: 227).

12. Heidegger and Merleau-Ponty (1962) both call this realm of being *primordial*, while Wittgenstein (1980a) notes that: 'When you are philosophising [i.e., conducting his kind of practical, descriptive investigations] you have to descend into primeval chaos and feel at home there.' (ibid.: 65).

13. Elsewhere (Shotter), I have called it a 'knowing of the third kind.'

14. The notion is not, of course, without its history in psychology. The notion of *mental set*, or of thought *directed* upon an object (intentionality), was already implicit in the act-psychology tradition dating back to Franz Brentano (1973).

15. It will be apparent that I have used the word 'difficulty', rather than the word 'problem'. The issue here is a matter of the logical grammar of the two words. Calling something a problem leads one to expect, one day perhaps, a *solution* to it. Whereas a difficulty is something that requires the achievement of a *resolution* to it in one's actions, in the immediate situation in which it is encountered.

16. Wittgenstein (1953) seeks in his poetic–descriptive approach to his philosophy of language: 'something that already lies open to view and that becomes surveyable by a rearrangement' (ibid.: § 92).

REFERENCES

Bakhtin, M. 1984. *Problems of Dostoevsky's Poetics* (edited and translated by Caryl Emerson). Minneapolis, MN: University of Minnesota Press.

———. 1986. *Speech Genres and Other Late Essays* (translated by Vern W. McGee). Austin, TX: University of Texas Press.

———. 1993. *Toward a Philosophy of the Act*, (with translation and notes by Vadim Lianpov, edited by M. Holquist). Austin, TX: University of Texas Press.

Barfield, O. 1999. *A Barfield Reader* (edited by G. Tennyson). Hanover and London: Wesleyan University Press.

Boje, D. 2008. *Storytelling Organizations*. London: Sage Publications.

Bourdieu, P. 2000. *Pascalian Meditations* (translated by Richard Nice). Stanford, CA: Stanford University Press.

Brentano, F. 1973. *Psychology from an Empirical Standpoint* (translated by A.C. Rancurello). London: Routledge and Kegan Paul.

Brooks, D. 2008. 'The Behavioral Revolution', *New York Times*, 28 October.

Czarniawska, B. 1998. *Narrative Approach in Organization Studies*. Thousand Oaks, CA: Sage Publications.

Foucault, M. 1973. *The Birth of the Clinic: An Archaeology of Medical Perception* (translated by A.M. Sheridan Smith). New York: Vintage Books.

Garfinkel, H. 1967. *Studies in Ethnomethodology*. Englewood Cliffs, NJ: Prentice-Hall.

———. 2002. *Ethnomethodology's Program: Working out Durkheim's Aphorism* (edited and introduced by Anne Warfield Rawls). New York & Oxford: Rowman & Littlefield Publishers.

Heidegger, M. 1962. *Being and Time* (translated by John Macquarrie and Edward Robinson). New York: Harper & Row.

Holland, J. 1998. *Emergence: From Chaos to Order*. Oxford: Oxford University Press.

Hume, D. 1910. *An Enquiry Concerning Human Understanding*. Harvard Classics, Vol 37. Adelaide: P.F. Collier & Son.

Hustvedt, S. 2008. 'America Has Been Listening to a President Who Has Cut the World in Two', *The Observer Review*, 2 November.

Katz, A. and J. Shotter. 1996. 'Hearing the Patient's "Voice": Toward a Social Poetics in Diagnostic Interviews', *Social Science and Medicine*, 43: 919–31.

Katz, A. and J. Shotter. 2004. 'On the Way to "Presence:" Methods of a "Social Poetics",
    on D.A. Pare and G. Larner (eds), *Collaborative Practice in Psychology and Therapy*,
    pp. 69–82. New York: Haworth Clinical Practice Press.
Kundera, M. 1993. 'Á la Recherche du Présent Perdu', in *Testaments Betrayed: An Essay
    in Nine Parts*, pp. 119–44. New York: HarperPerennial.
Lewes, G.H. 1875. *Problems of Life and Mind* (First Series, Vol. 2). London: Trübner.
Merleau-Ponty, M. 1962. *Phenomenology of Perception* (translated by C. Smith).
    London: Routledge and Kegan Paul.
———. 1964. *Signs* (translated by Richard M. McCleary). Evanston, IL: Northwestern
    University Press.
Prigogine, I. 1996. *The End of Certainty: Time, Chaos, and the New Laws of Nature*.
    New York: The Free Press.
Ryle, G. 1949. *The Concept of Mind*. London: Methuen.
Schumacher, E.F. 1977. *A Guide for the Perplexed*. London: Jonathan Cape.
Shotter, J. 1993a. *Cultural Politics of Everyday Life: Social Constructionism, Rhetoric, and
    Knowing of theThird Kind*. Milton Keynes: Open University Press.
———. 1993b. *Conversational Realities: Constructing Life through Language*. London:
    Sage Publications.
———. 2005. 'Inside Processes: Transitory Understandings, Action Guiding
    Anticipations, and Withness Thinking', *International Journal of Action Research*,
    1(1): 157–89.
———. 2007. 'With What Kind of Science Should Action Research be Contrasted?',
    International Journal of Action Research, 3(1+2): 65–92.
———. (in press). *Getting It: Withness-Thinking and the Dialogical... in Practice*.
    Cresskill, NJ: Hampton Press.
Shotter, J. and A. Katz. 1998. 'Living Moments' in Dialogical Exchanges', *Human
    Systems*, 9: 81–93.
Steiner, G. 1989. *Real Presences*. Chicago, Ill: University of Chicago Press.
Todes, S. 2001. *Body and World*, with introductions by Hubert L. Dreyfus and Piortr
    Hoffman. Cambridge, MA: MIT Press.
Voloshinov, V. 1986. *Marxism and the Philosophy of Language* (translated by L. Matejka
    and I.R. Titunik). Cambridge, MA: Harvard University Press, first published
    [1929].
Williams, R. 1977. 'Structures of Feeling', Chapter 9 in *Marxism and Literature*, pp.
    128–35. Oxford: Oxford University Press.
Wittgenstein, L. 1953. *Philosophical Investigations* (translated by G.E.M. Anscombe).
    Oxford: Blackwell.
———. 1980a. *Culture and Value* (introduction by G. Von Wright, and translated by
    P. Winch). Oxford: Blackwell.
———. 1980b. *Remarks on the Philosophy of Psychology* (Vols. 1 and 2). Oxford:
    Blackwell.
———. 1981. *Zettel*, 2nd ed. , G.E.M. Anscombe and G.H.V. Wright (eds). Oxford:
    Blackwell.

5

PERPLEXITY, ECOLOGY AND TECHNOLOGY

Richard Ennals

> *Silence resides in the gaps between the known islands of explicit knowledge in the overall ecosystem.*
>
> *Rather than expecting to be able to build technology-based systems with complete information, we take a human centred approach. Individual people are integral.*
>
> *They need to be active, to engage in dialogue and to be aware of the importance of tacit knowledge. As societies, we recognise the incompleteness and inconsistency of our discourse, and the differences between participants. Perplexity continues.*

*Whereof one cannot speak,
thereof one must be silent.*

The closing words of Wittgenstein's (1922) *Tractatus Logico-Philosophicus* expressed, in the clearest terms, the perspective of logical positivism. It was argued that we can only talk meaningfully about areas of life and experience when we can produce propositions which can be verified, and, preferably, quantified. Meaning was defined in terms of the means of verification. This excluded areas such as aesthetics, religious belief and romantic love, which, for many, define what it is to be human.

This approach was revived by the most optimistic enthusiasts for artificial intelligence, who argued, with Feigenbaum (Feigenbaum and McCorduck 1983), that the technical obstacles would soon be overcome which had inhibited access to the knowledge of experts. It was simply a matter of developing the right techniques for knowledge elicitation. They foresaw a brave new world in which disembodied expertise could be made explicit and widely available. The human experts themselves would no longer be required. In the workplace, there was a return to Taylorist scientific management, and a definition of tasks in terms of sub-tasks, resulting in new vocational qualifications, based on competence rather than skill (Göranzon and Josefson 1988).

Practical experience of building expert systems and other applications of artificial intelligence led to the widely shared view that success in processing knowledge could only be partial. Although it is indeed possible to represent explicit knowledge in the form of facts and rules, using formalisms such as predicate logic, in forms which can be regarded by computers as programmes (Kowalski 1979), there are limits. We discover the gaps in the new systems, following processes of automation, outsourcing or early retirement, when key knowledge is absent (Ennals and Molyneux 1993).

TACIT KNOWLEDGE

There has been considerable recent debate concerning tacit knowledge (Gourlay 2006, 2007), and how access can be gained through dialogue and reflection. It is clear that converting implicit knowledge, such as knowledge of procedures, into documented rules, is not necessarily difficult. This has been demonstrated in recent quality campaigns, resulting in new procedure manuals, which have then been used to control operations in organisations. However, this leaves a vast residue of knowledge, that we may know individually or collectively, but is not amenable to direct conversion into explicit form. This information is not being consciously withheld. However, it is not easily accessible to analysis. Such issues are culturally situated: we need preparation if we are to understand apparent gaps in knowledge in other contexts (Toulmin 2001).

We may need to deploy analogical thinking, in contrast to conventional analytical approaches. Within a discipline there are structured approaches to the analysis of data, 'drilling down'. However, this may not prove to be an effective means of gaining access to personal experience. The Dialogue Seminar Method (Göranzon et al. 2006), developed at the Swedish Royal Institute of Technology, involves a process of reflection on text. Companies engage in collective reflection on impulse texts or theatrical performances. Management is then seen as the orchestration of reflection, transforming organisational cultures as the silences become audible. We can learn through engagement in the culture, the form of life.

SILENCE

As tacit knowledge cannot straightforwardly be spoken about, it is argued by the positivists that we must be silent. At least in the sense of giving verifiable descriptions of the world, our utterances can have no meaning. They may, however, be understood as actions, or 'speech acts'.

We miss a great deal if we fail to listen to silence, and do not seek to understand what it means. We need to go beyond conventional academic debates, and take account of theatre and music. This is consistent with the approach taken by Wittgenstein (1968) in his lectures and conversations on 'Aesthetics, Psychology and Religious Belief'. Rather than simply analysing propositional content, he was concerned to see how beliefs were expressed in action.

Wittgenstein was a great admirer of Henrik Ibsen, for whom silences were to be identified and explored. His accounts of families and communities gripped by their past, such as 'Ghosts' or 'The Pillars of Society', normally included areas of silence, where the characters found it impossible to be explicit (1980a, 1980b). Gradually, during the play, the truth would begin to emerge. At a certain point, typically in the third act, the picture was transformed, as the implications of previously undisclosed facts were worked through. It was no longer possible for the characters to view the world in the same way as before. Having been 'seen as' one picture, an irreversible change could come about. A tipping point was reached.

There will be cases where we prefer to remain silent. Just as the meaning of a word may be seen in its use, the same applies to silence. What is more, given the limits of what can be expressed in direct terms, we are obliged to consider the meanings of systems which include silences. We have to consider systems in the context of their use, and not just as programmes comprised of symbols. This requires a critical understanding of institutions.

When it comes to information technology, we have tended to demand explicit representations, as we seek to model reality. In order to have confidence in our conclusions, we demand completeness and consistency, or act as if we had complete information, with equal access available to all, although these conditions are rarely met. All too often we end up with an impoverished picture. Not only do we lack certain details, we are denied an appreciation of silence. We might reflect on Gödel's conclusion, published in 1951, that within a particular level of language and formalism, one can either be complete or consistent, but not both (Gödel 1995). This provides a context for considering the numerous cases of information systems disasters (Ennals 1995).

EVIDENCE

Discussions of history and current policy have conventionally been based on the analysis of explicit knowledge, in the form of documents. So much more would have been known by the historical characters, implicitly and tacitly, but is not available to us, separated by time.

In one of the most successful example programmes for 'Logic as a Computer Language for Children' (Ennals 1983), the pilot school class developed a 'murder mystery', with an incomplete database, which supported initial investigation but did not provide a ready made solution. There were vital gaps. Successive investigating detectives would have to find additional evidence, or indeed fabricate it, adding it to the database in order to build a convincing case against a particular suspect. As a result, simultaneous investigations by subsequent classes could reach different conclusions. We tend to assume that others draw the same conclusions as we do. We add something of ourselves to the database, but it is not usually made explicit. Detectives are supposed to be constrained by rules of evidence. They cannot avoid interpretation.

We need to find a way to enter into the particular form of life, and understand the language games, if we are to make sense of the silences, and interpret fragments. This requires us to reflect on our own experience, and make an empathetic leap. With contemporary cases, we can start by reflecting on our own experience, and setting it against the background of other cases (Ennals and Gustavsen 1999; Gustavsen et al. 2007).

The 'evidence-based' approach is increasingly popular in official circles, applying analytical techniques to data, and attributing extra validity to conclusions and recommendations with strong quantitative support. There is a tendency to measure what can be measured, concentrating on 'hard' data, based on financial figures, at the expense of, for example, 'softer' data about health or learning. Where nothing quantifiable can be said, it may indeed be easier to remain silent. This philosophical conclusion is echoed by management consultants, who concentrate on what can be measured.

However, this approach can only deal with the explicit tip of the iceberg. It tends to perpetuate illusions. In reality, all too often, it is pre-determined policy which determines what is to count as evidence. Areas which cause difficult complications may be added to the silence.

Thus, amid our accounts of complex topics, as Pålshaugen (2006) has observed, there will often be two bodies of information, one of which is made explicit while the other remains silent. Wittgenstein's *Tractatus* can be seen as consisting of two volumes, only one of which could be written.

STAR WARS

Silences arise in the context of problems where there are tensions and sensitivities. We need to be able to hear what is not said, and locate it in context. As was found with investigative research concerning the American Strategic Defense Initiative (Ennals 1986), in areas of secrecy, sensitivity and confidentiality, we will inevitably be restricted to partial accounts. Each of us has to make a decision as to what we need to know, and what we are prepared to take on trust. This may not be conscious, but may be a result of professional training or conditioning.

The child in the fairy story had not been told that it was not officially permissible to point out that the emperor had no clothes. President Ronald Reagan had followed the example of Lewis Carroll's Alice, who 'believed six impossible things before breakfast'. He asked the civilian population of the United States to believe that, using the best available technology, a 'peace shield' could be created which would protect America and her allies from the threat of international ballistic missile attack. The cartoons were reassuring.

There was silence regarding the accumulating test evidence that the technology would not work, in the absence of a spare planet, and regarding the international treaties which would be broken. Indeed, these treaties were then broken by ex-President George W. Bush, with his Missile Defence systems.

Computer scientists were asked to accept lucrative contracts to undertake work on projects which they did not believe to be technically feasible. They were asked to maintain silence over their areas of concern, and simply take the money. They were to refrain from commenting on issues in different technical areas in the same overall programme, such as laser physics. They were to assume that other domain experts had concluded that what was proposed was indeed feasible. They had been divided into disciplines, to be ruled. The general public, and the President of the United States, were to be left with the impression that the proposed defence system could protect the USA and their allies from intercontinental ballistic missiles. The Pentagon remained silent about what might be done to counter threats from bombs in suitcases or cars, or terrorists armed with box cutters. Today we have a richer understanding of these particular threats. Doubtless new gaps will emerge, following shoes and liquids.

The questions on defence and security were not wholly new. Indeed, they were addressed by Abelson (1973) at Yale, where he developed the 'ideology machine', which modelled the behaviour of a State Department spokesman when giving a press conference, setting out the position according to a pre-determined script, which required emphasis on some points, and silence on others. The system was set to simulate the position of a right-wing ideologue such as Barry Goldwater. It worked quite well in modelling the American régime led by George W. Bush, including Dick Cheney, Donald Rumsfeld and John Bolton.

The challenge for the cross-disciplinary researcher, based in the United Kingdom, was to avoid asking a question to which the answer was likely to be an official secret, but to listen carefully for what was not said by ministers and officials. By not asking a direct question, it could become easier for the answer to be made available. The Memorandum of Understanding between the UK and USA in December 1985 was to remain 'secret in perpetuity', but, as they had not been asked, the UK Ministry of Defence provided off the record explanatory briefing.

The apparent surface meaning of a statement could be transformed by the use of silence, by individuals and institutions. An office based in Whitehall, that supposedly existed to encourage UK companies to participate in Strategic Defense Initiative (SDI), turned out, in reality, to have the role of discouraging ill-advised participation. If the intention had been to encourage participation, it would be hard to explain some of the appointments, and the actions taken. This interpretation could not be made explicit, but, in the context of a more general press conference, it could be implied, with supportive body language. Thus we began to understand the resignations of two British cabinet ministers, Michael Heseltine and Leon Brittan in January 1986: neither was allowed to explain their reasons.

Both Arthur Conan Doyle (creator of Sherlock Holmes) and Earle Stanley Gardner (creator of Perry Mason) wrote crime stories where the vital clue was 'the dog which did not bark'. We need a feeling for what is usual, if our attention is to be caught by the unusual. We need to be aware of our presuppositions (Collingwood 1946). We are in practice constantly comparing our expectations with reality. These feelings, instincts and comparisons are beyond the scope of computer systems, even ideology machines.

SLAVERY

Silence surrounds slavery. In 2007 there were celebrations of the Bicentenary of the Abolition of the Transatlantic Slave Trade by the British Parliament, yet the published historical accounts are still sparse. Those who were engaged in the slave trade tended not to talk or write about it, and the activity was conducted largely off shore, out of sight. Slaves were taken from Africa to the Americas, and rarely landed in Europe. When returning to their home towns and acting as civic benefactors, slave traders and plantation owners did not mention their links to slavery. In polite society, where family incomes were derived from West Indian plantations, as was the case with Jane Austen and the Knight family plantations, silence would be maintained on the subject of slavery.

The British school curriculum has largely avoided the subjects of the slave trade and the British Empire. Students, teachers, journalists and politicians are left with defective accounts of their pasts, with potentially dangerous consequences for the future. Where nothing is said, there is scope for speculation as to what could be said. In an increasingly multicultural society, the silence must be broken, meeting the government's curriculum requirements for schools from September 2008. What is now to be said? The past cannot be changed. The future needs to be built.

In order to make sense of the silence, we need to test models, and find the metaphors which enable the silence to be broken (Ennals 2007). For the African Diaspora communities, the silences about slavery and the slave trade have meant that African Diaspora people have in essence been rendered stateless, and left without a history. The bicentenary may force a change. For the majority British population, the realisation has grown that the history which has been published and taught has been at best partial, and at worst profoundly misleading. As the country is encouraged to reflect on 'Britishness', with widely proclaimed values of tolerance and democracy, the contradictions are uncomfortable. Few had realised that when the slaves were eventually freed in 1838, compensation was paid to the owners, including the Church of England. Numerous public buildings and stately homes, right across the United Kingdom, were financed by the slave trade.

Following traumatic periods, such as Apartheid in South Africa, the objective has been to find healing, to break through barriers of silence, and to be able to continue in dialogue. Individuals have had to be prepared to participate in difficult dialogue, disclosing facts about which silence had been maintained. Continued support has then been provided, enabling reconciliation.

In the case of the Transatlantic Slave Trade, sensitivities continue. The slave trade determined the futures of millions in the African Diaspora over several generations. Some would like a series of explicit apologies, by people present today, on behalf of those who had been involved in slavery in the past. The initial problem appears to be that the preservation of silence has resulted in widespread denial. It has not been acknowledged that much of the current prosperity of the UK, and in particular banks in the City of London, can be attributed to the economic impact of the slave trade.

Denial

When an individual or a society is in denial, there tends to be an assumption that if silence is maintained about particular sensitive topics, then certain truths will not be made more widely known. It then becomes increasingly difficult to continue a full life, in a modern complex society, steering clear of difficult issues. Many European countries continue to have difficulty discussing aspects of the Second World War, over 60 years after it ended. The 'ghosts' can include wartime collaboration with Nazism, or complicity with the treatment of the Jews in the Holocaust.

The result can be a reliance on public relations, on 'spin doctors', who use an extended version of social constructionism to create a synthetic interface to the outside world, intended to provide immunity to attack from probing questions. Wishful thinking underpinned the evidence given to public enquiries, in the late 18th century, that slaves were well accommodated on the Middle Passage to America, and that they lived an idyllic life on plantations. In 2007 there were efforts to focus on the abolition movement, and the role of William Wilberforce, rather than what was abolished, an international trade in some 12 million human beings, in which British ships and merchants played a dominant role.

Virtual Realities

It helps to have convincing accounts. The energy company Enron developed a complex 'virtual reality' account of their business, in which key transactions were undertaken off the balance sheet, in a complex maze of technical arrangements. Their ingenious business model was designed by McKinsey and Arthur Andersen. The same team also designed the Private Finance Initiative (PFI) in the UK. PFI provides a means of expenditure on public sector projects, without being included in calculations of public sector debt, and without disclosure of the costs of servicing the private sector contributions (Craig 2006). If such costs, estimated at over £40 billion, are now disclosed, they would represent a sudden increase in the official annual figures of public borrowing.

Less comfortably for university academics, a similar account might be given of public sector pensions in the UK, which are guaranteed in law, but have not been funded. They will constitute a major drain on public finances when they are paid out.

Silence could be maintained over such matters. Where silence is deliberate business strategy, the short-term rewards can be golden for the financiers concerned. A focus on balance sheets, and on items which can be quantified, makes this strategy easier to execute. When the truth is more widely known, the consequences could be both painful and controversial.

INSIGHTS FROM ARTIFICIAL INTELLIGENCE

Herbert Simon (1981) discussed *The Sciences of the Artificial*, ways of making sense of the activities of man-made structures and organisations. We can model these structures, explore their modes of operation and test the consequences of change. The researcher is able to consider the original case, and compare it with the emerging model, which he/she can adapt and refine. Where silence has been maintained, the relevant information can be added to the model. Where this is successfully accomplished, it may result in new understanding of information which had previously not been seen as connected.

It could be argued that this approach long pre-dates artificial intelligence, and can be seen in the work of Richard Collingwood (Collingwood 1946). It has been later developed further by the French archaeologist Jean-Claude Gardin (Ennals and Gardin 1989; Gardin 1988). For him, artificial intelligence provided a means of reconstructing the reasoning of archaeologists. Experts would not normally make their reasoning explicit, so it now has to be rationally reconstructed, overcoming years of silence.

SYSTEMS AND CITIZENSHIP

Those from the human centred tradition are interested in using tools which can give us access to greater understanding of the complex world in which we live. There are some ambitions associated with the building of complete systems, which we disavow. We are not seeking to develop artificial intelligence systems to replicate the full operations of the human brain. In John Searle's (1984) terms, we are engaged in 'weak AI', not 'strong AI'. We want control to remain with the human user.

We reject the idea of systems which could have complete knowledge of a complex area of human activity, such that the system could sensibly be given control. With all its limitations, Ronald Reagan's 'Star Wars' system would have had to operate automatically, with a launch on warning, as there would have been no time to wake the President. To rely on such a system was to regard it as the implementation of a fundamentalist ideology, encompassing the answers to all questions before they were put.

As human beings, we recognise that we can never provide a complete explicit account of our actions and situations. Areas of silence remain. Sometimes we can be helped to gain access to the content of those silences. Where we term the content 'tacit knowledge', it can be made more accessible through dialogue.

Some silences, however, are more profound. Psychotherapists operate with individuals and groups. There are examples, such as the Transatlantic Slave Trade and its legacy, where the emerging truth, as silence breaks, may require us to change many previously accepted accounts of individuals and institutions in history.

Having broken the silence, we enter a perplexing new world. In this world, we are not simply observers, but need to be active citizens of the world. We recognise the pragmatic case for efficiency, security and the use of the latest technologies, but we set these against the requirements for the preservation of our humanity, both individual and collective. In this imperfect world, where complete knowledge is not available, we recognise the importance of dialogue, of learning from differences, and of silence.

REFERENCES

Abelson, R. 1973. 'The Structure of Belief Systems', in R. Schank and K. Colby (eds), *Computer Models of Thought and Language*. Freeman: New York.

Collingwood, R. 1946. *The Idea of History*. Oxford: Oxford University Press.

Craig, D. 2006. *Plundering the Public Sector*. London: Constable and Robinson.

Craig, D. and R. Brooks. 2006. *Plundering the Public Sector*. London: Constable.

Ennals, R. 1983. *Beginning Micro-PROLOG*. Chichester: Ellis Horwood.

———. 1986. *Star Wars: A Question of Initiative*. Chichester: Wiley.

———. 1995. *Preventing IT Disasters*. London: Springer Verlag.

———. 2007. *From Slavery to Citizenship*. Chichester: Wiley.

Ennals R. and B. Gustavsen. 1999. *Work Organisation and Europe as a Development Coalition*. Amsterdam: John Benjamin.

Ennals, R. and J-C. Gardin (eds). 1989. *Interpretation in the Humanities: Perspectives from Artificial Intelligence*. London: British Library.

Ennals, R. and P. Molyneux (eds). 1993. *Managing with Information Technology*. London: Springer Verlag.

Feigenbaum, E. and P. McCorduck. 1983. *The Fifth Generation: Artificial Intelligence and Japan's Computer Challenge to the World*. New York: Addison Wesley.

Gardin, J-C. (ed.). 1988. *Artificial Intelligence and Expert Systems: Case Studies in the Knowledge Domain of Archaeology* (translated by R. Ennals). Clichester: Ellis Horwood.

Gödel, K. 1995. 'Some Basic Theorems on the Foundations of Mathematics and Their Implications', [1951], in *Collected Works*, Vol. III (edited by Solomon Feferman), pp. 304–23. Oxford: Oxford University Press.

Göranzon, B., M. Hammarén and R. Ennals (eds). 2006. *Dialogue, Skill and Tacit Knowledge*. Clichester: Wiley.

Göranzon, B and I. Josefson (eds). 1988. *Knowledge, Skill and Artificial Intelligence*. London: Springer-Verlag.

Gourlay, S. 2006. 'Towards Conceptual Clarity Concerning "tacit knowledge": A Review of Empirical Studies', *Knowledge Management Research and Practice* 4(1): 60–69.

———. 2007. 'An Activity Centred Framework for Knowledge Management', in C. McInerney and R. Day (eds), *Rethinking Knowledge Management: From Knowledge Management to Knowledge Processes. Information Science and Knowledge Management*, Vol. 12, pp. 21–64. London: Springer-Verlag.

Gustavsen, B., R. Ennals and B. Nyhan (eds). 2007. *Learning Together for Local Innovation: Promoting Learning Regions*. Luxembourg: Cedefop.

Ibsen, H. 1980a. *Ghosts*, in *Ibsen Plays*, edited by M. Meyer. London: Methuen.

———. 1980b. *The Pillars of Society*, in *Ibsen Plays*, edited by M. Meyer. London: Methuen.

Kowalski, R. 1979. *Logic for Problem Solving*. Amsterdam: Elsevier.

Pålshaugen, Ö. 2006. 'Reading and Writing as Performing Arts: At Work', in B. Göranzon, M. Hammarén and R. Ennals (eds), *Dialogue, Skill and Tacit Knowledge*, pp. 216–28. Clichester: Wiley.

Searle, J. 1984. *Minds, Brains and Science*. London: BBC.

Simon, H. 1981. *The Sciences of the Artificial*. Cambridge, MA: MIT Press.

Toulmin, S. 2001. *Return to Reason*. Cambridge, MA: Harvard University Press.

Wittgenstein, L. 1922. *Tractatus Logico-Philosophicus*. London: Routledge.

———. 1968. *Lectures and Conversations on Aesthetics, Psychology and Religious Belief*. Oxford: Blackwell.

6

PERPLEXITY AND ETHICS

Ian Steers

There are limits to language and, by positioning the body at these limits we can reveal an embodied ethics.

In an embodied form ethics emerges through bio-social processes. The first process is questing which constructs meaning through the normative turbulences of ethical dilemmas. The second, narrating, makes the ethical process apparent in the social body.

Questing and narrating, self-enacting and self-disclosing, managers are celebrated as complex and perplexed humans who organize part of their lives within organizations.

Words, words, mere words,
no matter from the heart
(Troilus, Troilus and Cressida,
viii, Shakespeare, 1602)

S tudies of the language–organisation relationship have since the 1980s taken two tracks (Westwood and Linstead 2001: 2–3). Instead of focusing on language as a mechanism of communication related to the pragmatic managerial problem of organisational effectiveness and language as a means of representing reality, one track puts language centrally in the creation of social behaviour and social structure. Rejecting correspondence picture theories of language that fix meanings and meaning is seen as prior to language, this track embraces aspects of social theory and philosophy such as social constructionism, the dramaturgical perspective and narratology. Human organising takes place in language and language constructs and creates a coherent world that excludes other worlds and, in doing so, reflects the language of particular communities. The second track, drawing from across the humanities such as historical theory, literary criticism, anthropology and social science, sees the language–organisation relationship as far more intimate. Language is not just central to organisation studies, but is indivisibly enfolded in the concept of organisation and organisation theorising. Organisation has no stable, autonomous meaning outside language. It is a linguistic process in which 'organisation' meanings emerge and defer. Organisation cannot therefore be codified and represented statically because organisation-is-language, and language-is-organisation. Language organises by controlling and creating order out of disorder, constructing boundaries as it interferes, punctuates, identifies and stops the flow of experience. As it interposes itself between living bodies, the body is forgotten, emotion silenced 'leaving something important unsaid, some necessary unspoken remainder', which creates 'monstrous openings' outside language. Decentred, the material body is subordinated to language and becomes a 'lifeless body, a cadaver' (ibid.: 332–33).

In *Hard Boiled Wonderland and The End of the World* Haruki Murakami tells a science fiction story in two parts each occupying alternating chapters in a book that, in the end, never converge completely. In one narrative, 'Hard Boiled Wonderland', a nameless human data encryptor, a 'Calcutec', works for the 'System', an all-knowing pseudo-governmental organisation dedicated to protecting data from the 'Semiotics', who steal data for the 'Factory'. To kill time in the 'System', 'Calcutec' counts the change, three thousand and fifty yen, in different pockets. With his hands in his pockets he runs a parallel count. In tandem the right and the left hands add up the yen and, when the counts do not match his expectations, he becomes anxious. Impossible to identify clearly, the 'System' evokes a dark reality involving conflict, competing organisations, close surveillance and an all-pervasive dominant power. Ripped from his modern profession as a 'Calcutec' laundering and shuffling numerical data, numeric's, in the 'System' he is swept by events beyond his control into 'The End of the World', a peaceful walled town which he cannot leave and where his shadow is cut off, and imprisoned within the town. Shadows carry memories and town residents are not permitted memories. Living in the present with no past or future, here, he is not employed as a 'Calcutec'. He is a dream reader. Dreamreading, he removes the minds of town residents by reading unicorn skulls for dreams. Resisting he struggles to reclaim his shadow and leave the 'The End of the World'. With less imagination, similar themes run through this chapter: parallel interdependent dual processes that mingle but never merge and disappear to reappear, incomplete ends, the interplay between conscious and unconscious, dreams and nightmares, choosing and being swept away, good and bad, working and living and memories in shadows that galvanise us to actions to discover and recover lost identities. Simply and with far less literary skill, this chapter seeks to keep the humanity of perplexed managers alive and argues this requires knowing our shadows, the past and future in the present.

The chapter is structured in three parts. Before remembering the forgotten body in the study of organisations, I outline 13 limits of language, which have been recognised particularly by moral philosophers. This section also serves to introduce an embodied ethics. Second, I appropriate and briefly outline my take of Capra's system to map humans organising life and focus on that 'leaving something important unsaid, some necessary unspoken remainder' (Linstead and Westwood 2001: 332). Capra's central project is to examine the complex question 'What is life?' He organises his holistic thinking of the complexity of social and biological human life with a complex dynamic human system. What's important that is missing in this 'unsaid' and 'unspoken'? I suggest it is an embodied ethics of a living human, which I construct as a 'dynamic system', and then retell as a 'moving story'. Third, from my interpretations of the narratives of these six Human Resources (HR) practitioners, I in/conclusively offer up a composite story of the ethical dilemma of an HR practitioner that, by glimpsing at the animality of humans, reemphasises the dual metaphysical processes, questing and narrating, that organise practitioners' living processes. Singling out a part, 'process', of Capra's four part system, centres human nature connected to and moving in a wider mobile nature, recognises humans are meaningful fluid matter and human living is more complex than other forms of life. The more complex a living being, the more complex are the ways by which they *process* their experiences, the *meanings* they construct, their *forms* of living and their interactions in, and with *matter*. Capra recognises the difference between life and death is the beginning of ethics and when we understand the meaning of non-life we are becoming living humans who seek to make their lives meaningful. Life belongs to organisms and humans are living animals that when treated as non-living machines deaden human life. So while organisation-is-language, the living body is not language and whilst language-is-organisation, it is not the only form of organisation. There is a process of organising beyond language and, in the constraints of language, it is the perplexing organising 'oughts' of living biological matter becoming 'human' which is the central focus of this chapter.

RAISING THE DEAD

Language does not live, and neither does it know the value of life. A child studying biology can tell you about Mrs Nerg. Biologists distinguish living matter from non-living matter by seven processes. Living organisms: <u>M</u>ove, <u>R</u>espire, are <u>S</u>ensitive to their environments, need <u>N</u>utrition, <u>E</u>xcrete, <u>R</u>eproduce and <u>G</u>row. Non-living matter is passive and inactive, dependant on circumstance and it cannot move. It can only be moved. Plants are active; they develop, move towards light and extend their roots through the soil. Plants exhibit some movement, they grow, and their growth is irreversible. But plants are mainly passive. Animals live by moving around and, unlike plants their movements are reversible, repeatable and rapid. In a complex evolutionary relationship among muscles, neurons and the environment, these animal movements are *'timed'* (Dawkins 2006: 48, emphasis original). In this biologically synchronised movement animals are also conscious and unconscious of time passing during which they experience an inner-life of happiness, unhappiness, confidence, fear, expectations and disappointment (Schumacher 1977: 26–27). Biologists also tell me that humans and chimpanzees share 99.5 per cent of their evolutionary history (Trivers 2006: xiv) and cognitive scientists underestimate that 95 per cent of all thought is unconscious and the 'hidden hand' of unconscious embodied thought shapes and structures all conscious thought (Lakoff and Johnson 1999: 13).

Moral philosophers have also long argued that our human animality is fundamental to the process by which we create meaning in our lives (Gerhardt 2006) and, here, I have no intention of ascending a ladder of nature suggestive of an animist apartheid that draws sharp dividing lines among different living species. This chapter privileges the 'human' animal body without reducing it to a 'biological specimen, a meaningless organism, walking bits of flesh and bone with a number attached' (Bernstein 2006: 382) and counters conceptions of perplexed managers and workers as bits of disembodied labour power. The processes of Mrs Nerg and the relationship between ethics and our embodied animality rarely make its appearance in studies of organisations. This strange omission has epistemological, ontological, moral, ethical and political implications. Scholars studying organisations and organising are coy to organise the human relationship of mind and spirit, united in substance with the flesh and engaged in the universe of matter (Maritain 1964: 452). Yet, we are social *and* biological animals and, in failing to celebrate our materiality, language is made sacred and given priority over life. Falling over in my haste not to anger lovers of language, I am not for turning away from 'the linguistic turn'. It is not possible to separate the speaking being from the living being. I have no desire to extract FOXP2, the language gene fundamental to the acquisition and development of language in humans. However, putting humans in language assumes human curiosity about living can be satisfied by knowing language and its conventions. Life is then made culturally and morally bound and what becomes meaningful are the words used, not the Good lives lived and whether forms of living are worth living because they are humanly meaningful. Language cannot turn without the body turning and all linguistic turns originate in the body. I am therefore for a body turn that *returns* ethics to its original place as a hybrid life process of embodied humans interacting with the material world. In my 'body turn' I invite an understanding for human life, not language, and for not assuming life inside or outside organisations can be understood exclusively by language. In this invitation is a normative imperative that organisational scholars ought to re-channel their energy away from the text to the body and to fight the paralysis of language (Linstead and Westwood 2001). Consequently, I point to monsters *and* wonders, nightmares and dreams, which infer uncertain openings beyond the limits of language.

Language's Limits

1. *Language decentres biology.* To equate human life with language disrupts the logic of biological discourse. It distorts the science that studies life. That distortion minimises the contribution of bio-centric understandings of human life that urge us towards a deeper respect for our animality, reduces the relevance of our evolutionary development to current understandings of being and becoming human and diminishes different political conceptions of human freedom (Singer 1999: 63). It encourages us to forget that, in DNA, we are the first generation to know our cellular ancestors, and, in that forgetting, language is privileged over life. We have an evolutionary human form because we are made human by matter and it is through our embodied humanity that we interact with the world. By our material nature we are human animals and, in decentring biology, any examination of the similarities between the biological organisation of living beings and humans organising their lives with a living *telos* is foreclosed. Withdrawing the materiality of humans levels all humans to the inanimate, the living become dead and we forget to think, act and feel materially. Biology, the science of living, shows us our mortality, our biological coexistence and socially reveals close and infinitely distant others.

2. *Language does not live.* Life lives and dies. We know life when we experience death. Death cannot be represented in language or imagined, but death exposes us to our finitude. It is not in knowing our own death but in the disappearance of the other which language cannot expound that we know our mortality, our finitude and our being-in-common (Nancy 1991). Being-in-common does not emerge in language but consists in the exposure of the in between you-and-I in which I know you share me, and I share you. The kiss of lovers is not speech, the speech of lovers is impotent and in the death of lovers we know love: ecstasy and joy touch their limits.

3. *Language stops anachronic time.* Language requires consciousness and memory. Outside language is the significance of the unconscious, the transitory nature of our memories, the importance of forgetting and an unimaginable future beyond individual existence. Levinas (Hutchens 2004: 67) identifies three modalities of time: synchrony, diachrony and anachrony. In synchrony a single self strives to empower itself over time by remembering the past, perceiving the present and predicting the future. He objects to this view of temporality because we do not expect every future, nor do we remember every past in the present. Our historical consciousness is based on events we have never experienced and could not possibly remember in language. In diachronic time, the entry of the other person introduces a past and a future the self cannot predict or remember. The approach of the face of the other is an unpredictable temporal event in which we encounter the future, a future that carries with it a past the self cannot remember. The immemorial past of the face has passed the self by, carrying with it an unpredictable future. No interested movement of conscious memory can capture this time. In anachronic time, the other person's others, the dead, the absent and the unborn open up a massive dimension of time that demands ancient and future responsibilities that language cannot appropriate. Anachronic time is therefore an 'indefinite number of inappropriable temporalities irreducibly immanent to the experience of the infinitely responsible self' (ibid.: 72).

4. *Language disembodies human nature.* Although language precedes a body that generates it and we are born into language, language does not organise the body. It is organised by the body. Language is not autopoietic and self organising, and the body is the centre of all the senses that organises language. Dealing discursively with Auschwitz is therefore, for Adorno, an outrage (Bernstein 2006) because it denies nature's ultimate authority over language. By denying nature's ultimate authority radical divisions are created

between ways of living (their form) and the human processes (ethics) by which we create meanings that extend beyond those of being a living biological member of a particular species or subject in a social discourse. Language identifies. The process of creating a social identity with language, the 'identity thinking' of the speaking being, is a linguistic process that abstracts from the living being. In the abstraction of language the unbearable physical agony to which humans were subjected to in the Nazi extermination camps was justified by who they were identified as being, not for what they had done nor the forms of life they lived. In an organising language of particular societies no one is other than what he has come to be and what he has come to identify himself as being: a useful, successful or frustrated member of vocational and national groups and representative of geographical, psychological and sociological types (Adorno and Horkheimer 1997: 84). Human nature and its material embodiment are then suppressed and we become disenchanted with the material world, consequently, our experience of normativity loses its 'animistic auratic' individuality (Bernstein 2001: 37).

5. *Language abstracts human motivation* from our material existence. Matter does not speak but it matters because matter moves us. By our embodied animality we are both (cf Vogel 1996) in nature and constructive of nature. Each finds in nature what he needs in ethics (Williams 1995: 203) and 'lost in the translation' to narration is the normative force of unique human experiences. In translating unique experience to language we make experience common to communicate it to ourselves, and to others. The more frequently experience is translated into language, the more it is socially constructed, the more social it is the more common it becomes. Further it becomes detached from its origins in a unique animal and as a human experience. Our empirical and material binding to the world is then displaced and movements towards others lose their material and normative force. The normative forces

of nature are replaced by what humans socially construct and the 'power of discourse' dominates the 'power of nature'. Yet, for Levinas ethics is an infinite openness to the other, an acceptance of the possibility to be changed by the experience of the difference of the other, and that difference can be expressed outside human language. He presents the possibility that the dog which barked its spontaneous greeting to Jews because it recognised them as human beings displayed more openness to the other than the soldiers and villagers that denied them that greeting (Jones et al. 2005: 77).

6. *Language conforms.* To truncate humans to discursive subjects and social narrators suggests all that is needed to realise our humanity is for the appropriate moral discourse to be provided by moral philosophers, institutions, managers and academics. And fat are the fees of those that talk ethics (Aristotle 1976: 335) and conform to prevailing moral discourses but fail to acknowledge our biological and material existence. Rorty (1999) argues 'language' and 'discourse' in the 20th century have become buzzwords, like 'science' and 'reason' in the previous century. Human beings are unique and their uniqueness lies partly in their ability to use language as a way of abbreviating their interactions with their environment. Language provides us with useful tools, useful for particular purposes such as regulating our existence, mediating our experiences and to restrict living to language is to stay with custom and therefore stability, security and order. We substitute knowledge for hope, certainty for imagination, today for yesterday and tomorrow and limit our ability to act as agents in creating new ways of being human. In not looking beyond language, organisational writers risk becoming '*levellers*—glib tongued and scribe-fingered slaves of democratic tastes and its modern ideas' (Nietzsche 1997: 31).

7. *Language clarifies.* Language seeks clarity and we invent form, such as words and stories that impose linguistic patterns on our intolerably chancy and incomplete lives because in narrative

we seek to organise life into coherent symbolic forms. These coherent forms clarify our lives by concealing the monsters and wondrous openings that exist beyond language. Again Levinas argues there is first ethics and then language. Language originates in ethics, the face-to-face relationship. The non-verbal command of the approaching face of the other person represents, through the language of its defenceless eyes: Here I am! You should not murder! The face, merely, approaching, is enough to force obedience to an indeclinable obligation. 'The face, itself speaks before any word is spoken' (Hutchens 2004: 49), and once it has spoken one must then find the words to explain and account for oneself. The Good is beyond being. Neither intelligible nor reducible to intelligibility, ethical responsibility is what we first catch sight of in the approaching defenceless face of the other. Through an appraisal of the approaching face of the other we know that other goods such as those organised in language are 'merely imperfect copies of the Good that makes them possible' (ibid.: 78). The Good is too fragile (Nussbaum 2001) and mysterious to be clarified and fractured by language.

8. *Language displaces human accountability.* When the human subject is situated in various social and discursive practices 'human' becomes merely another position or product of language. Moral responsibility is situated in language and humans are replaced by authorial positions in particular moral discourses; there are linguistic performances without subjects, 'deeds without doers' (Benhabib 1992: 215) and 'sins without sinners, crimes without criminals, guilt without culprits' (Bauman 1993: 18). Language, by reducing ethics to the problems of conflicting social moralities, performs a conjuring trick. It makes an embodied individual interacting with nature disappear. In the collective language of social moralities, humans cease to be accountable for the mortal lives they live and the empirical lives of others stop being the

paradigmatic heroes and villains we might wish to follow and avoid. The lives of Christ, Mohammed, Mandela and Gandhi cease to be exemplars of human living and we are forced to accept, and not condemn those such as Eichmann who followed the organising linguistic order of the Nazi cause.

9. *Language makes lives sensible, not meaningful.* In sense making (Weick 1995: 36) humans seek a narrated plausibility and a narrative is made intelligible by its completion in a story; what is necessary in sense making is therefore a 'good story', not a good life. Yet, what makes life worth living is not only what sense we make of life, but also its meaning. A story can simultaneously be sensible and insignificant, unimportant, trivial and disposable. But such a life story has little meaning, and would not be a life worth living. A meaningful life (Metz 2002) is one in which we come to by fulfilling a purpose God has assigned to us, maintaining our souls in a condition that makes life worth continuing, fulfilling our feelings of satisfaction and love, desiring something and getting it, being true to oneself, doing what is right, not harming others, by an active engagement with others, being creative, being virtuous. Sense making does not make meaningful sense of the value or worth of the identity, the life lived or the story narrated. Language also diminishes the significance of stories that ought not to be said because, for example, they are so painful they cannot be said. Discourse of life being story denies our debt to the living and the dead and suggests the living realities of Auschwitz never happened: there is only that which is said about it. Such a discourse is an insult to the dead; they are killed twice (Ricoeur 1991: 186).

10. *Language censors.* It closes down knowledge of what cannot be said. Art, music and poetry are often intended to be aesthetic, obscure and ambiguous in meaning. Such arts do not seek a human response in language because such a response affirms or glorifies the language that organises the response. If all the

arts could be said then these arts can be dispensed with because language would be sufficient to create them. Designed to make us speechless these arts often promote discomfort and a conscious dissatisfaction with our lives. All art is not intended to be expressed in language because language creates a form of self-censorship (Geus 2005: 127). By suggesting human experience is thought and identified in language we foreclose the mimetic, the idiosyncratic, the original and the potentially subversive often reflected in art. Languages vary and so do the realities they construct and relying on language to understand pictures such as Figure 6.1 suggests art is relativistic, which displaces the possibility of universals in art. Prince (2004) cautions against understanding pictures as discourse when body motions such as gestural and facial expressions express pan-cultural meanings, cinema communicates globally, picture perception abilities involve 3D skills developed in real world experiences that are transferred to 2D situations, unconditioned and unlearned spontaneous responses have been identified empirically across black and white, still and motion pictures. Picture recognition abilities have been demonstrated across a wide range of non-human subjects such as primates, birds, fish, reptiles and insects, which suggests a biologically basis of pictorial communication without a verbal label. Consequently, 'we can have mental concepts or ways of abstracting from our sense data which are beyond our current stock of words, but for which we could develop a vocabulary if communicating such concepts became important' (ibid.: 103).

11. *Language creates borders* that mark an inside, and an outside. Inside are the values, stories we tell to ourselves and to others, living with our nearest and dearest, social frames of reference, jokes, religion, culture and history which all draw upon a shared language that creates and sustains moral identities and moral communities. These moral narratives also bring with them relations with other moral narratives, of victory and

defeat, grievance and revenge, of Jew and German, of Croat and Serb, of Christian and Moslem. Inside a shared discourse of moral identities and moral communities are vendetta, genocide, racism, tribalism, nationalism, death camps and ethnic cleansing. Inside language are the monsters that need to be caged and tamed, and left outside this shared communal language is an ethic humanised (Glover 2001).

12. *Language silences emotion.* Language does not laugh, cry or curl its lips as it greets another, and a necessary condition of ethics is our embodied emotions. Emotions cannot be divorced from action. Language neither acts nor feels emotion. In language we reflect but it is in moral salience (Sherman 1990), in our emotions of compassion, sympathy, pity and indignity we act spontaneously, without conscious thought, towards the plight of others. Without the need to translate into language, emotion propels us towards others and, after our conduct and in the emotions of shame and guilt, joy and pride, we also know the value of life.

13. *Language simplifies experience.* Language reduces the complexity of living to language and in this reduction it fits and identifies. Identifying a living experience in language stops the flow of experience and the fluid movements of living beings are fitted into linguistic categories. Experience leaves everything in, and language talks its way out of human experience. Nishida (1990), drawing together eastern and western moral philosophy, argues experience does not exist because there is an individual translating experiences. An individual exists because there is experience. Experience is more fundamental than an individual who reflects or expresses experience in words that can be transmitted to self or others. In Nishida's 'pure experience', the knower and known are not separated but one. The self does not experience something, but is experienced actively, creatively and constructively. In 'pure experience' the ultimate reality, the Good, is to fulfil

one's nature in unity, as merged with the universe, realised cognitively and through knowing from without (in language) and also volitionally and emotionally from within (outside language). Irrespective of how much a seed is nurtured from without, it cannot become a plant unless it has, from within, the power of growth and no plant grows if there is only a seed (Nishida 1990: 53). Lying in my mother's womb and knowing her presence, playing the air guitar at a Led Zeppelin concert, head banging to Black Sabbath's 'Paranoid', the look in a woman's eyes, the down on her face, our orgasms, the birth of our children, the grip of their small fists around my finger, the student who thanks you for knowing that they are now not 'thick', sitting in a turquoise sea, ageing and the approach of death are places and times beyond language. In the translation of our material experience (from within) to communicative experience (from without), experience becomes appearance, the unique becomes common, private becomes public, possibility becomes actuality, the unconscious becomes conscious, indeterminate becomes determinate, consciousness becomes forms, forms become life, life becomes abstracted, abstraction becomes reason without embodiment, disembodied and abstracted dispassionate reason becomes principle, principle becomes rules, rules become theory, theory becomes coherence, theoretical coherence becomes commensurating, complex human living is made coherently simple and all perplexity becomes solvable. Paradoxically, as social and biological animals, we respond to the human compulsion to communicate coherently to within, ourselves, and to without, others. Yet, the complexity of experience and the materiality of human lives are, if viewed solely as linguistic performances, dehumanised, externalised, simplified, sanitised of emotions and rationalised. The without is wrenched away from the within and the living being is dismembered from the speaking being.

Figure 6.1: Capra's System

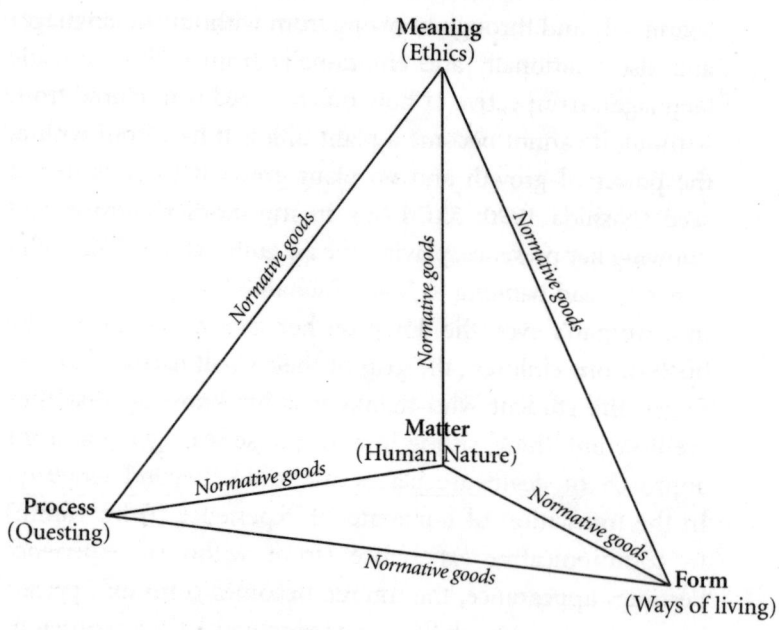

Source: Adapted from Capra (2003: 64).

Simply, when language dominates understanding human life inside and outside organisation humans become lifeless, a 'cadaver'; language then makes human inhuman. Humans are disembodied, lose their living vitality and become units of language subject to social conventions and the power of language. Discourse becomes the Gorgan, which turns animated lives into inanimate language. Language then destroys the animality and vitality of human life; the power of language displaces the power of nature. Managers and workers cease to be living beings and are detached from their material existence. Immaterial and disembodied, humans cease to coexist with other sentient beings, are disconnected from being part of nature and living processes are stilled. An ethics that celebrates life is displaced and, replaced by language, the pleasures and pains of living cease to be relevant to organisation and we become indifferent to the organisation of the living.

Organisation-is-language and language-is-organisation but language is not life. Language originates in our material coexistence and language is only one form of organising.

Numerous questions trouble this chapter. How can I make intelligible the mutually opposing, complementary and transformative duality that waxes and wanes its way through human nature? How can the yin–yang of being and becoming a complete social *and* biological animal be organised in a chapter that seeks to write and talk about that which cannot be said, namely, the ethics of an animate HR practitioner living part of a whole life in organisations? How do I *not* cover-up (O'Doherty 2007: 21) the broader irresolvable, perennial philosophical questions, about human nature; 'who we are and are and ought to be', 'who I am and who I ought to be', 'what I ought to be and do' about 'what is humanly possible'. In the writing and the saying how do I write and talk about the unsaid, cannot be said, and ought not to be said? How do I simultaneously research, celebrate and commiserate an ineffable living humanity? How do I speak for that which cannot speak for itself, human nature? The rest of this chapter, working in the constraints of language, offers the ethical dilemma of an HR practitioner as a dynamic complex system, and as a composite empirical moving story. Although both 'story' and 'system' merely provide stationary concepts of moving realities and do not constitute an ethical dilemma, Capra's dynamic system, with its parts connected by articulating normative goods symbiotically coupled to a perpetually changing natural environment, provides a holistic map of an ethical dilemma. After describing 'human' as a living system, I tell an empirical story of the combined narratives of six HR practitioners interviewed as part of my research. In picking up 'process' from Capra's system and examining its movements in more depth and within a story, I promote both a systemic or *'world-centred'* and an *'agent-centred'* (Oderberg 2004: 128, emphasis original) appreciation of ethics. Picking up the themes in the science fiction *Hard Boiled Wonderland and The End of the World* such as the conscious and unconscious, I tell an empirical story, not of a 'Calcutec' but of an imaginary manager, an HR practitioner, being and becoming human. This story, 'I am the organisation', elaborates the social (narrating) and biological organising (questing) processes of an ethical dilemma. So let me start with the complete system of Capra and later I will tell you this incomplete moral story.

ORGANISING LIFE: A COMPLEX DYNAMIC SYSTEM

The organisation of a living being is a process of '*autopoietic organization*' (Maturana and Varela 1998: 43, emphasis original) that defines the moment when life began on Earth and recognises that, as humans, we share life's molecules and also its basic principles of organisation (Capra 2003: 60). *Forms* of human living and *meanings* are always trans/forms. Trans/forms are temporary 'slow downs' in the continuous evolving *processes* of humans experiencing normative disturbances provoked by normative goods arising from their *material* existence.

Process (Questing)

The natural world exhibits a continuous process of movement. Every organism, from the plant that turns to face the sun and the human that turns away from its blinding light, moves towards the good and away from the bad. All living animals consciously move and this animal movement, *oregō* (Nussbaum 2001: 289), is a movement in and towards nature apparent in stories told about animals moving symbiotically towards others. Dolphins altruistically save sailors' lives, and elephants are self-aware and show affection towards the bones of their ancestors. Stickleback fish hunting together are more likely to put their lives at risk for the partner who also reciprocates by taking a risk, wolves hunt together in packs, the communicative skills of apes, friendships among different species. All these stories suggest animals are both selfish and co-operative (Ridley 1996) and do *not* live in a basic relationship of the 'survival of the social and biological fittest' (Bernstein 2001: 138; Dawkins 2006: 48; Richards 1999; Singer 1999; Varela et al. 1993: 214).

By this animal movement, '*questing*' (Cooper 2001: 323, emphasis original), humans are connected to nature. Life is an ongoing generalised '*process*' (Dawkins, 2006: 137 emphasis original) of natural movement towards the Good life. All animals evolve, change and exhibit movement. From the womb to the morgue, individually and collectively, humans, as living organisms, are inextricably related. Entangled in a web of life (Capra 1996) humans are becoming. They are consciously and unconsciously socio-biological animals moving symbiotically and teleologically towards what is good for them experiencing emergent realities and possible worlds whose absences are always present in their lives.

Questing is the primal animal living process of moving towards the Good and away from the bad; its *telos* is a Good life that responds to the quest/ion how ought I to live? Hybrid, questing encompasses all other forms of thinking such as narrative, episodic, mimetic, mythic, theoretical and mechanical. It is the evolutionary life process, the 'basic process of life' (Capra 2005: 34) of moving closer and further away from a Good life. Questing, an autopoietic life process of human production therefore begins all forms of thinking and acting. It is a lateral and creative holistic movement that expands infinitely sideways to construct forms of the Good life, which it continuously redefines as new forms of living evolve. Questing changes and moves because the Good life changes and the Good life changes as questing moves. Yet, in this change there is permanency because all human life moves, and it moves towards something, the Good Life. This movement is a process of 'distanced nearness' in which 'we all reach out, being incomplete (Adorno 2005: 90; Nussbaum 2001: 289). It is a dynamic process of consciously questing in which the structures of mind maps lose their meanings, yet, some sense of their parts remains. The Good is preserved.

Humans are in evolving relationships, connected to a mobile material word in which we grow and decay, live and die, talk and write, think and act. As Sid Lowe highlights in Chapter 1, there are no black and white photos or inanimate maps available for perplexed managers because we are living organisms with embodied animate maps that we create and are created for us as we interact with moving cinematic emergent realities. Living matter, organisms, is always evolving so each living human entity is in an animated process of moving, questing, in a web of life that is never completed. When life stops moving, ceases evolving and becoming, it ceases to be alive.

Meaning (Ethics)

Without meaning, questing animals move closer towards good lives, bare organic and biological lives, that evoke vivid images of humans working as 'Calcutecs' or existences such as that of Neo in the film *The Matrix*. Before he is released from the machines Neo exists in a capsule of pink fluid that feeds his body, whilst his brain is fed his 'life' by an electronic cable controlled by a malign machine which, originally created by humans, now uses them as a source of energy.

Radically different from this energy sapping mechanised process is questing. The questing, of living material organisms interacting with matter and non-matter makes, and remakes, different meanings of their biological experiences and represents them in varied meaningful forms that guide their actions in the world. Never ending, always provisional, and never complete, this conscious/unconscious meaning-making process, questing, is *also* a narrative movement for different forms of deities, stories, theories, performances, pictures, concepts, solutions that will ostensibly cohere the complexity of living. Triggered by normative disturbances in their moral environments, discords in the concords of living, humans become conscious of their animality, their questing movements towards their Good lives. Ethics is questing made conscious and meaningful in the narratives of human living. Ethics is a conscious practical reasoning about the final ends in our lives (Richardson 1994) and these transient emergent forms of the Good life go by way of their context. In ethics we narrate human ends that are loose, unfixed and revisable. When we revise our ends we move to a less precise end and, in changing this end, we appeal to another end that we then specify, as we relate to the material world. I map that process visually in Figure 6.2.

Questing humans are social animals that narrate their lives and, as they narrate, they translate their unconscious embodied

Figure 6.2: A Map of Meaning

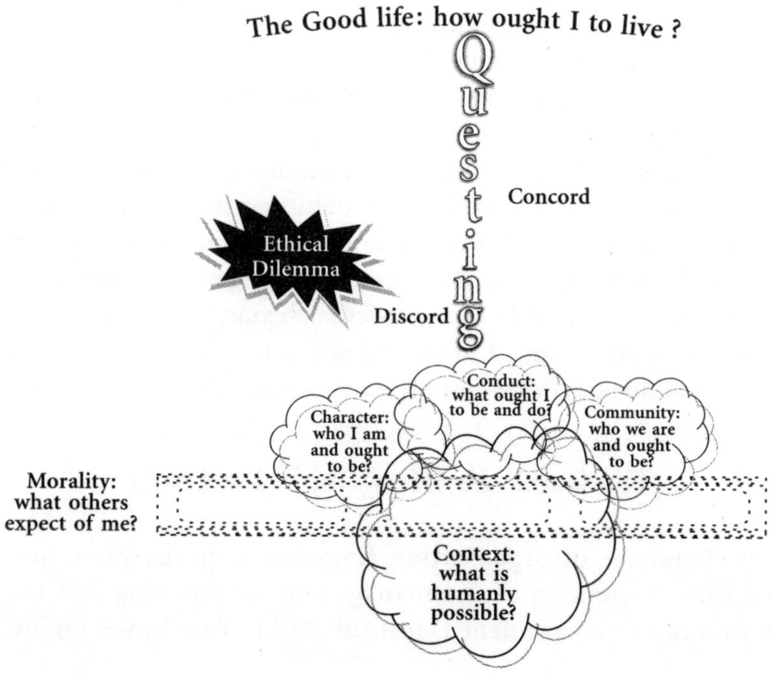

The Good life: how ought I to live ?

Questioning

Concord

Ethical Dilemma

Discord

Conduct: what ought I to be and do?

Character: who I am and ought to be?

Community: who we are and ought to be?

Morality: what others expect of me?

Context: what is humanly possible?

experiences of questing into language. In this translation of our animality we simplify the complexity of our embodied experiences by converting, with language, our knowing into thinking and in this translation we seek meaning in their lives. In narratives we simplify by excluding other complexities we could have told, circumstances we could have included, contingencies we could have imagined and limit the meanings that could have emerged. Seeking but never reaching narrative coherence every narrated experience is an incomplete human story that leaves remainders; '*missing remainders*' (Cooper 2006: 64, emphasis original) accompany every narrative, and every story. Ethical meaning represented in different narrative forms fixes and slows down questing movements by incompletely representing ethics in a type of form such as a 'story' of the sublime and the divine. Questing humans move towards a Good life and in the transitory place between different forms, humans slow down, think, create coherent meanings, fix those meanings in different forms and narrate their animated experiences as 'ethical' as they continue to quest a Good life. All narratives are partial, temporary slow downs in living movements that we socially construct and, in our conscious narrative creations, we leave behind fragments of 'left out' experiences. Narratives are a continuous process of linguistic 'forming–fixing' and creating ethical meaning of the complexities of human life that is never, in narrative, completed. This continuous construction of the manifest out of the latent and the continuous inspiring of the manifest by the latent (Cooper 2005: 1693) is a social linguistic feat, a narrative, that, by its embodiment in our human nature, in our bio-social animal natures, is never complete or accomplished.

The Good Life (How Ought I to Live?)

The language of organisation frequented by the plain and rhetorical speaking of the management of meaning and the meaning of management (Linstead 2001) often leaves unsaid meaningful work (Overell 2008) and the part meaningful work plays in meaningful lives (Metz 2002). The meaning of life 'goes beyond' and is outside language. Humans organise to make life meaningful and this meaning is not language and is reflected, for example, spiritually as Brahman in Hinduism, Dharmakaya in Buddhism, Tao in Taoism and the Holy Trinity in Christianity. Humans practically cohere (Richardson 1994: 195) goods believing that organising conflicting normative goods is significant to their living meaningful lives. Humans conduct their lives believing their normative bargains with imperfectly imagined futures (Oakeshott 1975: 44), their reliable bets (Swanton 2003: 85) will make their lives coherent and therefore meaningful.

A Good life, 'the unqualifiable final end that is uniquely suitable for the regulation of human life' (Richardson 1994: 202) evolves. Each partial or temporary realisation of the Good life of each human animal creates new imaginations, possibilities, aims, desires, aspirations and imperatives, and from these dynamic and organising relations we imagine new possibilities about living meaningful lives. Examining our lives we look forward and backward in time, and our aspirations for the future and our memories of the past provide us with the normative reasons and emotions to act in the present. The present is not therefore the centre of our existence. The 'what is' may reflect the present but the 'what was' and the 'what ought to be' or 'what ought to maybe' equally feature in our living presents. Grounded in the past, present and our concern for the future the 'ought' is never fully realised in language or action for it grows on what it feeds on (Macmurray 1993: 52). The process of questing the Good life cannot be stopped in language, it can only be slowed down by narrating, because when life stops moving, organising, it dies. Continuously participating in the living process of its creation (questing), the Good life cannot be stilled in language because it moves us as we move towards it, making us as we are shaped by it.

Morality (What Others Expect of Me)

In this complex system conduct, character and community are overlapping parts of meaning that foregrounds morals relationships. Whilst acknowledging self/other, singular/plural, subjective/objective, individual/collective, personality/organisation, psychology/sociology, identity/society are relevant to understanding organisational lives, I appropriate the moral language of 'conduct' 'character' and 'community' to emphasise a moral ying–yang of a communal–individual in moral relationships. Morality is a 'congealed wisdom' and a 'vernacular language of colloquial discourse' (Oakeshott 1975: 63) learned by *speakers,* which enables them to express, prescribe and learn the value of, for example, vice and virtue. In this moral discourse they can identify, and speak good and bad. Moral discourse provides the public and private 'moral goods' that enable humans to narrate their lives. In this moral language we are social, live communally and are connected socially to others in a web of narratives. Moral language enables humans to live out their characters and communities, to lead moral lives.

The human world is ordered and we organise our lives through the discourse of rights, obligations, justice, shame, guilt, pride, honour, virtues and vices (Scrutton 1997: 297). Morality enables character and communities to think and act on the language of right and wrong, good and bad, and to understand relationships between the non-moral and the moral. But, morality constrains individual conduct (Mackie 1977: 106; Whitely 1970: 23). Its purpose is to protect social groups by creating moral obligations that regulate the individual and their movements towards the Good. Morality is the 'stiff armour' (Bauman 1993: 33) of moral codes and duties that constrains our conduct and imposes normative obligations from the outside. Morality imposes a moral obligation on us whereby we are summoned to responsibility by others (Ricoeur 1994: 170) and this summons can demand and constrain, fulfil and inspire. Humans, questing the Good life, pass through the sieve, the texture

(Benhabib 1992: 50) of moral discourse and, shaped and reshaped by this discourse, they are made moral, not human. Humans live moral lives, which they narrate, and animal lives, which they quest.

Conduct (What Ought I to Be and Do)

Questing the Good life and sensitive to their moral environments, humans consciously experience normative disturbances in their moral lives and in these disturbances they conduct; they self enact and self disclose (Oakeshott 1975). Conduct is bifurcating. In self-disclosure we translate our experiences into language and in language we are narrators, moral discursive subjects. Connected by the communicative contingencies of our moral discourses we, in the process of narrating, move closer to identified others, known persons, and our conceptions of personal failure give rise to moral censure; we experience guilt (ibid.: 72). Self-disclosing is a narrative movement arising from a normative disturbance in a specific morality. It organises and seeks its *telos* in a coherent story, made ostensibly coherent by a narrative plot. As humans are self-disclosing to themselves and identified by others they communicate in language, they are narrating and, as they narrate, they are also self-enacting. Self-enacting, released from their contingent contexts, their particular social moralities, identified others and a narrative web, humans are in a web of life; they commune in and with human nature. Humans self-enact and failing to self-enact produces another form of self-censure; they experience, not guilt, but shame (ibid.: 77). These movements of self-disclosing and self-enacting, in the immediacy and particularity of ethical dilemmas and their contingent moralities, are narrating and questing transformed by normative disturbances that arise from humans experiencing specific discursive moralities. Humans are social and biological animals that are becoming and these processes of becoming, self-enacting and self-disclosing, originate as questing and narrating and, after the specific anxiety of a particular normative disturbance, these processes mutate. This duality of connected movements change to return in renewed forms of questing and narrating. In this metamorphosis of their dual living processes, humans remain the same. In self-disclosing they are discursive social subjects seeking coherent and sensible life stories, and in self-enacting, they are biological animals questing a Good life.

Character (Who I Am and Ought to Be) / Community (Who We Are and Ought to Be)

Debates in ethics between liberalism, the promotion of individual goods of liberty and freedom, and communitarianism, the promotion of collective goods of community for example welfare and equality, are well rehearsed (Pettit 1994). In this map character/community acknowledges both collective and individual moral goods constitute identities of who I am and ought to be in a communion of who we are and ought to be.

In my map 'character' is the morality of I/dentity work. It refers to an ethics of identity, which emphasises individuals making sense of their lives by narratives that 'cohere in the way appropriate to a person in my society' (Appiah 2005: 23). Identifying social and linguistic constructions of, for example, human, citizen, person, mother, father, public servant and manager it centres individual goods of character. Character goods are expressed for example as authenticity, self-understanding, self-respect, forgiveness, learning, humility, courage, wisdom, creativity, imagination, temperance, conscientiousness, confidentiality, discretion, integrity, regret, remorse, consistency, ambition, patience, modesty, righteousness indignation, moderation and pride.

A portrait of the isolated individual is incomplete until it includes the presence of other individuals who make up social groups. 'Community' counters the individualism or rational egoism in character (Brink 1990) and here refers to social systems that create shared collective identities. These shared identities celebrate communion, a sense of belonging, social attachment and have an 'unfashionable status in sociology' because of their definitional difficulties and their *value* laden and normative nature (Sherlock 2002: 1.3). Co/mmunity is other-than-I/identity, and community goods are expressed as citizenship, love, friendship, reciprocity, mutuality, equality, nurturing, social accomplishment, empathy, generosity, compliance, obedience, diligence, promise keeping, industriousness, detachment, restitution and professionalism. The premise of an ethic of community is 'fraternity' or 'civic friendship in civic communities' (Spragen 1995: 47)

In the yin–yang of character-goods/community-goods is, for my purposes, moral, not natural. By foregrounding moral discourse and therefore language, 'morality' decentres the metaphysical and an ethics of non-identity in which the dialectic cognition of non-identity is the secret '*telos*' of identification (Adorno 1973: 145, emphasis original). The ineffable Good life and its quest cannot be known *solely* in language. We are more than self–other identifying discursive subjects situated and organising in the language of particular social moralities. Universally we are biological and embedded in particular social contexts, we are relatively social.

Context (What is Humanly Possible)

'Ought' implies is, and can. This 'context' enables and disables meaning-making and to ignore that what can be done, what is possible, centres 'what may be', idealises ethics, disconnects ethics from human lives, dissociates experience from our expectations, disconnects economics and power from ethics. It makes human possibilities, nightmares, dreams, aspirations, ideals and stories irrelevant to the practicality of who humans are, what they do and ought to do with their lives. The language of organisation teaches us, through Foucaultian bio-politics that social institutions, calculating and administering bodies, bring human life within the boundaries of social institutions. In these social institutions that bind our bodies others cannot expect us, and we do not expect ourselves, to do what we cannot do and we cannot blame others and ourselves for not doing what we do not know, or, for what cannot be done.

What is possible is both human and personal. Humans enact and disclose what is 'humanly' and 'personally' possible (Adams 1934). We expect generalised others to be human and particular others to be and act within the immediacy of their knowledge and power. Expecting others to be human, we forgive or excuse them and their actions when they act, in their particular and individual personal circumstances, in ignorance. Knowledge and power foreground what is personally and practically possible for an individual embedded in a particular context. Power, ethics and moral discourse are inextricably linked. Without knowledge and power there is no conception of social institutions binding and bidding our minds and bodies. Lost is an ethics of moral excuses, will, autonomy, choice, responsibility, rationality, social justice and, without the situated ethics of a singular individual living in particular institutions there are no subjective judgements about morality. Unless norms are internalised by a particular individual there is no emotional sensitivity to shame and guilt, and ethics disappears as it is replaced by 'moral'.

Matter (Human Nature)

To live is to experience life, and living experience is embodied in matter. This living timed experience is the questing that moves the fluid matter of genes, proteins, pathways, cells, tissues, organs and, as the human organism moves, it makes and is made by its interaction with its material environment. In that ebb and flow of internal/external activity and connections, there are no genes (Noble 2006: 112). The unity of intactness and self-organising that comes naturally to all animals, this timed movement of complete embodiment by which living animals negotiate the physical world, is firstly a physical and then a social and narrative accomplishment. In matter we are firstly questing and secondly narrating our quests. We are neural, phenomenological and meaning–making humans (Lakoff and Johnson 1999; Varela et al. 1993) bound to and acting in the material world from which we cannot be detached. In our umbilical connections we begin to know living community and are then, born into languages. From this embryonic connection, we enter a web of narratives and, physically breaking off this mother–child connection, we are reconnected to the web of life: 'a cosmos of organic patterns of land, climate, vegetation, animals and man are interwoven in a vast web pulsating with life' (Richards 1999: 124).

By their timed movements animal bodies enter into the multiplicity and incommensurability of language and, in this entrance, they attain their bodies. For Lacan infants mature and come to have ownership of their bodies; we attain the body we already are, by the seen images of our own or others' bodies. The uncoordinated and uncertain child reaches out for the complete image of the mother because the mother possesses the coordinated unity, the sureness, that the child quests and this organic completeness becomes in the early months of childhood socially mediated and therefore always normative (Bernstein 2006: 49). Biological forms, bodies, become social constructions, which reconstruct the image of the animal body. Biological humans become bio-social and, on claiming ownership of the whole of their bodies, they maintain the normative integrity of their own and other bodies. I am my body. It is my dignity. I am not a story. My body connects me to your body. The dignity of the socially contingent person is nothing other than the integrity of the complete body that represents what must never be seen, dismembered bodies, bodies in fragments.

Form (Ways of Living)

Biologically and socially humans have various forms, unity-patterns of organisation, which mark them out as human. They have 'a certain range of power and tendencies, a repertoire, inherited and forming a fairly firm characteristic pattern' (Midgley 1995: 74) that is their human nature. By their human nature they move towards form A, to other patterns of organisation form B. Such a movement from A to B suggests a continuity of movement in which humans are incomplete and destined to experience living in the process of being 'in-between' forms, in the process of questing they are 'becoming'. Humans are complex living systems, not another form of matter such as dead DNA or machines; humans are biologically the same and socially different from each other.

Human cognition is animate and embodied minds create forms. The amoeba, as it quests, naturally categorises what it encounters into food and non-food, what it moves towards and what it moves away from (Lakoff and Johnson 1999: 13, 17). Humans also make patterns of organisation and they have a unique way of organising that makes them a form of animal, a human species-form, living a variety of different possible lives, 'life-forms' in which they think and act out a variety of different social roles, 'role-forms', thinking in a variety of different ways, 'thinking-forms', creating an infinite number of 'cognitive-forms'. So when thinking theoretically they construct theories, mimetically they construct performances, mechanistically they manufacture machines, and ethically they narrate, often completing their narratives into stories. In all these processes and forms humans never leave their bodies. They take their bodies with them as they construct conscious meanings from their experiences of living. Experiencing these different forms of living they move meaningfully towards those forms, which they construct as being good meaningful lives to live. Humans are ethical as they normatively construct narrative meanings of their animate quests.

LEAVING SOMETHING IMPORTANT UNSAID, SOME NECESSARY UNSPOKEN REMAINDER

In short Linstead and Westwood (2001: 332) suggest a linguistic lacuna that points to the limits of language. Although empty of language, this lacuna is not a vacuum. It contains human nature or, more precisely, the mystery of embodied humans being and becoming human. Nature, human or otherwise, cannot speak for itself. The timed movements of humans naturally seeking meaning of the mystery of their lives hold a normative silence broken by language. Unable to escape their biologies and biographies, self-organising humans naturally experience imperatives, normative goods, to do this and that, to live this life and not that life. Orientating actions and organising lives in infinite ways these normative goods are limitless and they speak to us (narrate) and move our bodies (quest). Immersed in the chaos of the different demands created by humans interacting with nature, inevitably, different individual constellations of normative goods collide, producing conscious conflict. Sensitive to normative disturbances in a regulatory moral orders, the organising 'oughts' of moral discourse, humans are hurt by these collisions and become conscious of who they are and ought to be in connection with others. Physically jolted by their emotional experiences humans become aware of their connectivity, their similarities and differences and their unconscious incomplete quests for the Good life. Normatively disturbed, they translate their quests into language. Ethics is made meaningful as humans transform their human quests into narratives and, in this 'narrative turn', humans know language's inability to organise life. They know language leaks.

Minimally, there are three features of human production that, because they escape organisation-is-language, leave narrative remainders: the residues of ethical dilemmas, translated losses of complex living movements and the ineffable Good life. Born into infinite human movements towards their Good lives in a perpetually changing world, humans create unsatisfied normative goods. In the normative disturbances of their ethical dilemmas (Hursthouse 1999: 43–87; Mason 1996; Sinnot-Armstrong 1988) they choose one constellation of normative goods over another and, in this choosing, they leave other normative goods unsatisfied. Opening one knocking door and its normative claims humans choose not to open other doors and therefore leave other normative demands unanswered. Second, seeking to make sense of life, humans turn to language and find it wanting. Desiring 'language-is-organisation' humans artificially and superficially create a linguistic order out of the chaos of the living movements of nature and, constructing these linguistic coherences, they translate the complexity of human living into narratives. An inadequate language trans/forms natural human quests for the Good life into ostensible coherent linguistic forms or patterns of organisation and language makers, seeking organising coherence, leave normative residues in their narrative efforts at 'organisation'. The complexity of living in between forms is, in its translation, made sensible and this incomplete narrative sense making also leaves narrative remainders. Third, questing the Good life and immersed in the normative power of particular moral discourse humans conduct. Self-disclosing and self-enacting in their particular moralities humans self-organise and self-organising they move towards their human production. The body stretches out and, in the process of moving closer and keeping their distance from the Good life, they are immersed in their particular moralities simultaneously conscious of an unknowable Good. Moving towards and never reaching the ineffable Good, humans are 'ethically' conscious of the incompleteness of narratives derived from particular moral discourses. 'Necessary unspoken remainders' are accumulated ethical reminders of past, present and future incomplete narratives, narrative remainders, of humans naturally questing the Good life.

Narrative remainders despite their normative silence, their speechlessness, make normative claims on our bodies. Life escapes representation and construction in language and yet the organising 'oughts' of living in and with nature are limitless. Questing and incomplete humans, in organising their lives, move and these movements cross over and mingle with the incomplete quests of other organisms. Every individual human ethical dilemma is an incomplete movement that emerges from being and becoming entangled with other different incomplete movements in nature.

Between this and that, between these 'oughts' and those 'oughts', incomplete and unresolved, each human movement is a natural questing that leaves 'oughts' behind. Nature lives and life is not motionless; it moves and all human living movements leave ethics in its wake. Entering and leaving the timed movements of others, every individual human movement mixes with other natural movements and, as these different natural movements mingle, there is 'normative turbulence'. Sensitive to these normative disturbances, ethics emerges as humans narrate their connected human natures. Ethics seeks to make human organisation, organisation-is-language and language-is-organisation, meaningful. Ethics moves in the normative silence created by autopoiesis and, knowing language's inability to organise the body, ethics struggles to create conscious meaning of humans' natural quests for the Good life. Questing and narrating leave narrative remainders that 'necessarily' remind us of our coexistence with others; non-linguistic residues that remind and organise, orientate and animate human lives. These residues, the fragmented 'oughts' of incomplete living movements, are a conscious reminder of language's limits, and orientate life's meaning.

Public moral goods, moral 'oughts', once internalised become private normative goods that 'ethically' point to an indeterminate future and endure in the present as tenuous memories of past experiences of language failing to organise life. These failings are conscious narrative remainders which normatively work on our bodies as guilt and shame (Fontaine et al. 2006; Lickel et al. 2005; Orth et al. 2006; Tracy and Robins 2006), achievements of success and joy, of living being incomplete, of being unable to speak the Good life and not being able to do both this and that, live this life and that life. This minimal threefold residue of language's inability to organise the living body is, collectively, the inescapable 'guilt context of living' (Bernstein 2001: 398) created by individual normative experiences of incomplete human productions. Individually, a product of the biological organisation of living things, autopoiesis, is the 'conscience' or the 'natural guide'

(Cottingham 2004: 25) that normatively pushes and pulls us, moves us, in different directions. By her conscience the morally sensitive HR practitioner, Joan, is ethical when she hears '*the monkey on the shoulder*', is emotionally aware of these reminders and, failing to move with these ethical reminders would be unnatural; she would be normatively deficient (Sherman 1990: 153). So managers necessarily and *naturally* pass '*monkeys*' onto Joan's shoulders and they 'wait for the monkey to come back suitably lightened and easy to carry. So I find by the time I go home I have quite a few monkeys on my shoulders and have to make some fairly serious decisions which is part of my job' (ibid.).

ORGANISING LIVING: A MOVING STORY

Despite appropriating Capra's system and its emphasis on bio-social human processes of being and becoming human, the word 'system' risks making 'human' an animal specimen of a particular form, a human biological kind, a 'Calcutec'. Systems evoke connections and relationships and potentially reduce the living individual and her/his processes of meaning construction to regulative principles that describe the operation of complex systems. Ethics is then regulated and deprived of its emotions and the emotional intensities of an individual consciously experiencing good and bad is lost. Material feelings, the body's immediate reaction to the fate of others, disappears into the dynamics of the 'System'. The processes of a complete and coherent 'system' replace spontaneous compassion and the history of ethics is transformed into a contemporary 'autopoiesis'. Consequently, below I recast the 'system' into a 'story' fashioned from the empirical narratives of HR practitioners and invite you, the reflexive reader, to participate emotionally in a particular managerial and human discourse that, paradoxically, transcends language and particular societies. It values the processes of the living body, its integrity, and the elimination of pain and suffering.

In the social conventions and traditions of language the significance of nature, planetary and human, is displaced. There is no common or ideal language available to all persons, therefore, moral language has as its reference point conventional moralities. Words are social conventions that have no normative compass that points to a common humanity and without a common humanity there is only insanity (Macmurray 1993: 9). We know each other subjectively and objectively, we know each other individually and as wo/men (Macmurray 1991: 40; 1993: xiv). In the 'Very Life of Things' Mullarkey (2007) acknowledges the similarities among Bergsonian metaphysics, biological self-organisation and complexity theory. In Bergsonian metaphysics metaphysic is movement, physics in process. This process is not singular, but a duality of movements that imply two ways of knowing. The first knowing is symbolic, relative and linguistic. It moves around the object. The second knowing is immanent, absolute and embodied. It enters us into the living object. Metaphysics becomes a serious knowing, *'just when it returns to life'* (ibid: xviii, emphasis original) and it enters life when it dispenses with symbols such as language. This second knowing experiences and sympathises with the object and, in the effort to experience the object and intuitively enter into it, we participate in its own becoming.

Responding to the other's recognition of the need to turn to metaphysics to understand human nature (MacIntyre 1999; Oderberg 2004: 161) and quests for the good life (Geus 2005: 78–86) I re-enter the movements of practitioners. By imagining from the centre (Harpham 1999: 261) of their human experiences of working in organisation-is-language of Human Resources Management (HRM), I compose a story of two living and organising movements. One organising movement, questing, is an open, inexhaustible, infinite, indivisible movement of knowing that moves towards the absolute, the unknowable Good life, which exists within the body and escapes translation in language. The second movement, narrating, is language-is-organisation and relatively closed. Expressed in symbols, this thinking movement reconstructs the body from the outside and whatever weight is attached to the artifices used to construct the object, such as visual diagrams, systems and stories, these human made artifices only describe shadows of the body (Bergson 2007: 13). Whereas Capra's system represents complexity with normative goods that travel across parts of a human system and integrates it with a holistic living nature, a web of life, this story also moves to create a whole. Moved by nature and moving, it moves inwards, to its narrative plot, towards its centre. 'I am the organisation' enters the very life of things by recreating, in Bergsonian terms, a dual unity of changing and complex movements; the absolute, knowing, and the relative, thinking. I narrate a story of a living body organising itself through a duality of relative and absolute changing movements towards the Good life, a human and integrated living nature that continuously changes. In the biology of knowing and in the sociology of thinking, questing and narrating, the living body organises itself with a duality of movements. Inescapably these biological and biographical movements are not constants; they change. An animal movement of questing and narrating becomes localised and disturbed by the painful anxieties of an ethical dilemma. In this emotional disturbance questing and narrating are transformed into self-enacting and self-disclosing. As the protagonist in the story naturally moves, she moves towards the consciously knowing, thinking, of her communal relations, and as she enters her co-becoming, the living body transforms itself. It becomes self–other enacting and self–other disclosing to return on its incompletion to different original forms of questing and narrating a new and transformed Good life. Perpetually changing and renewing its self as the Good life naturally guides and organises the living body and its processes, she is becoming human.

Mainly using the words of six HR practitioners, I create a composite empirical story of a human dilemma. Capra's dynamic system of human production is holistic and clear, but these strengths carry with them their weaknesses. The system loses particularity, ambiguity and a sense of the emotional turbulence experienced in living in between matter, meaning, process and form. At the edge of chaos and in their dilemmas, practitioners are continuously buffeted by those endless 'oughts', normative goods, of innumerable others. With the fables narrated by six HR practitioners, I imagine a story of their narratives of working in multiple organisations. These narrators did not refer to a single law, principle or deity that holistically organised their narratives. They did not associate ethics with a dominating reason, contract, duty, utility, virtue or specific singular Good that enabled them to resolve their dilemmas, assuage their guilt and shame and fill their linguistic lacunae. Instead their normative experiences were characterised by emergence, anxiety, emotions, uncertainty and incompleteness. There were no stories of SAT NAVS or Google Earths that holistically organised their mind maps and conclusively guided practitioners towards a clean and clear resolution of their ethical dilemmas. Without any commensurating principle or finite sets of unconditional goods to organise their complex human experiences, their narratives spoke of a thorough incommensurability of normative goods (Richardson 2004). What made its empirical appearance is a human animal spontaneously and compassionately moved and moving towards the Good life, and so in writing this empirical incomplete story, this moving fable of human production, I reconfirm:

> The history of ethics itself constitutes powerful evidence that ethics can never hope to resolve its internal difficulties and offer itself as a guide to the perplexed. Articulating perplexity, rather than guiding, is what ethics is all about. (Harpham 1999: 27)

IN/CONCLUSION

I am the Organisation

Evolving, ageing and continuously changing to remain the same, 'a constantly changing core' and 'wriggling line', she is a moving part of a moving living system that make normative claims on her movements towards her Good life. From the multiple forms of life that are humanly possible for her to live, she lives one life 'cos *of where I'm coming from*' and her '*history and ancestors*'. She is '*formulating her own kind of life*' that she finds impossible to express because she doesn't fall '*into any camp*'; she '*is Indian but not quite, British but not quite and therefore in the middle, not part of any of them*'. She lives one form of life and being, '*nothing in particular*'. She is transforming; constantly being and becoming by moving towards another form. In her '*sleepless nights*' she quests and unconsciously knows her 'oughts': '*Am I allowed to do that? Should I be doing that?*', and the 'oughts' of others who have '*a right to be themselves*'. Moving and entering the harmonious and disruptive movements of others she is, naturally, continuously quest/ioning herself '*Did I do the right thing? Did I make the right decision? Did I do the right thing for the wrong reasons?*' Experiencing the movements of others, she thinks that these normative demands insist she ought to transform her living into a life that '*fits in someone else's values*' and '*act in a way that isn't naturally*' her. Entering the movements of others she moves with and against her own quest and questing 'herself', she quest/ions her Good life. The Good life changes as she moves towards it. Sensitive to human polymorphic movements and their normative goods she becomes thoughtful. She thinks in language. She begins to narrate. She thinks of the discordant movements of others and consciously entering these movements she becomes anxious and, in this painful experience, seeks some form of order in her life. Starting to narrate her anxiety about '*what's right for her*' and '*worrying about the person that I was*' she is emotionally entering an organisation-is-language. Entering the institution that employs her: '*Do you "just" do what the organisation wants you to do or do you do what is right, or what you think is right in the context*' and leaves this organisational living as she feels '*a very deep pull towards India*'. In this entering and leaving of her local and national institutions she knows no borders between good and bad *because* '*everybody is doing it*' when they '*shouldn't be doing it*'; '*it becomes the nor*'. Beginning to narrate her life, she starts to make her identity. Becoming an HR practitioner, being '*expedient*', '*dealing with crap*' in the '*department of Truth and Lies*' and '*helping somebody to develop genuinely*' she is in a '*constant*' dilemma. She is '*rocked*' because she is constantly '*responding to someone else's values*'. '*Wrenched away*' from her '*emotional side*' and '*going against my principles, I had to go against my belief*' she conducts. Her dual movement of questing/narrating is transformed as she enters the moral institutional discourses that she knows and enables her to think and organise in language. In the moralities of her unique and individual experience, she changes. She conducts; questing and narrating become self-enacting and self-disclosing. In the regulatory moral 'oughts' dominated by economic imperatives that pay her to humanise and dehumanise herself and others she painfully self-enacts and self-discloses. Hurting from this rupture of her human nature, she makes her 'self' and others a '*contextual being*'.

In character, communal and institutional relationships she coexists and conducts with others. Remembering and forgetting her other conducts in which she failed and succeeded in satisfying the goods of others, she is continuously changing, twisting this way and that, arranging and accommodating her goods as others continuously adjust to her movements. Living her way of life with living others who are also moving towards their goods, inevitably, these relational and integrated human movements of chaotic goods collide. Co/becoming she is sensitive and, becoming conscious of colliding goods, she is ethically reminded of her other moral experiences and of those goods she is never satisfied. Spontaneously, her movements of questing and narrating are transformed. Self-enacting and self-disclosing she changes and, as she transforms, she becomes guilty and ashamed of being diverted from her dual movements of questing and narrating her Good life. Her *emerging dilemma* changes her as it emerges and, as it emerges, she starts transforming her anxiety into guilt and shame. In this emotional transformation, she increases her anxiety. In her emerging dilemma she seeks meaning to her life in an 'organisation-is-language' in which she is '*fearful for the future*'. In the dominating morality of the economic normative goods of her paid work to humanise by '*nurturing*', '*developing*' and '*creating the assets of the organisation and growing those assets'* that dehumanise others she experiences and witnesses moral and immoral movements. Buffeted by the normative demands of living movements that disconfirm her way of living, discordant goods that demand she is '*whiter than* white', and those that affirm it, concordant goods that make her '*stronger and shape decisions better*', and enable her to develop her '*as a person and as a professional as well*', she feels compelled to make discordant goods concordant with her quest for the Good life. Pausing in her natural movement towards the Good life, her nascent dilemma begins to appear as she enters 'language-is-organisation'.

A dilemma of anxiety emerges from her conscience and, as this dilemma emerges, she gives birth to a *nascent dilemma* of guilt and shame. She is reminded of her human nature and her natural questing for the Good life. In this nascent dilemma she is entwined in the movements of others and moving to disentangle her body from the living movements of others of which she is an inseparable part she reaches out for clarity and coherence in language. In this 'linguistic turn' of organisation she turns to language because she '*needs in her own life to reflect on what she did and why she is in the situation she is in and what she does next*'. In language she thinks and begins to translate her experiences of the emerging discord in the concord of her life. Confronted by wondrous and monstrous openings, she enters '*Dystopia*'. Frightened and beckoned, she has to escape the unknown. Questing and narrating she starts clarifying her life in language. She begins to make linguistic forms. Seeking meaning, she starts formulating her experience as a moral experience of '*getting into a club that you didn't want to get into, but now can't get out of it*', and organisational goods that are '*much like the 10 commandments, that is everywhere and goes in unconsciously*'. In the institutional '*eye of suspicion*' she identifies and narrates this nascent dilemma as a *narrated dilemma*. It is, for her, an 'HR ethical dilemma'.

In this 'HR ethical dilemma' she is naturally compelled towards self-enacting and self-disclosing her Good life and pausing with the question, can I live an ethical life being paid to dehumanise and humanise others? She becomes conscious of life forces in her life. In communion with living forces that connect her with infinite others, she is pushed and pulled by normative forces beyond language, and beyond her control. Simultaneously obliged and committed by these forces of good and bad, she must do this or that. Moving closer to '*Dystopia*' she must regain control. She must organise. She must move. She bifurcates; she is between linguistic forms A and B. She becomes '*schizophrenic*'; she self-enacts and self-discloses. In the morality of her schizophrenic experience she is self-disclosing and social and self-enacting she communes with human nature.

Interrupted in her questing and unstable, she self-discloses; she steps '*into the HR field you put on the coat of being an HR professional*' and in this public and private dressage (Jackson and Carter 1998) she is '*saying more than you are as an individual*'. Self-disclosing she begins to make sense of endless articulating pushing and pulling goods, which commit and oblige her towards different forms of living. Making sense of her life she carves out a field of having a '*core*' of '*what's right as a person*', '*fundamental personality*', of '*naturally being truthful and honest*', '*being true your self*', of '*worry about the person that I was*' and of '*reason as a comforting belief*'. With this linguistic field of goods she is integrated in the discursive movements of others. She moves to organise goods. Self-disclosing she temporarily and partially translates her Good life. She starts making sense; she wants to make coherent sense of her experience. In her self-disclosure she finally makes sense of her story but inadequate meaning of her life. Self-disclosing she is slowed down by narrating her moral identity but energised by her humanity. Simultaneously, '*urged*' by her coexistence, her co-becoming, and also '*rocked*' she is unstable and imaginatively productive. Intuitively, she continues to reach out for her Good life so she can cohere her narrative remainders, and make her life holistically meaningful. As she self-discloses, she simultaneously self-enacts.

Self-enacting in the morality of her particular experiences, she stretches out for her Good life and this animal movement is natural and unstoppable. She is conscious of the possible and impossible, the 'oughts' and 'cans and can'ts' in her life. She experiences inexhaustible and ineffable normative demands to do this or that about her coexistence in a material world. Unable to translate her normative anxiety, '*rocked*' by the organisational inadequacy of her language, a coherent but incomplete story, and reminded of other persistent and ineffable narrative remainders of '*movement and shuffles and things that happen to people*' she simultaneously experiences moral/ethical forces that push/pull her in infinite directions. In this field of '*ethical consequences*' she seeks meaning more than sense.

Self-enacting in her conduct, the particular and contingent circumstances of her dilemma, she is self-enacting her quest for the Good life and, in moving towards an uncertain Good she keeps her distance, and is held back by the limits of her language. Self-enacting the morality of her experience she organises and is organised by her experience. Inseparably connected to the movements of living forces, she is moved by her human experience and moves. She self-enacts her quest to be human. Self-enacting, she produces her humanity as a '*fundamental personality*', and autopoietically she arrives at her *telos*: '*I am the organisation*'. Self-enacting to organise the '*monkeys*' of her narrative remainders, she moves nearer and keeps her distance from her Good life, which she cannot self-disclose. Facing the unknown, its monsters and wonders, and seeking relief from her anxieties she moves imaginatively and productively towards an uncertain and ineffable Good life. Moving towards an unknown that cannot be identified, responding to normative demands of a moral discourse in which she is changing; she makes and is made by her social and material environment. Co be/ing and be/coming, self-other enacting and self-other disclosing, she bifurcates by moving concurrently in two different directions. Morally sensitive to her material conditions, her contingent personal and organisational life and its human possibilities, she bifurcates again. This time she bifurcates life, not language. At her '*crossroads*', in the between of life forms A and B she bifurcates by trans/forming her life. Choosing between multiple life forms A and B she decides on her '*kind of life*', life B, and leaves behind the normative demands of life A unanswered. Confronted by the normative demands of her immediate and particular personal life, her organisational life and other human possibilities she is pushed and pulled towards and away from her HR organised life. Ashamed of dehumanising others and witnessing the dehumanisation of others as she lives her HR life, she believes she copes with her human shame by covering it, dressing it in language. Covered in language she is released from her monsters and wonders and, safe from the chaos presented by her linguistic lacunae, she breaks its normative silence. She makes therapeutic sense of her life (Phillips 1986). By narrating, she partially convinces herself of her ability to leave life, she can if she wishes abstract from her human relations. She believes she can uncouple her material and embodied co-existence. She can arrest her co-becoming. She makes herself sovereign: '*I don't feel the need to detach myself*'.

But she never relieves herself of her normative anxieties. Translating experiences that refuse translation (losses in translation), aware of unconscious and conscious normative demands which she does not choose (residues of ethical dilemmas) and she cannot and ought not to narrate (an ineffable Good life), she is continuously committed and obliged to move. She has a human conscience. She is sensitive to traces of unorganised human movements and normative demands: demands that are '*always around us*', '*lurking around somewhere*', '*everywhere*' and '*they go in unconsciously*'. Aware of these narrative remainders she narrates. Identifying and translating her experience but unable to identify and organise her life into a coherent form, a coherent thought, she knows she leaves these narrative and normative 'oughts' behind her as she moves forward in her questing. Constantly, on edge she knows she is unable to reconcile the 'demands of her job' with the 'demands of her Good life'. Paralysed by organisation-is-language and language-is-organisation she is, in this powerful discourse of 'organisation', made helpless. In organisation-is-language she is in an organisational discourse that suggests she is a social text and in language-is-organisation she is persuaded she is sovereign; she can organise; she can make sense of her organisational life. She can think all that she knows. In the dressage of language she clothes and masks her body. She is linguistically fashionable but without an ethical life-line by which she can make her life in 'organisation' meaningful. Disembodied, she has no normative material compass. She is the 'lifeless body, a cadaver' of the language of 'organisation'. In language her embodied life of making and being made human has less, not more meaning.

ACKNOWLEDGEMENTS

This work has developed from comments and conversations with numerous individuals. However, I owe a particular debt to Mary Golden, Jon Baggot and John Thompson at the Thames Valley University. Generous with their time and gentle with their feedback, this chapter would not have been possible outside their academic community.

REFERENCES

Adams, G. 1934. 'What Makes Possibility Possible?' in G. Adams (ed.), *University Publications in Philosophy*, Vol. 17, pp. 1–24. London: Cambridge University Press.

Adorno, T. 1973. *Negative Dialectics*. New York: Seabury Press.

————. 2005. *Minia Moralia: Reflections on a Damaged Life*. London: Verso.

Adorno, T. and M. Horkheimer. 1997. *Dialectic of Enlightenment*. London: Verso.

Appiah, K. 2005. *The Ethics of Identity*. Oxford: Princeton University Press.

Aristotle. 1976. *The Ethics of Aristotle: The Nicomachean Ethics* (translated by J. Thomson). London: Penguin.

Bauman, Z. 1993. *Postmodern Ethics*. Oxford: Blackwell.

Benhabib, S. 1992. *Situating the Self: Gender, Community and Postmodernism in Contemporary Ethics*. Cambridge: Polity Press.

Bergson, H. 2007. 'An Introduction to Metaphysics', in J. Mullarkey and M. Kolkman (eds), *Henri Bergson: An Introduction to Metaphysics*, pp.1–54. Basingstoke: Palgrave Macmillan.

Bernstein, J. 2001. *Adorno: Disenchantment and Ethics*. Cambridge: Cambridge University Press.

Bernstein, J. 2006. 'Intact and Fragmented Bodies: Versions of Ethics "after Auschwitz"', *New German Critique*, 97: 31–53.

Brink, D. 1990. 'Rational Egoism, Self and Others', in O. Flanagan and A. Rorty (eds), *Identity, Character and Morality: Essays in Moral Psychology*. Cambridge, MA: MIT Press.

Capra, F. 1996. *The Web of Life: A New Synthesis of Mind and Matter*. London: Harper Collins.

———. 2003. *The Hidden Connections: A Science of Sustainable Living*. London: Flamingo.

———. 2005. 'Complexity and Life', *Theory, Culture and Society*, 22(5): 33–44.

Cooper, R. 2001. 'Un-Timely Mediations: Questing Thought', *Ephemera*, 1(4): 321–47.

———. 2005. 'Peripheral Vision: Relationality', *Organization Studies*, 26(11): 1689–710.

———. 2006. 'Making Present: Autopoiesis as Human Production', *Organization*, 13(1): 59–81.

Cottingham, J. 2004. 'Conscience, "Nature", and Moral Experience', in D. Oderberg and T. Chappell (eds), *Human Values: New Essays on Ethics and Natural Law*, pp. 798–817. London: Palgrave.

Dawkins, R. 2006. *The God Delusion*. London: Transworld Publishers.

Fontaine, J., P. Luyten, P. Boeck, J. Corveleyn, D. Herrera, A. Ittzes and T. Tomcsanyi. 2006. 'Untying the Gordian Knot of Guilt and Shame', *Journal of Cross Cultural Psychology*, 37(3): 273–92.

Gerhardt, C. 2006. 'The Ethics of Animals in Adorno and Kafka', *New German Critique*, 97: 159–78.

Geus, R. 2005. *Outside Ethics*. Princeton: Princeton University Press.

Glover, J. 2001. *Humanity: A Moral History of the Twentieth Century*. London: Yale Note Bene.

Harpham, G. 1999. *Shadows of Ethics: Criticism and the Just Society*. Durham, NC: Duke University Press.

Hursthouse, R. 1999. *On Virtue Ethics*. Oxford: Oxford University Press.

Hutchens, B. 2004. *Levinas: A Guide to the Perplexed*. London: Continuum.

Jackson, N. and P. Carter. 1998. 'Labour as Dressage' in A. Mckinlay and K. Starkey (eds), *Foucault, Management and Organization Theory*, pp. 49–64. London: Sage Publications.

Jones, C., M. Parker and R. ten Bos. 2005. *For Business Ethics*. London: Routledge.

Lakoff, G. and M. Johnson. 1999. *Philosophy in the Flesh: The Embodied Mind and its Challenge to Western Thought*. New York: Basic Books.

Lickel, B., T. Schmader, M. Curtis, M. Scarnier and D. Ames. 2005. 'Vicarious Shame and Guilt', *Group Processes & Intergroup Relations*, 8(2): 145–57.

Linstead, S. 2001. 'Rhetoric and Organizational Control: A Framework for Analysis', in R. Westwood and S. Linstead (eds), *The Language of Organization*, pp. 217–40. London: Sage Publications.

Linstead, S. and R. Westwood. 2001. 'Meaning Beyond Language? Monstrous Openings', in R. Westwood and S. Linstead (eds), *The Language of Organization*, pp. 329–47. London: Sage Publications.

MacIntyre, A. 1999. *Dependent Rational Animals. Why Human Beings Need Virtues.* London: Duckworth.

Mackie, J. 1977. *Ethics: Inventing Right and Wrong.* London: Penguin.

Macmurray, J. 1991. *Persons in Relation.* London: Humanities Press International.

———. 1993. *Conditions of Freedom.* Atlantic Highlands, NJ: Humanities Press.

Maritain, J. 1964. *Moral Philosophy: An Historical and Critical Survey of Great Systems.* London: Geffrey Bles.

Mason, H. 1996. *Moral Dilemmas and Moral Theory.* Oxford: Oxford University Press.

Maturana, H. and F. Varela. 1998. *The Tree of Knowledge: The Biological Roots of Human Understanding* (revised edition). London: Shambhla.

Metz, T. 2002. 'Recent Work on the Meaning of Life', *Ethics*, 112: 781–814.

Midgley, M. 1995. *Beast and Man: The Roots of Human Nature.* London: Routledge.

Mullarkey, J. 2007. 'The Very Life of Things: Thinking Objects and Reversing Thought in Bergsonian Metaphysics', in J. Mullarkey and M. Kolkman (eds), *Henri Bergson: An Introduction to Metaphysics*, pp. ix–xxxiv. Basingstoke: Palgrave Macmillan.

Murakami, H. 2003. *Hard Boiled Wonderland and The End of the World.* London: Vintage.

Nancy, J. 1991. *The Inoperative Community.* Oxford: Oxford University Press.

Nietzsche, F. 1997. *Beyond Good and Evil: Prelude to a Philosophy of the Future.* New York: Dover Publications.

Nishida, K. 1990. *An Inquiry into the Good* (translated by H. Abe and C. Ives). London: Yale University Press.

Nussbaum, M. 2001. *The Fragility of Goodness: Luck and Ethics in Greek Tragedy and Philosophy.* Cambridge: Cambridge University Press.

Noble, D. 2006. *The Music of Life: Biology Beyond the Genome.* Oxford: Oxford University Press.

Oakeshott, M. 1975. *On Human Conduct.* Oxford: Clarenden Press.

Oderberg, D. 2004. 'The Structure and Content of the Good', in D. Oderberg and T. Chappell (eds), *Human Values: New Essays on Ethics and Natural Law*, pp.127–65. London: Palgrave.

O'Doherty, D. 2007. 'Organization: Recovering Philosophy' in C. Jones and R. ten Bos (eds), *Philosophy and Organization*, pp. 21–38. London: Routledge.

Orth, U., M. Berking and S. Burkhardt. 2006. 'Self-Conscious Emotions and Depression: Rumination Explains Why Shame But Not Guilt is Maladaptive', *Society for Personality & Social Psychology*, 32(12): 1608–19.

Overell, S. 2008. 'Inwardness: The Rise of Meaningful Work', *The Work Foundation, Provocation Series*, 4(2): 1–54.

Pettit, P. 1994. 'Liberal/Communitarian: MacIntyre's Mesmeric Dichotomy', in J. Horton and S. Mendus (eds), *After MacIntyre: Critical Perspectives on the Work of Alasdair MacIntyre*, pp. 176–204. London: Polity Press.

Phillips, D. 1986. 'Authenticity or Morality', in. R. Kruschwitz and R. Roberts (eds), *The Virtues: Contemporary Essays on Moral Character*, pp. 22–35. Belmont: Wadsworth.

Prince, S. 2004. 'Discourse of Pictures: Iconicity and Film Studies', in L. Braudy and M. Cohen (eds), *Film Theory and Criticism*, pp. 187–205. Oxford: Oxford University Press.

Richards, R. 1999. 'Darwin's Romantic Biology: The Foundations of His Evolutionary Ethics,' in J. Maichenschein and M. Ruse (eds), *Biology and the Foundation of Ethics*, pp. 113–53. Cambridge: Cambridge University Press.

Richardson, H. 1994. *Practical Reasoning About Final Ends*. Cambridge: Cambridge University Press.

———. 2004. 'Incommensurability and Basic Goods: A Tension in the New Natural Law Theory' in D. Oderberg and T. Chappell (eds), *Human Values: New Essays on Ethics and Natural Law*, pp. 70–101. London: Palgrave.

Ricoeur, P. 1991. 'Life in Quest of a Narrative', in D. Wood (ed.), *On Paul Ricoeur: Narrative and Interpretation*, pp. 20–33. London: Routledge.

———. 1994. *Oneself as Another*. London: University Press.

Ridley, M. 1996. *The Origins of Virtue*. London: Penguin.

Rorty, R. 1999. *Philosophy and Social Hope*. London: Penguin.

Schumacher, E. 1977. *A Guide to the Perplexed*. London: Harper Perennial.

Scrutton, R. 1997. *Modern Philosophy: An Introduction and Survey*. London: Arrow Books.

Sherlock, K. 2002. 'Community Matters: Reflection From the Field', *Sociological Research* 7(2): 1.1–7.8. Online, http: www.socresonline.org.uk/7/2/sherlock.html (Downloaded 28/6/04).

Sherman, N. 1990. 'The Place of Emotions in Kantian Morality', in O. Flanagan and A. Rorty (eds), *Identity, Character and Morality. Essays in Moral Psychology*, pp. 149–70. Cambridge, MA: MIT Press.

Singer, P. 1999. *A Darwinian Left*. London: Yale University Press.

Sinnot-Armstrong, W. 1988. *Moral Dilemmas*. Oxford: Oxford University Press.

Spragen, T. 1995. 'Communitarian Liberalism' in A. Etzioni (ed.), *New Communitarian Thinking: Persons, Virtues, Institutions and Communities*, pp. 37–51. Charlotsville, VA: University Press of Virginia.

Swanton, C. 2003. *Virtue Ethics: A Pluralist View*. Oxford: Oxford University Press.

Tracy, J. and R. Robins. 2006. 'Appraisal Antecedents of Shame and Guilt: Support for a Theoretical Model', *Society for Personality and Social Psychology*, 32(10): 1339–51.

Trivers, R. 2006. 'Foreword to the first edition', in R. Dawkins (ed.), *The Selfish Gene*, 30th Anniversary edition, pp. xix–xx. Oxford: Oxford University Press.

Varela, F., E. Thompson and E. Rosh. 1993. *The Embodied Mind: Cognitive Science and Human Experience*. London: MIT Press.

Vogel, S. 1996. *Against Nature: The Concept of Nature in Critical Theory*. Albany, NY: State University New York Press.

Weick, K. 1995. *Sensemaking in Organizations*. London: Sage Publications.

Westwood, R. and S. Linstead. 2001. 'Language/Organization: Introduction', in R. Westwood and S. Linstead (eds), *The Language of Organization*, pp. 1–19.London: Sage Publications.

Whitely, C. 1970. 'On defining moral', in G. Wallace and A. Walker (eds), *The Definition of Morality*, pp. 141–60. London: Methun and Company.

Williams, B. 1995. 'Replies', in J. Altham and R. Harrison (eds), *World, Mind, and Ethics: Essays on the Ethical Philosophy of Bernard Williams*, pp. 185–224. Cambridge: Cambridge University Press.

7

PERPLEXING IMAGES: RELATIONAL IDENTITIES IN CULTURAL *TEMPOSPACES*

Sławomir Jan Magala

Relational identities involve weaving our "red thread" of personal identity through the rich texture of social processes in cultural 'tempospaces'.

Do we want to understand how relational identities can be developed without too much fear, control and awe vis-à-vis sovereign professional bureaucracies but with individual moral sensitivity and responsibility of creative social entrepreneurs?

We might as well risk replacing robust identities guaranteed by professional bureaucracies and ideologically protected from new social movements on the one hand and market pricing mode of building relationships on the other.

Universalism is implicated in both imperial schemes to control the world and liberatory mobilizations for justice and empowerment. Universalism inspires expansion— for both the powerful and the powerless.
(Tsing 2005: 9)

I am very excited about the idea of a relational self. (...) if the first period of Enlightenment—which solidified the concept of the self-contained individual—brought forth democracy, public education, and human rights, then what flowering of practices may now be anticipated?
(Gergen 1999: 138)

All identities are equally relational and relative, but not all of them are equally salient and relevant in all social contexts and during all individual projects. Some are more robust (influencing more of an individual's decisions) and fertile (facilitating creation of better networks and organisations), while some degenerate and decline more easily, spawning antisocial networks (such as mafias, drug cartels) and pathological organisations (ENRON). All identities change, although social sciences do not provide precise answers to the question 'how do they change?' Historical mutability of cultural identities has frequently been an object of historical studies (how did ethnic groups become ideological nationals of nation-states, how did various employees of industrial companies become ideological members of working class parties, and so on) but transformations of collective and individual identities are still an under-researched domain of social studies. Are newer collective identities more conclusive, inclusive and/or exclusive than the more traditional ones? Do they allow more tolerance of personal identities? Is there a progress in the construction of more egalitarian relational identities and in facilitating more tolerance towards them?

Identities matter, but they should not be studied according to positivist essentialism (let thousand qualitative methodologies bloom, let quasi-monopolies of the 'one and only scientific truth' disappear) and they should not be packaged as neutral knowledge constructs while contributing to the sustainability of global inequalities and negative national, racial, gender or religious stereotyping. We should be more aware of the fact that we socialise ourselves into acceptance of inequalities. We do so usually in a tacit way, as we interact, communicate and reflect on how we relate and to whom. We do so usually weaving our 'red thread' of personal identity through the rich texture of social processes in cultural *tempospaces*. Relational identities are much more flexible and hybrid than 'essentialist' ones. Relational identities are much more mutable and reversible than a collectivist and job-centred approach implies. If there is a progress in social construction of identities, then it is to be found in increasing competence in tracing tacit exclusions and accepted negative stereotypes, in exposing them and overcoming their consequences. Norbert Elias had once studied the evolution of table manners and summed this process up as a 'civilising' process—nobody had tried to sum the other manners, for instance sexual ones, from the same point of view. Is there a progress in a social construction of our sexual personae? If there is progress in social construction of identities, then it is to be found in growing courage to test emotionally safeguarded identities against evolving relationships, increasing inequalities and shifting domains of relevance.

The 'state of the art' image of progress, of the idea, of the vision and of the construction of 'sustainable and desirable progress' is perplexing indeed. A brief survey of the idea of universal humanist values slowly but surely implemented in increasingly egalitarian institutions and in increasingly inclusive rules for interactions makes us uneasy. Even if we apply new creative ontologies of social being understood as 'becoming' rather than 'being', we are still ill at ease. We keep trying to capture the ebb and flow of social processes (social processes flowing through time and space, through *tempospaces* thus, are simply what is usually labelled 'society' tout court). Even then, however, a very brief survey of such ideas (linear or spiral ascendance to the heaven of the end of history) still makes us uneasy. Rousseau did not become obsolete at all. Man and woman are still born free but everywhere they are in chains. The Enlightenment project is still unfinished, deadlines long forgotten, plans still far from completed, designs abandoned, re-engineered, re-juvenated, re-advertised. The grand edifice of a just and fair society is still under construction. The scaffoldings are still around the social institutions, and they are still in use because we are changing institutions according to our changing designs.

In social life, nothing signals sudden invention and rapid arrival of the best possible institutional design (there is no 'halo' around the best historically achievable design for social institutions). Movements are still being born, but professional bureaucracy working through formal hierarchies of managed organisations is more dominant than ever. There is some hope for genuine success in the battle for recognition and democratic inclusion with respect to some socially defined minorities (women in professional bureaucracies, African Americans in the USA, environmentalists in sustainability politics). Apocalypse can be postponed. The end of history came and went, while we are still talking of Michelangelo and Kant, Bartolomeo de las Casas and Shakespeare. Work of designing better social forms and implementing those designs goes on, while changing teams of architects, urbanists, visionaries, politicians, craftsmen and volunteers, critics and defenders, artists and researchers, media wizards and therapeutic coaches mill around, reinforce some scaffoldings, break down the others. How to find our way in this world in the making? We are used to metaphors of maps and navigation, which we live by in explaining how to 'make our way in the world' (Archer 2007). But we are also increasingly aware of the perverse continuity of inequalities and of their exploitation under the new guises (Sennett 2003). Colonialism gave way to the liberation of the Third World's nation-states from European rule, but 'Third World' turned into 'emergent economies' under creeping neocolonialism. Ghana and Kenya are represented in the United Nations, but still Morocco and The Philippines deliver underpaid domestics rather than fellow teachers and researchers to the

European shores, low skill labourers rather than inventors, investors and patent-holders (cf. Eicher and Turnovsky 2003; Memmi 2006). Racism and sexism are more morally repulsive than ever before, but still there are more white male professionals in the upper ranks of corporate and public bureaucracies than black females, black males or white females. *Et puis ça change, plus c'est la meme chose* (The more it changes, the more it remains the same).

The above judgement could only have been made with the help of a value system, a justification scheme, an ideological 'audit' measuring socioeconomic and sociocultural realities to our value-laden visions and criteria of successful practice (cf. Boltanski and Thevenot 2006). We may notice, ironically, that traditional humanist navigational devices, solid middle-class novels, of the Bildungsroman type (established from Cervantes to Mann and from Balzac to Coetzee), have stepped back from centre stage of our perceptive attention. When is it that a politician has last quoted Orhan Pamuk or Ryszard Kapuscinski? When did the secretary general of the United Nations quote Dereck Walcott or Wislawa Szymborska? Novels and poems used to be mirrors walking down the city streets and roaming the country roads according to the French definition. They used to determine the moral climate in which moral judgements have been made. 'All happy families resemble one another' wrote Tolstoy on the first page of *Anna Karenina*, but 'all unhappy families are unhappy in their own way'. This is a clearly formulated principle of moral falsificationism, which Popper introduced to philosophy one century later. If you want to understand human values and identities, you should study their failures, since case studies of failures to live up to one's dreams and expectations deliver more useful knowledge and even more useful pragmatic warnings than success stories. Dostoyevsky imagined a meeting between the Grand Inquisitor standing for the multinational corporation of a Catholic Church and Jesus Christ who stands for the core message of Christianity. They talk, and the Grand Inquisitor asks Jesus to leave the project of salvation to the church professionals: they are better in dealing with human individuals fearing freedom and independence. Christianity, according to the author of *Brothers Karamazov*, is as unfinished a project as Enlightenment is (the latter being but a slightly secularised version of the former). The moral climate of the epoch could not remain uninfluenced by these and other novels about imperfect search for personal and collective identity. Hans Castorp of *The Magic Mountain* (*Der Zauberberg*) by Thomas Mann went to the trenches of World War I leaving Settembrini and Naphta to battle for his soul. 'Soul' was a nickname for social identity torn between middle class liberalism and working class Bolshevism as recipes for the future that works. Benedetto Croce inspired Mann to create the character of Settembrini, while Gyorgy Lukacs, a Marxist with a mix of Jesuit charm and Bolshevik ruthlessness prompted the character of Naphta. Those two, a liberal and a humanist, and a Jesuit and a Bolshevik fought for Castorp's citizen's soul. Yossarian emerged from World War II in Joseph Heller's *Catch 22* to issue a stern warning against the 'military–industrial complex' of professional bureaucracies closing around individual liberties as a seamless spider's web. Both Dwight Eisenhower's warning against the 'military–industrial complex' and Heller's warning against 'catch 22' of state bureaucracies were sounded in 1961. Political identities had still been frozen through the Cold War, but a thaw had been eroding them both east and west of the iron curtain.

Novels are still being written and read after 2000 and Nobel prizes in literature go to the best authors who pen them. But are novels and poems also consulted for charting one's way through life, for one's personal self-coaching project, for career pathing and balanced quality of working, family and beyond? Have they perhaps withdrawn to the niches for the retired, the overeducated, the professionals, the middle class, the feminine, those who can afford sophisticated leisure, high-brow cultural consumption and conscious life-style self-styling?

Have these solid novels—as far as majority of social groups exposed to publishers' advertising are concerned—given way to visually overloaded telecommunications in networked global villages, which claim our attention without a break, ready to catch us through a mobile phone or portable laptop or liquid screen in public spaces any time any place any way? If so, no need to herd us into Plato's cave anymore—we have herded and shepherded ourselves, we have escaped from our freedoms to explore social realities and bonds in new relationships hidden in our social imaginaries. We have eagerly embraced the multimedia miracle, mystery and authority reinforced by spin doctors and delivered instantly 24 by 7. After all, we voluntarily wear our chains of instant availability and receptivity. We carry our mobile miniaturised individual chains with us and settle into cave-like dimly-lit cavities of car or airplane seats, office chairs or sweet home couches switching on the multimedia connections, zapping and zipping, unzapping and unzipping to our heart's delight. Linking up to these instant communications we switch on our mobile portable navigational devices as if we were told to do so by an invisible hand of the Panopticon master disguising his decisions as caprices of conspicuous, random fashion.

These new media offer instant navigational maps through realities (Castells 2001). But they spread as many stereotypes and sustain as many biases and prejudices as they prick with occasional critical insights (Joselit 2007). Hence they provoke critical mobilisation (Fischer 2003; Jenkins et al. 2003). Will the critical mass suffice for major paradigmatic shifts in mapping, coding and interpreting social processes to emerge and by doing so, facilitate critical deconstruction and dismantling of tacit stereotypes? There are some grounds to suspect that the processes of emergence of the alternative paradigmatic options have accelerated, particularly compared to the past experiences of successful marginalisation of alternative option providers. But there are also some grounds for suspicion that the exploitation of (s)lower classes continues unabated and these new critical research projects, new identities available for social scientists and humanist scholars, are still neutralised and marginalised as successfully as ever before. In order to see how it happens let us compare the critical identities in social research of the 1920s and 1930s with the present predicament of critical theories of managerial practices.

Among the alternative 'paradigmatic option providers' the representatives and contemporaries of the 'critical theory' of the Frankfurt School loom large. Among them Walter Benjamin merits attention as one of the most fascinating and most successfully marginalised critics of the emergent mass media. In the 1920s Walter Benjamin wrote about the inevitable loss of an aura of a work of art in the age of this work's mechanical reproduction (for the early English version of the famous essay, see Benjamin 1969). In the 1920s another rebellious German author, more interested in drama than art criticism, more in mobilising the masses than entertaining the bourgeois, Bertolt Brecht, wrote about the egalitarian, participatory and democratic road, which had not been taken at this crucial point, when radio entered the communicating *tempospaces*.[1] Brecht called for a radical departure from the development of the radio as a machine for distributing the views of the rich and the powerful (Brecht 2000). He urged the politically organised masses to start organising listeners as suppliers of the 'contents' of social communications. Brecht's views attracted hardly any attention and they had been resuscitated only after analogies with the Internet became clear at the turn of the 21st century to some of the more perceptive art and literary critics. Both Benjamin and Brecht were marginalised by history and driven out of Germany and Europe by the Nazis. Benjamin remained marginal until his death, hovering on the edges of the Frankfurt School, which itself remained a marginal voice in Germany and subsequently in the US academia. Brecht remained hesitating between disgust with the McCarthy hearings on the one hand (he had a wartime episode in Hollywood) and with Soviet tanks crushing East German Berlin revolt of 1953 (he ground his teeth and stayed in East Berlin, a loyalty rewarded by the communists with the Stalin Peace Prize) on the other. Benjamin committed suicide in 1940 and had been rediscovered in the last two decades of the 20th century by the postmodernist authors, for whom his 'passages' became a work of postmodernism *avant la lettre*, primarily in theory of literature, philosophy of culture and aesthetics. Brecht's ambiguous flirt with the communist party drove him into semi-oblivion, in spite of the relative popularity of *The Threepenny Opera* (Jack the Knife tune) or disturbing actuality of *Mother Courage* (war and business and what they do to the human heart). In short, their maps are not readily available in amazon.coms of the early 21st century. Which maps are easier to come by, then?

The answer is both older and newer. First, the metaphor with the novel as a walking mirror should be partly resuscitated. Novels are being written and they do matter. In the fall of 2008, when the text of the present chapter had been drafted, readers could navigate through the world as mirrored in Philip Roth's *Indignation*, John Updike's *The Widows of Eastwick*, Coetzee's *Diary of a Bad Year* and Alaa Al Aswany's *Chicago*. Readers of Roth would be able to see the frustration of a Jewish immigrant, whose upward social mobility is thwarted by the Korean war. They would see drafting to the army of those who failed to be saved by the university as a powerful mechanism for controlling the poor and undereducated inside the USA. They would see analogies among the Korean, Vietnam and Iraq wars in terms of their domestic uses discovered, sustained and promoted by the power elites:

> and that was it for the butcher's son, dead three months short of his twentieth birthday—Marcus Messner, 1932–1952, the only one of his classmates unfortunate enough to be killed in the Korean War, which ended with the signing of an armistice agreement on July 27, 1953, eleven full months before Marcus, had he been able to stomach chapel and keep his mouth shut, would have received his undergraduate degree from Winesburg College—more than likely as class valedictorian—and thus have postponed learning what his uneducated father had been trying so hard to teach him all along: of the terrible, the incomprehensible way one's most banal, incidental, even comical choices achieve the most disproportionate result. (Roth 2008: 231)

Readers of Updike and Coetzee would see the decline of the middle-class paradise designed as a version of 'consumer immortality', with increasingly older and despairing 'western citizens' watching decay of their 'best' West and the gradual but unstoppable arrival of their feared barbarian 'Rest'. They would recognise the melancholy of opulent decadence of the western consumer unable to exercise the role of a versatile and active citizen of 'the west', while the long march upwards of 'the rest' reorients global flows. Coetzee lets his porte-parole, an ageing white male novelist, try to measure up to Tolstoy and Dostoyevsky:

> Only now, late in life, do I begin to see how ordinary people, Nitezsche's bored higher animals, really cope with their environment. They cope not by becoming irritated but by lowering their expectations. They cope by learning to sit through things, by letting the mental machinery run at a slower rate. They slumber and because they do not mind slumbering they do not mind being bored. (Coetzee 2007: 219)

Readers of Al Aswany would see long and painful way of Egyptian students at the US universities towards a recognition and acceptance in an open society in spite of and beyond old and new biases hammered by the media into our willing eyes, ears and noses (the role of the smell of oriental spices in sustaining Western racist bias towards the immigrants is hard to underestimate). These readers would agree with the moral condemnation of the long shadow cast by the authoritarian regimes of 'the rest' onto those young members of their nation-states who were sent to study in 'the west':

> Nothing can replace a people's need for self-governance, as was shown during the various decolonization movements. They must recover their wealth and, to do that, begin by freeing themselves of the raïs and caudillos, the putchists and accomplices of the privileged, internal and external, of their leader maximo, the comic title given to Fidel Castro, and their 'supreme combatants', the paranoid title assumed by ageing Bourguiba, along with the political imams and compensatory myths that perpetuate stagnation, and, sometimes, regression. Only a rediscovered freedom will create an environment where a pragmatic balance can be maintained between economic liberalism and a centralized economy based on actual circumstances and the specific needs of all individuals. (Memmi 2006: 139–40)

Second, mirror had been turned back onto the authors of the post-novelist navigation systems, namely the coaches of modern princes, that is ourselves, academic researchers and teachers in schools of business. We are the primary (and the preferred) professional producers of certified 'business managers'. Our graduates, according to our commercial advertising, should be capable of working both with private firms and inside (preferably on top of) public authorities. Their credentials signal their potential competence in running governance structures and networks—large, small and medium, female friendly, antiracist, diversity-promoting, next door and around the globe. In the official publication of the mainstream academic, Western-centred, imperially US-focused Academy of Management—'The Academy of Management Review'—this competence is being questioned in a paper entitled, quite tellingly, 'Mirror, mirror on the wall: *Culture's Consequences* in a value test of its own design' (Ailot 2008) and in a paper questioning the concept of distance in drawing maps of organisational realities entitled 'From "Distance" to "Friction": Substituting Metaphors and Redirecting Intercultural Research' (Shenkar et al. 2008). Both texts are part of a special topic forum on 'international management; critique and new directions' edited by Gavin Jack, Marta Calas, Stella Nkomo and Tuomo Peltonen.

The contrast between early warnings of the 1920s, which had been marginalised within a conservative academic establishment (and survived by clinging to the less conservative artistic and literary bohème) and recent warnings, which are voiced on the main stage of professional communications among those who shape the minds (of those, who will be running professional bureaucracies and thus shaping social realities in future), could not have been greater. Moreover, the publication coincided with a financial meltdown triggered by the US sub-prime mortgage loan market, which bankrupted large banks and reintroduced government intervention into 'free markets', putting an abrupt end to the neoliberal ideology presenting globalisation as the surrender of all localities and communities to the universal wisdom of multinational corporations in their global search for shareholders' bliss. In this context, the tendencies, which had already emerged throughout the 1990s and in the first eight years of the 21st century, became clear to those of academic professionals who:

> ...reflect on some of the changes between the 1960s and 1990s sciences as institutional enterprises, sketching three areas of difference: the ethics and institutional context of science; the way in which activists of all sorts, including scientists, become media players, complicating questions of who speaks for whom; and the palimpsest of continuities and differences between the human biology research projects (population genetics, sociobiology, human genome diversity project, health and epidemiological transition) of the 1960s and the 1990s. The differences ... have to do as well with the increasing pressure for the participation of publics in decision making about scientific research that affects their welfare: a pressure towards accountability, if not transparency. (Fischer 2003: 25)

This hypothesis had been stated in an academic book in 2003 and had been read by a limited number of fellow-researchers and students of cross-cultural encounters in the postcommunist world. It would have remained tucked away in a relatively academic segment of social communications, without the spillover effect into other areas, those areas, where more direct influence is exercised upon the making of the managers and the managing of organisations. However, only five years later, in the autumn of 2008, a number of top academic researchers launched the special topic forum on international management as a domain defined within the professional community of academic researchers/teachers in the sciences of management and published it in *The Academy of Management Review. AMR* is a mainstream publication of the dominant organisational platform (Academy of Management annual conference) inside the hegemonic power in contemporary academic world. The Academy of Management annual conference always—well, almost always since the 2010 meeting is planned in Montreal—takes place in one of the US cities. In an attempt to rescue the relevance of academic research in times of the financial meltdown and a dramatic breakdown of the neoliberal ideology of globalisation, Homi Bhabha and Antonio Gramsci had been mobilised, along with Edward Said, Jacques Derrida, Michel Foucault and the others (cf. Frenkel 2008; Levy 2008). It is not hard to see why Gramsci had been resuscitated; his idea of an ideological hegemony as an important mechanism of social control and his idea of a collective prince as a flexible agency for political change outlived historical materialism of the 1930s and are as attractive for contemporary critics of commercial advertising and political propaganda as they had been for the Marxist opposition to Mussolini in Italy before World War II. Equally important is the attempt to analyse globalisation 'from below', from empirically accessible power struggles and cultural influences 'on the ground'. In particular, the concepts of *mimicry, hybridity* and the *third space,* as introduced by the 'postcolonialist' author, Homi Bhabha (the author of *Nation and Narration* and 'DissemiNation', cf. Bhabha 1994, 1996) are picked up from the side alley of global research networks (parked under 'the postcolonial theory' or 'new media') and reinserted into the 'main street' research on multinational corporations and social realities they co-shape with their power games and economic expansion:

> ...for example, the centrality attributed in I(nternational) M(anagement) studies to the national affiliation of the MNC, its daughter companies, its expatriate or local managers, and its workers prevents current research from revealing the complex and varied ways in which the abovementioned actors draw on a multiplicity of cultural and institutional repertoires that temporarily become for them a third space of in-between. By adhering to essentialist categories of nation and culture, this literature is liable to become less relevant as the various actors in the organization are increasingly exposed to a wide range of repertoires, both through the electronic and digital media and as part of the increasingly frequent movement of people between different parts of the world. (Frenkel 2008: 939)

What is being pointed out in the above quotation is the limited nature of the so-called cultural relativism. The concept of universal values had often been employed as an ideological device legitimising Western colonial and neocolonial practices. This does not necessarily imply that the concept of relativism is always the best vehicle for counter-mobilisation of the poor and the excluded. Relativism can also be an instrument of ideological domination. For instance, the approach which reduced the concept of relativism to a neutralised comparison of 'softwares' implanted in individual minds during collective socialisation in families, nations and corporations is tacitly privileging the Western academic industries in spite of an explicit embracing of diversity issues. Some very significant assumptions are being made. We are assuming that all human individuals, who will interact around the world, have gone through three 'identity labs'. All have been influenced as children by their families and churches, as citizens by their nation-states, by their organisations, institutions, corporations, firms, companies, job-holding entities as employees. This approach is based on what had been called positivist essentialism—identities are generated in privileged loci (family, school, job), at strictly defined times (individual childhood, school-age youth, job-holding maturity) and covering everybody from cradle to grave, with a seamless web of three giant, overlapping matrixes. These matrixes are churning out individual clones of a collective national soul, character, personality, *esprit de corps*.

Note that at least four assumptions about the making of an individual identity merit criticism.

- First, the essentialist nature of these matrixes for reproducing culture by stamping identical clones as if they had been assembly lines for mass production of identical value boxes inserted into individual minds.
- Second, the homogeneity of culture as resource tool-kit available to individuals looking for guidance in actual interactions and within their changeable networks of relationships.
- Third, the passivity of an individual subjected to socialising and acculturating influences—he or she never talks back and never fuses hybrids, there is no room for creativity and deviance.
- Fourth, the universe of cultures and nations is frozen in hierarchic pecking order reflected in stereotypes, which tend to be confirmed by neoneopositivist, that is by making it neo-neopositivism research.

All of these assumptions should be undermined and critically examined. All of them could eventually be rejected, leading to the following counter-recommendations:

- Socialisation and acculturation processes are much more flexible, contingent and unpredictable than essentialists assume because individual cultural competence is an open source rather than a ready-made matrix and can generate different behaviours in different contexts. Creating ideological climates does matter.

- Moving through *tempospaces* an individual continually manages and recombines webs of relations (society) and webs of meaning (culture) changing him or herself both in different contexts and at different times. Learning from unique patterns (case studies) increases heterogeneity and diversity of interaction flows.

- Individuals are constantly talking back and responding to the socialising and acculturating individuals and collectives, producing hybrids, exercising creativity and gambling for future outcomes. Their frantic activity is the fuel of hope, especially in view of the necessity of talking back to the electronic, digital, tele-multimedia.

- The universe of cultures and societies (nation-state organised) is fluid and mutable, expanding not only in 'content' of processes and interactions but also in their 'forms' (hence there is no 'quasi-genetic' code of social organisation or change, no core pattern of elementary relational models).[2] Pattern recognition is not reducible to the excavation of 'deep structure' and resembles 'surfing' more than 'mining'.

The temptation to reduce complexity of organising and managing knowledge-intensive organisations through recombining individual and collective agencies supported by flexible and changeable competences remains very strong. One of them is *epistemological*. For instance, Fiske's neat distinction among communal sharing, authority ranking, equality matching and market pricing is a case in point. He claims to have 'discovered' the core matrix of organising relationships among individuals, while he is actually describing the results of his 'surfing' of the interactions streams in contemporary Western society. He reports on pattern recognition in a society, where market pricing is the hegemonic mode of relating individuals and which is continually reshaped in changing patterns of all four modes of relating and many more (for instance by the state injecting US$ 700 billions into market pricing agencies when their 'elementary forms of human relations' collapse). Legitimising this financial injection requires ideological skill—especially in an instant organised forgetting of the neoliberal ideology of a free market. This is the *ideological* temptation to reduce the complexity of organising and managing through recombine-able agencies and mutable agents. Let us add that the 'legitimising' of market pricing and the construction of an individual identity as a rational calculating human being (which is the consequence of the hegemonic enthroning of market pricing as the highest stage of managing relations among human beings) is also a very complex and ongoing activity (cf. du Gay 2007; Hirschman 1977; Perelman 2000). It requires a defence of the assumptions which—if my reasoning above is accepted—should be rejected and replaced by their counterparts also spelled out above:

> It is a profound mistake, therefore, to assume that the state should be 're-invented' or 'modernized' to accord with the nitty-gritty facts of social and moral life as conceptualized either in 'social-constructionist' academic analyses or in expressivist liberal and communitarian conceptions of 'governance'. Both strive to prove that the 'independence' and 'autonomy' of the 'sovereign state' is a fiction. But the fiction with which the sovereign state sustains its role is in fact the assumption (no more or less vulnerable than any other) that constitutes its role; take it away and you remove the role and all the advantages it brings to bear.(…) To actively attempt to de-autonomize the state under the aegis of its status as a 'social construct' or the imperatives of moral expressivism is effectively to re-theologize it (Hunter 1998). One need only to point to the rise of democratic and nationalist movements in the nineteenth century armed with similar expressivist concerns to indicate the dangers such re-theologization poses to social pacification, the rule of law, and the practice of religious toleration. (du Gay 2007: 171–72)

Paul du Gay defends robust organised identities in a way which resembles the famous exclamation of a Russian captain in the tsar's army, whom revolutionary terrorists try to convince that God does not exist in Dostoyevsky's novel *Demons*. 'If there is no God', replies the desperate officer who had previously agreed with their condemnation of social injustices, 'then what kind of a captain am I?' The poor captain's response reveals the ideological belief that behind the hierarchy of a professional bureaucratic organisation there is another hierarchy, ultimately legitimised by the higher, transcendent, divine being. The author of *Organizing Identity* does not evoke political theology a la Carl Schmitt (cf. Mouffe 1999). To the contrary, he rejects openly theological legitimisation of a bureaucratic identity as based on a 'will to power'. But Carl Schmitt as the new ideological patron saint of the new left is not his only victim. He manages to reject also social movements for change as 'theological'. His blanket condemnation covers not only theology and political theology, but also the working class movements of the early 20th century and the movements for democratisation of professional bureaucracies symbolised by the student rebellion of 1968, the emergence of the Polish 'Solidarity' in 1980 and the fall of the Berlin Wall in 1989. His argument rests on ideological defence of the calculating self (individual identity) protected by state bureaucracy ('individual rights and community freedoms ... are an enforced uniformity, enforced that is by sovereign states', du Gay 2007: 173) and legitimised by the historical ideologies of early modern Europe emerging from religious wars and accommodating economic, urban and colonial growth to the nation-state framework for regulating the flows of interactions.

Should we heed this plea for a return to a safe fold of robust identities guaranteed by professional bureaucracies and ideologically protected from new social movements on the one hand and market pricing mode of building relationships on the other? Or should we go ahead with the reconstruction of the above assumptions? If we want to understand how relational identities can be developed without too much fear, control and awe *vis-à-vis* sovereign professional bureaucracies but with individual moral sensitivity and responsibility of creative social entrepreneurs, we might as well risk replacing them.[3] Can we expect that this replacement of assumptions will help a perplexed manager? It will certainly make him or her re-examine his or her way of thinking about organising. And, as we all know, unexamined managerial career is not worth pursuing.

NOTES

1. Ever since Whitehead suggested the term 'eventism' for an ontology, whose basic component is an event rather than an object, the idea of a *tempospace*, or spatiotemporal environment housing all our activities, seems mild and tame in spite of a common sense use of spatial or temporal metaphors separately (cf. Whitehead 1925).
2. Cf. Fiske 1991.
3. Feyerabend (2001) spoke of developing 'science for a free society', Gergen (1999) speaks of therapy and art as role models liberated from the dictatorship of the illusory idea of progress.

REFERENCES

Ailot, G. 2008. 'Mirror, Mirror on the Wall: Culture's Consequences in a Value Test of Its Own Design', *The Academy of Management Review*, 33(4): 885–904.

Archer, M. 2007. *Making our Way through the World: Human Reflexivity and Social Mobility*. Cambridge and New York: Cambridge University Press.

Benjamin, W. 1969. 'The Work of Art in the Age of Mechanical Reproduction', in H. Arendt, (ed.), *Illuminations*, pp. 217–51. New York: Schocken.

Bhabha, H. 1994. 'DissemiNation: Time, Narrative and the Margins of the Modern Nation', in H. Bhabha (ed.), *The Location of Culture*, pp. 139–70. London and New York: Routledge.

———. 1996. 'Cultures in Between', in S. Hall and P. du Gay (eds), *Questions of Cultural Identity*, pp. 53–60. London and Thousand Oaks, Ca.: Sage Publications.

Boltanski, L. and L. Thevenot. 2006. *On Justification. Economies of Worth*. Princeton and Oxford: Princeton University Press.

Brecht, Bertolt. 2000. 'Brecht on Film (Diaries, Letters and Essays)'. London: Methuen.

Castells, M. 2001. *The Internet Galaxy: Reflections on the Internet, Business and Society*. Oxford and New York: Oxford University Press.

Coetzee, John M. 2007. *Diary of a Bad Year*. London: Harvill Secker.

Dostoyevsky, F. 2002. *Brothers Karamazov*. New York: Farrar, Straus and Giroux.
———. 2008. *Demons*. London: Penguin.
du Gay, P. 2007. *Organizing Identity*. Los Angeles, London, New Delhi, Singapore: Sage Publications.
Eicher, T. and S. Turnovsky (eds). 2003. *Inequality and Growth: Theory and Policy Implications*. Cambridge, MA and London: The MIT Press.
Feyerabend, P. 2001. *The Conquest of Abundance: A Tale of Abstraction vs the Richness of Being*. Chicago and London: The University of Chicago Press.
Fischer, M. 2003. *Emergent Forms of Life and the Anthropological Voice*. Durham, NC and London: Duke University Press.
Fiske, A. 1991. *Structures of Social Life: The Four Elementary Forms of Human Interaction*. New York: The Free Press.
Frenkel, M. 2008. 'The Multinational Corporation as a Third Space: Rethinking International Management Discourse on Knowledge Transfer Through Homi Bhabha', *The Academy of Management Review*, 33(4): 924–42.
Gergen, K. 1999. *An Invitation to Social Construction*. London, Thousand Oaks and New Dehli: Sage Publications.
Heller, J. 1961. *Catch 22*. New York: Simon and Schuster.
Hirschman, A. 1977. *The Passions and the Interests*. Princeton, NJ: Princeton University Press.
Hunter, I. 1998. 'Uncivil Society', in M. Dean and B. Hindess (eds), *Governing Australia*, pp. 242–65. Sydney: Cambridge University Press.
Jenkins, H., D. Thorburn and B. Seawell (eds). 2003. *Democracy and the Media*. Cambridge, MA and London: The MIT Press.
Joselit, D. 2007. *Feedback: Television Against Democracy*. Cambridge and London: The MIT Press.
Levy, D. 2008. 'Political Contestation in Global Production Networks', *The Academy of Management Review*, 33(4): 943–63.
Mann, T. 1924. *Der Zauberberg*. Frankfurt am Main: Fischer Verlag.
Memmi, A. 2006. *Decolonization and the Decolonized*. Minneapolis, MN and London: University of Minnesota Press.
Mouffe, C. (ed.). 1999. *The Challenge of Carl Schmitt*. London and New York: Verso.
Perelman, M. 2000. *The Invention of Capitalism: Classical Political Economy and the Secret History of Primitive Accumulation*. Durham and London: Duke University Press.
Roth, P. 2008. *Indignation*. London: Jonathan Cape.
Sennett, R. 2003. *Respect in a World of Inequality*. New York and London: Norton.
Shenkar, O., Y. Luo and O. Yeheskel. 2008. 'From "Distance" to "Friction": Substituting Metaphors and Redirecting Intercultural Research', *The Academy of Management Review*, 33(4): 905–23.
Tsing, A. 2005. *Friction: An Ethnography of Global Connection*. Princeton and Oxford: Princeton University Press.
Whitehead, A. 1925. *Science and the Modern World*. London: Macmillan.

8

PERPLEXITY AND STRATEGY: MOVING TOWARDS AN ENROLMENT ADVANTAGE PARADIGM

Jonathan Gander

The perplexity inducing dominance of prescriptive strategy models is the target of an enrolment advantage paradigm.

The application of Actor Network theory in strategy involves a move from a 'ties that bind' view of networks and competitive advantage to a 'ties that (per)form'.

It is not essentialist accounts of individual motivation or the power of immutable economic laws that guide organizations; their interests are constructed pan-relationally by an actor-network.

Richardson (1972: 883) proposed that firms are not 'islands of planned co-ordination in a sea of market relations' but are highly inter-related, engaged in 'dense networks of co-operation and affiliation'. It follows that we shouldn't look inside the firm for sources of competitive advantage but across a network of connected organisations. The work on network structure (Burt 1992), collaborative advantage (Kanter 1994) technology brokering (Hargadon 2003) and strategy as ecology (Iansiti and Levien 2004) all build on this increasingly recognised insight (Foss and Loasby 1998). Such work while varied in approach, contains a common position; that a firm's connections are a factor in its organisational performance. So far, so good. However, this welcome 'relational turn' is hampered by the concrete terms in which firms are discussed (Morgan 2006). Treating firms as entities that engage in relations problematises the relations but stops short of reflecting on the influence of those connections on the firm. In this gap essentialist rational economic assumptions on the nature of the firm are reasserted and the relational project is captured. It is proposed that managers follow through with the logic of relational thinking and view the firm, not just its capabilities, as an outcome of its connections. Not something made that then follows economic or social structures or preferences but something performed, continually enabled by the practice of its relationships. From this perspective a subtle but rewarding shift in thinking and analysis can be made, and the promise of Richardson's network view of firms realised. Strategy becomes not the practice of making favourable connections among firms but the practice of making firms, constructing relationships that conscript or enrol others in routines and meanings. It is the difference between attempting to outcompete rival firms and organising the rules of competition. Strategy involves creating the rules of competition and in other words it is recommended that managers engaged in strategic analysis move from a 'ties that bind' view of networks and competitive advantage to a 'ties that (per)form' paradigm.

THE PROBLEM

Strategy is usually viewed as involving the study and pursuit of differential performance; why one particular firm or industry is more successful than another (Porter 1991, 1996). Framed in this way managers tackle questions on the nature and scope of organisational structure, means and degrees of control, position of the firm's boundary, resource acquisition and utilisation and industry position. To aid them in this endeavour, managers are offered models and approaches that contain prescriptions for success. The position school (Porter 1980) for example, recommends increasing the bargaining power of the firm with its suppliers and customers, the boundary school (Volberda and Elfring 2001) considers the limits of the firm's activities and nature and management of its relationship with partners, while the resource based position recommends the identification, generation or acquisition of valuable and difficult to copy resources (Barney 1991; Wernerfelt 1984).

It is suggested that these prescriptions, often couched in recipe styled imperatives, doom the ambitions of those who follow its directives. For how can a comparative advantage over another firm be achieved if the solution selected by comes from a text that has sold half a million copies, a course delivered in hundreds of universities or a consultancy that provides strategic services to hundreds of clients, often in the same sector? Of course there are explanations for superior performance that respond to this paradox. Advantage may be achieved through historic or path dependent means that bar the progress of certain firms and equip others with rare abilities (Arthur 1994; Dierickx and Cool 1989). Organisations may utilise tacit knowledge that cannot be identified and copied (Nelson and Winter 1982), or enjoy regulatory conditions that restrict the entry or competition (Porter 1985). However these explanations are vulnerable to the charge of tautology (Mackenzie 1990; Priem and Butler 2001) and in any case offer little help to the managers of those less privileged firms. To make matters worse when the dominance that results from the possession of such superior resources is overturned, it is explained either as a catastrophic managerial failure attributable to a few key executives, the brilliance of the new entrant, the emergence of a new economy or the destructive effect of technology. None of these are especially constructive for the managers aiming to develop a basis for competition that will deliver some degree of competitive advantage for their organisations. Such explanations either produce unwise bandwagon type investment decisions to invest in the emerging economy or new technology, or in the cases where managerial prowess or inadequacy are offered as the reason for organisational performance, serve as largely non-transferable lessons anchored in a particular set of circumstances.

It is not suggested that the prescriptive approaches to the search and generation of advantage are entirely without merit. What is proposed is that without the realisation of their limits and underlying assumptions, and a recognition of the way they shape the user and organise the situation of the firm, then the manager risks trapping herself into analytical procedures that in the best case scenario result in only marginal and temporary competitive advantage, and in the worst ensure a commonality of approach among competitors that reduces the possibility of differential organisational performance. To help break the spell of the attractively designed and persuasively elaborated models and approaches that populate strategic management literature and managerial publications such as the *Harvard Business Review*, it is useful to consider that it is not the case that such theories and analytical procedures have been made for managers attempting to create superior performance for their firm, but that managers and firms are made for the models and theories. If we reflect on this possibility then strategy, or the pursuit or organisational advantage is better understood as a contest to enrol suppliers, employees, competitors, regulators and consumers in a set of practices and identities that work to a particular firm's advantage, rather than as a contest among organisations over resources or market share.

This chapter joins with others in this text in warning managers of the problems of reaching toward the airport shelf for the solution to complex dynamic conditions of competition and management. The task is a difficult one as their number is overwhelming, and their promise seductive. Yet is not reasonable to remove the undeniable comfort these well-constructed texts provide (no matter how dangerous the direct implementation of the ideas they espouse could involve) without offering something in its place. That something is more of an attitude than a model, one that seeks to encourage and support the mental flexibility that can help managers work through rather than reduce, the complexities of contemporary business competition. In order to do this it is recommended that managers draw on Actor–Network Theory (ANT) (Callon 1986, 1998; Latour 2005; Law 1992, 1999) a post-structural approach that rejects the use of pre-formed identities and practices. This approach takes the view that the organisation of people, practices and objects that make up an organisational field are the outcome of a particular configuration of relations and things not a cause. ANT is therefore one device to take the perplexed manager out of the 'dead mapping' of simple causality. Viewed from this perspective, managers, firms and their strategies are the consequence of the types of associations constructed by a network of relations not the input to a system guided by reductively expressed laws of human behaviour, economic practice or organisational dynamics. In Capra's terms (1997, 2002) ANT therefore requires an equal engagement with the criteria for understanding relationships, identity, language and structure.

Once managers view the strategies adopted by firms as the result of a network of relationships the search for differential performance becomes more hopeful. For rather than strategy involving the attempt to follow the rules of a game, and by rarity, luck or speed outperform one's rivals, strategy becomes the organisation of the game itself. The construction of a network made up of ideas, people, practices and objects that are enrolled into associations that benefit particular actors within it.

THE MANAGERIAL CONDITION

Before we consider the insights offered by such an enrolment paradigm to our understanding of organisational performance, we need to visit the managerial condition that is an outcome of the currently dominant prescriptive approaches to the pursuit of organisational advantage; perplexity.

The current managerial condition is characterised by the uncertainty that surrounds decisions made on projections of a particular future and the models of advantage offered by the position school or resource based view scholars. Looking through these theoretical lenses produces high levels of causal ambiguity when attempting to understand the performance outcomes of large complex organic entities such as firms, within dynamic markets and societies. Challenged to determine how a firm came up with a new product, or why one particular project came out so well, while the latest one seems to be heading for failure, managers are enticed to reach for solutions rather than embrace the complexity of the task. The danger is that if strategy is described as a solution for uncertainty and the manager as the role tasked with selecting and implementing that solution, the outcome is to live in a kind of thraldom as Schumacher (1977: 79) described. Lurching from one managerial fix-it to the next, managers attempt to create competitive advantage through the adoption of models and approaches that by their widespread diffusion and reliance upon fixed essentialist assumptions of products, firms and markets, can offer little true, sustainable, competitive advantage. The result is disappointment tinged with self-doubt as the failure of the strategy is reasoned as an execution failure, due to the weakness of the implementation, or a misunderstanding of the core message of the text.

The perplexity inducing dominance of prescriptive strategy models (Lilley 2001) was not how the development of the strategy discipline began. Early recognition of the limits of rationalist perspectives based on normative assumptions of competition and organisation was evident in the works of writers such as Lindblom (1959) and Wrapp (1967: 74) and later reprised in Quinn (1980), Mintzberg (1987, 1994) and Knights and Morgan (1991). However, supported by the *Strategic Management Journal*, these more critical accounts of the strategy task have been largely overcome by the rationalist project. In this version strategic management approaches treat the market, firm and manager as stable pre-formed entities largely unaffected by the perspectives and problem solving methods they adopt. In such circumstances strategy becomes a matter of design, a question of selection from a tool-kit of approaches and methodologies. Unquestioning acceptance of this tool-kit usage of strategy research not only takes the user down the well-trodden paths of her competitors encouraging a profit destroying isomorphism but builds in dependence, constructs logic and the search for a better tool. Ironically this pursuit for a more effective tool, is ridiculed in management texts as the myopic search for a better 'mousetrap' rather than the concentration on the more fundamental needs of the customer (Levitt 1960). Yet while business texts carry this warning on product development, the lessons are not carried over to the task of organising competitive performance. Managers building better mousetraps are condemned to a narrowing set of practices that deliver marginal and decreasing returns while blinding them to opportunities to reorganise and liberate their thinking.

Viewing strategy as a set of prescriptive tools reduces strategic analysis and development to the level of technique, not reflection. Desire to stay ahead of diminishing returns brought about by the rapid diffusion of managerial techniques, managers pursue new and improved solutions, in the form of popular management texts, effectively rejecting the past as a place of limited relevance. This fetishisation of the new helps dissuade managers from reflecting on their past actions and reconceptualising their experiences and adjusting their behaviour (Argyris 2000). In the case of the most extreme examples of these managerial texts, the guru books, the possibility for real damage is made explicit both in the admission and the consequence of this statement from Tom Peters, 'I decide to write a new book when I feel disgusted and embarrassed by my previous one' (Crainer 1997: 74). The norming effect of the buzzwords that populate their writings can act to reduce the degree of critical interrogation of the resulting plans (Jackson 2001). The result is a dumbing down of the managerial function that 'undermine(s) managers' understanding of the real complexities that pertain to their work' (McGill 1988: 202).

A highly visible example of this was seen in the business process re-engineering dictum of 'Don't automate, obliterate' (Hammer 1990). This message was enthusiastically embraced by managers seeking more efficient working structures yet it obscured from consideration the effect on staff commitment to the company, the costs of change especially of radical change, the informal communication and working practices that supported organisational structures and the damage to previously established projects whose value was reduced by the withdrawing of resources. Indeed, in what is a rare case for such texts that sweep through management practice, the authors acknowledged the failures of an approach 'that was insufficiently appreciative of the human dimension. I've learned that's critical' (White 1996: 1).

The oft quoted, smart, but unhelpful remark of the consultant, who when asked for his/her opinion on a problem facing the firm responds with 'Well I wouldn't start from this position' is of relevance to our discussion. In the same way that solutions to a problem lie outside the frame of reference selected by those framing the problem, the construction of sustainable competitive advantage is not to be found in the well worn models of strategy textbooks (no matter how efficient and effective the implementation) nor in the latest management best seller or presentation book tour. Rather, sustainable competitive advantage is achieved by managers recognising that strategy models and paradigms are constructive, forming the user, the problem as well as the 'solution'. Self-awareness is required to halt this 'drifting along in captivity' (Schumacher 1977) and realise the way ideas are performative; they organise identities and needs not just problems and answers. They construct their own reality, they do not reflect it.

Treating models of competition as neutral instruments with which to generate and calibrate actions is to follow the map believing it is the territory and trap oneself within another's game.

One example of the performative character of words and actions is found in the word strategy itself. There are, as Czarniawska (2004: 782) argues, 'no innocent terms'. The term strategy is part of the network of discursive practices that set out the game, encouraging the problematisation of competition and organisational performance in the kinds of models and managerial practice recipes that, due to their insular readings of firms and static assumptions of competition, can lead to disappointment. Strategy as a word, carries with it, its military origins of generalship, from the Greek '*strategos*'. Due to this etymology, lay notions of military activity; battle, conflict, surprise, leadership, and so on, are introduced into the question of attaining organisational advantage. It is not necessary to discuss the similarities and differences between armies and businesses, of war with trade, or generalship with that of management. The important point is to consider the constitutive effects of likening one to the other (Tsoukas 1991). In the present discussion on strategy and perplexity these effects include the damaging and limiting belief in superior planning accompanied by a zero sum reasoning that sees market share as some version of physical territory that must be wrestled away from the present occupier.

STRATEGY AS ENROLMENT

The immediate benefit to the perplexed manager of framing her condition within actor network theory is to help break the positivistic assumptions of strategy that the problem solving paradigms encourage. One of the central questions posed by ANT perspectives is who does the organising and who is organised? The value of business ideas does not lie in their correspondence with some 'truth' of competition. Core competencies, Blue oceans and balanced scorecards do not reflect reality, they 'enrol' managers in the construction of it. Introduced by academics or guru practitioners, popular management texts do not satisfy the needs of managers as they maintain their position of dependence. It is recommended that managers view themselves as participants rather than just observers. From this position managers are better equipped to reflect on the effectiveness of implemented business strategies and reflexively generate a way of understanding the manner in which the firm competes and might compete.

In other words actor network theory offers managers a way of making living maps of their experiences and action; of producing frameworks for decisions without constraining their perspective in self-reinforcing dead maps whose use only enrols the manager in the perplexity of rationalist topographies of organisational competition. ANT allows the practice of strategy to shift from one of map reading, following the contours given to us, to that of map making; not of redrawing to populate with our own set of dimensions and key, but as a process that both constructs and guides (Chia and Holt 2006).

Actor network theory, as befits a theory of becoming, is still developing and changing and is not a unified field of work (Law and Hassard 1999). This, plus its rich conceptual and terminological frameworks makes ANT a challenging perspective to employ (ibid.). However its benefits outweigh these difficulties and its use in management and organisational studies (Czarniawska 2004; Law and Hassard 1999; McLean and Hassard 2004; Newton 2002; Neyland 2006; Steen et al. 2006) point to an increasing relevance. ANT's main contribution to the understanding of organisational advantage lies in its reconceptualisation of networks and resources and its explanation for the ability of firms or individuals to maintain a privileged role within and over them respectively. The use of a 'network' view is a highly contested term with a wide variety of applications (Nohria and Eccles 1992). Network in an ANT sense does not refer to the technological networks of the internet, water supply or electricity. Nor does it share the meaning used by organisational and managerial writers to refer to 'a set of actors connected by a set of ties' (Borgatti and Foster 2003: 992). Neither does it, as in Castells' (1996) usage, refer to a mixture of both where network structured organisational forms operate within production and consumption relations shaped by informational technologies. Network in ANT has a very different meaning. It refers to the performance of something. A network, as Latour (2005: 131) defines it 'is a tool to help describe something, it is not what is being described'. The word network is a way of describing the flow of translations that stabilise relations among people, ideas, routines and physical objects. Organisations seen this way are not 'in' networks but are made by them. This enables the step towards the contentious portrayal of agency as the performative outcome of a stabilised network rather than an input to action. By flipping the view of agency as a cause to that of an outcome we remove the need to navigate between the determinism of structural explanations and the reductionism of agency to atomised, maximising individuals. More productively our attention can now be placed on how the agency of an organisation or individual is described and maintained. Rather than seeing strategy as a matter of building links among actors and sharing resources and benefits such as in the brokerage perspectives of Burt (1992) and Hargadon (2003), who consider strategy as the creation of actors and resources with interests that benefit the firm.

Resources in strategic management theory are usually presented as assets or capabilities that are drawn on by actors in pursuit of some performance advantage (Barney 1991; Pfeffer and Salancik 1978). This substantialist position misdirects the analysis of organisations away from their own part in constructing the advantage of others and towards the vain task of tracking circular arguments where the performance of an organisation is due to their possession of 'valuable' resources (Priem and Butler 2001).

Adopting this performative view of the contribution of networks and resources to the construction of organisational advantage is not straightforward. A characteristic of such networks is the way they blackbox the performative process, creating what appear to be fixed entities of firms and markets, subjects and objects, establishing roles and rationalities that take on a self-evident air. Established models of industry analysis and organisational advantage only serve to recreate the fixed entities obscuring how they come to be stabilised. If we begin with an acceptance of this map of competition then what needs to be explained; such as the presence of switching costs, the operation of market power, or the sale of premium priced products and services, become the things that do the explaining. We mistake cause for outcome and consign ourselves to analysis based on self-reinforcing logics drawn from economic or management theory and limited by holding organisations and practices as stable pre-formed entities. Within such assumptions, the strategising of managers is constrained and their organisational strategy becomes more vulnerable to an organisation that can go beyond established orthodoxies of the industry. ANT offers a way to 'displace more conventional organizational thinking' (Calàs and Smircich 1999: 664).

Both the positioning school and resource-based approaches to the generation and maintenance of organisational advantage have at their basis the view that industries are organised power networks. However rather than imputing the source of power to the operation of 'economic laws', managerial characteristics or the constraints of socially embedded institutions, we need to concentrate on how these networks are 'actually constituted and reproduced' (Clegg 1989). By reframing this question of understanding the distribution of power within a sector to one of acceptance of the 'reality' of economic or social forces and interests, while acknowledging their constructed nature ANT achieves a very useful, from a managerial perspective, double movement. The challenge of strategic analysis immediately becomes more rewarding and in a sense more strategic. The challenge is not simply to compete within these constructed rules but to also consider how the stabilised set of relations can be reorganised to better suit the organisation in question. Strategy involves the organisation of the game, not the outperformance of others who play the game.

So if we wish to see beyond the constructed logics of an industry and conduct a 'performative' analysis of organisational advantage we need to adopt an attitude towards the analysis of organisations as becoming not being (Clegg 1989; Latour 2005). However this project faces a significant obstacle; the tendency of networks to conceal the nature of their assembly behind apparently bounded entities and the action of immutable economic laws or managerial characteristics and social structures. The task is made easier during what Callon (1998) terms a 'hot situation' when the roles, identities, practices and organising rationalities become controversial, and the organising rationality less stable. Such hot situations occur when breakthrough technologies offer new functionality, organisations experience catastrophic failure and the boundaries around organisational fields become less stable. During such periods the co-construction of the actors and the nature of their associations can be revealed and the view of the organisation as a performed outcome, rather than a 'natural' entity, may be revealed.

Callon (1986) offers four stages through which actors seek to rearticulate a network that reconstitutes interests, structures and entities in their favour. These four stages of 'translation' are problematisation, interessement, enrolment and mobilisation. These moments of translation begin with the actors reframing themselves as the solutions to the problems being experienced by others, then attempting to fix this association, by categorising roles, meaning and identity, these are then strengthened by forming alliances and membership groups and finally extended by getting others to maintain the system of associations. This translation is achieved through the circulation of meaning carrying intermediaries; texts, technical artefacts, people and money. These intermediaries, through their adoption in the practices of the network configure their users and enrol them in the project of the actor who circulated them. Intermediaries are thus distinguished from actors as those who are organised rather than those who achieve the organising (Murdoch 2006). Actors maintain their power to organise these intermediaries by establishing nodal points in the network or obligatory points of passage through which they must pass. These nodal points operate as centres of calculation where metrics are applied, meanings reinforced and judgements of quality made. These measurement and valuation devices enable the network to be regulated and governed at a distance. The result is the actor-network, where the network is the actor and the actor the network.

The hybrid nature of actor-networks where agency is performed by assemblies of text, people and objects rather than by bounded individuals or organisations acting according to rational economic preferences is in the pluralist tradition exemplified in Frankl's (1969) attack on nihilism. Schumacher (1977: 15) quotes Frankl 'The true nihilism today is reductionism. Contemporary nihilism no longer brandishes the word nothingness; today nihilism is camouflaged as nothing-but-ness.' ANT offers a way of avoiding the reductionist trap produced by rational economic reasoning and atomised views of the nature of the firm that still grips much strategic management literature.

CONCLUSION

Strategy is commonly described as a competitive activity aimed at capturing the maximum value from within an organisational field. Strategy from an ANT perspective shifts the focus to one of value being the constructed outcome of the assembly and maintenance of an organisational field. This orientation produces a number of liberating alternatives to established strategy perspectives. Organisational advantage is performed by an organisational field (actor network), not deployed within it. It is not the position of the firm within a network, but the capabilities of the firm achieved through the nature of the network (Pratt 1997). It is not access to resources that describes relational advantage but the network enabling capabilities that a firm embodies (Zaheer and Bell 2005). Resources are not entities to be deployed within networks

(Dyer and Singh 1998), they are a property of a network. It is not essentialist accounts of individual motivation or the power of immutable economic laws that guide organisations, their interests are constructed by an actor-network.

I have portrayed the managerial condition as one of dependence upon techniques of analysis aimed at out-competing others within a field acted upon by immutable laws of competition, economics or the interests and motivations of individuals. Use of such techniques rather than offering the possibility of advantage actually trap the manager into a cycle of disappointment where the failure of their strategies is used to demonstrate the need for ever improved products of analysis. The way out of the thraldom into which they have been cast are periods of organisational failure or the availability of new technologies, which produce what Heidegger (1962) termed a broken tool moment. A point where, just as when the door handle breaks in our hand and the previously unacknowledged union of door, mechanism and body, separate and are revealed, the assembled nature of their world is made visible. Instead of stable phenomena such as subjects and objects, individuals and organisations, the manager is able to see the flow of things, the processes of subjectification or organising (Weick et al. 2005; Weick 1979). Managers who seek to understand and engage in the construction of organisational advantage need to grasp these opportunities and seek to translate the interests of others and enrol them in a set of discursive practices stabilised through the operation of centres of calculation fixed by obligatory passage points.

REFERENCES

Argyris, C. 2000. *Flawed Advice*. New York: Oxford University Press.

Arthur, W. 1994. *Increasing Returns and Path Dependence in the Economy*. Ann Arbor, MI: University of Michigan Press.

Barney, J. 1991. 'Firm Resources and Sustained Competitive Advantage', *Journal of Management*, 17(1): 99–121.

Borgatti, S. and P. Foster. 2003. 'The Network Paradigm in Organizational Research: A Review and Typology', *Journal of Management*, 29(6): 991–1013.

Burt, R. 1992. 'The Social Structure of Competition', in N. Nohria and R. Eccles (eds), *Networks and Organizations: Structure, Form and Action*, pp. 57–91. Cambridge, MA: Harvard University Press.

Calàs, M. and L. Smircich. 1999. 'Past Postmodernism? Reflections and Tentative Directions', *Academy of Management Review*, 24(4): 649–71.

Callon, M. 1986. 'Some Elements of a Sociology of Translation: Domestication of the Scallops and Fishermen at St Brieuc Bay' in J. Law (ed.), *Power, Action and Belief*, pp. 196–233. London: Routledge and Kegan Paul.

———. 1998. *The Laws of Markets*. Oxford: Blackwell.

Capra, F. 1997. *The Web of Life: A New Synthesis of Mind and Matter*. London: Flamingo.

———. 2002. *The Hidden Connections*. London: Flamingo.

Castells, M. 1996. *The Rise of the Networked Society*. Oxford: Blackwell.

Chia, R. and R. Holt. 2006. 'Strategy as Practical Coping: a Heideggerian Perspective', *Organization Studies*, 27(5): 635–55.

Clegg, S. 1989. *Frameworks of Power*. London: Sage Publications.

Crainer, S. 1997. 'Tom Peters', *Management Today*, May: 74–75.

Czarniawska, B. 2004. 'On Time, Space and Action Nets', *Organization*, 11(6): 773–91.

Dierickx, I. and K. Cool. 1989. 'Asset Stock Accumulation and Sustainability of Competitive Advantage', *Management Science*, 35(12): 1504–11.

Dyer, J. and H. Singh. 1998. 'The Relational View: Cooperative Strategy and Sources of Interorganizational Competitive Advantage', *Academy of Management Review*, 24(2): 660–79.

Foss, N. and B. Loasby (eds). 1998. *Economic Organization, Capabilities and Co-ordination; Essays in Honour of G. B. Richardson*. London: Routledge.

Frankl, V. 1969. 'Reductionism and Nihilism', in A. Koestler and J. Smythies (eds), *Beyond Reductionism*. London: Hutchinson.

Hammer, M. 1990. 'Reengineering Work: Don't Automate, Obliterate', *Harvard Business Review*, July–August.

Hammer, M. and J. Champy. 1993. *Reengineering the Corporation: A Manifesto for Business Revolution*. New York: HarperBusiness.

Hargadon, A. 2003. *How Breakthroughs Happen*. Cambridge MA: Harvard University Press.

Heidegger, M. 1962. *Being and Time*. Oxford: Blackwell.

Iansiti, M. and R. Levien. 2004 'Strategy as Ecology', *Harvard Business Review*, 82(3): 68–78.

Jackson, B. 2001. *Management Fads and Management Fashions*. London: Routledge.

Kanter, R. 1994. 'Collaborative Advantage: The art of Alliances', *Harvard Business Review*, 72(4): 96–108.

Knights, D. and G. Morgan. 1991. 'Corporate Strategy, Organizations, and Subjectivity: A Critique', *Organization Studies*, 12(2): 251–73.

Latour, B. 2005. *Reassembling the Social*. Oxford: Oxford University Press.

Law, J. 1992. 'Notes on the Theory of the Actor-Network: Ordering, Strategy and Heterogeneity', *Systems Practice*, 5: 379–93.

———. 1999. *After ANT: 'Topology, Naming and Complexity'*, in J. Law and J. Hassard (eds), *Actor Network Theory and After*, pp. 1–14. Blackwell: Oxford.

Law, J. and J. Hassard. (eds). 1999. *Actor Network Theory and After*. Oxford: Blackwell.

Levitt, T. 1960. 'Marketing Myopia', *Harvard Business Review*, July–August: 3–13.

Lilley, S. 2001. 'The Language of Strategy', in R. Westwood and S. Linstead (eds), *The Language of Organization*, pp. 66–68. London: Sage Publications.

Lindblom, C.E. 1959. 'The Science of Muddling Through', *Public Administration Review*, 19: 78–88.

Mackenzie, D.A. 1990. *Inventing Accuracy: An Historical Sociology of Nuclear Missile Guidance*. Cambridge, MA: MIT Press.

McGill, M. 1988. *American Business and the Quick Fix*. New York: Henry Holt.

McLean, C. and J. Hassard. 2004. 'Symmetrical Absence/Symmetrical Absurdity: Critical Notes on the Production of Actor Network Accounts', *Journal of Management Studies*, 41(3): 493–519.

Mintzberg, H. 1987. 'Crafting Strategy', *Harvard Business Review*, July–August: 66–74.

———. 1994. 'The Fall and Rise of Strategic Planning', *Harvard Business Review*, January–February: 107–14.

Morgan, G. 2006. *Images of Organization* (updated edition). London: Sage Publications.

Murdoch, J. 2006. *Post-Structuralist Geography*. London: Sage Publications.

Nelson, R. and S. Winter. 1982. *An Evolutionary Theory of Economic Change*. Cambridge, MA: Belknap Press of Harvard University Press.

Newton, T. 2002. 'Creating the New Ecological Order? Elias and Actor-Network Theory', *Academy of Management Review*, 27(4): 523–40.

Neyland, D. 2006. 'Dismissed Content and Discontent', *Science, Technology and Human Values*, 31(1): 29–51.

Nohria, N. and R. Eccles (eds). 1992. *Networks and Organizations: Structure, Form and Action*. Cambridge, MA: Harvard University Press.

Oxford University Press. 1971. *Oxford English Dictionary*. Oxford: Oxford University Press.

Pfeffer, J. and G. Salancik. 1978. *The External Control of Organizations: A Resource Dependence Perspective*. New York: Harper & Row.

Porter, M. 1980. *Competitive Strategy*. Free Press: New York.

———. 1985. *Competitive Advantage*. Free Press: New York.

———. 1991. 'Toward a Dynamic Theory of Strategy', *Strategic Management Journal*, 12: 95–117.

———. 1996. 'What is Strategy?' *Harvard Business Review*, November–December.

Pratt, A.C. 1997. 'The Emerging Shape and Form of Innovation Networks and Institutions', in J. Simmie (ed.), *Innovation Networks and Learning Regions?*, pp. 124–36. London: Jessica Kingsley Publishers.

Priem, R. and J. Butler. 2001. 'Is the Resource Based View a Useful Perspective for Strategic Management Research?', *Academy of Management Review*, 26(1): 22–40.

Quinn, J. 1980. *Strategies for Change: Logical Incrementalism*. Homewood IL: R.D. Irwin.

Richardson, G. 1972. 'The Organisation of Industry', *Economic Journal*, 82: 883–96.

Schumacher, E. 1977. *A Guide for the Perplexed*. London: Jonathan Cape.

Steen, J., C. Coopmans and J. Whyte. 2006. 'Structure and Agency? Actor–Network Theory and Strategic Organization', *Strategic Organization*, 4(3): 303–12.

Tsoukas, H. 1991. 'The Missing Link: The Transformational View of Metaphors in Organization Science', *Academy of Management Review*, 16(3): 566–85.

Volberda, H. and T. Elfring. 2001. *Rethinking Strategy*, London: Sage Publications.

Weick, K.E., D. Sutcliffe and D. Obstfeld, D. 2005. 'Organizing and the Process of Sensemaking', *Organization Science*, 16(4): 409–21.

Weick, K.E. 1979. *The Social Psychology of Organizing*. Reading, MA: Addison–Wesley.

Wernerfelt, B. 1984. 'The Resource–Based View of the Firm', *Strategic Management Journal*, 5(2): 171–80.

White, J. 1996. 'Reengineering Gurus Take Steps to Remodel Their Stalling Vehicles', *Wall Street Journal*, 26 November.

Woolgar, S. 1991. 'Configuring the User: The Case of Usability Trials', in J. Law (ed.) *A Sociology of Monsters: Essays on Power, Technology and Domination*, pp. 57–102. London: Routledge.

Wrapp, H. 1967. 'Good Managers Don't Make Policy Decisions', *Harvard Business Review*, 45(5): 91–99.

Zaheer, A. and G. Bell. 2005. 'Benefitting From Network Position: Firm Capabilities, Structural Holes and Performance', *Strategic Management Journal*, 26(9): 809–25.

PART TWO

PERPLEXITIES IN SELECTIVE INTERNATIONAL CONTEXTS

9

PERPLEXITY AND INDIGENOUS LEADERSHIP

Karl-Erik Sveiby

This chapter encourages further exploration of indigenous leadership as a horizontal paradigm; it may progress the indigenous leadership discourse towards recognising the value of 'pure', traditional horizontal leadership. Perhaps even more importantly, a horizontal leadership paradigm is one of the unique contributions that indigenous leadership can make to the mainstream leadership discourse. The chapter also identifies a generic framework for shared leadership derived from a traditional Aboriginal law story. It draws upon Australian Aboriginal traditional knowledge and anthropological studies on contemporary African Bushmen bands.

INTRODUCTION AND PURPOSE

In a thorough study of leadership theories House and Aditya (1997) found that 98 per cent of theories and empirical evidence at that time were distinctly American in character, such as individualistic rather than collectivistic, stressing follower responsibilities rather than rights, assuming hedonism rather than commitment to duty or altruistic motivation and assuming centrality of work, and emphasising assumptions of rationality rather than asceticism or religion. Existing leadership models are perhaps better described as supervisory leadership models (Seers et al. 2003) produced under one paradigm cemented by 'thousands of years of cultural conditioning' (O'Toole et al. 2003): the (mostly) implicit theory that vertical hierarchical leadership under the single command of a top-chief is required to 'prevent organizational chaos and anarchy' (Locke 2007).

This chapter is an attempt to question this paradigm by examining indigenous leadership represented by hunter–gatherer bands. They have no leaders at all, not even top chiefs. Band organisations go back to Palaeolithic times, that is, before the advent of agriculture some 11,000 years ago, a time never visited by leadership scholars, not even writers contributing to management history (see Pindur et al. 1995) or describing leadership paradigms (see Avery 2004). 'The ever more rigorous application of the scientific method to all subjects and disciplines has destroyed even the last remnants of ancient wisdom' (Schumacher 1977: 14).

The chapter is a contribution to the discourse on indigenous leadership (IL) and the argument is that far from being a recent phenomenon, shared leadership was once humanity's dominant leadership paradigm, maybe even the first. This chapter argues that the IL discourse needs to recognise that the roots of Indigenous Leadership come from a horizontal paradigm not a vertical one. This is why the study of leadership in prehistoric and contemporary bands is of value for both the IL discourse and the general leadership discourse; bands represent what can be called a 'pure' *horizontal leadership–followership paradigm.*

The chapter draws on empirical data from 10 Aboriginal law stories, preserved through oral tradition by the Nhunggabarra people that once lived in north-western New South Wales in Australia, as told and interpreted by their last custodian Tex Skuthorpe. Secondary data from social anthropology studies of contemporary hunter–gatherer societies are used to broaden the perspective to band organisations in general. A general framework for shared leadership is derived from the story 'The Black Swans', arguably one of the oldest surviving records of a code of conduct for leaders, and its implications for the discourse on shared and distributed leadership is discussed.

The Band Organisation

'Band' is in social science a term used primarily in social anthropology. Although scholars in the field argue about the definition and how to classify different cases (Berndt and Berndt 1999; Lee 1979; Service 1979), the term generally refers to a society of lowest known complexity. The band has no formal institutions, such as formal laws, police and treaties; it has no leaders with positional powers and no other regular economic specialisation except by age and sex. It has no permanent single base of residence, but moves regularly around a territory with defined borders and its members live primarily from hunting and gathering. Social anthropologists regard hunter–gatherers in bands as the oldest of all organisations going as far back as humanity, several hundred thousand years; 15,000 years ago all humans still lived in band organisations (Sanderson and Alderson 2005). This means that the dynamics; how humans in prehistory developed their version of shared leadership is cloudy. Data are available however, to study highly evolved 'end states', represented by Aboriginal traditional law and anthropological studies of contemporary bands. This is the aim of this chapter.

Australian Aborigines—The Nhunggabarra People

The current generally accepted archaeological theory is that the first people arrived in Northern Australia some time between 40,000 and 60,000 years ago (Flood 1999). The band organisation and nomadic life of the central desert-living Aborigines was (with some exceptions, see below), similar to African bushmen bands. However, very little is known, besides traditional tales, about how the Aborigines in the relatively fertile Australian southeast lived before the Europeans disrupted their societies.

It seems that people living along the rivers—like the Nhunggabarra people—were probably living a more sedentary life. Their camps resembled villages according to the early explorer Thomas Mitchell (1839, 1847). The Nhunggabarra and their 25 neighbouring peoples were loosely united in a federative structure; they may once have had a population exceeding 15,000, that is, 500–1,000 people per community on an area approximately the size of Belgium (Sveiby and Skuthorpe 2006). When the white settlers arrived in this area, outbreaks of diseases, unwittingly introduced by the British colonialists, had already severely depopulated it. Atrocities and massacres committed by the early white settlers completed the tragedy, (Broome 2005; Reynolds 1981). Today the original Nhunggabarra people have disappeared almost entirely from their home country—their language is not spoken, and not even the name of their country remains in official records.

Australian Aborigines differ from contemporary African hunter–gatherers in that they had developed more institutionalised codes of behaviour. In addition to the most elaborate kinship rules found among hunter–gatherers (Barnard 1999) and the most complex cosmology [Dunbar et al. (1999)], Australian Aborigines also have a totem system, which among others regulates land custodianship, and marriages (Berndt and Berndt 1999). Unlike the African Bushmen the Australian Aborigines also have a specialist function, the *wiringin* (shaman), the custodian of sacred law. Aboriginal law stories contain spiritual knowledge, cosmology, sustainable land management, diplomatic codes and how to behave in times of birth and death (Berndt and Berndt 1999; Sveiby and Skuthorpe 2006). Some law stories regulate leadership practice and this chapter features one of them—'The Black Swans' story below.

The 'Law'

Nhunggabarra 'law' was a code of moral and social behaviour contained in stories. The law regulated life in the community and among communities. Its authority was unquestionable and considered to have been given to the Nhunggabarra at the time of creation by the first law maker, an early ancestor. Although the code was not a law in the Western sense its power over individuals' minds and behaviours was probably higher than the behavioural rules in our societies today. Hence, both Aboriginal people today and anthropologists use the term 'law' because the behavioural code provided a moral authority outside the individual. Offences were recognised and carried both social sanctions and, in severe cases, penalties, which were enforced by the *wiringin* (Berndt and Berndt 1999: 336ff).

The law stories tell the ideal behaviours and they do not show how the Nhunggabarra actually behaved before the white people arrived. It is not possible to know how common offences were in the pre-European Aboriginal societies, but what matters for the purpose of this chapter is what was considered to be 'normal' behaviour.

'THE BLACK SWANS'—A STORY ABOUT LEADERSHIP

The following law story was told and interpreted by the custodian Tex Skuthorpe. The paragraphs are numbered for ease of interpretation.

1. When Wurunna returned to his people he brought with him some hunting tools never seen by men. These, he said, were made in a country where there were only women and they had given them to him in exchange for his possum skin rug. They had told him that they would trade more hunting tools for more possum rugs. The people agreed to trade and to go to the women's country.

2. Wurunna warned his people that there were unknown dangers on the plain because he was sure the women were spirits—they had told him there was neither death in their country nor any night. However, Wurunna said there was an evil smell on the plain which seemed to have death in it.

3. Wurunna planned to smoke all the men so that no evil would be carried back to their people. Wurunna also arranged a plan for warning the men to leave if they stayed too long on the plain. He would take his two brothers with him and would turn them into two large swans. As there were no birds or animals on the plain they would be noticed quickly.

4. As soon as everyone was ready Wurunna would send these swans to swim on the lake opposite the women's camp. Seeing them, the women would be frightened and forget the men, who could then go on to the plain and get what they wanted. He told every man to take an animal with him and if the women tried to interfere, they should let the animals go and again the women would be distracted and the men could make their escape with the tools.

5. They set out—Wurunna and his brothers went to the far side of the plain and Wurunna lit a fire to smoke his people. From inside himself he brought out a large crystal and with its power he turned his brothers into two swans. 'bibil, bibil,' they said. When the women saw the smoke they ran towards it crying, 'Wi-balu, Wi-balu,' but then they saw the two large white birds swimming on their lake and ran towards them.

6. The men seized the opportunity and took all the tools they wanted from the women's deserted camp but the women saw them and came angrily towards them. Then each man let go of the animal he had brought—far and wide on the plain went possums, bandicoots and others. While the women chased the animals, the men dropped the possum rugs and, taking the tools, rushed towards Wurunna's fire.

7. The women, seeing the men leaving with all their tools, ran after them but the men passed into the darkness and smoke and the women were afraid to follow—there was no dark or fire in their country. The women were so angry they began to fight among themselves and their blood flowed fast so that it stained the whole of the western sky where their country is. Now, whenever the people see a red sunset they say the Wi-balus must be fighting again.

8. Wurunna now travelled on his journey to the sacred place where Baayami lived. He forgot about his two brothers even though they flew above him crying, 'bibil, bibil', so that he would change them back into men. By the time Wurunna reached the sacred place, the swans were very tired and rested on a small lagoon.

9. The eaglehawks, messengers of the spirits, who were flying to deliver a message, saw the two swans on their own lagoon. In their rage they swooped down, drove their claws and beaks into the poor white swans, and then carried them far away from the sacred place. As they flew, they plucked out the feathers of the swans, which fluttered down the sides of hills and lodged in between the rocks with blood dripping beside them—these formed flowers which are now known as paper daisies.

10. The eaglehawks flew on until they came to a large lagoon near the big salt water. At one end of the lagoon were rocks on which they dropped the swans. The eaglehawks then remembered the message they had to deliver and left the swans almost featherless, bleeding and cold. The swans

thought they were going to die far away from their country and their people.

11. Suddenly, they felt a soft shower of feathers falling on them, warming their bodies. High on the trees above they saw hundreds of crows similar to those they had sometimes seen on the plain but had believed to be a warning of evil. The black feathers covered the swans except on their wings, where a few white ones had been left. Also the down under the black feathers was white. The red blood on their beaks stayed there forever.

12. The swans flew back to their country and their people. Wurunna heard their cry, 'bibil, bibil', and knew it was his brothers, although when he looked he saw not white birds, but black birds with red bills. Sad as he was to hear their cry, Wurunna could not change them back into men. His power as a *wiringin* had been taken from him for daring to go, before his time, to the sacred place.

Interpretation of the Story

'The Black Swans' story describes the dire consequences of a seemingly innocent action—the trading of possum skin for tools. As is so often the case in Aboriginal stories, the story teaches by showing us the consequences of abuse—in this case abuse of the personal power that superior knowledge can give. What follows is the interpretation by Tex Skuthorpe.

1—Power as Ego-trip

Wurunna, who started the chain of events, did so because personal curiosity and ego drove him, not the needs of his people. He desired the tools because the new technology represented something new and different and it would have value as a new form of power. However, he did not understand the technology he was taking, not the women nor the customs of their land. He did not know the concept of trade—his only concept was to steal what he wanted.

2 –Use Fear to Gain Power

Wurunna did not respect the people he had just met and did not care to learn. He did not even realise that the death he could smell on the plain was the smell of the possum skin rug, which he carried himself. His ignorance did however, not prevent him from using the little he knew to instil fear into his own people—the fear for that which is different—so they would go along with him and his plans.

3—Use Superior Knowledge to Gain Power

Wurunna then abused his status position as a person of superior knowledge to persuade people to change without telling them why. He ruthlessly induced his own people to invade another country to get what he wanted. He even used his own brothers to protect himself and to achieve his own ends. He showed disrespect to his people by exploiting the power he had been given for his own benefit.

4—Manipulate the Ignorant

Wurunna showed disrespect to the innocent animals to achieve his ends. The animals were taken into a foreign country and had no choice but to follow him. The people followed blindly even though it was going against all they had been taught.

5—Conceal the True Purpose

Wurunna then again abused his knowledge and his power to generate 'smoke and mirrors'. He showed disrespect to the women when he confused and concealed the true purpose of his actions.

6—*Ignore the Risks*

In their ignorance the people brought change that would last forever without understanding the consequences of their actions. They brought anger to the women's country and because they were blinded by their anger, the women became blind to the innocence of the animals—all they wanted to do was hurt them. By stealing the tools, the people brought dishonesty and disrespect into their lives.

7—*When Things go Awry: Blame Others*

The women turned on each other as soon as something went wrong. By their actions, they brought chaos, dishonesty, distrust of each other, disloyalty and disrespect into their world. They realised the consequences of what they had done and tried to blame each other—but their realisation came too late to change it. They made decisions without considering the consequences and then turned on each other when it went wrong.

8—*Do not Take Responsibility ...*

Wurunna finally walked away from the disaster of his creation. He made a final show of disrespect by forgetting his brothers. All he wanted was even more knowledge—he went to a place that could give him more knowledge and power. He did not want to see what was happening around him or have any knowledge or responsibility for the actions he had taken.

9—*... and Leave the Followers to Save Themselves ...*

The brothers now got in real trouble, but Wurunna ignored his team and everything that happened to them. He was focused solely on himself and what he wanted to achieve so he did not see—or did not want do see what he had done. Chaos and death followed him and he still did not see it.

10—Impose Dire Consequences on the Followers

The pain of his brothers, Wurruna's teammates, was severe. Not only were they suffering and would die; even worse was that if they died outside their country they would not be buried properly, an eternal curse.

11—Do not Learn From the Mistakes

Because they now understood their mistakes and what had happened, what the brothers had thought was evil actually offered them help! One of the morals of the story is that out of all the 'bad' comes a great deal of learning if we take notice of what is happening and if we take responsibility for what we do wrong. By facing our mistakes we learn.

12—Avoid the Issues for too Long

Even Wurunna at last understood the consequences of what he had done, but it was now too late to change it. He had to live with remorse, shame, distrust, guilt, disrespect, loss of his powers—he had sacrificed all that we need to live a happy and fulfilled life.

Summary of the Interpretation

'The Black Swans' story follows the common style in Aboriginal law stories; in showing us the antithesis and the punishment incurred the story expects the listeners to infer the opposite as the ideal to strive for.

According to the Nhunggabarras, ideal leaders should be characterised, not by their ego-driven quest for personal power, but by a genuine motivation to serve their people. They were expected to respect all people; in particular the less knowledgeable and the less fortunate. They should have considered the consequences of actions and asked for advice before they acted; reasons for their decisions were supposed to be transparent and they were expected to review the results of their actions. If things went wrong, the leaders had to own up to their mistakes, take personal responsibility for any negative effects and try to compensate any followers who suffered. They should have acted with wisdom and broadmindedness in their relations with the communities outside their country. They had to honour and respect their differences and encourage their people to learn from different ways of being and the different perspectives of other countries.

Respect

Respect is a recurring theme in the Nhunggabarra law stories. When Aborigines use the word 'respect', it does not carry the conventional meanings of today—that is, to convey a feeling of admiration of someone or obedience towards a higher authority. 'Respect' in the Aboriginal sense is an action verb. It means that you allow people to see you in 'your true form'; authentic, as you are. You show your authentic self only to people you respect, people you think worth the effort, and who you consider as having the capacity to understand what you mean and who you are. Showing your authentic self to another person is, as such, a sign of respect. Tex Skuthorpe sometimes thanks a group of listeners for 'the respect'. He is not thanking them, as most of them probably believe, for listening to him, but he is thanking them for allowing him to see them as they truly are.

Respect permeated one's understanding of what it was to be a Nhunggabarra person. At the core was a general respect for knowledge itself. The respect for knowledge gave all knowledgeable individuals automatically an influential position. Their influence, however, was balanced by respect the opposite way: knowledgeable people supposedly respected the integrity of others and had to lead without imposing themselves on others and without giving outright orders. The followers would, in turn, respect the leader and not try to usurp the leader's role.

Horizontal Leadership in Theory Today

In mainstream leadership theory the discourse on shared and distributed leadership (SL/DL), comes nearest to a horizontal leadership paradigm. The term shared leadership (SL) can be traced to education management (Peters and Scoville 1984; Reid 1967), but has risen to prominence only in the last few years as an umbrella term covering a broad range of alternatives to the dominant vertical leadership paradigm (Pearce and Conger 2003a). The term distributed leadership (DL) was discussed in 1986 (Brown and Hosking 1986) in conjunction with management in social movements, but it was not considered as a concept worthy of scholarly attention until it emerged as an alternative to single chain of command in a programme funded by the US Department of Education in 1996 (House and Aditya 1997).

The SL/DL discourse can be understood as being an early pre-paradigm era; a reaction against the dominant vertical leadership paradigm. Pre-paradigm eras are often random (Kuhn 1970) as the SL/DL field indeed appears to be. Research is in an embryonic stage, exploring new metaphors like 'transmission' (Buchanan et al. 2007) and characterised by a wide range of definitions. Contributions are predominantly theoretical and often uncritical (see Gronn 2002; Pearce and Manz 2005). One can treat SL and DL as synonyms; other terms that have been used are 'dispersed leadership' (see Currie 2007) and 'peer leadership' (House and Aditya 1997).

Pearce and Conger (2003a) trace efforts to find alternatives to the dominant individual–focused vertical paradigm theories back to 1924 with Follett's (1951) notion of 'the law of the situation', that is, the person with the most knowledge and experience in any given situation should be appointed leader, regardless of rank or hierarchical position. They argue that leadership seen as a process or as an activity is a more useful perspective and they define shared leadership as: 'a dynamic, interactive influence process among individuals in groups for which the objective is to lead one another to the achievement of group organizational goals or 'both'.

To see leadership as a process means that organisation is both the outcome of action and a vehicle for it (Gronn 2002), and that leadership is but one of a number of inputs to the process influenced by environmental factors, which can substitute leadership (Kerr and Jermier 1978). Gronn provides an indicative taxonomy of three stages of concertive action which lead to conjoint agency. The taxonomy, however, lacks reference to its conceptual origin, concertive control, originally developed theoretically by Tompkins and Cheney (1985) to describe a group of people acting 'in concert'. Concertive control in teams develops through the values and norms of team members and becomes manifest in the interaction processes of the team members themselves by peers within the team, who enforce the concertive control system on each other (Wright and Barker 2000). Team members are expected to conform to the team norms and rules with violation resulting in various forms of sanctioning by the team. It is a form of community policing that can be 'more powerful, less apparent, and more difficult to resist than that of the bureaucracy' (Barker 1993: 408).

SL/DL literature generally presupposes an environment where SL/DL is emerging or implemented within an organisation, public or private, characterised by the vertical leadership paradigm (see Gardner et al. 2005; Hooker and Csikszentmihalyi 2003; Mayo et al. 2003), which may be more or less benevolent toward SL/DL or even actively driving it (see Jackson 2000), for instance, as a Super Leader (Houghton et al. 2003). Contributions discuss ways to empower or encourage SL (see Manz and Sims 1987, Pearce et al. 2008), emancipate (see Auwal 1996, Jaros 2006) or facilitate (Houghton et al. 2003) the rise or emergence of SL.

The issue is the dearth of organisations built under a horizontal paradigm. Today's mainstream organisations are built and governed under the vertical paradigm and they function in societies with vertical paradigm institutions. Hence the paradoxical situation

(Fletcher and Käufer 2003) is that SL/DL can exist only if an existing vertical leadership structure introduces it. But even in those cases members will have an implicit leadership theory (Seers et. al 2003) coloured by the vertical paradigm. As the 18 historical bases of shared leadership SL/DL listed by Pearce and Conger (2003b) bear witness of: It is virtually impossible to find a 'pure' state of shared leadership 'untainted' by the vertical leadership paradigm in today's organisations. SL is portrayed as being dependent on a vertical power, which can change its attitude overnight. Disappointment with the progress of the discourse is evident (see O'Toole et al. 2003); Gronn (2008) considers 'hybrid' leadership a more accurate description of the current SL/DL practice.

Contemporary Hunter-gatherer Bands—Common Traits

Comparative studies (Barnard 1992, 1999; Gluckman 2006; Sanderson and Alderson 2005; Service 1971, 1979; Woodburn 1982) on the organisation of hunter–gatherer bands find similarities across all continents. The following summary is taken from empirical studies on African Bushmen bands. Australian Aborigines are different in some respects, as discussed above.

African Bushmen bands consist of family units, each comprising some 2–8 people. The bands are rarely larger than 50 people and regularly disperse into family units for the winter season, when food is less abundant. Social groups are flexible and constantly changing in composition. There are no strict rules regarding group affiliation. Movement of all types, in bands, between bands and geographical areas are seen as healthy and desirable in themselves. Adults are free to join and leave the band at will and they frequently do. Some, particularly men, even choose lives as eremites.

Adults are not dependent on *specific* other people for access to basic requirements. Relations among people stress sharing and mutuality, but do not involve long-term binding commitments and dependencies. No tightly defined group monopolises resources.

Contemporary hunter–gatherer bands assert strong egalitarian values; equality is repeatedly acted out and publicly demonstrated. The value of sharing is emphasised and reinforced by peer pressure on a daily basis. Sharing of more valuable resources, such as meat, are regulated by strict rules, which ensure wide distribution.

Leadership Without Leaders

One might believe that hunter–gatherer societies, which tend to be characterised by fluid organisation and 'chaotic social arrangements' (Lee 1979: 54) and absence of formal governmental and legal systems, would require 'strong men' to act as judges and policemen. However, there are (and were) no leaders at all in hunter–gatherer bands. Instead, there are several codes of behaviour, among them the kinship system. Guided by these rules adults have and feel a responsibility for the functionality of the band and they initiate and apply 'management practices' to influence the functionality.

Personal Influence

There are no differences in material wealth and no formal leaders in hunter–gatherer bands. But equality in status is not there; some band members are more influential than others. Anthropologists measure influence as the extent to which opinions attract public support during decision processes. Under that criterion knowledge and experience of the matter in question and personality are characteristics that carry most weight.

However, a person, who has expertise in one matter, will not necessarily, be influential in another; for instance Silberbauer (1981: 138–90) observed little or no 'overflow' of prestige in the G/wi band he studied. Leadership shifted quite unpredictably among acknowledged experts with an occasional 'dark horse'. Discussions tended to be emotionally calm with a lack of competitiveness.

Barnard (1992), in searching for personality qualities that make persons more influential in a !Kung band, concludes that an absence of certain traits is the most common attribute. The most influential people are the 'opposite of arrogant, boastful, overbearing or aloof'. These traits absolutely disqualify a person as leader (ibid.: 345). Modesty in all respects is the hallmark of an influential !Kung band member.

Generally, older people are more influential than the young in bands (Barnard 1992; Berndt and Berndt 1999; Service 1979; Silberbauer 1981). Also, in some hunter–gatherer societies, particularly among Australian Aborigines, men have a more visible role than women in decision making. But the main common criterion for leadership, irrespective of continent, seems to be generally acknowledged expertise in the matter under deliberation (Berndt and Berndt 1999, Silberbauer 1981) and the situation (Tonkinson 1988).

Conflict Resolution

While the anthropologist literature consulted for this study agrees that hunter–gatherer bands generally can be characterised as non-authoritarian, sharing and caring, avoiding hostility rather than fighting and cooperative rather than competitive, intra-band conflicts are not uncommon. The general approach to conflict resolution is to make sure that grievances are addressed at as early a stage as possible before they become serious enough to cause serious damage in relations. The first and most important conflict resolution is to talk. In fact, the !Kung have been characterised as the most talkative people in the world (Lee 1979: 372ff). Much of their talking seems aimed at testing the air for any potential grievances.

The potential for conflict is further minimised by the codes of behaviour. Kinship and values provide criteria by which a range of actions can be judged right or wrong. Kinship also regulates how to behave and communicate towards all members in the band in order to resolve a conflict. Other 'management methods' to resolve a budding conflict can be to organise a feast and make sure the people involved are forced to communicate. Exorcising dances (also known as trance dances) are performed to dispel non-specific tensions among bushmen societies. The initiatives to such occasions may come from men and women, old and young (Service 1979).

If a conflict grows to involve the whole band, consensus is applied. Consensus is not unanimity of opinion or decision—it is a process that ends when most members of the team agree on a clear option and the few who oppose it think they have had an opportunity to influence that choice.

Discussion

This chapter has presented an analysis of shared leadership in hunter–gatherer bands, which once probably was humanity's dominant leadership–followership paradigm. The paradigm has proven to be remarkably resilient in the few contemporary hunter–gatherer bands that still survive the onslaught on their habitats.

Contemporary hunter–gatherer societies and band organisations have given important contributions to social exchange theory (Sahlins 1974), but they are absent from organisation theory and leadership research. This is unfortunate because studies from a leadership perspective on the vast empirical research accumulated in, for instance, social and evolutionary anthropology represent non-mainstream data, which would be valuable at this stage of the field.

At a general level, therefore, the study encourages further exploration of the horizontal leadership paradigm; it is one unique contribution that the discourse on indigenous leadership can make to the general leadership discourse.

The chapter also identifies two specific contributions, developed under a horizontal paradigm, to further understanding of shared leadership in today's organisations. One is a generic framework for shared leadership derived from 'The Black Swans' story. The other is what we may learn from the meetings between horizontal and vertical paradigms in bands.

A GENERAL FRAMEWORK FOR CONJOINT AGENCY UNDER A HORIZONTAL PARADIGM

Gronn (2002) suggests three successive stages in a process of institutionalisation of concertive action: Spontaneous collaboration, intuitive working relations and institutionalised practices. 'The Black Swans' story prescribes practices in the third or even a fourth stage: they have become institutionalised in the form of an explicit code of conduct. Wurunna, the archetypical self-enhancing (Michie and Gooty 2005) and corrupt (Pearce et al. 2008) leader, is punished; hence the opposite is the self-transcending behavioural ideal. The story identifies 12 ideal leadership codes and one ideal followership code of conduct. They are outlined in a 'modern' form by the author in Table 9.1. Other stories (see Sveiby and Skuthorpe 2006) prescribe further follower behaviours; they are summarised in Table 9.2.

One Nhunggabarra law story ('The Crane and the Crow', cited in Sveiby and Skuthorpe 2006) prescribes 'role-splitting'; a mechanism for division of labour. Roles can be seen as patterns of behaviour (Katz and Kahn 1978), which allow individuals to know both what others expect of them and what to expect from others. The individual Nhunggabarra roles may once have emerged organically, but the process for allocating roles described in the law stories had become highly institutionalised; the roles were pre-planned by the women already at the stage of determining suitable marriage partners and finally allocated at birth.

The roles connected with fishing (net-making, trapping, catching, cooking), hunting (tracking, spearing, collecting and cooking), teaching of stories and many other activities were divided in this

Table 9.1: Code of Conduct for temporary leaders derived from 'The Black Swans' (1–12) and Crane and Crow stories (13)

Leadership Code of Conduct

1.	Do not take the leadership role for ego reasons–you are there on behalf of the followers.
2.	Do not use fear to influence (fear of competition, job losses, and so on).
3.	Do not keep information to yourself—share.
4.	Do not exploit ignorance (of customers, of followers, and so on).
5.	Do not say one thing and do another—walk the talk.
6.	Do not ignore risks for others (in the operation, when launching new products, and so on).
7.	Do not blame others when things go wrong.
8.	Do not conceal problems occurring—take responsibility.
9.	Do not leave the followers alone to save themselves (in times of downsizing, and so on).
10.	Do not inflict damage on the innocent bystanders (such as society).
11.	Do not repeat mistakes—acknowledge and learn from them.
12.	Do not avoid the issues—change direction before it is too late.
13.	Do not impose your own view on other people.

Source: Sveiby and Skuthorpe 2006.

way. For example, every story had four custodians; all four would know the whole story, but each was allowed to teach only their own part. Each hunter would hold all the knowledge about an animal and its related ecosystem, and each would be able to perform all

Table 9.2: Code of Conduct for temporary followers derived from 'The Black Swans' (1) and other stories (2–3)

Followership Code of Conduct

1.	Do not follow a leader who shows disrespect toward followers.
2.	Defer to more knowledgeable people.
3.	Do not usurp the role of another person.

Source: Sveiby and Skuthorpe 2006.

four roles (for instance in an emergency), but each was allowed to perform only their own role. Role-splitting reduces the risk that someone would develop a power monopoly; it increases the number of interfaces between leader and follower roles and it forces leaders and followers to interact, that is, it increases interdependencies (Gronn 2002) by creating complementary roles.

A multitude of roles created a multitude of role leaders and the law added support and authority to the role owners by also requiring respect for the person fulfilling their role. This meant that leaders were safe in the role—but only as long as they showed respect to the followers. The Nhunggabarra person with a certain role had undisputed leadership and power in that field of knowledge, but at the same time they had to accept the leadership of others and be the follower in other knowledge fields. So every adult had both leader roles and follower roles. Both roles were temporary; who had the leader role and who had the follower role depended on situation, task and context. This is crucial; unless the roles are transient the follower code of conduct may lead to permanent subservience.

Figure 9.1 depicts conjoint action as the outcome of a process of interactive influence between leaders and followers moderated by mutual respect and supplemented by substitutes for leadership. It is a generic framework developed under a horizontal paradigm; it avoids the vertical paradigm, both the predominant top–down leadership dyad and its 'radical' vertical opposite, to turn the leadership–followership dyad upside down and to see leaders as dependent on followers (Meindl 1995). The framework does not predetermine the number of leaders and followers; examples from contemporary bands suggest that the numbers fluctuate depending on task, situation and context.

The framework allows for at least two possible leadership approaches leading to conjoint action; one is the serial emergence model originally suggested by Conger and Pearce 2003 with either explicit or implicit coordination (Gronn 2002). Implicit coordination and role differentiation have been found to increase

Figure 9.1: A Generic Horizontal Paradigm Framework for Shared Leadership Derived from Aboriginal Law: Conjoint Action as the Result of Interactive Influence Moderated by Mutual Respect and Substitutes for Leadership

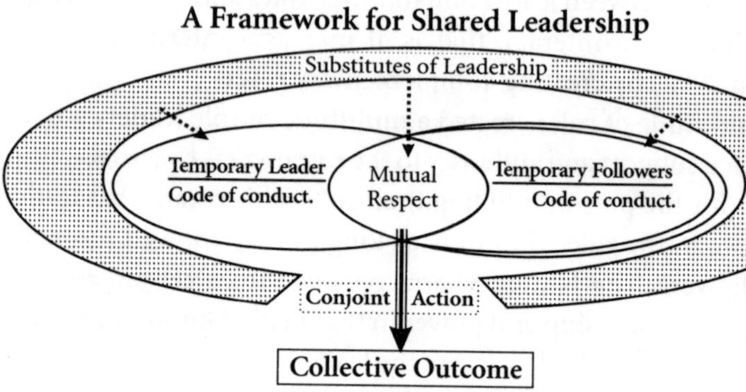

A Framework for Shared Leadership

Substitutes of Leadership

| Temporary Leader Code of conduct. | Mutual Respect | Temporary Followers Code of conduct. |

Conjoint Action

Collective Outcome

team efficiency (Seers et al. 2003). An example of serial emergence with implicit coordination and/or role differentiation (unclear which) comes from the memoirs of the Australian labour activist Mary Gilmore (1986). She describes a team of Aborigines, who were felling and positioning trees as a barrier in a river, probably in the 1870s: 'Every man was alert; no man got in another's way; and each was captain in his own place.'

The other approach is a process where all members of the organisation feel a responsibility for maintaining harmony and act accordingly. Examples from contemporary Bushmen bands described above can illustrate. One is the constant watch-out for potential causes of disharmony, addressed by constant talking among the !Kung. The other is 'management actions' to keep the cohesion of the group, maintain harmony and avoid internal conflict (Barnard 1992; Lee 1979).

A key component in the framework is respect. Respect—downwards, upwards and sideways—prevents leaders' power abuse and follower alienation/obstruction. Respect also counteracts negative effects that may come of concertive control. The concept of respect in the Aboriginal sense is quite similar to the concept of authenticity proposed by Avolio et al. (2004) and Gardner et al. (2005). The difference is that their concept of authenticity is developed under the vertical leadership paradigm while respect assumes a horizontal relationship between temporary leaders and temporary followers. Rule #13 in Table 9.1, which states that leaders should lead without imposing their views on the followers, forces leaders to lead by example, an authentic leadership ideal also identified by Avolio et al. (2004).

The shared leadership process is supported by substitutes of leadership (Kerr and Jermier 1978). In hunter–gatherer bands they are numerous and combined, they become quite strong. Unlike substitutes identified in modern organisations, the substitutes in bands give clear rules on how to behave also in contentious tasks and on how to communicate to reduce conflict and they define criteria against which proposals can be measured when members are faced with difficult decisions. The most important substitutes among hunter–gatherer bands are kinship, high skills levels and abilities of the adults and closely-knit groups (ibid.), strong shared values in general (Podsakoff and MacKenzie 1997), shared collective values and team orientation (Day et al. 2004) and, since all adults were potentially self-sustainable, the capability for self-leadership (Manz and Sims 1980).

One might say that in bands the substitutes of leadership function as live 'law books' and 'management counsel' embedded in people; they do not replace formal chiefs and judges, but they empower adult band members to do their jobs. These are positive aspects of strong substitutes, and vertical paradigm organisations lack them to a large degree. The negative aspect, however, can be rigidity. There was and is in bands no mechanism to change the kinship rules and the codes of conduct—except by evolution. For organisations of our times this is unthinkable, so the generic framework in Figure 9.1 needs to include codes of conduct for both leaders and followers about how to change the rules.

Leadership under a horizontal paradigm such as the one above can be summarised under a Golden Rule: *Lead others as you wish them to lead you.*

VERTICAL MEETS HORIZONTAL

The first written record of the meeting between the vertical leadership paradigm and the horizontal paradigm of a hunter–gatherer band is from 29 January 1789. The author was the captain of the marines, Watkin Tench, who came across a group of Australian Aboriginal men walking on the beach three days after the First Fleet arrived in what was to become Sydney Harbour. Tench (1996 [1789]: 57) makes this entry in his diary:

> It would be trespassing on the reader's indulgence where I impose on him on account of *any civil regulations, or ordinances, which may possibly exist* among this people. I declare to him that I know not of any, and that excepting a little tributary respect which *the younger parts appear to pay to those more advanced in years, I never could observe any degrees of subordination among them.* (emphasis original)

His condescending entry resonances with disbelief—both attitudes were to dominate the British colonial governments in the years to come. The British leaders, governed by the vertical paradigm, could not cope with a people, who neither recognised chiefs with positional powers nor political leaders. During 1800s the British, therefore, instituted a system of appointed 'chiefs', who were given brass plaques as a token of their 'distinction'. The forced introduction of vertical leadership on people familiar only with the horizontal paradigm had disastrous social effects, which still prevail in Aboriginal society today. However, they are outside the scope of this chapter.

'The Black Swans' story shows a horizontal paradigm opinion about the vertical leadership paradigm and it is not a pretty picture—almost Machiavellian. It tells the band members that a self-enhancing individual, who exploits hierarchical status, must be stopped early on or else the band's existence is in danger. Also the constant watch-out behaviours of contemporary bands suggest high risk awareness in this respect.

This begs the question about the stability of the horizontal paradigm, a question raised by both Conger and Pearce (2003) and Seers et al. (2003). The resilience and longevity of the horizontal paradigm in bands from prehistory into our days shows that it can be stable over a very long time indeed. However, the data of this study suggest that SL requires constant maintenance if it is to remain stable—maybe even more so today when the implicit leadership theory (Seers et al. 2003) of both leaders and followers is ruled by the vertical paradigm.

How do/did members of bands maintain stability? Studies on contemporary African hunter–gatherer bands indicate that their form of shared leadership requires members, who are willing and capable to take on both leader roles and follower roles, just as the SL/DL discourse postulates (see Conger and Pearce 2003).

One factor seems to be transactive memory (Seibert et al. 2003) aided by education; skills and knowledge are traded across generations via socialisation, explicit codes of conduct and stories. The Nhunggabarra law stories contain explicit leadership and followership codes of conduct, which were taught and internalised during adolescence (Sveiby and Skuthorpe 2006).

A third factor is the strength of leadership substitutes. In bands they formalise relationships and communications, thereby empowering adult band members to deal also with difficult situations and conflicts of interest, tasks which in modern societies and organisations are considered to be the roles of judges and top chiefs. Although substitutes of leadership have generated much scholarly interest since Kerr's and Jermier's seminal paper in 1978, it has never been suggested that substitutes may replace top management.

A fourth factor is the size of the group, an issue raised also by Conger and Pearce (2003). Contemporary African hunter–gatherer bands vary between 10 and 100 individuals; thereof perhaps half are adults with capacity to influence. Above that size they tend to disintegrate. When individual band members have a free choice many seem to prefer to opt out (Barnard 1992) rather than to face a polarised situation (Seibert et al. 2003) head on. On the other hand, contemporary bands form loose co-operative structures; there is also some evidence of federative structures in prehistoric Australia comprising much larger groups and with quite elaborate institutions and processes (See Sveiby and Skuthorpe 2006 for more details). This suggests that large organisations built under the horizontal paradigm may look quite differently compared to organisations built under the vertical paradigm.

Last but not least, a large number of other practices and factors found in Nhunggabarra law (NL) and in anthropological studies on contemporary bands (AR) facilitate SL and counteract barriers. This suggests that bands have had the group leadership capacity (Day et al. 2004) to respond to environmental factors and new situations and develop measures accordingly from prehistory onwards. These factors became interwoven in the context of all other measures, together creating an almost ironclad paradigm, resilient and stable over time.

In Table 9.3 a list of those factors is compared to the list by Seers et al. (2003) (SKW) and other studies.

LIMITATIONS AND FUTURE RESEARCH

How did leadership in bands emerge? Why did leadership in those early days of humanity become dominated by a horizontal rather than a vertical paradigm? Were there prehistoric bands where vertical leadership was tried and failed? In what settings did the vertical paradigm later replace the horizontal paradigm? These are among the questions beyond the scope of this chapter, partly

Table 9.3: Facilitators and Barriers of Shared Leadership—A Comparison

Facilitators of Shared Leadership in theory	Nhunggabarra Law (NL) and contemporary bands in anthropology research (AR)
Task requires role differentiation (SKW)	Role splitting (NL). Creates division of labour
Multiple exchange relationships (SKW)	Role splitting (NL). Increases interdependencies
Group size; larger than 6, up to a point where coordination requires formalisation (SKW)	Band sizes vary between 10 and 100; bands above 100 tend to disintegrate (AR)
Generalised exchange norms (SKW)	'Sharing' and generalised exchange characterise h-g bands (NL, AR)
Team agrees on shared explicit codes of conduct for concertive control. (Wright and Barker 2000)	Explicit codes of conduct contained in law stories were taught and internalised (NL)
Shared collective values (Day et al. 2004; Podsakoff and MacKenzie 1997)	Shared values emphasising equality, sharing and community characterise hunter – gatherer bands (NL, AR)
Barriers to Shared Leadership in theory	**Nhunggabarra Law (NL) and contemporary bands in anthropology research (AR)**
Scepticism toward the idea of shared leadership among both leaders and followers (SKW)	Bands enforce shared leadership (AR) and outlaw a vertical paradigm (NL, AR)
Evolutionary evidence of status differentials among both humans and animals (SKW)	Wide range of rules (NL) and concertive control (AR) to counteract differentiation
One or two leaders usually emerge in leaderless groups (SKW)	Wide range of rules (NL) and concertive control (AR) to restrain status seeking individuals
Individual differences in status seeking—non-competitive individuals defer (SKW)	Roles allocated to all adults and rules to ensure parity leader-follower (NL), community policing (AR) and rules (NL) to suppress competitive behaviours
Implicit leadership theories; group members expect members, who fit cognitive schemas to act in leadership roles (SKW)	Probably the same—except that cognitive schemas in bands generate expectations of leadership and followership under an Horizontal paradigm (AR)
Individual lack of receptivity to SL (Conger and Pearce 2003)	Non-receptive band members could be expelled (AR)

because of space limitations, partly because it has drawn from comparative studies with the aim to generalise. More specific studies on bands, examining the differences rather than similarities may shed light on those issues.

There is none or little work done on followership in shared leadership settings—only implicitly can a reader sometimes deduce that it can be both emotionally taxing (see Brown and Hosking 1986), and time consuming. Confusion among followers and leaders alike (Manz and Sims 1995) in self-organising teams is therefore sometimes seen as evidence that SL is inadequate and impractical in modern organisations. A more likely reason is a lack of knowledge about how to share leadership among people in modern organisations, as Conger and Pearce 2003 suggest. There must be a huge difference in skills among today's organisations about how to share leadership effectively compared to those of the members in prehistoric and contemporary bands. What are the skills we have lost?

This chapter argues that substitutes of leadership can empower members of an organisation to make decisions independent also of top chiefs; in Aboriginal bands the substitutes had become quite institutionalised. Research on substitutes has been done primarily under the vertical paradigm, so it has focused on amending Kerr's and Jermier's original list or finding empirical evidence that substitutes actually do replace leaders (see Podsakoff and MacKenzie 1997 for an overview). No studies have been made to examine substitutes from a horizontal paradigm and no studies have been made on whether substitutes can also replace top chiefs. The example of bands suggest that substitutes have to be on the one hand powerful enough to give members skills and concrete tools to deal with difficult situations, on the other hand flexible enough to allow change. What are those substitutes in modern organisations? They may exist under our nose; existing and successful shared leadership practices have a tendency to 'get disappeared' (Fletcher and Käufer 2003) in organisations ruled by the vertical paradigm. Which substitutes are the most effective from followers' perspective? Empirical studies in non-corporate settings might shed light on this issue.

A theoretical contribution would be to explore the concept of respect (in the Aboriginal sense) in modern organisations. A horizontal paradigm version of the authenticity concept by Avolio et al. (2004) suitable for empirical testing under the horizontal paradigm could be a starting point.

METHODOLOGICAL ISSUES

This chapter combines empirical data from traditional indigenous stories and secondary sources, such as anthropological research. Traditional indigenous stories are unusual as sources in management and leadership research, except in research fields, such as anthropology, where indigenous people are the object of study. In such studies their stories are used to understand the indigenous society in question, but the knowledge is not considered relevant for drawing conclusions valid for the Western industrialised societies. The issue is what is considered legitimate knowledge. The scientific concept of knowledge has not much in common with the knowledge of indigenous people, which is largely based on personal experiences and uncontrolled, undocumented observations and conveyed in stories via oral tradition. 'Modern materialistic scientism leaves all the questions that really matter unanswered', as Schumacher (1977: 14) stated in his critique against the Western scientific reductionism. Hence much of humanity's oldest wisdom is lost.

Traditional indigenous stories are highly unusual as sources in organisational and leadership research. They are vulnerable compared to documents in one respect: oral tradition cannot guarantee word-by-word accuracy. This raises several critical issues. How authentic is 'The Black Swans' story? How can we know that the story is not just a recent invention? How can we know that the interpretation is valid?

There are some aspects that suggest a fair degree of authenticity and validity. One is the message of the story, which displays values consistent with anthropologists' accounts from contemporary hunter–gatherer societies both in Africa and Australia. Another is that the Australian Aborigines lived without much contact with the world outside Australia until 1789; the Nhunggabarra people probably had no contact before 1828. Since archaeological evidence shows a high level of cultural consistency in Aboriginal Australia as far back as 30,000 years (Flood 1999), it matters less how old the story is in years. Given the conservatism of hunter–gatherer societies, even a young story would probably reflect very old traditions and values. One might speculate that the complexity of 'The Black Swans' story suggests a gradual evolvement over time. The story in its current form could therefore be fairly young, while the core message could be quite old. A final guarantee is the elaborate system for maintaining consistency and safekeeping the law stories across generations that the Nhunggabarra had devised, (see Sveiby and Skuthorpe 2006). The accuracy of their system has been tested to some degree; seven of the 10 stories (not the Black Swans story, however) published by Sveiby and Skuthorpe (2006) had been collected and published 110 years earlier in 1896 by K. Langloh Parker (1978). A comparison between the versions reveals a remarkable consistency.

The capacity of stories to capture and convey the essence of complex knowledge beyond the text itself has made story telling recognised as an effective communication method (Denning 2007; Martin and Powers 1983), and stories have been the basis for study in linguistics (Schank and Abelson 1995), who claim 'that from the point of view of the social functions of knowledge, what people know consists almost exclusively of stories and the cognitive machinery necessary to understand, remember, and tell stories'. In organisation studies and related disciplines the recognition came in the 1990s, with a 'methodological turn to language' (Alvesson and Kärreman 2000) and development of methods for analysing narratives (Czarniawska 1999) and discourses (Potter 1997). Lately, stories have also been recognised as an effective knowledge management method (Denning 2000; Snowden 2002).

What we know about band organisation is primarily through observations made among present-day hunter–gatherers made by anthropologists, which raises the question as to what degree conclusions about the past can be inferred. The anthropological primary research instrument, participant observation is not effective when the society under study has undergone dramatic changes (Aboriginal Australia) or no longer exists (the Nhunggabarra people).

African bushmen are these days regarded as the most primal of people living today, with genetic compositions that have been traced back more than 100,000 years. However, as people their societies have not been isolated from influence by other African peoples or white colonists—but the contrary. Hence, detailed conclusions about past leadership practices cannot be inferred with certainty. One reason why anthropologists maintain that inferrals are possible is the extraordinary resilience of the hunter–gatherer culture and their vigilant defence of their value system when exposed to other cultures (Woodburn 1988).

CONCLUSION

This study has drawn upon Australian Aboriginal traditional knowledge and anthropological studies on contemporary African bands to argue that humanity's first leadership was indigenous: a horizontal leadership–followership paradigm, which is still practiced in contemporary bands. The existence of an indigenous horizontal leadership paradigm shows that the common tendency to believe that vertical leadership is 'needed' for an organisation or a society to be successful is a paradigmatic belief—no more rational, realistic or logical than any other belief. The IL discourse can see this as an opportunity to make a unique contribution to the leadership discourse. The study encourages further exploration of indigenous leadership as a horizontal paradigm; it may progress the discourse towards recognising the value of a horizontal paradigm. Perhaps even more importantly, a horizontal leadership paradigm is one of the unique contributions that IL can make to the mainstream leadership discourse.

The chapter does not suggest that modern organisations should apply the practices and the values of hunter–gatherer bands—but the contrary. But we can learn from the underlying Golden Rule: *Lead others as you wish them to lead you.* We cannot develop as strong substitutes of leadership in today's organisations as bands did in prehistory—but we can learn from the principle: 'substitutes of leadership can replace managers and even top-chiefs'. We cannot apply all the methods of bands—but we can develop our versions of them. This requires a research effort aimed at developing the indigenous horizontal paradigm further on its own terms. Fertile ground for studies can be organisations which exist as far outside from the vertical paradigm as possible. By deriving a framework for shared leadership from Aboriginal law and anchoring it in the leadership discourse this chapter has tried to demonstrate the value and the relevance for the IL discourse in doing so.

ACKNOWLEDGEMENT

The author acknowledges with gratitude the contribution of Tex Skuthorpe in interpreting the 'Black Swans' story and other Aboriginal law stories used in this chapter.

REFERENCES

Alvesson, M. and D. Kärreman. 2000. 'Varieties of Discourse: On the Study of Organizations Through Discourse Analysis', *Human Relations*, 53(9): 1125–49.

Auwal, M. 1996. 'Promoting Microcapitalism in the Service of the Poor: The Grameen Model and Its Cross-Cultural Adaptation', *Journal of Business Communication* 33(1): 27–49.

Avery, G. 2004. *Understanding Leadership: Paradigms and Cases*. London: Sage Publications.

Avolio, B., W. Gardner, F. Walumbwa, F. Luthans and D. May. 2004. 'Unlocking the Mask: A Look at the Process by Which Authentic Leaders Impact Follower Attitudes and Behaviours', *The Leadership Quarterly*, 15: 801–23.

Barker, J. 1993. 'Tightening the Iron Cage: Concertive Control in Self-Managing Teams', *Administrative Science Quarterly*, 38: 408–37.

Barnard, A. 1992. *Hunters and Herders of Southern Africa: A Comparative Ethnography of the Khoisan Peoples* (Cambridge Studies in Social and Cultural Anthropology; 85). Cambridge: Cambridge University Press.

———. 1999. 'Modern Hunter-Gatherers and Early Symbolic Culture', in R. Dunbar, C. Knight and C. Power (eds), *The Evolution of Culture: An Interdisciplinary View*, pp. 50–68. Edinburgh: Edinburgh University Press.

Berndt, R. and C. Berndt. 1999. *The World of the First Australians* (fifth revised edition). Sydney: Aboriginal Studies Press.

Broome, R. 2005. *Aboriginal Victorians: A History Since 1800*. Sydney: Allen & Unwin.

Brown, M. and D. Hosking. 1986. 'Distributed Leadership and Skilled Performance as Successful Organization in Social Movements', *Human Relations* 39(1): 65–79.

Buchanan, D., R. Caldwell, J. Meyer, J. Storey and C. Wainwright. 2007. 'Leadership Transmission: A Muddled Metaphor?', *Journal of Health Organization and Management*. 21(3): 246–58.

Conger, J. and C. Pearce. 2003. 'A Landscape of Opportunities: Future Research on Shared Leadership', in C. Pearce and J. Conger (eds), *Shared Leadership: Reframing the Hows and Whys of Leadership*, pp. 285–304. London: Sage Publications.

Currie, G. 2007. 'A Critique of Transformational Leadership: Moral, Professional and Contingent Dimensions of Leadership Within Public Services Organizations', *Human Relations*, 60(2): 341–70.

Czarniawska, B. 1999. *Writing Management. Organization Theory as a Literary Genre*. Oxford: Oxford University Press.

Day, D., P. Gronn and E. Salas. 2004. 'Leadership Capacity in Teams', *Leadership Quarterly*, 15: 857–80.

Denning, S. 2000. *The Springboard: How Storytelling Ignites Action in Knowledge-Era Organizations*. KMCI Press.

———. 2007. *The Secret Language of Leadership: How Leaders Inspire Action Through Narrative*. New York: Jossey Bass.

Dunbar, R., C. Knight and C. Power. 1999. *The Evolution of Culture: An Interdisciplinary View*. Edinburgh: Edinburgh University Press.

Fletcher, J. and K. Käufer. 2003. 'Shared Leadership: Paradox and Possibility', in C. Pearce and J. Conger (eds), *Shared Leadership: Reframing the Hows and Whys of Leadership*, pp. 21–47. London: Sage Publications.

Flood, J. 1999. *Archaeology of the Dreamtime: The Story of Prehistoric Australia and its People*. Sydney: Angus & Robertson.

Follett Parker, M. 1951. *Creative Experience*. New York: Peter Smith. Available online at http://link.library.utoronto.ca/booksonline/ (downloaded on 12.04.2008).

314   *Karl-Erik Sveiby*

Gardner, W., B. Avolio, F. Luthans, D. May and F. Walumbwa. 2005. '"Can You See the Real Me?" A Self-Based Model of Authentic Leader and Follower Development', *Leadership Quarterly*, 16: 343–72.

Gilmore, M. 1986. *Old Days, Old Ways* (Illustrations by Robert Avitable). Sydney: Angus & Robertson.

Gluckman, M. 2006. *Politics, Law, and Ritual in Tribal Society*. New Brunswick, NJ: Aldine Transaction. Originally published in 1965 by Oxford: Basil Blackwell.

Gronn, P. 2002. 'Distributed Leadership as a Unit of Analysis', *The Leadership Quarterly*, 13: 423–51.

———. 2008. 'The Future of Distributed Leadership', *Journal of Educational Administration*, 46(2): 141–58.

Hooker, C. and M. Csikszentmihalyi. 2003. 'Flow, Creativity and Shared Leadership: Rethinking the Motivation and Structuring of Knowledge Work', in C. Pearce and J. Conger (eds), *Shared Leadership: Reframing the Hows and Whys of Leadership*, pp. 217–34. London: Sage Publications.

Houghton, J., C. Neck and C. Manz. 2003. 'Self-Leadership and Superleadership: The Heart and Art of Creating Shared Leadership in Teams', in C. Pearce and J. Conger (eds), *Shared Leadership: Reframing the Hows and Whys of Leadership*, pp. 123–40. London: Sage Publications.

House, R. and R. Aditya. 1997. 'The Social Scientific Study of Leadership: Quo Vadis?' *Journal of Management*, 23(3): 409–73.

Jackson, S. 2000. 'A Qualitative Evaluation of Shared Leadership Barriers, Drivers and Recommendations', *Journal of Management in Medicine*, 14(3/4): 166–78.

Jaros, S. 2006. 'Skill Dynamics, Global Capitalism, and Labour Process Theories of Work', *TAMARA: Journal of Critical Postmodern Organization Science*, 5(1/2): 5–16.

Katz, D. and R.L. Kahn. 1978. *The Social Psychology of Organizations*. New York: John Wiley.

Kerr, S. and J. Jermier. 1978. 'Substitutes for Leadership: Their Meaning and Measurement', *Organizational Behaviour and Human Performance*, 22: 275–403.

Kuhn, T. 1970. *The Structure of Scientific Revolutions*, 3rd edition. Chicago: University of Chicago Press.

Langloh Parker, K. 1978. *Australian Legendary Tales* (Contains both 1896, *Australian Legendary Tales: Folklore of the Nhunggahburrahs as Told to the Piccaninnies* and 1898, *More Australian Legendary Tales*). London: Bodley Head and Angus & Robertson.

Lee, R. 1979. *The !Kung San Men, Women, and Work in a Foraging Society*. Cambridge: Cambridge University Press.

Locke, E. 2007. 'Shared Leadership Theory, Letter 1', *The Leadership Quarterly*, 18(3): 281–88.

Martin, J. and M. Powers. 1983. 'Organizational Stories: More Vivid and Persuasive than Quantitative Data', in B. Staw (eds), *Psychological Foundations of Organizational Behavior*, pp. 161–68. Glenview, IL: Scott Foresman.

Manz, C. and H. Sims. 1980. 'Self-Management as a Substitute for Leadership: A Social Learning Theory Perspective', *The Academy of Management Review*, 5: 361–67.

———. 1987. 'Leading Workers to Lead Themselves: The External Leadership of Self-Managing', *Administrative Science Quarterly*, 32(1): 106–28.

Manz, C. and H. Sims. 1995. *Business Without Bosses: How Self-Managing Teams Are Building High- Performing Companies.* New York: Wiley.

Mayo, M., J. Meindl and J-C. Pastor. 2003. 'Shared Leadership in Work Teams: A Social Network Approach', in C. Pearce and J. Conger (eds), *Shared Leadership: Reframing the Hows and Whys of Leadership,* pp. 193–214. London: Sage Publications.

Meindl, J. 1995. 'The Romance of Leadership as a Follower-Centric Theory: A Social Constructionist Approach', *The Leadership Quarterly,* 6(3): 329–41.

Michie, S. and J. Gooty. 2005. 'Values, Emotions, and Authenticity: Will the Real Leader Please Stand Up?', *The Leadership Quarterly,* 16(3): 441–57.

Mitchell, T. 1839. *Three Expeditions Into the Interior of Australia* (Volumes 1 and 2, Limited facsimile edition). London: Boone.

———. 1847. 'Account of the Exploring Expedition Into the Interior of New South Wales', *Tasmanian Journal of Natural Science,* 3(3): 165–82.

O'Toole, J., J. Galbraith and E. Lawler III. 2003. 'The Promise and Pitfalls of Shared Leadership: When Two (or More) Heads are Better than One', in C. Pearce and J. Conger (eds), *Shared Leadership: Reframing the Hows and Whys of Leadership,* pp. 250–68. London: Sage Publications.

Pearce C. and J. Conger (eds). 2003a. *Shared Leadership: Reframing the Hows and Whys of Leadership.* London: Sage Publications.

———. 2003b. 'All Those Years Ago', Preface in C. Pearce and J. Conger (eds), *Shared Leadership: Reframing the Hows and Whys of Leadership,* pp. xi–xii. London: Sage Publications.

Pearce, C. and C. Manz. 2008. 'The New Silver Bullets of Leadership: The Importance of Self- and Shared Leadership in Knowledge Work', *Organizational Dynamics,* 34(2): 130–40.

Pearce, C., C. Manz and H. Sims. 2008. 'The Roles of Vertical and Shared Leadership in the Enactment of Executive Corruption: Implications for Research and Practice', *The Leadership Quarterly,* 19: 353–59.

Pearce C.L. and C. Manz 2005. 'The New Silver Bullets of Leadership: The Importance of Self- and Shared Leadership in Knowledge Work', *Organizational Dynamics* 34(2): 130–40.

Peters, D. and G. Scoville. 1984. 'Shared Leadership in the Graduate Classroom', *Innovative Higher Education,* 8(2): 124–33.

Pindur, W., S. Rogers and Suk Pan Kim. 1995. 'The History of Management: A Global Perspective, *Journal of Management History* 1(1): 59–77.

Potter, J. 1997. 'Discourse Analysis as a Way of Analysing Naturally Occurring Talk', in D. Silverman (ed.), *Qualitative Research: Theory, Method and Practice,* pp. 144–60. London: Sage Publications.

Podsakoff, P. and S. MacKenzie. 1997. 'Kerr and Jermier's Substitutes for Leadership Model: Background, Empirical Assessment, and Suggestions for Future Research', *The Leadership Quarterly* 8(2): 117–25.

Reid, S. 1967. 'Pastoral Care Through Small Groups', *Pastoral Psychology,* 18(3).

Reynolds, H. 1981. *The Other Side of the Frontier: An Interpretation of the Aboriginal Response to the Invasion and Settlement of Australia.* Melbourne: Penguin.

Sahlins, M. 1974. *Stone Age Economics: The Original Affluent Society.* London: Tavistock Publications.

Sanderson, S. and A. Alderson. 2005. *World Societies: The Evolution of Human Social Life.* London: Allyn & Bacon (Pearson Education).

Schank, Roger C. and P. Robert Abelson. 1995. 'Knowledge and Memory: The Real Story', in Robert S. Wyer Jr. (ed), *Knowledge and Memory: The Real Story*, pp. 1–85. Hillsdale, NJ: Lawrence Erlbaum Associates.

Schumacher E. 1977. *A Guide for the Perplexed.* London: Jonathan Cape.

Seers A., T. Keller and J. Wilkerson. 2003. 'Can Team Members Share Leadership? Foundations in Research and Theory', in C. Pearce and J. Conger (eds), *Shared Leadership: Reframing the Hows and Whys of Leadership*, pp. 77–102. London: Sage Publications.

Seibert, S., R. Sparrowe and R. Liden. 2003. 'A Group Exchange Structure Approach to Leadership in Groups', in C. Pearce and J. Conger (eds), *Shared Leadership: Reframing the Hows and Whys of Leadership*, pp. 173–92. London: Sage Publications.

Service, E. 1971. *Primitive Social Organization*, 2nd edition. New York: Random House.

———. 1979. *The Hunter*, 2nd edition, Englewood Cliffs, NJ: Prentice-Hall Foundation of Modern Anthropology Series.

Silberbauer, G. 1981. *Hunter and Habitat in the Central Kalahari Desert.* Cambridge: Cambridge University Press.

Snowden, D. 2002. 'Complex Acts of Knowing Paradox and Descriptive Self-Awareness', *Journal of Knowledge Management*, 6(2).

Sveiby K-E & Lloyd T. 1987. *Managing Knowhow.* Bloomsbury London.

Sveiby, K-E and T. Skuthorpe. 2006. *Treading Lightly: The Hidden Wisdom of the World's Oldest People.* Sydney: Allen & Unwin.

Tench, W. 1996(1789). *A Narrative of the Expedition to Botany Bay and a Complete Account of the Settlement at Port Jackson* (edited and introduced by Tim Flannery). Melbourne: Text Publishing.

Tompkins, P. and G. Cheney. 1985. 'Communication and Unobtrusive Control in Contemporary Organizations', in R. McPhee and P. Tompkins (eds), *Organisational Communication: Traditional Themes and New Directions*, pp. 179–210. Beverly Hills, CA: Sage Publications.

Tonkinson, R. 1988. '"Ideology and Domination" in Aboriginal Australia: A Western Desert Test Case', in T. Ingold, D. Riches and J. Woodburn (eds), *Hunters and Gatherers: Property, Power and Ideology (Explorations in Anthropology)*, pp. 150–64. University College London Series, London: Berg Publishers.

Woodburn, J. 1982. 'Egalitarian Societies', *Man* 17(3): 431–51.

Wright, B. and J. Barker. 2000. 'Assessing Concertive Control in the Team Environment', *Journal of Occupational and Organisational Psychology*, 73(3): 345–61.

Woodburn, J. 1988. 'Hunters and Gatherers Today and Reconstruction of the Past', in T. Ingold, D. Riches and J. Woodburn (eds), *Hunters and Gatherers, Volume 1: History, Evolution, and Social Change (Explorations in Anthropology)*, pp. 431–41. London: Berg Publishers.

10

PERPLEXITY, MANAGEMENT AND BUSINESS IN INDIA

Balakrishnan Muniapan

This chapter explores transformational leadership using ancient Indian Vedic philosophy that provides significance lessons to leaders.

It draws upon hermeneutics, which also originally involved study, understanding and interpretation of ancient or classical text.

The Bhagavad-Gita provides an 'inside-out' approach to leadership and human capital development which is self leadership first before leadership of every other thing. This inside-out perspective is also similar to Schumacher's description of the need for a leader to be self-aware to enable moving up Schumacher's 'ladder' to higher being.

INTRODUCTION

Leadership theories and concepts from the West have dominated the world for over two centuries. This dominance is due to colonisation and the widespread use of English in many countries and the readily available leadership literatures in English language. However, a careful analysis reveals that many of the recently popularised Western leadership theories and concepts have been in practice in the East for centuries. These practices however were not in the context of business organisation but in the state or political governance. Sharma (2001: 1) argues that for a leadership system, to be effective, it has to be rooted in the cultural soil of the country, where it is practiced. Many communities and countries in the world are now trying to discover and explore their own indigenous system of leadership and management, which includes financial management, human resource management, customer relationship management, corporate social responsibility and also corporate governance.

In recent times, Maruyama (1994) was one of the authors who explored the Asian context of leadership beginning with wide understanding of Japanese leadership. Besides Japanese, the interest in exploring other Asian philosophies and also religion in the context of leadership has seen a tremendous growth over the past two decades. As such, several research studies and books had been published to explore Islamic perspective, *Vedic* perspective and Confucianism perspective in the context of leadership. In Malaysia, the current Prime Minister, Datuk Seri Abdullah Ahmad Badawi has promoted an approach, which includes leadership, called Islam Hadhari or civilisation Islam (Swee-Hock and Kesavapany 2006: 36). The Islamic perspectives of leadership have also been explored extensively by several scholars such as Abuznaid (2005), Beekun and Badawi (1999) and Tayeb (1997).

The present growth in the studies of Asian leadership is also due to the growth of the many Asian economies especially Japan, the four tigers (Singapore, South Korea, Taiwan and Hong Kong, which is now part of China), China and India. India, in terms of geography, population size and cultural influence, is currently an important nation in Asia due to the consistent high economic growth rates over the recent decades. As a result an interest in studying leadership systems culture in the Indian context is necessary not only for the foreign multinationals operating in India but also for the Indians themselves who live in India and around the world. The Indian civilisation is also one of the oldest civilisations in the world, with recorded history of more than 5,000 years. The contribution of India and Indians to this world is enormous in various fields of knowledge (Rosen 2002: 7). Several ancient Indian classics such as the *Valmiki Ramayana*,[1] *Mahabharata*,[2] the *Upanishads*[3] and also the *Purana*[4] offer several leadership lessons which are useful even in the modern context, even though many of these texts were written more than 50 centuries ago.

THE BROAD PURPOSE OF THIS CHAPTER

From the perspective of the author the research on leadership lessons and concepts from the Asian context, although growing, is still limited. Most studies are general in nature and not in-depth studies. Even this chapter is also not an in-depth analysis of the *Bhagavad-Gita* and transformational leadership as it attempts to explore the transformational leadership only from the *Bhagavad-Gita* and its significance for human capital development. Asian leadership studies, to a larger extent, are still focusing on applying Western models of leadership practices due to the wealth of Western leadership literatures and concepts available. Besides, many of the new generation of Asian managers have received their education in leadership and management from Western countries [(especially from the UK, USA and Australia (Muniapan and Shaikh 2007: 50–51)]. Furthermore, there are also some fears among the Asian academics that the leadership philosophy, concepts and ideas from Asia will not be able to get acceptance from the West due to Western intellectual dominance and also the mentality of the Asians themselves.[5]

In the context of India,[6] leadership for example, according to Arindam Chaudhuri (one of the advocates of Theory 'I' Management or Indian management) is underdeveloped. Although India has some of the best management schools in the world, most Indian organisations have struggled to progress internationally. Among the reasons cited by Chaudhuri is the failure of Indian management to develop an indigenous leadership style, which revolves around Indian cultural roots and upbringing. He further asserted that an Indian grows up in a system, where family ties and sense of belongingness gets top priority. With this type of background, he may[7] not be able to adjust or fit into the job environment practicing American philosophies of individualistic, direct (low context communication), low power distant and contractual style of leadership.[8]

Recently, some Western countries have begun to take Indian management and leadership seriously. Indian organisations are being mentioned and discussed in MBA classes of various international business schools. Parts of the Western academic community are investing time, resources and intellect to understand Indian culture, leadership and organisations (Panda and Gupta 2007). According to a Goldman Sachs (one of the world's most prestigious investment banks) report recently, Brazil, Russia, India and China can become a much larger force in the world economy over the next 50 years. The report said India could emerge the world's third largest economy as it had the potential for achieving the fastest growth over the next 30 to 50 Years.[9]

In an earlier study by Hofstede (1983) on 'National Culture in Four Dimensions', India is high in power distance as employees acknowledge and respect for the authority of the leader is based on power legitimated by ascribed characteristics such as age and they seldom bypass the chain of command. Besides high power distance, India has a low uncertainty avoidance, which means leaders have a propensity for low risk aversions and employees exhibit little aggressiveness in businesses. India also has low masculinity and low individualism, which means group, family and society are more important than individuals. As such a leadership culture, which is based on high individualism, masculinity, uncertainty avoidance and low power distance, might be inappropriate in the context of Indian leadership and management culture (Gorden et al. 2007). From this objectivist perspective, it is imperative that Indians should focus their effort on transformational leadership development from their own cultural roots.

As a result ancient text such as the *Bhagavad-Gita* can be useful to develop and provide lessons in the Indian context of leadership. Spiritual leaders like Swami Chinmayananda (2003) asserted that from time to time an ancient philosophy like the *Bhagavad-Gita* needs intelligent re-interpretation to apply effectively in the context of modern times. A careful study of the text provides the potential to reveal several lessons in leadership. However there are many corporate leaders from outside India and Indians themselves who are not aware of what the *Bhagavad-Gita* can offer to enhance their leadership effectiveness. The purpose of this chapter is to provide them with transformational leadership lessons from the *Bhagavad-Gita* and also to create awareness to readers of leadership on the existence of many ancient indigenous texts from India such as the *Bhagavad-Gita* which provide many valuable lessons in efficient and effective organisational leadership.

METHODOLOGY

This chapter is based on the qualitative research methodology of hermeneutics. Hermeneutics is related to the name of the Greek god Hermes in his role as the interpreter of the messages of the gods. In the current context, hermeneutics can be described as the interpretation and understanding of ancient literatures and religious texts. It is also used in contemporary philosophy to denote the study of theories and methods of the interpretation of all texts and systems of meaning. The concept of 'text' is here extended beyond written documents to any number of objects subject to interpretation, such as symbols, images and experiences. A hermeneutic is defined as a specific system or method for interpretation, or a specific theory of interpretation. The scope of hermeneutics also includes the investigation and interpretation not only of ancient texts, but of human behaviour generally, including language and patterns of speech, social institutions and ritual behaviours. Hermeneutics is widely applied in many fields of social science such as philosophy, religion and theology, law, sociology and also international relations.[10] Besides social science, hermeneutics is also used in the field of management and organisation such as in the study of organisational culture, information systems, accounting and international management (Noorderhaven 2000).

The *Bhagavad-Gita* was written in the Sanskrit language, one of the oldest languages in the world. The translation of the *Bhagavad-Gita* requires a good mastery of Sanskrit. As the author only has some knowledge of Sanskrit, the main English translation of the *Bhagavad-Gita* verses quoted in this chapter is based on the authoritative translation of A.C Bhaktivedanta Swami Prabhupada (2003). This translation of the *Bhagavad-Gita* (*Bhagavad-Gita As It Is*) is one of the most authoritative editions and also one of the best selling *Bhagavad-Gita* translations in the world and has won praises of some of the world's leading scholars in religious studies, philosophy, theology, history and literature not only in India but around the world.

For this chapter, the *Bhagavad-Gita* is analysed by using the above methodology. The analysis is done based on four stages; namely identification, investigation, interpretation and integration. The identification stage involves searching for the relevant direct and indirect leadership verses or *slokas* from the text; this will be followed by a detailed investigation of the verses in terms of text and context. The next stage involves interpretation by providing the meaning and the relevance of the verses in the modern context. The final stage in the integration of the verses involves adopting, modifying the lessons from the verses and providing commentaries from the perspectives of transformational leadership.

LEADERSHIP THEORIES

Leadership is one of the most researched subjects and interesting topics of discussions in management around the world. Leadership is generally defined as the process of influencing the activities of an individual or a group in efforts towards achieving certain goals. The word 'influencing' can be substituted with other words such as transforming, empowering, driving, motivating and inspiring. In leadership the leader is the key in transforming the followers. The leader is the most important element in leadership. The personality, behaviour and character of the leader are important influences upon the success of any organisation, society or country. Napoleon Bonaparte once said that he would have an army of rabbits led by a lion than an army of lions led by a rabbit (Sheh 2003: vi). It is the leader who navigates and influences the vision and mission for an organisation. In most organisations, societies and countries, the failure or poor performance whether economically, politically or socially are not only due to poor administration but poor leadership. Therefore, leadership is the life force and the spirit of an organisation that holds everything together. The wise leader uses the force from within to inspire and motivate his people. Without the leader, an organisation, a society and a country are a disparate collection of people.

TRANSFORMATIONAL LEADERSHIP

Burns (1978) defined leadership as inducing followers to pursue a common purpose that represents the values and motivations of both leaders and followers. He was the first to define the term 'transformational leadership'. He proposed that leadership process occurs in one of two ways; either transactional or transformational. According to Burns transformational leadership occurs when a leader engages with a follower in such a way that both parties are raised to higher levels of motivation and morality with common purpose. Transformational leaders exhibit charisma, encourage followers to question their own way of doing things, and treat followers differently but equitably based on their follower needs (Bass and Avolio 1994).

Transactional leadership, on the other hand is a set of leadership behaviour that emphasises exchanges or bargains between the leader and the follower, and focuses on how the current needs of the followers can be fulfilled (Maher 1997). The exchanges can be economical, political or psychological in nature. Psychological exchanges are the primary characteristics that distinguish transactional from transformational leadership. Transactional leadership behaviour includes contingent reward, which involves an interaction between the leader and follower based on exchange of resources and management by exception, in which leaders intervene only when problems emerge (Bass and Avolio 1994). Most leaders engage in both transformational and transactional leadership however they do so in differing proportions.

Transactional leadership involves an exchange of valued things based on current values and motivations of both leaders and followers. Transactional leaders emphasise the clarification of tasks, work standards and outcomes. In contrast, Burns (1978) characterised transformational leadership as a process that motivates followers by appealing to higher ideals and moral values. Transformational leaders are able to define and articulate a vision for their organisations and their leadership style can transform their followers towards higher motivation and performance.

THE DIMENSIONS OF
TRANSFORMATIONAL LEADERSHIP

According to Bass and Avolio (1994), also cited in Krishnan et al. (2004), transformational leadership consists of four primary dimensions. They are as follows:

(a) Inspirational Motivation (IM): This dimension is reflected by behaviours that provide meaning and challenge to followers' work. It includes behaviours that articulate clear expectations and demonstrate commitment to overall organisational goals, and arouse a team spirit through enthusiasm and optimism. Krishnan (2000) asserts that inspirational leadership also involves envisioning a desired future state, making followers see that vision, and showing followers how to get to that state. Envisioning is translating intentions into realities by communicating that vision to others to gain their support as the right vision attracts commitment, energises people, creates meaning and establishes a standard of excellence. Vision inspires followers to transcend the outcome and gets people to commit voluntarily and completely something worthwhile.

(b) Idealised Influenced (II): Idealised influence is described as behaviour that results in follower admiration, respect and trust. Idealised influence involves risk sharing on the part of leaders, a consideration of follower needs or personal needs and ethical and moral conduct. Idealised influence also refers to the leader's charisma. Krishnan (2000) define charisma as a form of social authority that derives its legitimacy not from rules, positions or traditions, but rather from faith in the leader's exemplary character. He further asserts that the charismatic leader is seen different from an ordinary person and treated as endowed with supernatural, superhuman or at least exceptional power and qualities. Only charismatic leaders, with their sense of vision and empowering behaviour could address the higher order needs of followers. Charismatic leadership is characterised by followers trust in the correctness of the leader's belief, unquestioning acceptance of the leader, affection for the leaders, willingness to obey the leader, and emotional involvement in the vision and mission of the organisation.

(c) Intellectual Stimulation (IS): Leaders who demonstrate this type of transformational leadership solicit new ideas and creative solutions for problems from their followers and encourage novel approaches for performing work. Krishnan (2000) asserts intellectual stimulation arouses in the followers the awareness of the problems and how they may be solved, and stirs the imagination and generates thoughts and insights. The intellectual stimulation provided by the leader forces the followers to rethink some of the ideas that they never questioned before.

(d) Individualised Consideration (IC): This is reflected by leaders listening attentively to the opinions and feedback of their followers and pay special attention to the followers' needs for achievement and growth. Krishnan (2000) refers individualised consideration as the developmental orientation of the leaders towards the followers. The transformational leader gives personal attention to the followers who seem neglected, treat each follower individually and help each follower to get what they want. These leaders have empathy or the capacity to sense intuitively the thoughts and feelings of others.

Bass (1985), on the other hand found that transactional leadership consists of two factors. They are as follows:

(a) Contingent Reward (CR): This refers to leaders who reward followers for their effort, support and doing what needs to be done by clarifying the followers' roles and task requirements to meet their personal goals and the organisational missions.

(b) Management by Exception (ME): This dimension of a transactional leader refers to leaders taking corrective action only when followers deviate from expectations or fail to meet goals.

A number of researches have suggested that transformational leaders, in general, motivate followers to perform at higher levels and to exert greater effort than do transactional leaders (Bass and Avolio 1994). Transformational leaders motivate others to transcend self-interest so as to benefit the group as a whole. Transformational leaders create vision and direction for their followers around a common mission and give them a sense of purpose.

Table 10.1 gives comparisons between the two leadership styles based on finding by Bass and Avolio (1994) also cited in Krishnan et al. (2004).

The transformational leader, unlike the transactional leader, does not use people as a means to get his organisational objectives fulfilled.

Table 10.1: Comparisons Between the Two Leadership Styles

Leadership Quality	Transactional Approach	Transformational Approach
Time Orientation	Short term	Long Term
Communication	Vertical, Downward	Multidirectional
Focus	Financial Goals	Customer (Internal and External)
Reward Systems	Organisational, Extrinsic	Personal, Intrinsic
Source of Power	Legitimate, Reward	Referent, Expert
Decision Making	Centralised, Downward	Dispersed, Upward
Employees	Liability, Cost	Asset
Coordination Mechanism	Rules and Regulations	Goals and Value Congruence
Compliance Mechanism	Directive	Rational Explanation
Attitude Towards Change	Avoidable, Resistant, Status Quo	Inevitable, Embrace
Guiding Mechanism	Profit	Vision and Values
Control	Rigid Conformity	Self Control
Perspective	Internal	External
Task Design	Compartmentalised Individual	Enriched, Groups

Source: Bass and Avolio 1994; Krishnan et al. 2004.

In fact, he is intent on the development of the people, who in turn get inspired by him and try to emulate him. The transformational leader is able to guide the destinies of many, because he changes the very visions and perspectives of the people around him. People get so influenced by him that they are naturally transformed. Ross and Offermann (1997) found that higher levels of need for change, self-confidence and dominance predicted transformational leadership. Some of the characteristics of the transformational leaders are as follows (Krishnan 1990):

(a) They identify themselves as change agents.
(b) They are courageous individuals.
(c) They believe in people.
(d) They are value-driven.
(e) They are life-long learners.
(f) They have the ability to deal with complexity, ambiguity and uncertainty.
(g) They are visionaries.

Muniapan (2007) found that a transformational approach is likely to be more effective in overcoming barriers to change in organisations than a transactional style that concentrates on technical problem solving which neglects people and organisation issues. Due to the increasing environmental turbulence, every organisation, society and country needs transformational leaders. Bass and Avolio (1994) argued that transformational leaders instil feelings of trust, loyalty and respect from followers.

The above approaches that identify 'dimensions' and 'factors' are, however, somewhat entitative from a hermeneutic viewpoint. Hermeneutics, with its emphasis upon process, language, communication and discourse regards transformation as a consequence of the cultural skill of the leader dwelling in the *habitus* of historicity and context. In other words, the transformational leader has a practical wisdom, a local 'know how' and not just a global 'know what', and consummate socio-linguistic skills of interpretation and communication. Transformational leaders will be highly in demand in the years to come; transforming the world with their soft, soothing, golden discursive touch that allows critical ascendancy of Schumacher's (1977) hierarchy through practiced command of all areas of Capra's kite. Consequently, transformational leadership skills need to be cultivated and nourished, as every organisation, society and country needs transformational leadership.

THE *BHAGAVAD-GITA*

The *Bhagavad-Gita* is a sermon given by Sri Krishna to Arjuna regarding the correct technique of life (Dharmaratnam 1987). Over the centuries many renowned scholars and philosophers from all over the world have commented on the *Bhagavad-Gita* and elucidated its teaching in many publications and lectures. It is universal and non-sectarian and its teachings are applicable not only to Indians but to everybody. The message of the *Bhagavad-Gita* is not only limited to spiritual development but also in other aspects of human capital development, including the development of transformational leaders. The original version of the *Bhagavad-Gita* is in Sanskrit language, which is one of the oldest languages in the World. Charles Wilkins translated the first English language version of the *Bhagavad-Gita* in 1785 (Muniapan 2005). At present there are more than 1,000 English language versions and commentaries of the *Bhagavad-Gita* written by many scholars in India and around the world. The *Bhagavad-Gita* has also been translated into more than 500 world languages other than English. The *Bhagavad-Gita* has exercised an enormous influence, which extended in early times to China and Japan and lately to the Western countries (ibid.). The two chief scriptural works of Mahayana Buddhism—*Mahayana Sraddhotpatti* and *Saddharma Pundarika*—are deeply indebted to the teachings of the *Bhagavad-Gita*. Mahatma Gandhi who preached the *Bhagavad-Gita* philosophy, said: 'I find a verse here and a verse there and I immediately begin to smile in the midst of overwhelming external tragedies—and if they have left no visible, no indelible scar on me, I owe it all to the teachings of the *Bhagavad-Gita.*' (Mahadevan 2001: 1).

The background for the *Bhagavad-Gita* is the epic *Mahabharata*, extolled as the 5th *Veda*.[11] *Mahabharata* is an encyclopaedia of life and its central theme is *dharma* (meaning occupational duty, righteousness and virtues). It deals not only with *dharma* but also *artha* which is the acquisition of wealth, *kama* which concerns the enjoyment of pleasures and *moksha* which is liberation. The *Mahabharata* was composed by Sri Vyasa Muni (son of Parasara Muni) and was written by Sri Ganesa more than 5,000 years ago and it has 100,000 verses (Rosen 2002). The *Bhagavad-Gita* appears in 700 verses (of which 575 are uttered by Sri Krishna) in *Bhisma Parva* of the *Mahabharata* and consists of 18 chapters.

The *Mahabharata* narrates the war between two cousins; the five *Pandavas*[12] and 100 *Kauravas* to claim the kingdom of Hastinapura. Sri Krishna, the champion of *dharma* offered to go on a peace-making mission on behalf of the *Pandavas* (this is a lesson to the world that peace is preferred at all costs). However the *Kauravas* refused to make peace and hence war became a certainty. Sri Krishna humbled himself into becoming the charioteer of Arjuna, the *Pandava* prince. In fact, Arjuna could choose unarmed Sri Krishna who would not engage in battle or Sri Krishna's army consisting of great warriors. Arjuna (*Pandava*) decided to choose Sri Krishna unarmed, while Duryodhana (*Kaurava*) was happy to get the large army from Sri Krishna. He (Duryodhana) felt that, without the army, and without weapons, Sri Krishna could not be of much help to the *Pandavas* (Subramaniam 2001).

The entire armies (7 *Pandava* divisions and 11 *Kaurava* divisions) of both sides were assembled at the battlefield of Kurukshetra. Thus the stage was set for the *Bhagavad-Gita.* The sermon was given on the battlefield before the commencement of the war. The battlefield also represents our body where an unending battle is raging between the forces of good and evil—the evil always outnumbering the good

(5 *Pandavas* against the 100 *Kauravas*; or 7 *Pandava* divisions of soldiers against 11 *Kaurava* divisions). On a spiritual level, the focus is on the battle between the higher self and the lower self, the war between man's spiritual calling and the dictates of the body, mind and senses for material pleasures (Rosen 2002).

THE *GUNA* LEADERSHIP THEORY FROM THE *BHAGAVAD-GITA*

The *Bhagavad-Gita* provides a composite framework to aid the understanding of the mental make-up of a person or a leader. This is similar to the trait theory of leadership developed in the Western context. The *Guna* leadership theory,[13] has also been called the tri-dimensional personality theory, to explain differences across individual leaders. There are three *Gunas*—*Sattva* (awareness), *Rajas* (dynamism) and *Tamas* (inertness). *Gunas* are the fundamental constituents of every being and each being is composed of all the three *Gunas*. When one of the three *Gunas* is dominant in a person, that person is said to be characterised by that *Guna* (Kejriwal and Krishnan 2004).

A leader could thus be *Sattvic*, *Rajasic* or *Tamasic* depending on which of the three *Gunas* is dominant. Of these, *Sattva* is free from evil, immaculate, flawless, and is expressed in qualities like purity, wisdom, goodness, fineness, bliss and a love for knowledge. *Rajas* is characterised by egoism, activity, restlessness, assumption of undertakings, craving, passion, lust, greed and the need for power. *Tamas* is exhibited in sloth, delusion, ignorance, heedlessness, inertia, procrastination, confusion and perversion in thought and action (Chakraborty 1987). According to the *Bhagavad-Gita*, the *Sattvic* leadership behaviour is quite capable of being learned through regular practice and training. A leader can develop *Sattvic* nature and can reduce *Tamasic* nature to enhance transformational leadership quality. This *Sattvic* leader of the *Bhagavad-Gita* corresponds to the transformational leader, while the *Rajasic* leader corresponds to the transactional leader. The *Bhagavad-Gita* indicates that the greater the influence of *Sattva* in leaders' personalities, the greater will be the transformational leadership abilities.

An analysis of the characteristics of transformational leaders and those of the *Sattvic* performers or leaders has been presented below based on the interpretation of Biswajit.

(a) Transformational leaders identify themselves as change agents. They will strive to the utmost to bring about the desired change that is felt necessary to improve organisational effectiveness. They bring about changes not only in the organisational working, but also in the moods, images, expectations, attitudes and goals of the followers. They exert such a tremendous influence that the entire organisational structure gets meaningfully transformed. The *Bhagavad-Gita* believes that the world is in a state of constant flux and that all that we perceive keeps changing continuously and we as human beings have also undergone and are undergoing changes (*Bhagavad-Gita*, 2.13). [14] So the *Sattvic* leader has to effect changes in his environment, if he has to set an example to the world. Merely following the existing practices will take him nowhere.

(b) Transformational leaders are courageous individuals. Once they take a stand, they are brave enough to take risks and ensure that their objectives are fulfilled. They don't back out of a process of change once they have initiated it. Fearlessness is an essential virtue that adorns these individuals. Fearlessness is the watchword of the *Bhagavad-Gita* philosophy and the *Sattvic* leader goes about performing his actions without any fear (*The Bhagavad-Gita*, 16.1). [15] According to Swami Vivekananda (2000), if there is one word that you find coming out like a bomb from the *Upanishads*, bursting like a bomb-shell upon masses of ignorance, it is the word 'fearlessness' and this is an essential characteristics of a transformational leader.

(c) The transformational leader believes in people. They have a very positive approach towards human beings. They believe in the innate ability and motivation of the people and work towards the empowerment of others in the organisation. According to the *Bhagavad-Gita* philosophy, all beings are but the sparks of that one divinity. The infinite potential is there in every being, and a being varies from another only in the degree of manifestation of the divinity (*Bhagavad-Gita,* 17.61).[16] The *Sattvic* leader has imbibed this knowledge and hence spontaneously has a great regard for all human beings. He has tremendous faith in their potential and capacity and lovingly takes care of their emotional and other needs. To him, faith in people is not a virtue to be practiced, but it is a natural part of his existence. This faith in turn, generates the feeling in the people that they can dream the impossible and achieve the improbable. This is also consistent with McGregor Theory Y leadership.[17]

(d) Transformational leaders are value-driven. They have a set of core values, which serves as their driving force and which permeates their actions. These values are regarded to be of paramount importance and are never compromised for anything; in fact, no price is regarded too heavy to uphold these deeply cherished values. The *Sattvic* leader is someone who has already transcended the state of *Rajas* denoted by passion and frenzied activity. The divine *Sattvic* values are a part and parcel of his life and he will not give way to emotional upheavals and manages his emotions well. Since he is characterised by fearlessness, he has the necessary courage to stick to his values (The *Bhagavad-Gita,* 4.22–4.23).[18,19]

(e) Transformational leaders are life-long learners. They view mistakes not as failures but as learning experiences. They have an amazing appetite for continuous self-learning and development. The tendency of learning goes along with a sense of humility and scientific enquiry. According to Swami Vivekananda (2000) education is the manifestation of the perfection already in man. This manifestation takes place continuously throughout a person's life. The *Sattvic* leader has a great flair for wisdom and knowledge; in fact his unique attribute is that he is endowed with both wisdom and action. He takes pleasure in intellectual reflection and at the same time performs actions for guiding the world. (The *Bhagavad-Gita*, 4.33, 4.34, 4.35).[20,21,22]

(f) Transformational leaders have the ability to deal with complexity, ambiguity and uncertainty. They have all the requirements of an increasingly complex world that demands complex problem-solving ability on the part of the leaders. They have a perfect balance between the cognitive and emotional aspects of their beings. The *Bhagavad-Gita* presents the concept of *Shraddha* or deep-rooted faith to attain supreme peace in the form of self-realisation and ultimately realisation of the Absolute. The *Sattvic* leader, because of his wisdom, is able to be constantly conscious of his infinite potential, which develops a lot of self-confidence in him. And as faith can move even mountains, the *Sattvic* leader is capable of handling any complex problem in the organisation. Also, because of his cool and complacent nature, the leader will not get excited or tensed and hence is able to tackle any issue in the best possible way. He is not at all overawed by the complexity or ambiguity of a problem because of the absolute faith or *Shraddha* that he has in himself (The *Bhagavad-Gita*, 3.31, 4.39).[23,24]

(g) Transformational leaders are visionaries. They have broad and inspiring visions. They not only have the capacity to dream, but also the ability to translate those dreams and images, so that their followers are inspired by the visions that they have. The net result is that they are able to change the way people think about what is desirable, possible and necessary. The *Sattvic* leader is constantly working towards the goal of perfection and all his values and his entire personality are perfectly attuned towards achieving this objective. He is a source of constant inspiration to all those around him and he always radiates cheerfulness to his surroundings. People look up to him for guidance and because of these gradual *attunements*; they start sharing his visions, images and ideas. Thus a *Sattvic* leader is able to exert a tremendous influence on those who come in touch with him (*Bhagavad-Gita*, XI. 3–8).[25]

THE *BHAGAVAD-GITA AND* TRANSFORMATIONAL LEADERS

Transformational Leaders Must Strengthen Their Minds

In the beginning of the *Bhagavad-Gita*, Sri Krishna, playing the role of teacher (human resource developer), to revive Arjuna's morale embarked on the following sermon[26]: 'O son of Prtha (Arjuna), do not yield to this degrading impotence. It does not become you. Give up such petty weakness of heart and arise, O chastiser of the enemy.'[27] (*Bhagavad-Gita*, Chapter 2, verse 3.)

The leaders are advised to cast off their weakness of heart in performing duties. Leaders who are mentally weak cannot attain an organisational vision and mission. The mind of the leader must be firm in driving the organisational resources (human resources) towards vision and mission. In the words of Sri Ramakrishna (Chidbhavananda 1992) 'he who is soft and weak minded like the puffed rice soaked in milk, is good for nothing. He cannot achieve anything great. But the strong and virile one is heroic. He is the accomplisher of everything in life'.

There is also a similar advice for leaders to arise and awake from the *Katha Upanishad*. Nachiketa, a young boy was offered three boons by Yamaraja. The first two boons (wishes) asked by Nachiketa were given by Yamaraja.[28] In the third boon (wish), Nachiketa asked Yamaraja for the knowledge of the Absolute (*Brahmavidya*). Yamaraja tried to dissuade him and offered all the other pleasures of life, however Nachiketa did not budge, and he was strong and determined. Yamaraja finally became pleased with Nachiketa and gave him the knowledge of the Absolute. In the process, he said 'arise, awake and stop not till the goal is reached. Although the path of realising this goal is like walking a long distance on a razor's edge in the middle of the night. That is what those sages say'.[29] This is an important lesson from leaders to be mentally strong and determined as in the case of Nachiketa.

Leaders also need to arise and strengthen their self. The concept of 'self' has many meanings from many perspectives. For the purpose of this chapter, the concept of 'self' is limited to the individual leader. The *Bhagavad-Gita* stresses that an individual leader must uplift himself by his own self and he must not let himself be weakened under any circumstances or when facing a crisis. Leaders must elevate themselves by their own mind (*Uddhared Atman Atmanam*) and this requires effective leadership and management of our mind. For one who has conquered the mind, the mind is the best of friends, but for ones who fail to control their minds, the mind will be the greatest enemy.[30]

An untrained mind is very weak and unstable; as a result even a small obstacle coming in its way may make it lose initiative. Even Arjuna found that the mind is not easy to control. He told Sri Krishna that his mind was restless, very strong and difficult to control. Arjuna said that controlling his mind was more difficult than controlling the wind.[31] Sri Krishna agreed that the mind is not easy to control, however he said that it is possible to control the mind by constant practice and detachment.[32]

In the practical world, leaders have to fight so many opposing elements, it is certainly very difficult to control the mind. Leaders need to use their intelligence effectively to direct their mind. In this aspect *Katha Upanishad* also for example describes the position of individual self as a passenger in the car of the material body, and intelligence is the driver. Mind is the reins and the senses are the horses. The self is thus the enjoyer or sufferer in the association of the mind and senses.[33] Therefore it is essential that a leader uses his intelligence in an effective way to control the mind and achieve the equality of mind or even mindedness. Intelligence (*buddhi*) gives the power to the leader to discriminate and decide what it is good for and what is not. It is the force behind the leader's wisdom. A leader of lesser intelligence is constantly driven by the senses and the desire for sense objects.

The practice as asserted by Sri Krishna to control and strengthen the mind in context of leadership is 'self' training and development. This also implies the importance of training and development in individual employees and organisational development in achieving competitive advantage. Leadership development programmes in organisations should therefore focus in creating and developing leaders and organisational members to be strong and be mentally fearless.

Transformational Leadership Through Duty and Setting Example

The concept of duty is given great importance in the *Bhagavad-Gita*. Duty in the organisational context goes beyond contractual agreement in the employment relationship. Both employer and employee need to understand their duties in order to create good working relationship and harmonious industrial relations. Sri Krishna motivates and encourages leaders to do their duties and not to run away from the duties—perform your prescribed duty, for doing so is better than not working. One cannot even maintain one's physical body without work.[34] Sri Krishna further stressed that duty needs to be done without attachment and for those who do their duty without attachment will attain the supreme goal.[35]

In his explanation, Sri Krishna gave the example of King Janaka (father of Sita and father-in-law of Sri Rama in *Ramayana*) who attained perfection solely by performance of his prescribed duties. Therefore leaders need to perform their work (duty) for the sake of educating the people in general (leadership by example). [36] The leaders in the context of organisation needs to set examples for their followers as whatever the leaders do, the followers will follow and whatever standards or example the leaders set people in general will follow.[37]

This lesson in leadership is not only limited to leaders in the work organisation but each and every leader, including kings, ministers, community leaders, fathers or teachers. People in general always follow the leader and the leaders teach the public by their practical behaviour. If leaders want to create a healthy work environment by leading 'no smoking campaigns' in their organisations, first they should themselves stop smoking to set the example. Sri Krishna reminded Arjuna, if he runs away from the battlefield, all others will follow and if he fails to do his duty, others will also follow. The leaders must always set examples, this is a simple but important lesson for leaders to be transformational leaders.

Transformational 'Self' Leadership

The *Bhagavad-Gita* stresses the importance of self leadership first before leadership of other. Self leadership includes all aspects of management of oneself such as managing life, time, stress, anger, fear and self-control. The ability to lead others depends on the leader's personality traits such as self-esteem, locus of control, self-efficacy and other traits. Besides personality traits, other psychological attributes such as perception, values, attitudes, motivation, and so on will also influence leadership effectiveness. The leader should be able to manage his anger and should not let anger gain control over him. Sri Krishna described that from anger, complete delusion arises, and from delusion bewilderment of memory. When memory is bewildered, intelligence will be lost and when intelligence is lost one falls down.[38] The control and the management of anger effectively, is a vital aspect of human relations management not only in organisations but also in our everyday life. Anger resides in *Linga Sarira* (astral body) but it percolates into the physical body just as water percolates through the pores to the outer surface of an earthen pot and just as heat melts lead, so also *kroda* (anger) melts the individual (Sivananda 1990).

Besides anger, the leader in the organisation must also be able to tackle his worries, anxieties, fear, stress, and so on. These are the enemies of a leader. Even Arjuna, before the commencement of the battle had worries, anxieties and fear and he was forwarding a lot of argument to Sri Krishna on the negative outcome of the war. Arjuna was speaking learned words, yet he was grieving for what is not worthy of grief. He was lacking in real knowledge, the knowledge of the self. One who is in knowledge would not grieve in any circumstances. The *Bhagavad-Gita* defines this stage as *brahma-bhutah*. At this stage one will become fully joyful. He will not lament nor desire anything. He will be in an equal and consistent state of mind and will be equal to all.[39]

The *Bhagavad-Gita* has elaborated many aspects of self-leadership. In explaining the position of a self realised leader (*Bhagavad-Gita* 18.51–18.53), among others, Sri Krishna stressed the aspects such as controlling the mind, determination, giving up sense of gratification, being free from attachment and hatred, body and mind control, power of speech, free from false ego, false pride and anger as essential aspects of self management. In describing qualities of *brahmanas* (intelligent managers) (*Bhagavad-Gita* 18.42), Sri Krishna stressed the qualities such as peacefulness, self-control, austerity, purity, honesty, knowledge, wisdom and religiousness and in describing the qualities of *ksatriyas* (administrative managers) (*Bhagavad-Gita* 18.43), Sri Krishna identified qualities such as heroism, power, determination, resourcefulness, courage in battle, generosity and leadership.

Sri Krishna also described that fearlessness, purification of one's existence, cultivation of spiritual knowledge, charity, self-control, performance of sacrifice, study of the *Vedas*, austerity, simplicity, nonviolence, truthfulness, freedom from anger, renunciation, tranquillity, aversion to faultfinding, compassion for all living entities, freedom from covetousness, gentleness, modesty, steady determination, vigour, forgiveness, fortitude, cleanliness, and freedom from envy and from the passion for honour are among the essential qualities which are needed for our self development. These qualities are in the mode of goodness (*satva guna*) and are considered essential not only for leaders but also auspicious for progress on the path of liberation. It is clear that the *Bhagavad-Gita* gives the importance to self-leadership before any other type of leadership. In this context the *Bhagavad-Gita* provides an inside–out perspective to leadership as compared to the Western outside–in perspective.

Transformational Leadership by Renunciation

Pujan Roka (2006) describes the 18th chapter of the *Bhagavad-Gita* culminates with an important transformational leadership lesson for effective leadership; this lesson is about leadership renunciation. The *Bhagavad-Gita* defines renunciation as abstaining from selfish acts (*sanyasa*) and detaching from the results of an action (*tyaga*). Sri Krishna mentions specific areas where true renunciation must be practiced, such as:

- Renounce negative thoughts, words and actions.
- Renounce inequality and promote equality.
- Renounce selfish desires and exercise selfless service.
- Renounce indiscipline, dishonesty, and lazy attitude; and exercise integrity and pro-activeness.
- Renounce arrogance and ignorance, and be open-minded.
- Renounce momentary happiness that is derived from selfish behaviours. Instead, seek happiness that is long-lasting and beneficial to all.

The definition of renunciation, according to the *Bhagavad-Gita*, suggests that leaders must practice selfless giving and strive for the common good. This concept is ironic in today's context as leadership in general is shrouded with deceit, dishonesty and selfish acts. We hardly see leaders who sacrifice their authority, position and incentives for the benefit of their people. Many leaders lure their followers with hefty promises only to be forgotten once they capture their leadership positions. Many leaders promise prosperity only to lose focus on people and their well-being.

Practicing renunciation requires focusing on people and demonstrating compassion toward them. Today, we know 'servant leadership' as a popular leadership concept. Servant leadership is similar to the concept of leadership renunciation. Servitude and compassion enable leadership renunciation, and also enable effective leadership.

In the *Bhagavad-Gita*, Sri Krishna defines the meaning of true renunciation. He says, true renunciation is one that is undertaken with courage and without selfish attachments. By acknowledging one's responsibilities and doing everything in his or her capacity to fulfil those responsibilities, a person performs a true renunciation. When leaders acknowledge their responsibilities, there is no judgement of the nature of work. They do not worry about the pleasantness or unpleasantness of the nature of work. This is true leadership renunciation according to Krishna in the *Bhagavad-Gita*.[40]

CONCLUSION

After hearing the *Bhagavad-Gita*, Arjuna's ignorance was dispelled. He had regained his memory by Sri Krishna's mercy, and he was free from doubt and acted according to Sri Krishna's instruction.[41] This is an exhibition of transformation leadership, as quoted by Narayana (1998) who explained what happened after the *Bhagavad-Gita*. He (Arjuna) stood steady on the ground with a bow and arrow in hands. He lifted his arms ready to fight the war. Sri Krishna demonstrated transformational leadership qualities in developing and guiding Arjuna to victory in the war.[42]

As organisations continue to change and progress, we will without doubt need transformational leaders who can effectively guide and facilitate their organisational change. Transformational leaders will be in great demand in the years to come. In this chapter, some lessons on transformational leadership have been highlighted from the *Bhagavad-Gita*. These transformational leadership lessons, as described in the *Bhagavad-Gita*, attest that the subject of leadership was profound in the ancient Indian text and its principles are still applicable and relevant to transformational leadership today. The prospects of analysis of the *Bhagavad-Gita* in other areas of organisational leadership such as strategic management, organisational behaviour, human resource management and employment relations are prescient for future research.

NOTES

1. The *Ramayana* was written by Sri Valmiki Muni and contains 24,000 verses in seven *kanda*s (books). The *Ramayana* is about a Raghuvamsa prince, Rama of Ayodhya, whose wife Sita is abducted by the demon Ravana. The *Ramayana* provides the essence of the Vedas.

2. The *Mahabharata* is one of the two major ancient Sanskrit epics of India, the other being the *Ramayana*. The *Bhagavad-Gita* contains in *Bhisma Parva* of the *Mahabharata*. The *Mahabharata* was composed by Sri Vyasa Muni and written by Sri Ganesa. The full version contains more than 100,000 verses, making it around four times longer than the Bible and seven times longer than the Iliad and the Odyssey combined.

3. The *Upanishads* are part of *Vedic Shruti* scriptures, which are philosophical. They are the commentaries on the *Vedas*.

4. The *Puranas* are old stories and histories written in the form related by one person to another. Sri Vyasa Muni is considered to be the compiler of the *Puranas*. There are 18 main *Puranas*.

5. This includes the attitude and belief that anything from the West must be good.

6. The author, although a Malaysian Indian (Tamil), born and bred in Malaysia, has visited India and is familiar with cultures in India.

7. Please note that 'he', 'his' and 'man' used throughout also means 'she', 'hers' and 'woman' in the context of this chapter.

8. For details see http://www.arindamchaudhuri.com/theory.htm.

9. *The Star*, Monday September 11, 2006 (Malaysia).

10. For details see http://en.wikipedia.org/wiki/Hermeneutics.

11. '*Veda*' means knowledge. *Rig, Sama, Yajur* and *Atharva* are the four *Vedas* in the Indian tradition.

12. The classical Malay texts *Hikayat Pandawa Lima* is derived from parts of the *Mahabharata*.

13. *Guna* theory is a theory of psychological energies or forces that determine individual propensities and dispositions. *Guna*s can be understood as attitudes with which the mind functions or as influences under which the thoughts function. *Guna* theory provides the explanation for the innumerable and distinctive nature of people in the world. For details see http://rstpq.com/research_on_guna_composition.php.

14. *dehino 'smin yatha dehe, kaumaram yauvanam jara; tatha dehantara-praptir, dhiras tatra na muhyati.*

15. *abhayam sattva-samsuddhir, jnana-yoga-vyavasthitih; danam damas ca yajnas ca, svadhyayas tapa arjavam.*

16. *isvarah sarva-bhutanam, hrd-dese 'rjuna tisthati; bhramayan sarva-bhutani, yantrarudhani mayaya.*

17. For details see http://www.12manage.com/methods_mcgregor_theory_X_Y. html.

18. *yadrccha-labha-santusto, dvandvatito vimatsarah: samah siddhav asiddhau ca, krtvapi na nibadhyate.*

19. *gata-sangasya muktasya, jnanavasthita-cetasah; yajnayacaratah karma, samagram praviliyate.*

20. *sreyan dravya-mayad yajnaj, jnana-yajnah parantapa; sarvam karmakhilam partha, jnane parisamapyate.*

21. *tad viddhi pranipatena ,pariprasnena sevaya;upadeksyanti te jnanam, jnaninas tattva-darsinah.*

22. *punar moham, evam yasyasi pandava; yena bhutany asesani, draksyasy atmany atho mayi.*

23. *ye me matam idam nityam, anutisthanti manavah; sraddhavanto 'nasuyanto, mucyante te 'pi karmabhih.*

24. *sraddhaval labhate jnanam, tat-parah samyatendriyah; jnanam labdhva param santim, acirenadhigacchati.*

25. *niyatam kuru karma tvam, karma jyayo hy akarmanah; sarira-yatrapi ca te, na prasiddhyed akarmanah.*

26. Prabhupada, B.S., (1994), *Bhagavad-Gita as it is*, Bhaktivedanta Book Trust, Los Angeles. Please note that the *Bhagavad-Gita slokas* (verses) quoted throughout this chapter is also based on the above edition.

27. *klaibyam mA sma gamah pArtha naitat tvayy upapadyate; ksudram hrdaya-daurbalyam tyaktvottisha parantapa Bhagavad-Gita 2.3.*

28. For a brief information of Nachiketa's boons (wishes), please see http:// en.wikipedia.org/wiki/Nachiketa.

29. *uttiSThata jAgrata prApya varAn nibodhata kSurasya dhArA nizitA duratyayA durgaM pathas tat kavayo vadanti, Katha Upanishad 3.14.*

30. *bandhur AtmAtmanas tasya yenAtmaivAtmanA jitah anAtmanas tu satrutve vartetAtmaiva satru-va t- Bhagavad-Gita 6.6.*

31. *caNcalam hi manah krsna pramAthi balavad drdham; tasyAham nigraham manye vAyor iva su-duskaram - Bhagavad-Gita 6.34.*

32. *asamsayam mahA bAho mano durnigraham calam; abhyAsena tu kaunteya vairAgyena ca grhyate - Bhagavad-Gita 6.35.*

33. *AtmAnam rathinam viddhi, sariram ratham eva ca; buddhim tu sArathim viddhi, manah pragraham eva ca. indriyAni hayan Ahur, visayAms tesu gocarAn; atmendriya-mano-yuktam, bhoktety Ahur manisinah-* Katha Upanishad 1.3.3-4.

34. *niyatam kuru karma tvam karma jyAyo hy akarmanah; sarira-yAtrApi ca te na prasiddhyed akarmanah Bhagavad-Gita 3.8.*

35. *tasmAd asaktah satatam kAryam karma samAcara; asakto hy Acaran karma param Apnoti pUrusah Bhagavad-Gita 3.19.*

36. *karmanaiva hi samdiddhim AsthitA janakAdayah; loka-sangraham evApi sampasyan kartum arhasi - Bhagavad-Gita* 3.20.
37. *yad yad Acarati sresthas tat tad evetaro Jana; sa yat pramAnam kurute lokas tad anuvartate - Bhagavad-Gita* 3.21.
38. *krodAd bhavati sammohah sammohAt smrti-vibhramah; smrti-bhramsAd buddhi-nAso buddhi-nAsAt pranasyati - Bhagavad-Gita* 2.63.
39. *brahma-bhutah prasannAtmA na socati na kAnksati; samah sarvesu bhUtesu mad-bhaktim labhate parAm - Bhagavad-Gita* 18.54.
40. For details see Pujan Roka at www.pujanroka.com.
41. *nasto mohah smrtir labdhA tvat-prasAdAn mayAcyuta; shito smi gata-sandehah karisye vacanam tava Bhagavad-Gita* 18.73.
42. *yatra yogesvarah krisno yatra pArtho dhanur dharahah tatra srir vijayo bhUtir dhruvA nithir matir mama- Bhagavad-Gita* 18.78.

REFERENCES AND SELECT BIBLIOGRAPHY

Abuznaid, S. 2005. 'Islam and Management: What Can be Learned?', *Thunderbird International Business Review*, 48(1): 125–39. Available online at http://www3.interscience.wiley.com/journal/117946257/grouphome/home.html

Bass, B. 1985. *Leadership and Performance Beyond Expectation*. New York: Free Press.

Bass, B. and B. Avolio. 1994. *Improving Organizational Effectiveness Through Transformational Leadership*. Thousand Oaks, CA: Sage Publications.

Beekun, R. and J. Badawi.1999. 'The Leadership Process in Islam', *Proteus*, 16(2): 33–38.

Biswajit, S. 2006. 'Transformational Leadership in the Bhagvad-Gita', *The Journal of Indian Management & Strategy*, (July–September): 6–9.

Burns, J. 1978. *Leadership*. New York: Harper and Row.

Chakraborty, S. 1987. '*Managerial Effectiveness and Quality of Work Life: Indian Insights*. New Delhi: Tata McGraw-Hill.

Chatterjee, S. and C. Pearson. 2000. 'Indian Managers in Transition: Orientations, Work Goals, Values and Ethics', *Management International Review*, 40(1): 81–95.

Chatterjee, S. 2007. 'Challenging the Dominance of Western Managerial Models: Reflections from the Wisdom and Traditions of Asia', presented at International Conference on Integrating Spirituality and Organizational Leadership, University of Delhi, India, 8–10 February.

Chidbhavananda, S. 1992. *The Bhagavad Gita*. Trichy, TN: Sri Ramakrishna Tapovanam.

Chinmayananda, S. 2003. *The Holy Geeta*. Mumbai: Central Chinmaya Mission Trust.

Dharmaratnam, K. 1987. *Bhagavad-Gita in Action*. Klang, Malaysia: Nathan Publishing.

Gorden, A., S. Thomas and V. Schmit. 2007. *Impact of Culture on the Style and Process of Management and Leadership in India*. Munich: GRIN Verlag.

Hofstede, G. 1983. 'National Culture in Four Dimensions', *International Studies of Management and Organization*, 13(2): 46–74.

Kanji G. 2003. 'A New Business Excellence Model from an Old Indian Philosophy', *TQM and Business Excellence*, 14(9): 1071–76.

Kejriwal, A. and V. Krishnan. 2004. 'The Impact of Vedic Worldview and Gunas on Transformational Leadership', *Vikalpa*, 29(1)(Jan–March): 29–40.

Krishnan, A., B. Muniapan, T. Lew and E. Kong. 2004. 'Exploring the Extent of Transformational Leadership in the Context of Miri Entrepreneurs', presented at ASEMAL 4 Conference on the 13–15 December 2004 in Penang.

Krishnan, V. 1990. 'Transformational Leadership and Vedanta Philosophy', *Economics Times*, Mumbai 11 January: 7. Available online at http://www.geocities.com/rkvenkat/1990et.html.

———. 2000. 'Training Programs on Leadership: Do They Really Make a Difference?', Proceedings of the Seminar on *Role of HR: A New Agenda*, September, IIT, Delhi, Available online at http://www.geocities.com/rkvenkat/

Mahadevan, C. 2001. *The Glories of the Gita: Stories from the Padma Purana*. New Delhi: Sterling Publishers.

Maher, K. 1997. 'Gender-Related Stereotypes of Transformational and Transactional Leadership', *Sex Roles*, 37(3–4): 209–25.

Maruyama, M. 1994. *Mindscapes in Management: Use of Individual Differences in Multi-Cultural Management*. Aldershot, UK: Ashgate Publishing Company.

Muniapan, B. 2005. 'The Philosophy of Bhagavad Gita and its Relevance to Human Resource Development in the 21st Century', presented at International Conference on Cultural and Religious Mosaic of South and Southeast Asia: *Conflict and Consensus through the Ages*, 1st South and Southeast Asian Association of Study of Religion (SSEASR) Conference under UNESCO, New Delhi: 27–30 January.

———. 2006. 'Can the Bhagavad-Gita be Used as a Manual for Management Development of Indian Managers Worldwide?', presented at 5th Asia Academy of Management Conference, 'Asian Management: Convergence and Divergence', Tokyo, Japan, 19–21 December.

———. 2007. 'Transformational Leadership Style Demonstrated by Sri Rama in Valmiki Ramayana', *International Journal of Indian Culture and Business Management (IJICBM)*, 1(1): 104–15.

Muniapan, B. and J. Shaikh. 2007. 'Lessons in Corporate Governance from Kautilya's Arthashastra in Ancient India', *World Review of Entrepreneurship, Management and Sustainable Development (WREMSD)*, Special Issue on: 'Accounting Standards Convergence, Corporate Governance and Sustainability Practices in East Asia', 3(1): 50–51.

Muniapan, B. and M. Dass. 2008. 'Corporate Social Responsibility: A Philosophical Approach from an Ancient Indian Perspective', *International Journal of Indian Culture and Business Management*, 1(4): 408–20.

Narayana, G. 1998. *Management Lessons from Gita, in Inspirations from Indian Wisdom for Management*. Ahmedabad: Ahmedabad Management Association.

Noorderhaven, N. 2000. 'Hermeneutic Methodology and International Management Research', Occasional Paper 2000/2, Department of Business Studies, Uppsala University.

Panda, A. and R. Gupta. 2007. 'Call for Developing Indigenous Organizational Theories in India: Setting Agenda for Future', *International Journal of Indian Culture and Business Management*, 1(1/2): 205–43.

Prabhupada, Swami. 2003. *Bhagavad-Gita As It Is*, 2nd edition. London: The Bhaktivedanta Book Trust.

Roka, P. 2006. *Bhagavad-Gita on Effective Leadership, Timeless Wisdom for Leaders*. Lincoln, NE: iUniverse.

Rosen, J. 2002. *The Hidden Glory of India*. Los Angeles: The Bhaktivedanta Book Trust.

Robbins, S. 2003. *Organizational Behavior*, 10th edition. Sydney: Prentice Hall.

Ross, S. and L. Offermann. 1997. 'Transformational Leaders: Measurement of Personality Attributes and Work Group Performance', *Personality and Social Psychology Bulletin*, 23(10): 1078–86.

Schumacher, E. 1977. *A Guide for the Perplexed*. New York: Harper & Row.

Sharma, G. 2001. *Management and the Indian Ethos*. New Delhi: Rupa & Company.

Sheh, S. 2003. *Chinese Leadership: Moving from Classical to Contemporary*. Singapore: Times Edition.

Sivananda, Swami. 1990. *Sure Ways for Success in Life and God Realization*. Rishikesh, India: The Divine Life Society.

Subramaniam, K. 2001. *Mahabharata* (11th edition), Mumbai: Bharatiya Vidya Bhavan.

Swee-Hock, S. and K. Kesavapany. 2006. *Malaysia: Recent Trends and Challenges*. Singapore: Institute of SE Asian Studies.

Tayeb, M. 1997. 'Islamic Revival in Asia and Human Resource Management', *Journal of Employee Relations*, 19(4): 352–64.

Vivekananda, Swami. 2000. *The Complete Works of Swami Vivekananda* (eight volumes). Calcutta: Advaita Ashrama.

11

PERPLEXITY IN SOUTHEAST ASIA: DE-PERPLEXING THE EXPAT

Astrid Kainzbauer

The first lesson for the perplexed manager is to accept perplexity. Being perplexed is not a sign of failure. Rather it can be an opportunity for learning—particularly in the area of self-awareness. Thus being perplexed in a new environment can be seen as positive if it is used as an impetus for exploration, discovery and learning. Living in a foreign culture supports the development of self-awareness. By stepping out of the 'normal' frame of reference and confronting a new frame of reference, managers have opportunities to learn as much about themselves and their own culture as the foreign culture.

Western managers often encounter Southeast Asia when they are sent by their headquarters to work in local subsidiaries. Often, the expatriate manager's roles are to teach, command and control the local employees. Inherent in this situation are attitudes of the superiority of the one culture (Western) to the host culture (Asian). When coupled with power differentials between headquarters and the subsidiary, almost inevitably this situation leads to an ethnocentric outlook on the host culture (Harris and Kumra 2000). The overseas territory tends to be seen by headquarters as a microcosm of the corporate entity. In post in the host country, the expatriate manager has limited freedom in decision-making and action (often within narrow parameters set by headquarters). The expatriate manager may be expected to follow closely preset goals and work parameters. When this is the case, the individual manager has minimal local flexibility in terms of responding to local cultural conditions.

With values shaped by their home corporate cultures, many managers then tend to see cultural differences in the host country as negative. This may lead to confrontations with the new experience. In an Asian setting where social harmony is expected, this is likely to be counterproductive.

In Asia, people who are aggressive or confrontational are seen as unsophisticated. Many—if not all—cultures in Asia stress harmony as a social virtue. Individuals are expected to preserve social harmony. For the Western manager, the Asian notion of desiring harmony is often seen as avoiding critical evaluation. In Asia, differences of opinion lead individuals to seek compromise. People consider that to address the differing opinions openly would be seen as unfair and may lead to anger. To preclude social embarrassment, contrary opinions are kept to oneself and public discussion is avoided. From a Western viewpoint, it would be a neglect of duty not to seek differing opinions in order to work out publicly the communal view. In the context of an Asian workplace, expressing a contrary opinion to the social norm would be seen as distinctly unprofessional and may be regarded as grossly impolite.

HOW CAN WESTERN MANAGERS THEN MAKE SENSE OF THEIR NEW ENVIRONMENT?

This task is complex. It can be exacerbated when managers bring Western cultural concepts to the Southeast Asian workplace. It becomes especially arduous when these managers are reluctant to let go of their cultural preconceptions even in the light of contrary experiences. Perplexity is guaranteed.

Cross-cultural preparation training aims at informing and educating expatriate managers of differences between the home and host culture. However, one crucial factor for success is the attitude and the mindset of the Western manager. With an ethnocentric perspective often imposed by expectations of corporate performance and compliance, unique learning opportunities tend to be downplayed or even overlooked. Learning can only occur with the right mindset, one of openness, curiosity and search for intellectual/cultural stimulation. Unfortunately, such mindsets cannot be readily taught.

The first lesson for the perplexed manager is to accept perplexity. Being perplexed is not a sign of failure. Rather it can be an opportunity for learning—particularly in the area of self-awareness. Thus being perplexed in a new environment can be seen as positive if it is used as an impetus for exploration, discovery and learning.

The opportunity to desensitise oneself from one's 'home' environment and to learn more about oneself from the new environment is a valuable first lesson in cross-cultural adjustment.

One attribute of the new environment is that it can be very disturbing; more so if the person experiencing this new environment is reluctant to 'let go' well-learned certainties from their own culture. The new environment is likely to present oddity and the unfamiliar. Successful responses to this strangeness require the newcomer's humility towards the new culture. Paradoxically, this represents an ideal situation for learning, particularly for unlearning and relearning. In essence, the newcomer needs to learn the skills of uncoupling from previously assimilated cultural values and to more readily accept the cultural norms of the new environment. An attribute of successful learners is their ability to suspend prior knowledge in order to learn new knowledge.

In many ways the Thai attitude of *mai pen rai* (it doesn't matter, never mind), is helpful. By adopting this attitude, an individual can better disengage from prior learning and recognise the potential learning of fluid situations. In Asia the Western manager will encounter several fluid situations per hour.

> For Westerners who first move to Thailand, the famous Thai smiles all seem like happy smiles and every Thai 'yes' seems to mean 'yes'. After living in Thailand for a while and getting attuned to local culture, it becomes easier to face the impossible task of differentiating the 12 meanings of a smile or the real meaning of a 'yes'. Being exposed to Thai culture and allowing yourself to 'dwell' in local structures of meaning helps to develop an intuitive understanding of the 'un-understandable'.

INTUITION IN MANAGEMENT

Traditionally, Western management education as well as practice emphasises formalised thinking and rational analysis. Decision making processes are based on rational, logical positivism. Managers are urged to produce quantifiable targets and forecasts. Western culture and education focus mostly on the left hemisphere of the brain. In our schools, colleges and universities, westerners are taught to analyse, evaluate facts and reach certainty. From the perspective of this tradition, intuition is seen as irrational and emotional. Intuition is therefore often considered entirely unsuitable for management decisions. Traditionally, intuition was recognised as an inexplicable phenomenon, and called 'inspiration, common sense, bright ideas' (Barnard 1968, cited in Novicevic et al. 2002: 993).

Western management literature is currently rediscovering intuition as an important skill in managerial decision making (see Bennett 1998; Novicevic et al. 2002; Patton 2003; Wozniak 2006). However, the concept of intuition has become more differentiated. Intuition can be characterised along a continuum (Patton 2003: 989). At the one extreme, intuition is unduly emotional and irrational and as such, it has no place in the managerial skills toolkit. At the other extreme, intuition is a sophisticated managerial skill that has been refined through years of experience, self-reflection and self-development. Managers who are well attuned to real-time information are better at developing effective intuitive talents (ibid.: 991). Self-checking and feedback are also crucial for sound intuitive decisions (ibid.: 994). Intuition naturally comes into play in situations of urgency and time pressure, such as in response to a crisis. Intuition is also called upon when dealing with situations of uncertainty or great complexity. Intuition allows managers to integrate unpredictable unforeseen factors (Bennett 1998: 594).

According to the Western rationalist worldview, managers are urged to discover the truth through the use of the brain, situated in the head, not the heart. In a rationalist world, relying on the heart is seen as interference: an unnecessarily emotional distortion of reality. However, Schumacher (as early as 1977: 54) pointed out that 'People, when seeing, they see not, because they fail to understand with their heart. Only through the heart can contact be made with the higher grades of significance and the higher levels of being'. Recent research in the areas of leadership and decision making emphasises the need for managers to draw more from the right brain hemisphere, the intuitive side. Managers need to learn to trust their intuition; as gut reactions often turn out to be right (Bennett 1998: 595). Weick (1983) proposes that intuition should be viewed as parallel processing rather than serial processing. In this sense, intuition·complements rather than replaces rational thinking and decision making. Management expertise is thus seen as a mixture of analysis and intuition (Patton 2003: 990). To achieve increased effectiveness, a manager needs to combine intuition, logic and emotions. 'The effective manager does not have the luxury of choosing between analytic and intuitive approaches to problems. Behaving like a manager means having command of the whole range of management skills and applying them as they become appropriate' (Simon 1987: 61). Managers can develop their decision making skills by tapping more into the right brain (intuitive, subjective) hemisphere and let tacit and explicit knowledge stimulate each other (Bennett 1998: 594).

While Western management is rediscovering intuition as an asset for intelligent decision making and leadership, Southeast Asians have for centuries been applying intuition as a natural element in decision making. In an Asian context, intuition informs decisions to a degree that would be found strange in a Western setting.

A Thai company is recruiting a foreigner into a management position. After the usual checking of background, education, experience of the foreigner, the candidate is invited to spend time with the CEO, conversations focus on seemingly unrelated topics. What seems to be a 'waste of time' for the foreigner is deliberately used by the Thai CEO to develop 'a feeling' for the foreigner. And based on a good feeling, the hiring process can proceed swiftly.

In an Asian business context, managers 'sense' that a relationship feels right based on personal contact and past experiences. Formalised information about an individual's background or business history is secondary to 'gut' feelings and personal recommendations. In Western settings this approach would be regarded as negligent. Business documentation, for example in the form of contracts, should ideally be consulted as a safeguard in future business dealings and as a process of due diligence. To the Asian mind, this would be offensive and would be regarded as strange.

Western thinking tends to be more low-context, logical and specific, Asian thinking tends to be more high-context, implicit, intuitive. Managers in high context cultures are used to relying more on tacit knowledge, ambiguous information and intuition. Western managers on the other hand have to justify their decisions and actions by rationalisation and logical justification. Eastern philosophy and religion lay the foundations for a preference of intuition over rationalisation. Buddhism teaches virtues of living in the 'present moment'—The Eightfold Path includes the 'right mindfulness, being in the moment, aware of what is going on right now (Johansen and Gopalakrishna 2006: 339). This can be achieved by meditation practice. Meditation supports the development of effortless thinking through a non-directed awareness of thoughts. This Buddhist notion can be linked to the literature on intuition in management which concludes that 'managers who are well attuned to real-time information are better at developing effective intuitive talents' (Patton 2003: 991).

Buddhist scholars traditionally use symbols and metaphor in their teaching and explanations are given in a figurative way. This encourages intuitive understanding. It is the student's task to make connections. A similar tendency can be identified in Confucianism—students are expected to elaborate on the hints of the master and attempt to draw the whole picture (Wozniak 2006: 91).

An emphasis on 'holistic thinking' is prevalent in Southeast Asian countries. Whereas Western thinking stresses analytic, de-contextualised and depersonalised thinking, holistic thinking emphasises the opposite—contextualised, integrative, personalised thinking. Holistic thinking is related to the strong Southeast Asian emphasis on social relationships. Holistic thinking involves greater attention to context and subtle changes in social situations (Buchtel and Norenzayan 2008; Nisbett 2003).

Western managers in Thailand are often accused of taking decisions without considering the consequences. They apply analytical rather than holistic thinking. Analytical thinkers separate facts so they become clearer. Holistic thinkers integrate facts and feelings to see the whole picture. From an Asian holistic point of view, the big picture, including relationships with others, is more important than detailed analysis of facts.

Holistic thinking in this context sees the big picture and attempts to place individuals, including oneself, into this environment. Holistic thinking is concerned with all aspects of daily living, including the possibility that individuals may have future valuable roles even though this may not yet be apparent. By way of contrast, Western thinking would tend to focus on the immediate and thus tend to overlook future trajectories.

Strikingly apparent in Western versus Eastern views of intuition is that Westerners have to justify their actions in the light of objectivity. In Asia objectivity is not even an issue. In Thai culture, subjectivity is seen as inevitable, in the West, objectivity is seen as obtainable (Whiteley 2002: 5).

SELF-AWARENESS FOR PERPLEXED MANAGERS

One of the hallmarks of a manager who is competent cross-culturally is the ability to see and take opportunities in the new environment for both self-awareness and personal self-development. In terms of self-awareness, there will be myriad opportunities for self questioning one's inherent presumptions about work, work roles and work engagement with others. Overarching concepts such as time, work activity, work-life balance and effort can be questioned from differing perspectives.

Living in a foreign culture supports the development of self-awareness. By stepping out of the 'normal' frame of reference and confronting a new frame of reference, managers have opportunities to learn as much about themselves and their own culture as the foreign culture.

Cultural self-awareness, that is, knowing one's cultural background and its innate, unquestioned preferences and assumptions, is by no means natural or obvious. Cultural preferences are acquired subconsciously, develop over time and acquire invisibility through familiarity. Everyone tends to view their own cultural preferences as universal, that is, we view them as natural, logical and correct. Everyone else is out of step.

This implicit assumption of universality can only be overcomed through confrontation with cultural difference (Varner and Palmer 2005). In cross-cultural interactions, processes of identity clarification and repositioning occur, ultimately changing an actor's image of themselves relative to all others.

A foreign manager in Thailand reports:

I saw myself as very flexible, easy-going, until I began to struggle with the Thai fluid concept of planning time. Thais are incredibly flexible. When we Westerners already want to call off a project for lack of time and preparation, the Thais come up with a solution. I learned a lot about myself and I think I became a lot more flexible myself. The Thai saying '*mai pen rai* (never mind)' really helps to let go of past inflexible expectations and move on to new ways of dealing with the situation.

Through the experience of variations of cultural preferences we become aware of the relativity of values and behaviour. Experiencing differences makes us recognise our own preferences and makes us see the blind spots in our universe. Self-awareness therefore forms the basis for a receptive learning attitude.

Schumacher (1977: 50) points out that in order to move up the ontological ladder of higher being and reach the highest level of knowing/being, one needs to develop self-awareness. 'The understanding of the knower must be adequate to the thing to be known'.

Schumacher identifies four fields of knowledge for the individual. Field one is being aware of your feelings and thoughts—this field most closely links with self-awareness. Field two is being aware of what others are thinking and feeling. Field three is being aware of how others see you. Field four is knowledge about the outside world. Schumacher concludes that one needs to study all four fields to have true unity of knowledge. Self-knowledge can only be achieved through a balanced combination of fields one and three (self-awareness and objective self-knowledge).

The notion of cross-cultural competence encompasses all four fields of knowledge as identified by Schumacher. In order to develop cross-cultural competence, one needs to develop self-awareness as well as awareness of others with the ultimate aim of being able to work effectively across cultures. 'As one achieves a significant level of interculturalness, one may be better able to make deliberate choices of actions in specific situations rather than simply being bound by the culturally normative courses of behaviour' (Gudykunst and Kim 2003: 384)

Recent literature in the field of cross-cultural competence even takes the claim one step further. Cultural intelligence not only means being able to recognise cultural patterns but to be able to switch between cultures in practice. Thomas et al. (2008) emphasise the dynamic nature of cultural intelligence which involves continuous learning from social interactions. This is achieved by observing cultural differences between oneself (self-awareness) and others.

> At its zenith, this skill may be seen as fostering a positive learning environment and projecting respect for other cultures in order to influence the cross cultural interaction context. That is, culturally intelligent individuals can shape the context of the interaction to create a unique environment, as opposed to merely adjusting to it. (ibid.: 131)

The notion of cultural intelligence therefore goes beyond the traditional claims of cross-cultural competence as development in four areas of awareness, knowledge, emotions and skills (Brislin and Yoshida 1994; Gudykunst et al. 1996) and asks for integration of these areas into the realisation of cultural synergy.

Cross-cultural competence, or cultural intelligence, will not develop just by merely living abroad. Living abroad however supports the development of self-awareness which is crucial for developing cross-cultural competence.

Living in Southeast Asia allows a number of insights useful for the perplexed manager not only in an Southeast Asian context, but worldwide.

MULTIPLE SELVES OR NO SELF?

One fundamental difference between Western and Asian cultures is the view of 'self'. Westerners construct the self as an independent, self-contained and autonomous entity. The focus is on individual needs, individual achievements and individual identity. And even though individuals measure themselves against others, the 'I' is viewed as an independent construct. In Southeast Asian societies, the 'self' is not an independent entity but exists only through and in relation to others. Self-concepts, goals and desires tend to be interpreted within the context of the group. People's behaviour is guided by the view of the self in relation to specific others, in particular contexts. The self therefore has to be constructed or reconstructed in every situation (Markus and Kitayama 1991; Triandis 1995).

Whereas the Western self is detached from context, the Asian self is viewed as interdependent self-in-relation-to-others and cannot be fully understood when separated from the context. The Asian view of self is relational, holistic and is based on the concept of a 'fundamental connectedness of human beings to each other. The others participate actively and continuously in the definition of the interdependent self' (Markus and Kitayama 1991: 227).

In cultures where context is important, the 'others' are assigned more importance and carry more weight. Relationships therefore become ends in themselves rather than just means for achieving personal goals. There is a requirement to read the other's mind. Attentiveness and sensitivity to others are crucial skills (Markus and Kitayama 1991: 227). *People with interdependent selves must 'develop a dense and richly elaborated store of information about others or of the self in relation'* (ibid.: 231).

Deciding which restaurant to go to or which movie to see with a group of Thai friends requires a lot of empathy. Rather than the Western approach of everybody just stating their opinion and deciding by majority vote, the decision is a much more subtle process influenced by group dynamics (seniority, *kreng jai* = attentiveness to others, group harmony) more than by individual opinions. Thais have learned from a young age to acquire sensors for social situations which allow them to 'go with the flow' rather than 'standing out' from the rest of the group.

Members of collectivistic cultures self conceptions include their relationships with others present in the situation and the context influences how they define themselves. They, therefore, must take the context and status relationships into consideration when deciding how to behave in a particular situation. (Gudykunst and Ting-Toomey 1988: 140)

In an Asian worldview, there is not only a single 'self', there are multiple 'selves' depending on context. These multiple selves are represented in language. The Thai language reflects the importance of the right way of addressing people in two different perspectives, the 'self/I' and the 'other/you'. Whereas in Western European languages addressing another person involves the choice of the right form of 'you', Thai language speakers have to choose the right form of 'I' as well. Chantornvong (1992) elaborates on the flexibility and sensitivity a Thai speaker must have in communication when there are up to 17 different forms of 'I' and up to 19 different forms of 'you' to choose from. The right form of 'I' depends on the degree of politeness, intimacy, role relationships, status, age, and so on, of the person addressed and must reflect your relative position and relationship towards this person. In the Thai language it is possible to insult someone by using an inappropriate form of 'I'.

Basic Thai values reflect this sensitivity to context and relationships. *'Kreng jai'* (literally translated as 'constricted heart') is defined as '... to be considerate, to feel reluctant to impose upon another person, to take another person's feelings (and ego) into account, or to take every measure not to cause discomfort or inconvenience for another person' (Komin 1991: 164). Komin rightly acknowledges that while it is a basic social norm in Thailand to be *'kreng jai'*, this is one of the most difficult concepts for Westerners to grasp.

What can perplexed Westerners learn from the multiphrenic self approach?

Independent selves (members of individualistic cultures) are conscious of their own feelings and desires and of the need to express their own thoughts, feelings and actions to others. However they are less conscious of the need to receive/perceive the thoughts, feelings and actions of others.

The Asian relativity of the concept of 'I' allows for switching among different perspectives and teaches flexibility. The absolute 'I' of the West is replaced by the 'relativistic I' in Asia. Seeing yourself as an Asian 'I' induces a relativistic perspective. Needing to choose the right kind of language for referring to yourself and your interlocutor in every context creates a greater awareness for the relativity of the concept of 'I'. The Asian view of 'self' requires an understanding of identity as process in the context of interaction with others.

> Experiencing interdependence entails seeing oneself as part of an encompassing social relationship and recognising that one's behavior is determined, contingent on, and to a large extent organised by what the actor perceives to be the thoughts, feelings, and actions of others in the relationship. (Markus and Kitayama 1991: 227)

Buddhist philosophy takes the learning even one step further. One central element of Buddhism is the notion of 'no-self', called '*anatta*'. *Anatta* implies that a permanent self does not exist in an ultimate sense, because no particular aspect of our psycho-physical being qualifies as 'Self'. The mind is just a combination of transitory mental states, constantly changing factors. People's anxiety and stress typically results from the illusion that we 'exist' as an independent permanent 'self'. By discarding the illusion of self, we can end the suffering (*dukkha*) resulting from attachment or clinging to anything belonging to 'oneself' (Gethin 1998: 133–62).

The Western manager's learning curve in Asia starts from the compulsive certainty of knowing the realist self via the Asian constructivist view of multiple-selves to the Buddhist 'no-self'.

BUDDHIST ECONOMICS AND THE CONCEPT OF 'GROSS NATIONAL HAPPINESS (GNH)'

Schumacher introduced Buddhist economics in his book *Small is Beautiful*. In essence, concepts of Buddhist economics relate to countries 'remaining faithful to their heritage' (Schumacher 1973: 38). This means avoiding the errors of inappropriate economics and following precepts guided by Buddhist teaching. Thus from a Buddhist point of view, work has a threefold function. First, it gives man a chance to utilise and develop his faculties. Second, it allows man to overcome his 'ego-centeredness' by joining with others in a common task. Third, it provides opportunities to bring forth goods and services needed for existence (ibid.: 38–42). Thus, Buddhist economics reflect social values in countries like Thailand where ego-centeredness is reduced in the interests of collaborative work with others, and where combined efforts are seen as necessary for social well-being. King Bhumipol Adulyadej of Thailand has contributed to this tradition by advocating his theories of a 'sufficiency economy', which asks that people use resources in moderation. Briefly explained, the notion of sufficiency economy is based on the principles of reasonableness, moderation and self-immunity (building resilience against external shocks). Following these principles can lead to equilibrium and sustainability in the national economy.

The subtitle of Schumacher's book is 'Study of Economics as if People Mattered'. The same notion was noted by Payutto (1994) in Thailand and by the King of Bhutan who introduced the concept of 'GNH—Gross National Happiness' as the Buddhist answer to GNP (Gross National Product). The concept of Gross National Happiness is 'deeply rooted in Buddhist philosophy' (Hewavitharana 2004: 496). The concept relates to national development which is 'people-centred'. The ambitions of this concept are to 'arrest the growth of material poverty and spiritual decline' (ibid.). Schumacher remarks that the Western notion of giving a higher priority to goods rather than people and consumption a higher priority than creative activity is, from the Buddhist perspective, 'standing the truth on its head' (Schumacher 1973: 41).

GNH is a holistic concept which pervades daily life. In Thailand, one central motivation feature of life is fun (in Thai *'sanuk'*). This extends into the workplace where *'sanuk'* is a guiding feature of work and working together (Kamoche 2000; Komin 1991: 241). In Thailand, work tasks are designated as fun or not fun.

In the Thai context, fun is social and involves groups of other people, colleagues, acquaintances and even friends of friends. If something is not fun, it is not worth doing. Social arrangements like shared work, shared food and shared experiences are an essential part of work life. Solitary activities are regarded with suspicion. It is regarded as antisocial to express a preference to be alone. In Western cultures, there is a more discreet separation between the social and the work environment, demarcated by the clock and social activities taking place outside work. The Thai environment does not perceive such stark and seemingly arbitrary separations among activities.

For the Thais, good interpersonal relationships and a high level of fun are regarded as crucial factors for staying in a job. When these are missing, people will very likely seek alternative employment even if other extrinsic or intrinsic needs are fulfilled. What foreigners often view as a lack of 'seriousness' in work attitudes are often an integral part of personal and group motivation and cohesion. Unlike in Western cultures, having fun is a legitimate and worthy aspect of work life. It is somewhat perplexing to the Western manager that having fun is a predominant feature of the Thai workplace. There are reasons for this, although these reasons may not be overly apparent to the Western mind. The fun and the serious side of one's personality are less separated in the Thai work context. It is permissible, even expected, that individuals do not live this emotional schizophrenia. Fun happens at work and fun happens at play. To the Western mind, the concept of including '*sanuk*' in work tasks and in social activities can be interpreted as a signifier of GNH. In essence, this is the difference between 'live to work' and 'work to live'.

Modern economics measures the standard of living by the amount of annual consumption assuming that 'a man who consumes more is better off than a man who consumes less' (Schumacher 1973: 42). In this materialist worldview consumption is the ultimate purpose of all economic activity. A Buddhist economist however would consider this irrational. The aim should actually be 'to obtain the maximum of well-being with the minimum of consumption'. Instead of trying to maximise consumption, Buddhist economics aims at maximising human satisfaction. Four precepts of Buddhism are *Metta* (loving kindness) defined as goodwill towards others, *Karuna* (compassion and the desire to help other people), *Mudita* (appreciation of the virtue of others) and *Upekkha* (equanimity) (Payutto 2000: 20). These four key concepts inform daily life as can be observed in Buddhist cultures such as Thai culture. Concepts such as loving kindness and compassion for others contribute to social dynamics. For example, the Thai concept of '*nam jai*' (kindness, empathy), covers such diverse actions as making merit for the benefit of others such as young men becoming monks in order to make merit for their parents. On the death of a close relative, young boys often become novice monks in order to make merit for the recently departed in the next life. In the business world, it is usual for companies to sponsor funeral rites for relatives of employees. At weddings, someone's boss or supervisor will give support through sponsorship or contribution to expenses. In Thailand, there tends to be no obvious separation between work obligations and social obligations. Senior people in organisations have responsibilities for people at lower levels. These responsibilities include helping either financially, materially or psychologically in times of personal trouble. In exchange people at lower levels are socially obligated to give loyalty.

A recent example of the benefits of combining Buddhism and business is demonstrated by Thai Ha company.

> Thai Ha company encourages use of Buddhist values in managing its business. *Dhamma* plays a crucial role at Thai Ha, a diversified packaged-rice company. Before holding any major business meeting, Thai Ha staff is encouraged to watch a video of a monk who preaches Buddhist principles. The CEO of Thai Ha says *dhamma* can complement business conduct by helping one wash out the 'dirt' in one's mind, relieving anger and through these efforts, gain wisdom. The proof of the efficacy of these beliefs is the improved business results that Thai Ha has achieved during the past three years. (*The Nation* 17 October 2008: 10A)

The CEO of this Thai company, an MBA graduate from the US, believes in combining a thorough and systematic business approach with a Buddhist mind-set in order to achieve sustainable results.

SUMMARY

An expatriate manager who has newly arrived in Southeast Asia will find that there is no shortage of new situations which provide learning opportunities. In the workplace on an hourly basis, there are likely to be unfamiliar practices, events and situations. As Southeast Asian colleagues go about their daily lives, the expatriate's cultural preconceptions will be affronted by the workaday realities. More interestingly, from a learning perspective, there will be few cultural safety rails to grasp for support. Familiar landscapes have become non-existent and the cultural confines are bounded in a new experience.

A key to survival is the ability to suspend prior cultural certainties. In this way one's psyche is more prepared to deal with uncertainties. Retaining rigid cultural preferences is almost a recipe for disaster.

As noted earlier, for Western expatriates the nurturing of intuition is a valuable skill. However, much depends on individual personalities and mental adaptability. The aim is to take any available opportunities to increase self-awareness. Part of this strategy includes sensing one's automatic responses to uncommon situations and attempting to analyse these from two diverse perspectives. The ability to take an empathetic stance tends to pay dividends in de-perplexing reality.

REFERENCES

Barnard, C. 1968. *The Functions of the Executive*. Cambridge, MA: Harvard University Press.

Bennett, R. 1998. 'The Importance of Tacit Knowledge in Strategic Deliberations and Decisions', *Management Decision*, 36(9), 589–97.

Brislin, R. and T. Yoshida. 1994. *Intercultural Communication Training: An Introduction*. London: Sage Publications.

Buchtel, E. and A. Norenzayan. 2008. 'Thinking Across Cultures: Implications for Dual Processes', in J. Evans and K. Frankish (eds), *In Two Minds: Dual Processes and Beyond*, pp. 217–38. Oxford: Oxford University Press.

Chantornvong, S. 1992. 'To Address the Dust of the Dust Under the Soles of the Royal Feet: A Reflection on the Political Dimension of the Thai Court Language', *Asian Review* (Institute of Asian Studies, Chulalongkorn University), 6: 144–63.

Gethin, R. 1998. The *Foundations of Buddhism*. Oxford: Oxford University Press.

Gudykunst, W. and Y. Kim. 2003. *Communicating with Strangers*. New York: McGraw Hill.

Gudykunst, W. and S. Ting-Toomey. 1988. *Culture and Interpersonal Communication*. Newbury Park, CA: Sage Publications.

Gudykunst, W., R. Guzley and M. Hammer. 1996. 'Designing Intercultural Training', in D. Landis and R. Bhagat (eds), *Handbook of Intercultural Training*, 2nd edition, pp. 61–80. Thousand Oaks: Sage Publications.

Harris, H. and S. Kumra. 2000. 'International Manager Development: Cross-Cultural Training in Highly Diverse Environments', *Journal of Management Development* 19(7): 602–14.

Hewavitharana, B. 2004. 'Framework for Operationalizing The Buddhist Concept of Gross National Happiness', in *Gross National Happiness and Development—Proceedings of the First International Conference on Operationalization of Gross National Happiness*, Centre for Bhutan Studies, available online at http://www.bhutanstudies.org.bt/main/pub_detail.php?pubid=64 (downloaded on 11 August 2008).

Johansen, B-C. and D. Gopalakrishna. 2006. 'A Buddhist View of Adult Learning in the Workplace', *Advances in Developing Human Resources*, 8(3): 337–45.

Kamoche, K. 2000. 'From Boom to Bust: The Challenges of Managing People in Thailand', *International Journal of Human Resource Management*, 11(2): 452–68.

Komin, S. 1991. *The Psychology of the Thai People: Values and Behavioral Patterns*. Bangkok: National Institute of Development Administration (NIDA).

Markus, H. and S. Kitayama. 1991. 'Culture and the Self: Implications for Cognition, Emotion, and Motivation', *Psychological Review*, 98(2): 224–53.

Novicevic, M., J. Hench and D. Wren. 2002. '"Playing by ear" … "in an Incessant Din of Reasons": Chester Barnard and the History of Intuition in Management Thought', *Management Decision*, 40(10): 992–1002.

Nisbett, R. 2003. *The Geography of Thought*. New York: The Free Press.

Patton, J. 2003. 'Intuition in Decisions', *Management Decision*, 41(10): 989–96.

Payutto, P. 1994. *Buddhist Economics: A Middle Way for the Market Place*. Bangkok: Buddhadhamma Foundation.

———. 2000. *A Constitution for Living: Buddhist Principles for a Fruitful and Harmonious Life*, 2nd edition. Bangkok: Saha Dhammikkha.

Schumacher, E. 1973. *Small is Beautiful: Study of Economics as if People Mattered*. London: Vintage.

———. 1977. *A Guide for the Perplexed*. London: Jonathan Cape.

Simon, H. 1987. 'Making Management Decisions: The Role of Intuition and Emotion', *Academy of Management Executive*, 1: 57–64.

The Nation Newspaper, 'Firm Takes Principled Path to Success', 17 October 2008, Bangkok, p. 10A.

Thomas, D., E. Elron, G. Stahl, B. Ekelund, E. Ravlin, J. Cerdin, S. Poelmans, R. Brislin, A. Pekerti, Z. Aycan, M. Maznevski, K. Au and M. Lazarova. 2008. 'Cultural Intelligence:

Domain and Assessment', *International Journal of Cross Cultural Management*, 8: 123–43.

Triandis, H. 1995. *Individualism and Collectivism*. Boulder, CO: Westview Press.

Varner, I. and T. Palmer. 2005.: 'Role of Cultural Self Knowledge in Successful Expatriation', *Singapore Management Review*, 27(1): 1–25.

Weick, K. 1983. 'Managerial Thought in the Context of Action', in S. Srivastava (ed.), *The Executive Mind*, pp. 221–42. San Francisco: Jossey-Bass.

Whiteley, A. 2002. 'Philosophy and Business Management 701 Thailand, 2002', *in Book of Readings Thailand, Philosophy in Business Management*, Unit No. 12767. Graduate School of Business, Curtin University of Technology, Perth.

Wozniak, A. 2006. 'Managerial Intuition Across Cultures: Beyond a "West-East Dichotomy"', *Education + Training*, 48(2/3): 84–96.

12

PERPLEXITY AND *OIKOMORPHOSIS*: MANAGING TRANSFORMATION

Ronnie Lessem, Alexander Schieffer and Sudhanshu Palsule

> What we term Oikomorphosis involves drawing upon a four-fold foundation, or archetype, of nature and culture that has been embraced by all civilizations over the millennia; southern, eastern, northern and western.

OVERVIEW

The essence of the oikomorphic principle is first that the individual unit of survival is simultaneously a unit of transformation, and second, the transformation process involves the engagement of the individual unit with other units thereby creating new, intelligent forms without losing the essence of the original. That is also the basis for natural diversity.

Natural Diversity and Cultural Diversity go hand in hand. The local (South) represents the source, providing the indelible links we share with our natural environment. It also represents our organic links with the community in which we originate.

The local/global (East) represents the catalytic zone of change in which we bridge the indigenous and exogenous and engage in the process of re-creation through the intermediary step of becoming a non-entity.

The global (North) represents the newly organised entity, emerging out of the bridging process. The global/local (West) represents the culmination of the transformative process in a resilient and fecund global integrity.

SOUTH	EAST	NORTH	WEST
(Local) *(Indigenous)*	*(Local/Global)* *(Indigenous/ Exogenous)*	*(Global)* *(Exogenous)*	*(Global/Local)* *(Exogenous/ Indigenous)*

The cultural and spiritual awakening underlying the prospective human metamorphosis is driven by two encounters: one with the cultural diversity of humanity and the other with the limits of the planet's ecosystem. A rapid increase in the frequency and depth of cross-cultural exchange is awakening the species to culture as a human construct subject to intentional choice. The spreading failure of natural systems is creating an awareness of the interconnectedness of all life. (Korten 2007)

Figure 12.1: The Transformation Fourfold of the Foundations (Nature/Culture)

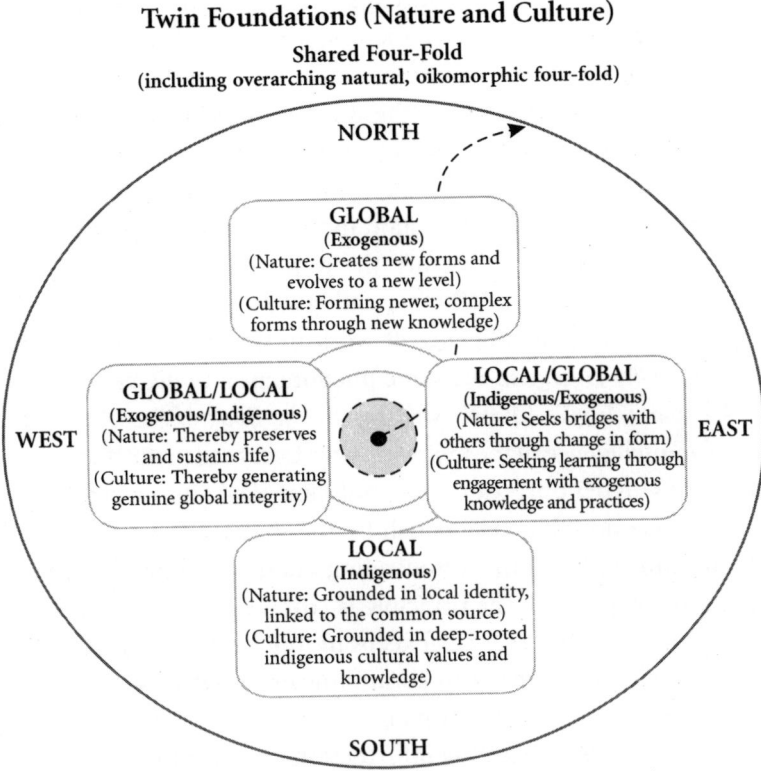

INTRODUCTION

We have anchored our approach to managing transformation (Lessem and Schieffer 2009), of self and organisation, community and society, fully and squarely in nature—inclusive of culture—as there is simply no other human-made process that can come close to the ability of ecological systems to transform themselves. We call this interaction between the indigenous, within nature and culture, and the exogenous our 'oikomorphic' principle.

It was only in the mid-1980s that medical researchers began to accept the notion that intelligence is not just a function of the brain but is spread over the body. Radical discoveries made showed how both the immune system and the digestive system are highly intelligent. In both the systems, molecules transmit and relay information to the brain and also function on their own. The scattered nerve cells of the digestive system are a highly sophisticated system that can respond instantaneously to information from the outside and 'think' before the brain has started to process the same information. What we call 'gut feeling' for example is a highly developed intelligence at work in several billion cells that co-creatively engage in the same phenomenon of *oikomorphosis*.

Deepak Chopra (2004), writing in *The Book of Secrets*, talks of cellular intelligence in the following way. Every cell in the body works towards a higher purpose of the whole and places its own individual welfare second. Skin cells perish by the thousands every hour, as do immune cells fighting off invading microbes. When it comes to a cell's own survival, the principle is co-creative, not competitive. This works because every cell keeps in touch with every other cell. Withdrawing or refusing to communicate is not an option. Cells adapt from moment to moment. They have to remain open to change and engage with the information on the outside to remain flexible, each cell engaging interdependently with each other at the same time. This behaviour keeps cells continuously transformative, and they are open to learning to deal with new situations.

This means although every cell has a set of unique functions, it is not bound by those functions. Moreover the behaviour of cells is governed by universal principles. Fluctuating hormone levels, blood pressures and digestive rhythms are examples of larger principles that govern the behaviour of cells. Chopra then goes on to add that due to their common genetic inheritance, cells know that they are fundamentally the same. The fact that liver cells are different from heart cells and muscle cells are different from brain cells does not negate their common identity. This is at the heart of life's co-creative principle, and at the heart of *oikomorphosis*. Take away the sense of the common source and you have cancerous growth: when one cell decides to go on its own and grow to the detriment of the whole.

Advances in medical science, quantum physics, microbiology and genetics are all pointing to an ecological worldview that has profound implications for how we run our societies and organisations, and how we perceive ourselves as individuals. The *oikomorphic* process also captures the underlying dialectic of the transformative process: the local-global process. It can be seen and understood in nature as a natural process that allows species to retain their core biological identities on one hand, and find a way of bridging across to combine with new species in order to build resilience. Partnership then, as opposed to domination, linkages between the private and the public, if not also with the civic and the animate, fusion between the 'south' and the 'north', all apply in this *oikomorphic* case. It is a similar process that enables cultures to retain their identities and reach out and engage with other cultures in order to build resilience and knowledge.

LEARNING TRANSFORMATION FROM NATURE: TRANSFORMATIVE PRINCIPLES

The Ecology of Transformation: *Oikomorphosis*

'To shake a tree is to shake the earth', is an ancient East African saying, vividly evoking an image of nature as an interconnected whole where dividing lines and boundaries are amorphous and permeable. So, for that matter, where does a leaf begin? And where does it end? Likewise, what are the boundary edges of a lake, or a sea? When systems are seen from the ecological perspective, clear-cut demarcations and boundaries just stop making sense. If a leaf, for instance, 'ended' at what we traditionally perceive to be its contour, it would die instantaneously. And so would the entire eco-system. The so-called edges of leaves are, in fact, highly amorphous linkages with the environment, and the sun itself. What every schoolchild learns to define as 'photosynthesis' is basically a scientific description of the leaf's relationship with the sun.

And ours too, for every time we breathe in a lung full of oxygen that keeps us alive, we are breathing in the relationship of leaf and sun. Where do we end, then? Certainly not at the contours of our body. Our skins too are highly porous linkages to the outside, without which we would not survive. What digests the meal you have just had is not 'your' digestive system, but a highly sophisticated alliance between your body and millions of microbes that live in your intestines.

Nothing in nature can be demarcated into individual entities. So for instance soil sustains life on earth and nutrients are recycled back into the soil with the help of certain bacteria. But where does the soil itself come from? In the old biology, it was taken as a given, something that exists as the environment. What we now know is that the soil is continually being created by the plant and animal life that lives off the soil. We know that carbon dioxide is pumped down by life on the surface after dissolution in water near the rock surfaces. The water may have come from rainwater or fed by nearby springs and rivers. This solution now causes rocks to weather. The microorganisms aid this process and more soil gets created. Without life there would be no soil, but only regolith, the rock rubble of dead planets.

What the new ecology teaches us is that the very emergence and the maintenance of life is itself an ongoing transformative process. While life emerges out of its environment, the environment needs to be continually transformed by life so that it remains life-supportive. Moreover, this is achieved by life being in a state of continual change itself, not opposing the forces of the environment, but flowing with them. Life and the environment are partners in co-creation. To take another example of this co-creative aspect, aquatic blades of grass reduce stream velocity, thereby forcing the waters to drop their silt load and the decaying plant material they carry along. Both these effects increase channel deposition, which creates more soil and nutrients for plant roots. Plants grow stronger, denser. This reduces velocity further, creating more deposition. Deposition displaces water. The stream overflows and spreads out, greatly expanding its surface area as it flows over. The water's energy drops drastically. Nourishing water and silt are spread over a broad channel, nourishing more lush growth. This growth creates greater accumulations of spongy, absorbent, plant material, spreading the slowing water even wider.

The interaction between natural energy and life's energy is the chief principle of co-creation. The interaction is often so subtle, so insignificant that we don't even see it. Each small shift in equilibrium creates another small shift. Each new equilibrium covers the tracks of the previous change. The power lies in the accumulative consistency with which these changes shift equilibrium in life's favour. Life creates conditions for more life, which in turn create conditions for more life. These loops create change, not stability. By shaping the development of its environment, life allows itself to be shaped by the environment. Co-creation provides us with a very viable, long-lasting, sensible and sustainable model of transformation. It is equally applicable to organisations and societies.

While life emerges out of its local environment, the environment needs to be continually transformed by global life so that it remains life-supportive. This is the essence of what we refer to as the '*oikomorphic* principle': the process of transformation in which first, the individual unit of survival is simultaneously a unit of transformation, and second, the transformation process is the engagement of the individual unit with other units thereby creating new, intelligent forms without losing the essence of the original.

The Four Worlds of *Oikomorphosis*

The purpose of transformation through co-creative *oikomorphosis* is to sustain a future in which resources become available to as wide a base as possible, and diverse units of local life work with a common global principle to sustain life as a whole. This twofold indigenous–exogenous undertone, to our *oikomorphosis*, turns, as we shall see, into a four-fold 'overtone'. We begin, as such in the South, then move East, then to North and end up in the West. In doing so we traverse the journey of humankind, as it were, from Africa through Middle, Near and Far East, through Europe ultimately reaching America, altogether underlying our transformative process.

Figure 12.2: Crucial Sub-processes for Transformation in Natural Systems

SOUTH	***The Formative—Ongoing generative principle***: The common indigenous (local) source is the ongoing generative principle behind every transformation that seemingly units participate in.
EAST	***The Re-formative—Openness to fluctuation and change***: Individual units are 'open' to indigenous/exogenous (local/global) fluctuation and change and engage with other units as well as to create new resilient forms.
NORTH	***The Normative—Resilience through interdependence***: Individual units are linked and interdependent with other now exogenous (global) units.
WEST	***The Transformative—Defined by new identity***: Individual units are no longer defined in terms of themselves but in terms of their transformed selves that are derived from the exogenous/indigenous (global/local) common source.

How does this process of *oikomorphosis* work its way? To answer that, we apply our Four World rhythm. In doing so, we shall be describing four sub-processes (See Figure 12.2) that are crucial for transformation in natural systems.

Together these four processes provide the basis for an ongoing transformation process. Clearly, if we are looking for a model of transformation, we need to look no further than the system of our natural environment that has successfully survived and flourished for millennia. As we saw earlier, nature engages in a continuous transformative process that seeks to sustain life.

We now take up each of the Four Worlds and explain how the process works.

Starting in the South: The 'Indigenous' Generative 'Common Source'

This rule of the common source is the same one that enables the transformation of a chrysalis into a butterfly. The caterpillar's organs and tissues dissolve into an amorphous soup-like state only to reconstitute into the structure of a butterfly's body that bears absolutely no resemblance to the caterpillar at all. The chemical complexity of turning into a butterfly is incredible and science still has no explanation for why this metamorphosis has evolved. But there is a clear picture emerging of how the process works. The two hormones that regulate the process ensure that the cells moving from larva to butterfly know how they are going to change. Some cells know when to die, others digest themselves, some turn into eyes, some into wings. The whole process of transformation requires a very delicate and precise rhythm between creation and destruction. This rhythm depends on day length, which in turn depends upon the earth's rotation around its axis. The transformation of a chrysalis into a butterfly is linked to its source in the rhythm of the cosmos. In the same way, the prolactin that generates milk in a mother's breast is unchanged from the prolactin that sends salmon upstream to breed, enabling them to cross from saltwater to fresh water. The insulin in a cow is the same as the insulin in an amoeba; both serve to metabolise carbohydrates.

How does each cell 'know' how to remain linked to the generative principle of the common source? The answer is simple: the universality of a cell or for that matter, any other unit, is contingent upon it being fully itself. What that means is that in the act of truly being yourself, you are at once universal.

Therefore the role of organisations and societies is to participate in continuously creating and sustaining a common future in which resources and benefits transcend the four walls of the organisation or society and encompass as wide an area as possible. The only way this can be done is when the society is simultaneously rooted in itself while engaging with other societies and the larger environment to bifurcate into other forms. So on the one hand business would naturally depend on society and its external environment for its growth and for resources, but on the other hand, it would participate in transforming its environment so that it's sustainable and conducive to doing business. This it can do only by engaging with other units of transformation. As we shall see later in the book, we refer to these as the four-fold perspectives of private, public, civic and animate.

Life is innately intelligent. White cells make intelligent decisions by being able to differentiate between invading enemy bacteria and harmless pollen. As we saw in the previous section, cells participate in the welfare of the whole without the slightest hesitation; if necessary they die to protect the body. Cells keep in touch with every other cell, adapting from moment to moment. They recognise each other as equally important and stay engaged in a continuous interplay of co-dependence. The very basis of life is *oikomorphosis*.

Moving East: 'Indigenous/Exogenous' Resilience via Fluctuation and Change

Another example of nature's ongoing transformative process of *oikomorphosis* is building resilience through diversity. David

Suzuki (1997), the renowned Canadian ecologist writing in *Sacred Balance* refers to the quaking aspen, the white-barked trees as an example of how nature operates as a system. Shoots may grow up from a root more than 50 feet away. So the aspen is really a super organism, a system that is made up of a network of interconnections. But for the system to remain healthy and thrive and grow, it has to have a diverse landscape. So some parts may grow in moist soil, and through their common underground roots, share the water with other portions, perhaps growing in mineral-rich soil higher up.

What Suzuki is saying is that if at each level of complexity—cell, organism and eco-system—new kinds of structures and functions emerge the totality of all life on the planet can be taken as a single entity too. But this totality of life: the convergence of all living and non-living matter into a single system is necessarily dependent on all the divergences that make the system possible. As Nobel laureate Roger Sperry (1982) points out, new properties that arise from complexes cannot be predicted from the known properties of their individual parts. These emergent properties only exist within the whole. No single species is indispensable, but the sum-total of all life maintains the fecundity of the earth.

How does life then achieve its extraordinary resilience? The answer is 'genetic polymorphism'. We shall be referring to this generally as the principle of *oikomorphism*. When a species such as the Siberian tiger is reduced to a few survivors, its long-term future is under threat because the range of its genetic variability has been radically diminished and therefore has fewer options to adapt to changes in the environment. Suzuki goes on to emphasise how a diverse mixture of gene variants is a fundamental characteristic of a vibrant, healthy species, a reflection of its successful evolutionary history and continued potential to adapt to unpredictable change. Population geneticists believe that the most successful species are found in places that are connected 'by bridges' to the outside. Thus each isolated community can evolve a set of genes adapted to its local habitat, while the migrants become a means of introducing 'new blood'—different genes with a new potential to respond to change.

This is precisely the grave danger that monoculture, naturally and culturally, presents to the world. Diminishing varieties of crops and widespread use of a single, selected strain of crop automatically makes a species vulnerable. In 1970, approximately 80 per cent of the 26.8 million hectares planted in corn in the USA carried a special genetic factor that was carefully positioned by the seed companies for higher productivity and profit. But that very trait rendered the species vulnerable to a specific parasite. Within three months, virtually all fields were affected and wiped out. Monoculture, physically and also for us in terms of humanity, is the enemy of life's evolutionary strategy.

Suzuki (1997: 27) goes on to talk about the assortment of climatic and geo-physical conditions on the earth:

> ... from the searing heat of deserts to the frigid cold of permafrost above the Arctic circle, from steamy equatorial river systems to dry grasslands, from the depths of the oceans to the soaring heights of rarefied mountain kilometres above sea level and to the inter-tidal junction between air, land, and sea.

Life flourishes in all these conditions. Even where species diversity is limited, the genetic variation within a species in one watershed will differ from that within the same species in another. Every ecosystem is special because it is simultaneously local and global.

The North: New Interdependent 'Exogenous' Forms

Elisabet Sahtouris (1996), contemporary biologist and thinker, writes about the enormous crisis we face because 'the most central and important aspect of globalisation, its economy, is currently being organised in a manner that violates the funda-mental principles by which healthy living systems are organised' (ibid.: 112). She writes about natural principles that operate in our bodies and in our families. We intuitively and collectively grasp such principles without any problem. So not many people starve three of their children to overfeed the fourth, or beautify one corner of the garden by destroying the rest of it. But strangely we begin to lose sight of those principles at the level of our local communities, towns or nations.

And globalisation of humanity definitely does not conform to the principles of living systems in that it flouts a critical principle of cooperation. A relatively small part of humanity is involved in decisions and has the power to serve its own interests, often at the expense of other parts. From a living systems perspective, if we treat globalisation as a process that is happening to a natural living system we call humanity, then we can see how economies that violate the fundamental principles by which living systems are organised, threaten the demise of human civilisation. Biological research of the last few decades, on the evolution of nucleated cells, multi-cellular organisms and mature ecosystems as cooperative enterprises, is updating our ingrained view of antagonistic competition as the sole driving force of evolution. As George Soros (2000) says, 'there is something wrong with making the survival of the fittest a guiding principle of civilised society. This social Darwinism is based on an outmoded theory of evolution'.

Once the polymorphic process has taken place, life settles into its newly normed form, assured in its resilience.

Heading West: Transformed Into a New 'Exogenous/Indigenous' Identity

Each species formed this way becomes part of the transformed ecosystem that thrives because of the simultaneity of individual and universal forces embodied in it. At each level of complexity—cell, organism and eco-system—new kinds of structures and functions emerge. The totality of life on our planet can be taken to be a single, resilient entity that has remained sustainable for so long because it is inherently transformative. Suzuki (1997) refers to the single envelope of atmosphere that encircles the earth, while water flows around the continents, creating great islands. The entire conglomerate of living things makes a wonderfully complex, interconnected community held together by the matrix of air and water. The entire layer of protoplasm (the living material within cells) on the globe is intermeshed into a living, breathing entity, which has survived through an immensity of time and space. All the living things, in their transformation, persist on their own, healing, replacing, adapting and reproducing in order to continue.

Ecosystems are highly resilient systems because their identities are not derived out of themselves but out of their relationships with their environment. So a corn stalk may be autonomous but its autonomy is derived from the fact that it is interdependent with its environment. That is the reason why the ecosystem is described as an autopoietic (from the Greek, meaning 'self-production') structure, based on the work of Maturana and Varela (1991) in the 1970s. The Chilean scientists compared autopoietic systems to allopoietic systems. So a car is the latter, as it contains the same molecules from showroom to junkyard. Its identity is given by the manufacturer and nothing changes. By contrast, autopoietic structures in life change molecules all the time and yet, somehow remain the same. So what exactly is this self-contained identity? That is precisely the connectedness between organism and environment.

So on the one hand, transformation in the West is effectively realised in the individual species and sub-parts that thrive through their separate identities. But paradoxically enough and from a more, authentically local–global perspective, what makes them and the whole ecosystem sustainable is the fact that they are inextricably a part of a pattern of relationships.

The overall *oikomorphic* process of transformation can be summarised in Figure 12.3.

Figure 12.3: The *Oikomorphic* Gene

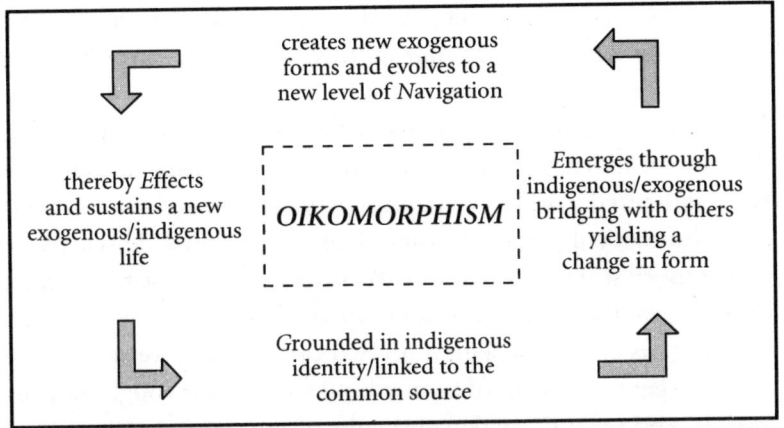

FROM NATURE TO CULTURE: THE TWIN
FOUNDATIONS OF TRANSFORMATION

The Case for Cultural Diversity:
Revisiting the Human Journey

Suzuki (1997) then goes on to say that human beings have extended
diversity to yet another level: that of culture. Using molecular
techniques to measure degrees of biological relatedness in DNA,
scientists have identified that just about 100,000 years ago the
ancestors of all of humanity arose along the Great Rift Valley of
Africa, in the communal 'south' of the four worlds. They moved
out from there, northeast across the Sahara, southwest into what
is now South Africa, northward across the Arabian Peninsula and
East to India. From there they fanned out to Europe and Russia,
from New Guinea to Australia, into Siberia and across the Bering
land bridge to the Americas. In time the most significant factor of
diversity became culture and language (ibid.). Whereas in animals,
it is genetically encoded instinctive behaviour that enabled them to

survive, for humans, culture has been the most crucial attribute. Cultural diversity and biological diversity go hand in hand. This is precisely why we hold that culture and nature are the twin foundations of transformation.

Like in the natural foundations that we explored earlier, revisiting the human journey provides us with the framework to challenge the fragmented worldview that has pervaded for so long in that it treats human cultures as disjointed and fragmented. This is made all the more seemingly real by treating culture as an artefact, a set of practices that codes a certain kind of behaviour. Our approach to culture is entirely different on two counts: first, we see culture in the larger movement of humankind's journey through the four worlds, and second, we perceive culture as a natural extension of nature (See Figure 12.4).

So as we can see, in terms of mankind's journey, the European 'north', and even more so, the American 'west' came very late in

Figure 12.4: 'Man's Journey' from South, to East, to North, to West

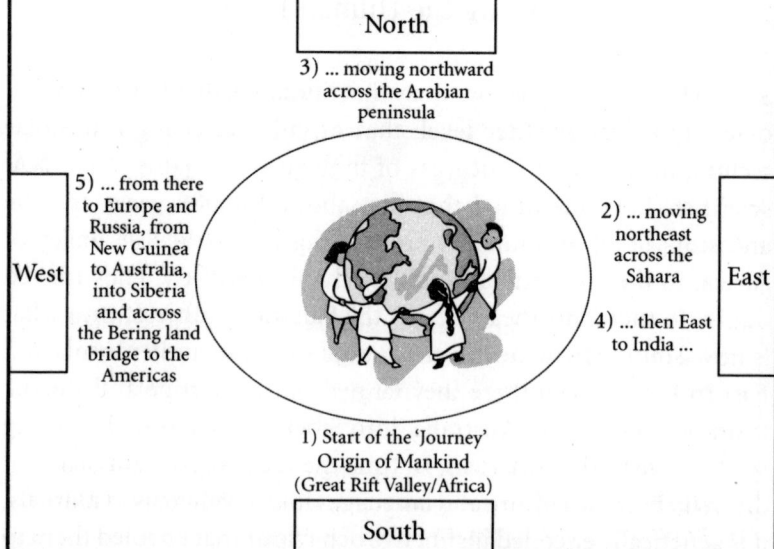

the day. Interestingly, this human journey starting from the south and extending to the west is like an archetype that provides us with a transformative tool and process (See Figure 12.5).

We start out, then, in the communal-natural 'south', and the spiritual–cultural 'east', before ending up in the individual 'west', via the organisational 'north'. As we have mentioned from the outset, each of the four worlds are divergences that are part of an overall, and centred, local/global system. The process of transformation involves each world engaging with and building upon successively the other three worlds.

The indigenous–exogenous dynamic is thus at the heart of the transformative process. To retain the core and the deep connectedness with the indigenous environment while simultaneously bridging with exogenous sources is what is needed to create an enriched and resilient global integrity. The crucial aspect here is that the state of global integrity depends irrevocably on each local identity. If that

Figure 12.5: The Transformation Journey

SOUTH: Ground	The south represents the localised identity, providing the indelible links we share with our natural environment. It also represents our organic links with the community in which we are *Grounded*.
EAST: Emerge	The east represents the local/global catalytic zone of *Emergence* in which we bridge with the exogenous and engage in the process of re-creation through the intermediary step of becoming a non-entity.
NORTH: Navigate	The north represents the newly global organised entity, emerging out of the bridging process, with its newly established structures and functions with which to *Navigate*.
WEST: Effect	Finally the west represents the global/local culmination of the transformative process, *Effecting* resilient, fecund global integrity.

gets obliterated as in the case of monocultural crops, there can be no global integrity. Isn't this then what the malaise of globalisation is all about?

A World Arises in Conversation

How then do we go about transcribing the *oikomorphic* process into human societies? To answer this question, we turn to the neurobiologists, Humberto Maturana and Francisco Varela (1991) who gave us the concept of autopoiesis; which literally means, self-creation (bringing forth). According to Maturana and Varela (1991), we as humans are grounded in biology.

> Our biology is our possibility. It is the grounding for all that we consider valuable in our lives; nothing we do, no art, no science, no religion—and no business enterprise—would be possible were it not for the particular biological configuration that we human beings have become along our particular path of evolution. (ibid.)

What they then say is, 'along this path we human beings have lived into being something unique among all living beings on earth; we have become fully languaging beings' (ibid.: 76).

Maturana and Varela (1991) make a case for language as the critical phenomenon in the development of human consciousness and culture. While the cohesion of social insects is based on the exchange of chemicals among individuals, the social unity of human societies is based on the exchange of language. Because of the world of consciousness, of concepts, ideas and symbols that arises with human thought, consciousness and language, the human social system exists not only in the physical domain but also in a symbolic social domain.

Since conversations are an interlacing of languaging and emotioning, both of which are flows in relational behaviour, conversations to take place as a flow of relational behaviours. All that we humans do, we do in conversation. The history of human beings has been a history of progressive generations of different worlds through different networks of conversations. Everything about human beings, including our body and brain has changed in accord with the conversation of living in language.

Conversations Transform Us

What Maturana and Varela (1991) say next is radical and explosive, most of all because it comes from scientists, not poets: 'The fundamental emotioning that enabled our ancestors to begin living in conversation is love.' They go on to say, 'love is that emotion in which one fully accepts the legitimacy of the other in coexistence with oneself'. Language is not an abstract entity but a process of transformation. 'Language entails the concreteness of doings; it is the coordination of doings' (ibid.: 86).

What Maturana and Varela (1991) are saying is that we understand human consciousness only through language and the whole social context in which it is embedded. As its Latin root—'conscire' (knowing together)—might indicate, consciousness is essentially a social phenomenon. The Indian concept of Maya meant the 'magic creative power' that brings the world forth through action, very much in the same way as Maturana and Varela describe it.

In a later work, Varela and Thompson interpretation (1993) of consciousness came remarkably close to the Buddhist notion that the ego is an intellectual concept that has no reality and that creates endless suffering and pain. What cognitive science says is that we bring forth the self just as we bring forth objects. Our self does not have any independent existence but is a result of our internal structural coupling.

'Independence is a political, not a scientific term', say Lynn Margulis and Dorion Sagan (2003). This sense of being autonomous, independent units is but an abstraction of thought and has robbed us of the visceral sensation of the link with the common source. But it is through language that we can regain that ancient connection. For us such 'language' is imbedded, most specifically, in the meeting of the local and the global, the indigenous and the exogenous, the tacit and the explicit, the 'south' and 'north' via the 'east' and 'west'. We are now ready to conclude.

CONCLUSION

We chose nature and culture as the foundations for transformation because both provide existing real-life models for transformation. The parallels between natural evolution and cultural evolution are stunningly visible. Begin with the local, whether it is a species in a certain specific eco-system or an indigenous culture. Both are linked to a common source; the species through the context of nature as a universal source of life, and culture through the common source of deep human values. Species and culture bridge gaps and engage with other counterparts, seeking to build new polymorphic forms by combination and learning, and eventually create resilience and what we refer to as global integrity.

We are also basing our work on the notion that culture is not a set of artefacts and practices that are external to the process of natural evolution, but is an extension of the evolutionary process. That is why Maturana and Varela's (1991) contribution of autopoiesis, or self-making is vital to the transformation process. According to their work in neurology, we 'bring forth' our world in the very act of cognition. The world does not exist as an objective entity separated from us, but is the outcome of our cognitive engagement with it. Transformation is about bringing forth a world that on the one hand is deeply rooted in its indigenousness but simultaneously engages with the exogenous and creates novelty and resilience.

The question is, how do we integrate the natural and cultural foundations of transformation into the transformational process? How do we transform as individuals, as organisations, as societies, rooted in local cultures and connected to nature?

By entering the Four Worlds, we will also have a closer look at the cultural diversity that the world produced and at the role each individual culture has to play.

REFERENCES

Chopra, D. 2004. *The Book of Secrets.* New York: Harmony Books.

Korten, D. 2007. *The Great Turning: Empire to Earth Community.* San Francisco: Berrett Koehler.

Lessem, R. and A. Schieffer. 2009. *Transformation Management: Towards and Integral and Sustainable Enterprise.* Farnham,UK, UK: Gower Ashgate.

Margulis, L. and D. Sagan. 2003. *Acquiring Genomes: The Theory of the Origin of the Species.* New York: Basic Books.

Maturana, H. and F. Varela. 1991. *Autopoiesis and Cognition: The Realization of the Living.* Boston: Kluwer.

Sahtouris, E. 1996. *Earthdance: Living Systems in Evolution.* Alameda: Metalog Books.

Soros, G. 2000. *Open Society.* New York: Little Brown.

Sperry, R. 1982. *Science and Moral Priority.* New York: Columbia University Press.

Suzuki, D. 1997. *Sacred Balance.* Vancouver: Greystone Books.

Varela, F. and E. Thompson. 1993. *The Embodied Mind.* Cambridge, Massachusetts: MIT Press.

EPILOGUE

Schumacher's hierarchy and Capra's kite provide us with mapping devices to navigate the 21st century. They show ways ahead for the perplexed manager and management researcher. Their maps requires us to add other orientations to the previously dominant scientific approach and expect us to seek wisdom in balance and in developing a practical knowledge that tells us when and how to act. As we move up Schumacher's hierarchy and begin to try to make Capra's kite fly, certain issues disguised by prior preoccupations with scientific rationalism come into consideration. We start to explore other metaphors to live by than the machine metaphor of 'dead-mapping', which has failed us. We begin to pay more attention to the invisible and imaginary and not just to the physical, we start to pay attention to the whole and not just to the detail of the parts, we focus more upon process and practice and realise that the only reality is in the present moment and we seek to heal the wounds of divisive fragmentation.

David Bohm (2004) identifies 'fragmentation' as a source of the woes of contemporary 'incoherence' as it diminishes the benefits of wholeness. Fragmentation is a consequence of the fragmentary philosophy of scientific reductionism and its partner in crimes of divisiveness—the ideology of individual rational choice and the privilege afforded to *homo economicus*. Fragmentation breaks things up (that are not really separate) so that they don't work. The broken up bits are 'at odds' with each other, uncoordinated, oppositional, dysfunctional, incapable of dialogue.

Dialogue, then, involves 'putting them back together' to make them work. It requires no preset agenda but benefits initially from employment of a skilful facilitator to tease out 'issues'. Emergent frictions have to be expected and overcome. They are a consequence of different underlying assumptions with separate historicities. An attitude of avoiding entrenchment and posturing can be avoided by putting a lens on the source of our differences (the assumptions). Movement towards greater fellowship and a more collective consciousness evolves problematically but is possible with an open attitude.

Communication should allow for similarity and difference. Overemphasis upon similarity can easily lead to factionalism. It is important to 'listen' to the slippery development of meaning rather than try to control it by insistent defence of your own meaning—the author is after all, dead. Vision requires focus upon the nature of the problems facing us, which are again inherited from historicity— from the previous evolution of ideas that now 'go without saying'. They are, based upon memories, the product of tacit representations that go unquestioned. A common error is to treat paradoxes within social relationships or with the 'self' as 'problems' that require solutions. This avoids the wisdom of living with paradoxes, which do not have 'solutions', requiring sustained reflective engagement and cultivation of the inspiration of new creatively different visions of realty. Bohm (2004) suggests we need to develop skills of wisdom, such as 'suspension' of assumptions, the mindfulness of thought tracking (a central tenet of Buddhist meditation) and the cultivation of 'participatory thought' (a kind of spiritual engagement with the 'becoming' of existence and the 'sublime').

So a creative future for the West and North may well need to be *very* different from the current rationalist, secular, materialist, utilitarian self-interested culture that we find ourselves in; an 'about turn'. The East and South, in acquiring Western technology and ideas, have to be very careful not, in the process, to abandon the spiritual wisdom that is their greatest asset.

REFERENCE

Bohm, D. 2004. *On Dialogue* (edited by L. Nichol). Adingdon, Oxon: Routledge.

INDEX